WILD EUROPE

Božidar Jezernik

WILD EUROPE

The Balkans in the Gaze
of Western Travellers

SAQI

in association with
THE BOSNIAN INSTITUTE

British Library Cataloguing-in-Publication Data
A catalogue record of this book is available from the British Library

ISBN 0 86356 574 3
EAN 9-780863-565748

© Božidar Jezernik, 2004

This edition first published 2004

Saqi Books
26 Westbourne Grove
London W2 5RH
www.saqibooks.com

in association with
The Bosnian Institute
14/16 St Marks Road
London W11 1RQ
www. bosnia.org.uk

To my late wife Bogna
For the difference she made

Contents

Illustrations

Foreword

Joel Martin Halpern

Professor Emeritus of Anthropology,
University of Massachusetts, Amherst

Božidar Jezernik has put together a fascinating volume. While his focus is on West European travel accounts from the fifteenth to the early twentieth centuries, he also cites Turkish and Russian authors, as well as some from the area of the former Yugoslavia. As he ably demonstrates, the literature is both vast and uneven. In the early twenty-first century the considerable academic literature on Orientalism would apparently offer a perspective for analysis of these writings. But the author suggests a more subtle approach and uses his analytical skills unobtrusively, enabling the reader to encounter views from the past directly without the too often suffocating special language of post modernism.

Jezernik's approach is apparent when he discusses the Western vision of the 'terrible' Turk and the image of persecution of Christian subjects. This view is, of course, most directly linked to the nineteenth century, when the Ottoman Empire was in terminal decline prior to its disappearance in the aftermath of the First World War. The earliest accounts cited, from the 16th century, paint a very different picture. As the author reminds us, 'In the sixteenth and seventeenth centuries the Ottoman Empire was perceived as possessing unlimited power, its army was the "the very terror of Europe".' (Chapter 10). Turkish talents and abilities in more peaceful aspects of human endeavour were also unrivalled: a prime example was the uncontested skill of Ottoman architects as builders of bridges of durability and beauty, like the famous Old Bridge in the city of Mostar in Herzegovina. A French traveller of the period described it as superior to and wider than the Rialto in Venice (Chapter 10). Jezernik also points out characteristic aspects of Ottoman rule which anticipated some much later aspects of British management of their empire. That is, as long as taxes were paid and political and military authority were unchallenged, the non-Muslim peoples were permitted to retain their own religious structures and belief systems.

In the early twenty-first century, a large portion of the Balkan lands where Muslims live, our principal area of concern, are occupied by NATO troops with UN participation; in Bosnia this has lasted for nearly a decade, in Kosovo half that. The Turk may no longer be terrible, the Balkans no longer wild and Islam no longer exotic, but the themes of culture conflict continue to be very much with us. In exploring Jezernik's collection of the views of observers of times past, we can easily see how they provide a necessary prologue to the present, even as our modern world has annihilated traditionally confining spatial boundaries.

Jezernik's work emphasizes historical process, a differentiated past. Thus, continuing with our example of the Mostar Bridge as an unchanging symbolic artefact, by the mid nineteenth century when Turkish power had notably declined, travellers no longer attributed the bridge to the Turks, but gave it classical origins. This point is abundantly illustrated in the cited sources. As might be expected, travellers reflected the dominant political perspectives of their times. Nevertheless the reflexive view is a complex one and mirrors not simply shifts in political power but accepted patterns of social status and even the gender of the observer. A nineteenth-century account of the bridge at Mostar by an Austrian noblewoman is illustrative. She had the insight to observe of the bridge that 'history mislabels it as Roman'. But her husband, who oversaw the publication of her book, added in his notes to it that the bridge was obviously classical, built by Trajan or Hadrian.

But what makes perceptions change? Jezernik provides different accounts for our comparison. One of the more distinguished scholars of the nineteenth century was the Englishman, Sir Arthur Evans, perhaps most widely known for his excavations of the Minoan palace of Knossos. He also wrote a widely cited work, *Through Bosnia and Herzegovina during the insurrection in 1875 by foot* (cited also in Chapter 10), in which he notes his agreement on the origins of the bridge with another famous English archaeologist from a generation earlier, John Gardner Wilkinson, referred to as 'the founder of British Egyptology'. Wilkinson was also a Balkan traveller and authored *Dalmatia and Montenegro: with a Journey to Mostar in Herzegovina* (1848). Evans notes that the 'grandeur of the work... attests its Roman origin'. Lest anyone doubt the probity of this view, the reader is informed that Sir John shares it. Clearly these Victorian travellers in the days of British imperial glory were so overwhelmed by their work on famous Mediterranean civilizations that in an area which was for them the peripheral Balkans the accomplishments of the Ottoman rulers were unworthy of careful consideration. How could something unique and of value come directly from the infidel Turks and be located in the Balkan back of beyond.

However, there were other views. In a book published in 1877 a German Consul General, Dr Otto Blau, claimed that nothing about the bridge related it to Roman architecture. Dr Blau's book was probably not widely read in Victorian England. Some travel accounts were rapidly translated, like Alberto Fortis's Italian classic which was issued in English (as *Travels into Dalmatia*) in 1778, only four years after the original appeared. But this case was a unique account, well predating Wilkinson's book (by some 70 years). It is hard to imagine that an English publisher would have rushed out a translated edition of Dr Otto Blau's *Reisen in Bosnien und der Hertzegowina* for the sophisticated British public: they were already well informed about the area by the writings of their own scholars, Wilkinson and Evans. Further, England then had no direct major strategic or imperial interest in the area.

Another thread is that, although Jezernik's book relies on multilingual sources, it is being published in English. Were its original publication to be in German and oriented to a German-speaking audience, we might perhaps be focusing on Dr Blau and the scholarly and administrative work that he did in Bosnia during his tenure there. He was, after all, based in Bosnia, while Wilkinson and Evans only passed through it. If this volume were to appear in French, one might begin with Charles Pertusier, who in his volume *La Bosnie considérée dans ses rapports avec l'empire Ottoman* (Paris, 1822) appears to be the first author to attribute the bridge to the Romans. Our brief survey of these accounts indicates how the historical period, the nationality of the author and the background of the writer influence perception. This complex layering of these supposedly individualized and independent observations is what makes Jezernik's approach intriguing and makes sense of the large number of sources that he uses to compile his survey. Thus this book is not simply an assemblage of a large number of travel accounts, but rather an analysis of how observers of the Balkans, mainly West Europeans, constructed their shifting images of otherness in the Balkans, an area geographically close but conceptually distant.

This matter of conceptual distance in the face of geographic proximity is clearly relevant to the image of Turkey in Europe. This same area of the south-east Balkans was also known as European Turkey in the period before the First World War. Just as relevant is the significance to West and Central Europeans of Islam in Europe, specifically Muslims in Europe. For Turkey was taken as a synonym for Muslim, i.e. non-Christian, civilization.

Although many bitter wars were fought between Catholics and Protestants in Western Europe, and although some of the Orthodox peoples in the eastern Mediterranean preferred to live under the more tolerant Ottomans than the Catholic Venetians, the foreign – i.e. non-Christian – Turkish-Muslim presence in Europe contributed to the enduring picture of the otherness of the Balkans, a strange and wild place.

Therefore, the historic date of September 1683 when the Ottoman armies were defeated by the Poles and Austrians at the gates of Vienna is as much a marker as 1492, when other infidel Muslims, the Moors, were finally expelled from Spain along with the only intermittently tolerated Jews. The complexity of contemporary relationships, often conflictual, between Islamic countries and the West remains a critical concern at the beginning of the twenty-first century, only now the focus is as much on Muslim immigrants as on external affairs (though the two are intertwined). Thus myriad observations, with often implicit and sometimes explicit feelings of fear and threat, are cited by Jezernik. Though taken from accounts of centuries past, these feelings remain very much with us today, although the encounter is now more pervasive. One can cite, for example, the Turkish immigrants who have been working in Germany for decades but are denied citizenship there. The contrast with Ottoman rule could not be more marked. In their lands the Ottomans offered their subject peoples a choice. They could remain in their own established communities and pay their taxes or, for some, take the opportunity to become part of the ruling Muslim administration.

The West/Balkan distinction, including the sense of otherness, continues, although some specifics of these perceived differences have altered. Thus the significance of spatial boundaries has been transformed, if only because we now mainly travel by air. But Jezernik documents a base line for evaluating these distinctions. He describes how travellers in the nineteenth century and earlier often felt as they traversed what they perceived as a marked cultural boundary: Crossing the Danube from Austrian-controlled Zemun to Belgrade and entering Serbia, a land with its mosques and Oriental architecture even after it became an independent state in the mid-nineteenth century, meant entering the strange Balkans, with its Eastern essence.

Now, in a curious or even ironic way, the tables are turned. In our time a traveller can encounter mosques and find sizeable Muslim communities in Berlin, Paris and London. A century ago, when Belgrade, Sofia and Bucharest and many smaller towns in these newly independent states emerged from Turkish rule, they entered upon a process of modernization which was a part of their desire to 'join Europe'. As a key element in this transformation, these new states began to obliterate their Oriental architectural heritage, a process still underway in the early twentieth century and not completed until after the second World War II.

Will a reverse process gather pace in the future in major West European countries, which need to import workers to generate the tax revenues essential for social benefits? Building mosques in Western Europe and the rise of Islamic-based political groups do not, of course, mean a new Turkey in Europe or a spread of earlier Balkan patterns to the West. But the presence of peoples from former colonies in the now diminished metropoles, and the long-term residence of migrant labourers in other parts of Western Europe, especially Germany, do reflect a movement from East to West, bringing a confrontation between different belief systems and cultural values which were formerly kept apart. The Danube is no longer the symbolic crossing point, but people in the Balkans still talk of 'joining Europe'.

This being the case, Jezernik's assertion at the beginning of his opening chapter that there is an 'absence of any obvious border' between the Balkan Peninsula and the rest of Europe (Chapter 1) takes on a historical significance. It is not geography which is at issue, although the Balkan mountain range is both a geographical landmark and a national symbol in Bulgaria, whose national airline was also called Balkan. What is really at issue is a state of mind, as Robert Walsh indicates in his volume published in 1836 where he speaks of a region of 'primitive quarrels and ancient ways of resolving them' (cited in Chapter 1).

Geographical proximity was accompanied by a sense of remoteness. The Balkans were seen by some 'as wild and remote as Tartary, darkest Africa or the wilds of Asia'. Many of these accounts show that the fundamental issue, continuing for most of the nineteenth century, was the continued presence of the terrible or infidel Turk, the two adjectives in a way synonymous. Further, to the mostly Protestant or Catholic authors, the Orthodox peasant population was, while not infidel, a group from which they felt historically and culturally remote. Appropriately Jezernik points out (Chapter 1) that Russian authors, themselves from an Orthodox Empire, saw the Orthodox Serbs as a fellow people, and the Muslims but also the Catholics were thought of as having undesirable qualities.

In this connection, just as an Orthodox Russian perspective gives a different view of Balkan peoples, so does a North American one with its ideology of assimilation and becoming part of a 'new' nation. In 1910 Emily Balch, a professor of economics from the women's college of Wellesley in Massachusetts, published a 536-page volume entitled *Our Slavic Fellow Citizens* sponsored by the Charities Publication Committee. Her primary concern was with the recently arrived immigrants, notably the Slovenes, Croats and Montenegrins. She was truly innovative because, for a full understanding of the immigrant problem in the United States, Balch thought it logical to carry her investigations to their recent homelands. Her title is more than symbolic:

Our Slavic Fellow Citizens describes her visits to villages and cities in Austria-Hungary, and contains interviews with peasant families as well as the more predictable contacts with officials and political leaders, thus directly linking the Old and New Worlds. The peasants described are not exotic strangers, but fellow participants in a civil society.

A socialist and pacifist, Balch's career contrasted with that of Mary Durham, who is extensively cited by Jezernik. Their visits to the Balkans overlapped but their approaches were dramatically different. Durham was a Balkan traveller and writer, intensively observing local life and customs, who subsequently became an advocate for the Albanians. Balch represents a beginning of professional scholarship dealing with Balkan populations. Her studies also reflect how emerging capitalist enterprises could affect distant lands. Long-distance mercantile trade had long been part of Balkan life – the network of inns and caravanserais, remarked on by almost all travellers, is ample testimony to its existence. Nevertheless, throughout the nineteenth century and even well into the twentieth, the picture given by travellers' accounts is of people essentially rooted in place and more or less isolated from the wider world. This is why the mass migrations to the New World in the late nineteenth and early twentieth centuries marked a departure in Balkan history.

The English novelist Joyce Cary went to Montenegro shortly after completing his studies at Oxford. Romantically setting out to participate in the First Balkan War, he was there during 1912–13 and observed much of the fighting. The defeat of the Turks in 1913 marked the beginning of the end of their power in the Balkans. His observations are among those cited in the chapter on 'Passionate about Head Hunting', on the taking of enemy heads in battle in Montenegro. Mary Durham's early twentieth century descriptions of this custom might seem a world away from immigrant life in the industrializing United States of the same period; but only a generation earlier in the struggle between US troops and the Plains Indians the taking of scalps in battle was a regular practice and not only on the Native American side. Following the culminating Battle of Little Bighorn in 1876, the Indians stripped and mutilated the bodies of all the uniformed soldiers, believing that the soul of a mutilated body would have to walk the earth forever, a view not dissimilar to those of Montenegrins and Albanians as described by both Cary and Durham. Being dismembered at death was believed by Muslims to block entrance to heaven (Chapter 7).

Jezernik also notes that the custom of severing the heads of enemies slain in war and of fallen comrades was seen by Western visitors, even after the end of the nineteenth century, as a strong symbol of barbarism. These observers felt that such behaviour marked a clear division between Balkan peoples and the civilized West. This distinction would certainly apply to the practice of carrying home the heads of enemies killed in battle, which were often dried and posted for public display. It would also apply to the custom of taking home the heads of slain comrades for a proper burial. But the Balkan war witnessed by both Durham and Cary was of an intimate sort where the killing was done in a very personal way and at close quarters, unlike modern warfare. The Turks and Montenegrins may have readily killed one another, as also did the Montenegrins and Albanians. Yet the latter peoples were culturally similar in many ways and the concept of physical racial differences did not exist. It certainly would appear true that, to the extent that heads were taken (and even preserved and stuffed), this was in large measure a symbolic rather than a strategic act. Indeed, the more time spent in the purposeful mutilation of killed foes, the less time for pursuing an active offensive intent on inflicting maximum damage to the opposition. It is further to the point that warfare was usually waged to the death and survival of the wounded was not a high priority. Emphasis was on the afterlife as much as on this world. Jezernik notes that when ritually sworn blood brothers went to war together, a primary duty was for one to cut off the head of the slain brother so that this symbolic body part would not fall into the hands of the enemy. Further, even the fatally or severely wounded comrade would have his head cut off by his fellow soldier for the same reason (Chapter 7).

The contrast between the types of fighting that occurred in Montenegro and on the Western Front in the years that immediately followed the end of the Balkan Wars is worth considering. The kind of trench warfare conducted on the Western Front, abetted by the use of poison gas, resulted in casualties measured not in dozens or even hundreds but in hundreds of thousands. Such organized mass slaughter does not appear to have been part of the conflict that Cary observed.

It is also worth mentioning that at Versailles the United States, then under President Wilson, advocated self-determination and democracy in the Balkans. At that time hundreds of black men were being lynched each year in the American South. Postcards of these events, depicting the violent killing and the mutilation of corpses, were sold as souvenirs. Further, given the specifics of the Second World War, with its concentration camps as part of the Holocaust where the Nazis experimented on their victims and used their skin for lampshades – violence carried out not against warriors met in combat but against defenceless civilians – the point could be made that Balkan head hunting was in a way a more restricted kind of warfare. Certainly if we add to our consideration the fire bombings and atomic attacks, terms such as 'civilized' when applied to Western Europe have either lost their meaning entirely or require the most stringent qualification. The atrocities committed

in the Yugoslav conflicts of the 1990s have also made the mass butchery
of civilians very much part of the continuing contemporary European
experience. While it does not seem appropriate to suggest that the taking of
heads was a humane custom, such a practice does not seem compatible with
strategies of extermination.

Mary Durham is cited as the source (Chapter 7) for the observation that
victims of war sometimes survived with their nasal bone hacked though and
the whole upper lip removed. Joyce Cary refers to 'all sorts of tales' of nose
cutting by Montenegrins and Albanians. He mentions that since they were less
bulky than heads, they could be evidence of how many were killed and what
bounty was due. But in the First Balkan War, in which he participated, Cary
thinks Durham was misled, but that if any incidents of this sort happened it
was the Albanian irregulars who were responsible.

In his style Jezernik is provocative, strikingly so in his chapter on the
bridge at Mostar, 'A Bridge between Barbarity and Civilization', as well as in
his two chapters on Montenegro, 'The Romantic Charm of Freedom' and
'Passionate about Head Hunting'. He makes no claim to be comprehensive
or definitive. Rather, he presents us with the numerous observations of
foreigners, most of them travellers passing through the Balkans. We might
call many of the observations sketch-books of travel. Jezernik is also explicit
that he is not presenting a series of 'truths' about the people observed:
rather, we are given points of view, some of them explicitly founded on
prejudices derived from the cultural background of the observer. In other
words an overall perspective on these travellers and other foreign observers
requires as thorough a knowledge of their background as of the cultures
they observed. But there is also another perspective: what the people thought
about themselves, a view from inside the culture. This approach is provided
by local scholars, folklorists and ethnographers, who began in the early to
mid nineteenth century to write about their own people. Their work was,
of course, closely related to the rise of national identity manifested in the
growth of formal institutions such as universities, academies of science and
museums. There is a rich tradition of this work in the Balkans, for example
among the Serbs and Montenegrins. The first such writer was Vuk Karadžić,
the folklorist, in the early nineteenth century. Another was the French-trained
human geographer, Jovan Cvijić, who founded a whole school of localized
ethnographic description concerned with origins and migrations. This work
had obvious political significance and it is not surprising that he participated in
the work of the Serbian delegation to the Versailles conference. But Jezernik's
focus is not upon the comprehensive descriptive accounts, based on detailed
local observation, that we can find in this literature. He is concerned with
broad historical patterns and encompassing judgements.

His collection of accounts is carefully phrased to encourage further thinking and speculation, for he constantly reminds us that he is a presenter of reports and observations, not a judge of the opinions expressed. That is, these accounts cannot be taken as a conclusive definition of the diverse cultural world that is the Balkans, but only as an introduction to it. These books are only one kind of viewing, a single dimension in the multidimensional reality of a given culture. Nowhere is this more true than in the complex world of gender relationships. Above we have discussed a way of looking at decapitation from within the community. However, in another chapter, 'The Romantic Charm of Freedom', we are told that visitors from abroad looked in vain for female beauty, perhaps because they were so taken by the dominant image of 'fearless fighters of gigantic stature', as one over-enthusiastic English visitor put it. Based on preoccupations with vengeance, heroism and death, Montenegrins may not have spent much time thinking about love, beauty, sex or even the pleasures of home life in the view of the foreign observer.

My focus here has been on selected individual accounts taken from the large number assembled by Jezernik. The variety of the sources cited is particularly remarkable in the chapters that deal with food and beverages, especially the one on coffee, 'Where Paradise Was but a Sip of Hellish Brew away'. Before the advent of hotels favouring international cuisine, the travellers cited in this book found that experiencing the local food and drink was the most accessible way to gain entrance into a foreign culture and its society. In sum, this book presents a point of departure for our reflections on the Balkans, whose past is ever present in influencing our ways of understanding the current dilemmas of the region.

ONE

The Land where the East Begins

Until the beginning of the nineteenth century the Balkan Peninsula had no name. Only in 1808 did the German geographer August Zeune give it the name of Hämushalbinsel, which he subsequently changed to the Balkan Peninsula, following the usual practice of naming a region after a prominent mountain range. Zeune's choice was rather arbitrary, however, as the Balkan Mountains, formerly called the Haemus (from *haima*, blood of Typhon), in what is now Bulgaria and known as Stara Planina (Old Mountain), constitute neither the most extensive nor the highest mountain system in the peninsula.[1] In English, the name 'The Great Balcan' was first used instead of the Haemus by Frederick Calvert in 1767.[2] However, almost from the beginning, the new name was considered an unworthy match of its predecessor. John Morritt, for instance, remarked in his journal in the 1790s: 'We slept at the foot of a mountain [the Šipka Pass], which we crossed the next day, which separates Bulgaria from Romania (the ancient Thrace), and which, though now debased by the name of Bal. Kan, is no less a personage than the ancient Haemus.'[3]

Moreover, it appears, the name itself was the result of a misunderstanding. The Turkish noun *balkan*, which denotes a rugged and thickly wooded mountain or mountain chain, was assumed to be the name of this specific range.[4] During the nineteenth century, this tautological title was imposed

The Šipka pass

on the area to meet the need for a short-hand label for the new states that emerged in the territory previously known as European Turkey or Turkey-in-Europe. Arguably, the choice was at least partly due to the fact that in the first half of the nineteenth century the mountain range became famous as the theatre of the Russo-Turkish wars and, till 1877, this natural bulwark formed the second and most important line of defence of the Well-Guarded City, as the Ottomans called their capital.[5] Thus, a British surgeon in the Ottoman army in the middle of the nineteenth century understood Balkans to signify 'mountains of defence.'[6]

In the absence of any obvious border between the peninsula and the rest of Europe, authors have often disagreed about the exact extent of the Balkans, rendering the geography of the peninsula a very inexact science. For one thing, its area has not been stable and constant but has expanded and contracted in step with shifting political boundaries. For instance, in 1911 the *Encyclopaedia Britannica* defined the Balkans as encompassing 'Albania, Bosnia and Herzegovina, Bulgaria, Croatia-Slavonia, Dobrudja, Greece, Illyria, Macedonia, Montenegro, Novibazar, Servia and Turkey.' During the twentieth century this definition underwent several changes. Eventually, the 1995 edition of the *Encyclopaedia Britannica Macropaedia* included not only Romania and Vojvodina but also Moldova and Slovenia among the Balkan states but excluded Greece. The Balkans' place in the topography of Western imagery was illustrated most precisely by a German author, who described it as a garden shed standing beside the noble West European villa and housing

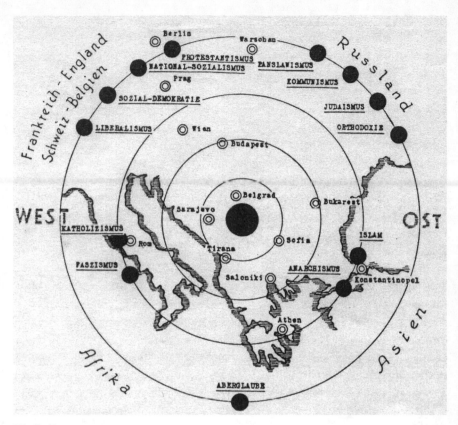

The Balkans as a target

many people who were unable to get on with each other and quarrelled incessantly among themselves.[7]

Agreement about the precise extent of the Balkans may have been lacking, but there has never been much disagreement about its non-European character or its intention to Europeanise itself: both were always taken for granted.[8] After the Age of Enlightenment, the Balkans was perceived as at once near (geographically) and far (culturally). Thomas Arnold, the headmaster of Rugby School and author of *History of Rome*, for instance, described the eastern coast of the Adriatic as 'one of those ill-fated portions of the earth which, though placed in immediate contact with civilization, have remained perpetually barbarian.'[9] Accordingly, in Western narrations of the area those qualities that made it different from the rest of Europe were quite often deliberately stressed and many travel reports were presented as journeys back in time, away from 'the eager, restless, hurried life of Western civilization' to 'the dreamy East.'[10] If the facts did not measure up to expectations, they could be changed or, if that was not feasible, disguised as picturesque and colourful survivals of the past: 'It is still the world of the "Arabian Nights," and here in Europe, within a day's journey of the railway that leads to Vienna, we are in the East and the Middle Ages.'[11]

If geographical terms are conventionally neutral, then the Balkans has been a notorious exception to this rule. Whenever the term is used to denote something more than a range of mountains in Bulgaria, a distinct ideological bias is introduced, with the negative connotations of filth, passivity, untrustworthiness, disregard for women, conspiracy, unscrupulousness, opportunism, indolence, superstition, sluggishness, unprincipled and overzealous bureaucracy, and so on. In the Balkan languages themselves, the term *Balkan* soon became a synonym for lack of civilisation and for backwardness. Thus, at the beginning of the nineteenth century a conversation between Westerners and the Balkan people often began: 'Your Excellency will find but poor fare in our country; but you are not in Christendom. What can be done amongst these beasts the Turks?'[12]

'The Balkans,' then, evoked not so much a specific area as the idea of localised chaos, of *balkanisation*, of primitive quarrels and primeval ways of resolving them. Reverend Robert Walsh pointed out that in western Europe 'humanity has tempered even the usages of war,' but it was not so in those countries 'and the Greeks, even at the most polished period of their history, perpetrated the greatest cruelties both on each other and on strangers, and always expected and suffered a similar retaliation.'[13] No wonder that polite and good-natured people thought it rude to say Balkans in the presence of a pacifist.[14]

The Least-known Corner of Europe

In the seventeenth and eighteenth centuries the peninsula was little known in the West. According to Diderot's *Encyclopédie* Bosnia bordered on Albania (1751, vol. ii, p. 337) and Herceg-Novi was the capital of Herzegovina (1765, vol. viii, p. 187). During the nineteenth century many books on the Balkans were published in the West, some very learned, others ephemeral, but the area remained nevertheless as unknown 'as the interior of Tartary or the centre of Africa,'[15] or 'the wilds of Asia,'[16] or even 'more completely than the heights of the Himalayas, or even of the Pamir!'[17] In the second half of the nineteenth century Western travellers thronged to see the area and published hundreds of travel reports, but, at the beginning of the twentieth century, it was still described as the 'least-known corner of Europe.'[18]

This is hard to explain. It seems to me, however, that the West in general has never been prepared to see the Balkans as it really is. Instead it has always

A Bosnian house

looked for characteristics that were clear-cut, unambiguous and, above all, unchanging, and this have been hard to find. As Martin Conway wrote, people in the West could 'form a picture of the mode of life of African savages, and some idea of their occupations, their tribal habits and superstitions, and the kind of world in which they live,' but they could understand 'nothing whatever about people and affairs in the Balkan Peninsula.' They found its geography too complicated, its ethnography too confused, its history too intricate and its politics too inexplicable. Although there were plenty of books dealing with these matters, each year that passed made room for more, as the situation continually changed, always introducing something new to record, a new subject to depict, a new problem to explain, a new complication to disentangle.[19] Thus, the images of Balkan people in Westerners' narration were not primarily, if at all, descriptions of real people, but rather projections of their own nostalgia and feeling of inadequacy. And the more books appeared, with their differences in focus and perspective, the more blurred was the picture.

In the first half of the seventeenth century, Sir Henry Blount asserted that our understanding of human affairs advances best through observing people whose institutions differ greatly from our own, 'for costumes conformable to our owne, or to such wherewith we are already acquainted, doe but repeat our old observations, with little acquits of new.'[20] Or, as several decades later another British traveller expressed his impressions of European Turkey:

It is not unpleasant sight, to behold a new Scene of the World, and unknown face of things, in Habits, Dyet, Manners, Customs and Language. A man seems to take leave of our World, when he hath passed a days journey from Rab, or Comorra: and, before he cometh to Buda, seems to enter upon a new Stage of the world, quite different from that of these Western countrys: for he then bids adieu to hair on the Head, Bands, Cuffes, Hats, Gloves, Beds, Beer: and enters upon Habits, Manners, and course of life: which with no great variety, but under some conformity, extend unto China, and the utmost parts of Asia.[21]

Many authors writing in the following centuries were strongly convinced that the points of difference between west European nations bore no proportion to their similarities. But visitors to European Turkey entered a 'new world,' finding there 'a total and striking change in the face of the country, the style of buildings, and the dress, manner, and general appearance of the inhabitants.'[22] Travellers who crossed the Ottoman border in the nineteenth century or later went 'not only from West to East, but from civilization to

Janissaries

savagery, from liberty to tyranny;'[23] they were entering 'on the field of the great battle between East and West – between barbarism and civilisation.'[24]

Given the difference in life-style, upon leaving Zemun for Belgrade some nineteenth-century travellers even thought they 'had done with the civilised world' and some organised their departure with nearly as much solemnity as if they had been 'departing this life.'[25] A British traveller to Tehran, James Fraser, wrote of his crossing the Danube in 1836 that there was something solemn in the ceremony of departure, for 'it was like quitting the living for the dead.' And when he shook hands with his last two friends and got into the boat, he 'could not help thinking of Charon and the river Styx.'[26]

In the nineteenth and twentieth centuries, hundreds and hundreds of Western travellers, who more or less shared Blount's opinion, crisscrossed the Balkans in every direction, but a lot of them did not see it for itself. The land and its people merely served as a kind of mirror in which they saw themselves and noticed, first and foremost, how advanced and civilised they were. In this respect, we can argue that there can be no Europe without the Balkans. Europeans had for centuries differentiated between members of 'civilised society' on the one hand and 'primitives,' 'barbarians' and 'savages' on the other, in order to define themselves as civilised people. For this they needed their opposite, their Other, and the Balkan people served this purpose excellently. It is in fact hard to imagine a more sharply defined Other than the Balkan people. It was as if they represented, in an extravagant and colourful way, everything that had been rejected by the West generations before. Conversely, they also embodied a combination that Julia Kristeva has called 'the disturbingly strange,' 'the otherness of our ourness,' which we do not know how to handle. In other words, they represented what Europeans had been but were no longer allowed to be.[27]

Accordingly, some writers on the Balkans could even find men with tails there in the twentieth century (see Chapter 4). And at the end of the twentieth century an American expert on the area did still better by explaining that Nazism could claim a Balkan origin.[28] Although a large majority of twentieth-century authors did not follow the extreme views of Paul Siebertz, Philip Thornton or Robert Kaplan, they still generally reckoned that the Balkan Peninsula does not belong to Europe, 'the most civilised of continents,' no matter what the atlas says.[29]

In order to substantiate why the Balkans was not part of Europe but rather part of Asia, Western authors made the forceful argument that its inhabitants rarely, if ever, class themselves as Europeans and always speak of Europe as a completely separate area. If inhabitants of the Balkans contemplated a journey to any of the countries to their west, they spoke of 'going to Europe.'[30] However, a west European might indicate a strong sense of achievement if in the course of a tour he visited a spot 'where no European traveller had preceded him,' be it in the heart of Albania or ancient Macedonia, on the coast of Crete or beneath Mount Olympus, the mythical home of gods and goddesses of ancient Greece.[31]

Images in Black and White

Before the end of the eighteenth century travel across the Balkans was mainly fortuitous. Most travellers had some business in Istanbul or further east and they journeyed across the Balkans because there was no other safe route from western Europe to Asia Minor. In their travel accounts they recorded what they happened to see and find out on their way, emphasising whatever was strange, unusual and picturesque. They wanted these descriptions of their journeys to please and amuse their readers with their detailed accounts of picturesque discoveries and adventures. If the experience itself was not as magnificent as the *Arabian Nights*, they did not hesitate to embroider the facts to make their readers marvel. The most perceptive of these writers gave their readers precise details of the interior of the sultan's harem – an amusing fiction, since merely to look at one of the sultan's women was a crime, which, in the words of an architect to Louis XIV, nothing could expiate 'but Death, or the loss of that which makes a man what he is.'[32] Nevertheless, some travellers were able to track the sultan's amorous pastimes with the ladies of his pleasure and portray for the readers 'all various Scenes of Love and Courtship, which are practis'd daily by their Lord and them;'[33] others knew whether the ladies entered the sultan's bed at the foot or at the side.[34]

Seventeenth-century authors discovered that in the East everything was different from what they were accustomed to at home, because the people of the East, as William Lithgow Scotus wrote, 'contrafact and contradict all the formes of Christians.'[35] This view was almost stereotypical of the period that followed; and those interested in such writing could have learned, for instance, that in the East in the eighteenth century nothing had changed, for 'In every Action of their Lives, the Turks oppose the European Customs.'[36] Again, at the beginning of the twentieth century, we are told that, 'These common instances of a general tendency of Orientals to do exactly the opposite of what Occidentals would do under the same circumstances, have an importance deeper than their picturesqueness when on exhibition.'[37]

From the end of the eighteenth century, travellers had a different purpose. Some even visited the Balkans out of curiosity, as tourists, but most came with a specific purpose in view: to study a particular country from a political, economic or military angle. They pursued their ends methodically and with a high degree of professional commitment, making precise observations, but they were not always above prejudice. The representation of the Balkans as 'a people of Antithesis'[38] continued: 'The habits and modes of the Turks are so much at variance with ours, that we visit them with the same kind of sentiments that we go on to exhibition.'[39]

The travel reports were written and published for a comparatively broad and enthusiastic public who found nothing more boring than plain facts. Like modern journalists, their authors shaped public opinion, expressing the dominant tastes and prejudices of their time.[40] Their reports had to fulfil the expectations of the public who, in their turn, took it for granted that the travellers saw 'strange things in strange lands.'[41] Hence, in travel writing the image of the Balkans was frequently seasoned with a liberal measure of partiality, prejudice and bias. Thus, according to several twentieth-century authors, in the Balkans people even indicate yes and no 'in a wrong manner.'[42]

Perceptions of the Balkans and its people were often coloured by the political sympathies of their authors and their readers. So, for instance, German-speaking authors portrayed the Bosnian Serbs as conspirators seeking to ignite the First World War. They portrayed the Orthodox people negatively and the Muslims positively, praising their discretion and restraint, their nobility and dignity.[43] Russian authors, on the contrary, were full of praise for the Orthodox people, while imputing to the Muslims and Catholics a range of negative qualities.[44] It is also important to bear in mind that the travel reports were not always the result of first-hand observation, but were often based on hearsay or on second-hand information taken from older authors. A fairly liberal attitude to borrowing other writers' work characterises many of them. They should, therefore, be taken with a pinch of salt, as the following extracts illustrate. At the beginning of the twentieth century a researcher named George Frederick Abbott made a tour of Macedonia under the auspices of Cambridge University in order to study the country's folklore. He described his adventures and noted his observations of men, women and government officials. Among many other things, his readers learn that his *teskereh* (Turkish passport for travel within the country) described him as 'exceedingly tall, with light hair, and eyes recalling the azure of the sky,' although in reality he was of 'a medium height (unfriendly observers might even call me short without being absolutely guilty of falsehood), black hair, and dark eyes.'[45] The police commissioner 'who played Cerberus at the Serres railway station' inspected the researcher's passport four times and each time entered into his register a similar description of his personal appearance. As the commissioner was not actually blind, Abbott thought that the only explanation of his tolerance must have been his way of reasoning: 'An Englishman... is tall, fair-headed, and blue-eyed. This gentleman is an Englishman. Ergo, he must be tall, fair-haired, and blue-eyed. That I happened to be the very opposite to all this was an accident which did not affect the Turkish official's syllogism.'[46]

Seven years later another traveller who visited the Balkans, with a rather different view in mind, also wrote about the land, its people and government officials. He also examined his *teskereh* and found, to his astonishment, that he was described as 'very tall, fair-haired, and blue-eyed,' although he was of 'barely medium height and decidedly dark.' He pointed this out, but was given the answer that most Englishmen were considered by the Turks to be tall, fair and blue-eyed, and consequently he must conform to the rule.[47] (Many years later, former internees from Auschwitz frequently showed that they had misperceived the notorious war criminal Dr Alois Mengele, describing him as 'very Aryan-looking' or as 'tall and blond,' although he was in fact a *Zigeunertyp*, no taller than 160 centimetres, with dark hair and a 'swarthy, almost gypsylike complexion.'[48])

How could the Turkish official(s) possibly have given such inaccurate descriptions of these Englishmen? Maybe they had read a book by one of their predecessors, claiming that the Englishmen 'could be easily distinguished from the Turks by reason of their fair complexion, clear blue eyes, neat figures, and general smartness.'[49]

The Magic Carpet of the East

For many travellers, the state of the roads constituted the basic criterion by which to assess the state of civilisation in the country they visited.[50] Given that in the Balkans the roads were 'none worthy of the name,'[51] a journey across the peninsula was not comfortable and travellers had to endure many obstacles and inconveniences. The lack of any direct roads between the various provinces was the first difficulty with which travellers had to contend, and so they and their baggage often had to proceed along horse tracks. In difficult terrain, in unfamiliar and mountainous country, it was easy to get lost even on the routes linking the larger Balkan towns. From Sarajevo to Mostar, for instance, is about 135 kilometres, but at the end of the nineteenth century the journey generally took three days in consequence of the nature of the roads.[52] This is why many travellers from the late seventeenth century on preferred to bypass the Balkan Peninsula altogether, and, if possible, went to Istanbul by boat via Malta, Marseille or Venice.

Along with roads, lodgings were an important criterion for the state of a country. The earlier Western travellers disliked the hostels beside the roads, because they were 'entirely on the Turkish style.' This meant that communal

Balkan roads

rooms, with bare walls, more often than not no windows and not a single article of furniture except straw mattresses, were used for eating, smoking and sleeping. Rich and poor were thrown in together, and travellers were obliged to sleep promiscuously among the 'Turks,' under the same roof as their horses and camels. In such lodgings nothing was private. Everyone could see what others were doing, except under the cover of night. Many travellers found it most uncomfortable because the habitual separation between seeing and being seen was blurred, as the local people stared at them while they ate, wondering at their customs.[53] In addition, as recorded by some twentieth-century travellers, there were no baths and usually only 'one basin and one towel for the common use of the entire hotel.'[54]

During the nineteenth century, Westerners generally saw themselves as a yardstick of correctness, travelling around with the firm conviction that 'There is no place like home.'[55] According to them, the 'primitive inns' they encountered during their journey across the Balkans were 'neither more beautiful nor more comfortable than those Abraham came across on his way to Canaan,'[56] and the people were 'still in the first stage of transition from Turkish barbarism to European civilisation.'[57] Till the middle of the twentieth century innkeepers in the Balkans generally let not rooms but beds, meaning that travellers who wanted to avoid sharing with a dozen 'doubtful travellers' had no alternative but to pay for accommodation for several people; that is, they had to pay 'Parisian prices' for 'Bulgarian comfort.'[58] If they happened to come across an inn with which they were satisfied, they saw it as a sign of progress and civilisation.[59]

Interior of a Balkan han

In the twentieth century railway travel became an important indicator of whether the Balkans was part of the East, an 'ahistorical realm of exotic pleasure,' or of the 'time-keeping' West. A key role was played by the Orient Express, which after 1883 ran between western Europe and Asia Minor. It was advertised in the 1920s as 'the Magic Carpet of the East.'[60] From western Europe it carried travellers directly to the ruins of the widely renowned castle of the Seven Towers in Constantinople, by way of London, Paris, Rome and Athens (exactly the opposite route to the one in which, according to Western understanding, world history had developed).[61] They did not have to struggle with Sir Walter Scott or Harrison Ainsworth; the Orient Express whirled them into the Middle Ages in three days.[62]

At the beginning of the twentieth century the Orient Express crossed the first 1,000 kilometres through France and Switzerland in sixteen hours. Its speed began to slow in Italy and then decreased further. Once over the Yugoslav frontier, its title of 'Express' became a kind of a mockery: the next 1,000 kilometres across Yugoslavia took twenty-six and a half hours.[63] In the first half of the twentieth century the whole world learnt that Turkish and/or Balkan trains 'never run up to time.'[64] If they did, it was taken as one more sign that 'the Balkans is not "Balkan" any more.'[65]

A lot of the inconveniences of journeying across the Balkans can be attributed to the local pashas' distrust of travellers, who were suspected of blazing a trail for future conquerors.[66] For instance, Felix who at the end of the eighteenth century was appointed French vice-consul in Sarajevo, waited in vain for a sultan's *firman*. It did not come and he could not take up his post, despite the interventions of the French ambassador in Istanbul.[67] This distrust was not without basis: as a French officer put it, the Bosnians were not so stupid as not to recognise political emissaries disguised as travellers, who crossed their country under various pretexts but, notoriously, with the aim of studying the state of the roads, the material riches of the country and the route which a conquering army could take. The writer added that Russia and Bonaparte 'not once' used this 'mean way' with their loyal ally, Turkey.[68] Travellers were often attacked, particularly by women who showered them with verbal abuse and by children who threw both verbal abuse and stones at them. Children even defied 'merciless' punishments from their fathers to attack foreign visitors in this way.[69]

Travellers' attempts to get to know local conditions were seriously hampered by their lack of knowledge of the local languages. Since Western travellers were generally ignorant of these languages and spent only a short time in passing through the Balkans, there were many obstacles to free communication. What they saw of the local people was their street life or their social hours at the *hans* (hostels) and coffee houses, where from time to time they engaged them in conversations comprising very few words and much gravity. The domestic life of the locals, especially the Muslims, remained 'an unknown quantity.'[70] Some travellers tried to overcome this obstacle by hiring an interpreter, thus adding an almost insurmountable impediment to communication, compounding the difficulties of different and contrasting prejudices, customs and opinions. The interpreters dared not embark on enquiries they thought might cause the slightest offence. Under pressure, both the questions and answers they reported were more often than not entirely their own invention.[71] Hiring an interpreter was not always a good solution for travellers, and could turn out to be a problem in itself, for the linguistic knowledge of hired interpreters did not always reach the expected level. When a certain British traveller, for instance, asked his interpreter for some explanation, his response would always be identical: "*Si, si.*" He asked him if he could understand Italian. The answer was: '*Si, si.*' Then he asked him if he could speak it and the answer was again: '*Si, si.*' And when he asked him why he did not speak it, the answer was once again in the affirmative: '*Si, si.*'[72]

River Deep, Mountain High

The earlier travellers saw nature with the eyes of practical men without much sense of the picturesque, or enough time to observe its beauties. For them, nature was principally a more or less dangerous obstacle which had to be overcome.[73] This attitude underwent a dramatic change in the age of romanticism, which brought with it a desire for distant and difficult journeys in search of those regions of romance where civilisation had not so far intruded as to eliminate all primitive features, where interesting ancient costumes and practices still thrived, where the wild, the sublime and the picturesque alternately presented their charms, where pomp and grandeur were profusely displayed and where the rude expressions of nature had never felt man's spoiling hand. As a result, some of those who thought of themselves as romantics and were 'dying of ardent desire' to observe local colour 'on the spot,' like Prosper Mérimée, the author of *La Guzla* (1840), could satisfy their curiosity by making just an imaginary journey to the Balkans. Those who actually went there were rewarded for their efforts by 'the striking features of Eastern scenery,' characterised by 'the magnitude and expanse of nature's beauties.' While in the West, they found the mountains and valleys 'circumscribed by limits which civilisation has, no doubt, contrived to make one feel to be more apparent than real.' But in the East, 'perhaps on account of the absence of that same civilisation,' they did not conceive any limits behind the gorgeous mountains.[74]

Not all of them were completely satisfied, however, for even Arcadia, the acme of picturesque beauty, the chosen home of faun, nymph and satyr, was more beautiful in the imagination than in real life. Visitors to the famous country were quite disappointed when they found that it was indeed 'as beautiful as possible,' with sheep and shepherds, 'though not the opera kind of *pastorelli* which one admires at the Haymarket. The people, indeed, disgrace the country, being a parcel of poor, miserable savages employed by the Turks, who are here few, but absolute.'[75]

In the nineteenth century travellers in the Balkans were still attracted by the material resources of the lands they traversed and quite often thought of the 'little pain that should be taken in order to become rich.'[76] However, they were concerned not only with what was visible on the surface of the earth but also with the natural resources hidden beneath it. They felt confident that the people of the East had much less interest in the treasures beneath the surface because, as an anonymous French traveller put it, for the Turks 'laziness was even stronger than love for silver.'[77] And since mining was 'foreign to the nature of the Turks,' they were, supposedly, 'content to let the rich mineral treasures of Bosnian mountains lie buried for the most part.'[78]

In the nineteenth and twentieth centuries, travellers in the Balkans were time and again fascinated by the romantic beauty of the wild and uncultivated mountains, gorges and inaccessible torrents. They indulged in elated epithets to describe those sights, which they found lovely beyond description.[79] They were always particularly excited to hear that they were about to cross a *balkan*; and disappointed upon discovery 'that this high-sounding title denotes only

Crna Peć in Herzegovina

a ridge which divides the waters, or a mountain pass, without its being a
necessary consequence that it offer grand or romantic scenery.'[80]

When the earlier travellers paid any attention to nature they were
disappointed because they found it 'mostly uncultivated, deserted, not
naturally, but due to the indolence of its inhabitants; it was full of terrible and
fatal forests, dangerous because of hayduks.'[81] With the new romantic attitude
the whole scene looked different, but disappointing once again. When fields
were cultivated, they became less romantic. 'Manifestly "civilization" kills the
traditional aesthetic sentiment, and it is a pity,' a Belgian baron maintained,
unable to share the enthusiasm of statisticians because

> It is not everything to double the number of our fat pigs and of our
> steam engines. *Non de solo pane vivit homo.* What is the use of being well
> off, if we cannot enjoy the beauties offered to us by nature, art, and
> dress? When manufactures cover the country with their ashes, dim with
> their smoke the blue sky, poison the water of the rivers, and abolish
> the costumes adapted to the climate and elaborated by the instinctive
> taste of the races.[82]

Romantic admiration for nature seized many of them so powerfully that they
were convinced that they alone were conscious of its beauty, while the 'Turks,'
it would seem, cared nothing for it. The beauties of nature were allegedly
hidden from the uneducated eyes of *rayah*, *Natursöhne* (the sons of nature):
'How enviable this poor Vlach would be, with nothing but a small corn-field
and a few goats, nestled down in the most wonderful spot of the Danube
current, if he only had developed sense for this beauty.'[83]

However, as early as the seventeenth century Edward Browne recorded
how the sultan spent over two months of the summer of 1669 on Mount
Olympus, not only for the coolness of the air but also to enjoy the view over
the plains and on to the Aegean Sea;[84] and the famous British orientalist of
the nineteenth century deemed that 'the beauties of nature seem always to
provoke hunger in Orientals, especially Turks, as good news in Englishmen.'[85]
How much such judgements reflected prejudice and how much the real state
of affairs can be assessed, for instance, by this description of the Pliva's fall
into the Vrbas in the town of Jajce, written by a Turkish adventurer and
traveller from the mid-seventeenth century, Evlija Çelebi. Çelebi was able
to find the proper words to describe the spectacle which many Westerners
found breathtakingly beautiful but 'indescribable,' many centuries later:

> In this very place the great river Pliva cascades down the sheer rock
> walls and flows into the lower river [Vrbas]. And the Pliva falls, high as

three minarets, make an arch, resembling the Milky Way. Then the two rivers flow together, raising a mist to the vault of heaven. Dew from this mist falls on the houses in the citadel. There are many water-mills in the river-bed on the rocks over which the Pliva flows beneath the town walls. Holes are pierced in the rocks above, bringing grist to the mills.

Lo, to sit in the cool chambers overgrown with greenery in front of these mills and watch the course of the river Pliva, wide as the sea, which flows with the knowledge and power of God, to watch its fall down the walls of rock, is such an interesting and unique spectacle that a man has to marvel at the Almighty and be struck with wonder. He who observes the stream of the river at midday is enchanted. The sight of the river Pliva, lit up by the sun which shines as a stone of Najaf, and the jumping of many great and small fish out of its water like lightning, is beautiful and wonderful![86]

The Balkan Ethics of Killing

Western travellers, then, stayed but a short time and their contacts with the locals were often limited to representatives of the Ottoman authorities, who were also their main source of information. For their part, the 'Turks' were often unfavourably disposed towards the Franks, as they called the people of the West, being much offended by 'that lightness in apparell, speech, gesture, &c. used of the Christians, whom for this cause they call Apes and Goats'[87] or 'Apes that have no Tails.'[88] These resentments persisted almost undiminished into the twentieth century when the Muslims of the Ottoman Empire still regarded those who differed from them as despicable dogs, hogs and devils, regardless of whether they were Russian or English Christians, French or German.[89]

On the other hand, the prevalent point of view in the West, especially from the nineteenth century on, was that the Christian population in the Ottoman Empire were deprived of their human rights. The British consul in Sarajevo, for instance, believed that oppression and wrong of every kind represented not merely the occasional but the constant state of things under the rule of the Turks, who divided the political body into conquerors and conquered, oppressors and oppressed.[90] In time, Christian subjects learned to exploit this prejudice for their own ends. They developed a list of classic horrors about the 'unspeakable Turk' to palm off on Westerners. Thus, Miss Durham found during her stay in Kosovo, just as she had earlier in Macedonia, that 'the approved method was to start a massacre and then to cry to Europe for help.'[91] She demonstrated this one-sided view by describing the Balkan ethics of killing:

When a Moslem kills a Moslem so much the better. When a Christian kills a Christian it is better not talked about, because people at home would not understand it; when a Christian kills a Moslem it is a holy and righteous act. When a Moslem kills a Christian it is an atrocity and should be telegraphed to all the papers.[92]

Islam versus Progress

Before the nineteenth century Christian subjects in the Ottoman Empire were not pitied, but were even viewed with contempt by Western travellers, who admired the proud bearing and strength of the Turks. Although the Christians had a 'wild look,' they lacked 'a dignified or martial air.' This was supposedly because slavery was 'too strongly marked on every feature' and sadly filled up 'many a profile that would appear to have been destined for a Miltiades, a Conon, or a Philopoemen.'[93] Thus, for instance, Bulgarians were described as 'Scythian Tartars that speak a sort of Sclavonian language,' who ate 'raw horse flesh' and put the author 'in mind of the horrid description Juvenal gives of the Anthropophagi in his fifteenth satire.'[94] Later such stigmatisation was reserved for the 'Turks,' 'the enemy to civilization and to the human race,'[95] since 'throughout Europe, and more particularly in England,... the word Turk has been applied as a mark of opprobrium, to designate ferocity, brutality, or savageness.'[96] In a comparable manner, a French consul in Travnik described the Bosnians as one of 'the most wild people in Turkey' and compared them to the Scythians and Hyperboreans. Another French traveller spoke of the Bosnian 'Turks' as 'exceptionally great ignoramuses' who were regarded 'as ignoramuses and barbarians' even by other 'Turks' from Macedonia, Greece and Istanbul.[97] In a book on the inhabitants of Bosnia, written by the French consul in Travnik at the beginning of the nineteenth century, readers would frequently come across terms such as 'wild,' 'ruthless' and 'cannibalistic.' In this light, the 'civilising' role of France might have seemed indispensable and could have been used as a pretext for the occupation of Bosnia. The author repeats several times in different words that this country and its inhabitants might change 'under some other rule.'[98]

The main reason for the bad state of the economy, in the Western view, was the corrupt Ottoman regime which prevented the material resources of the Balkans, magnificent as they were, from being developed for the good of its civilisation, 'while the enterprise of Europe has first to satisfy what is impossible- the avarice of the Divan.'[99] However, if it was impossible to

Audience at Sultan Suleiman's court, 1530

change 'the nature of the Turk,' it was possible to give him good government and thus to improve his social conditions.[100] This logic led the European powers to give Austria-Hungary the mandate for the occupation of Bosnia-Herzegovina in 1878. Before the occupation, Bosnia-Herzegovina was reportedly 'the poorest, most barbarous, most inhospitable country in Europe.'[101] Only a few years of Austro-Hungarian occupation, however, changed everything for the better, so much that 'a country which, but yesterday was steeped in barbarism' was miraculously transformed into 'a model object-lesson to the civilised world.'[102]

Western authors regarded the military and political conditions of a given country among the most important items of evidence for their judgements about it. Thus, when the Ottoman Empire was a great power, they visited it to admire its magnificent court and the military prowess of this 'great and mighty' empire. In the sixteenth and seventeenth centuries, European ambassadors to the sultan kissed his hand.[103] In 1593 when Queen Elizabeth sent Sir Edward Barton to be her ambassador to the Sublime Porte, it was recorded in the words of the capitulation that 'the queen had sent a noble person with presents to the victorious Porte, which is the refuge and retreat of the kings of the world.' From that time the custom was continued by every successive European ambassador of giving either gifts or money to the Ottoman government on every change of embassy.[104] The consular records of the seventeenth century show that the English Levant Company also adopted a very humble and respectful attitude towards the sultan, defended its rights by bribery rather than by arms, and never dreamed of resorting to naval action, as the great powers did from the second half of the nineteenth century.[105]

As long as the Ottoman Empire was expanding, its civil and military institutions were idealised as far superior to those of their contemporaries. Emperor Ferdinand II's ambassador to the Porte under Sultan Suleiman in 1554–62 Augerius Gislenius argued that while the Ottomans had 'a mighty, strong and wealthy Empire, great Armies, Experience in War, a veteran Soldiery, a long Series of Victories, Patience in Toil, Concord, Order, Discipline, Frugality and Vigilance,' on Western side there was 'public Want, private Luxury, Strength weakened, Minds Discouraged, an unaccustomedness to Labour or Arms, Soldiers refractory, Commanders covetous, a Contempt of Discipline, Licentiousness, Rashness, Drunkenness, Gluttony.' Worst of all, he found that the former were 'used to conquer' and the latter 'to be conquered.'[106]

Due to the defeat of the Ottoman army in wars in 1683 and at the beginning of the following century, the overall prestige of the Ottoman Empire and its civilisation declined. One of the first and the most obvious signs of the new state of affairs was a change in fashion. Till the beginning of the eighteenth century the ambassadors of the kings of Europe were compelled to wear Turkish dress when meeting the sultan. This 'humiliating masquerade' was formally abolished by the Treaty of Požarevac (1718). The ambassadors of England and Holland, who acted as mediators in the treaty, took advantage of the declining state of the Ottoman Empire to establish the custom that the European ministers should appear at these audiences 'in whatever dress they pleased.'[107] However, those diplomats who were given audience at the sultan's court in the first half of the nineteenth century had to hand over their swords and were still given pelisses which entirely covered their own clothes, not as a mark of honour, as some of them claimed, but to make them look like vassals of the sultan.[108] For it was an old custom that 'a Robe is the Present of a superiour to his inferiour, or to a slave.'[109]

When, in the nineteenth century, the tables were turned, what had been a formidable empire was personified as 'the Sick Man of Europe.' By then, the more or less idealised images had faded away, being replaced by duskier and more obscure ones. In the eyes of Westerners, the Ottoman Empire in general and its Balkan territories in particular were a symbol of backwardness, even for their neighbours in Croatia.[110] For the Western authors it was beyond all doubt that Islam was the main reason for the unenviable conditions of the Ottoman Empire and from the end of the seventeenth century they repeatedly stated that 'true Muslims' loved neither progress, innovation nor education; that the Koran was enough for them; that they were satisfied with their lot:

> And provided their Wives be handsome, their horses well Curri'd, and their Servants Submissive and Respectful, they never give themselves the trouble of inquiring after the Affairs of the rest of the World. Contented with their Lot, they sit whole Days on Sopha, without any other Occupation than drinking Coffee, smoking Tobacco, or caressing their Wives: So that their whole Life is a continual Revolution of Eating, Drinking, and Sleeping, intermixt with some dull Recreations.[111]

They subscribed to the view that as long as Muslims continued to be fatalists ('that is, as long as they continue to be Muslims'), there was little hope of their advancing in civilisation, for the stunting of the faculties produced by 'this benumbing principle' must necessarily render them unfit for the long struggle against the difficulties and obstacles which they would encounter in their progress towards a better order of things.[112]

If in the nineteenth century the mere sight of a 'passive' subject made the people of the West 'nervous,' in the pre-industrial East at the beginning of the twentieth century time had not yet become money.[113] However, Western authors had no doubt whatsoever that such a state of affairs was a consequence of the Turks' laziness and lack of ambition, for their sole aim in life, supposedly, was to enjoy *kayf*, and have enough food and no work to do. Supposedly, they spent their time in coffee houses, smoking their pipes and listening to stories, which saved them the trouble of thinking; and they watched passively as one cultural epoch after another passed them by.[114]

European Luxuries in the Hands of Barbarians

Travellers from abroad perceived any difference in the customs and manners of the local people from their own not as mere difference, but rather as an expression of their otherness, of their lack of civilised behaviour and of their backwardness. On the other hand, they perceived images and scenes which they associated with civilisation and progress as a sort of a foreign body in the Balkans.[115] Arthur John Evans who crossed Bosnia-Herzegovina on foot in 1875 found Bosnian people wearing turbans even 'more stupid.' He disliked 'the sometimes too obtrusive familiarity of these people' and he found it unpleasant, if those 'barbarians' called him *brat* (brother): 'I, who write this, happen to be told by every barbarian I meet that he is a man and a brother. I believe in the existence of inferior races, and would like to see them exterminated.'[116]

Although a large majority of twentieth-century authors did not follow such extreme views, they still found it impossible to like the Balkan people, for they were 'so unclean, uncouth, ignorant, and animal-like, and they live in such miserable hovels amid such appalling smells.'[117]

In the West during the nineteenth century hygiene became an important factor in assessing levels of civilisation. Many writers on the Balkans focused their comments on concepts of hygiene that they came across during their Balkan travels. The more important was hygiene as an indicator of civilisation, the more 'dirty' were the 'Turks' in these comments. 'As dirty as a Turk; as filthy as a Turk' became a byword. The 'Turks' were accused of being ignorant of the most elementary knowledge of the principles of cleanliness, though they washed their feet at least twice a day to obey the laws of the Koran. Since the book does not say how much water should be used, it was alleged that 'many a Turk merely spat upon his hands and rubbed them on the soles of his feet, fully believing that he had fulfilled the letter of the law.'[118]

Such observations applied not only to 'Turks,' but to the other Balkan people as well, who seemed 'heinously unclean.'[119] This is why Frederick Moore, for instance, was of the opinion that compulsory military service had provided useful training to the Bulgarian peasants. According to him, the natives of Macedonia 'bathe as they marry, only once or twice in a lifetime.' Newborn babies were not washed for fear of their catching cold, not even when they were baptised, for oil was used in the ceremony. He cited an open letter from a Greek priest to American missionaries concerning the use of oil instead of water during the baptismal rite: the priest defended the use of oil on the ground that, following their anointing at baptism, the Macedonian peasants, though they never wash, carried with them no foul odour, as did peasants baptised with water.[120] Yet some authors saw in the Bulgarians 'the strange contrast of their cleanliness, with the filth of the Turks, living under the same government.'[121]

Until the sixteenth century people in Western Europe blew their noses into their hands and ate with their fingers. Two centuries later the use of handkerchiefs became fashionable among people who laid claim to 'good manners,' this became a weapon against social inferiors, a means of distinction, because, like forks and plates, handkerchiefs assumed a particular social prestige value.[122] As the following passage shows quite clearly, travellers in the Near East in the nineteenth century still had an eye for this distinction:

> European luxuries of divers description are now beginning to be understood by the Osmanlees in Constantinople, but sometimes rather curiously applied. I remember seeing a Turkish military captain, who had occasion to blow his nose, in the first instance make use of such means as nature supplies, and lastly, as a finishing stroke only, he resorts to the handkerchief, which is furnished by art and refinement.[123]

Even in the twentieth century travellers were much surprised at how differently this instrument was used in Turkey, if it was used at all.[124]

Yet another reporter, with a certain disregard for truth, reported that, 'the Turks evidently, in many cases, did not know how to deal with their weapons.' This he illustrated by the Turks' use of an umbrella: apparently, they carried it straight in front of them, pointing upwards if it was shut, and sideways and away from their heads if it was open.[125]

Such reports generally say more about the customs and manners in the West than about the customs and manners of the East. To give one more example, at the beginning of the eighteenth century, when spitting was regarded as a seemly topic of conversation a famous French traveller informed his readers at length of how the Turks 'swallow their Spittle out of Custom and out of Cleanliness, and without any Prejudice,' adding that when he 'went to bridle my self before Persons of Fashion, and forbade to spit, it made me heart-sick: Decency however requires one to spit into a Handkerchief, in order to save the Carpet upon the Floor, or else one must sit at one Corner, and take up the Carpet, and spit upon the Boards.'[126] However, it is impossible to find any information on spitting in reports by authors of the second half of the eighteenth century, because by then the topic could no longer be mentioned in respectable company. Since in the middle of the nineteenth century it could be talked about with disgust as a revolting habit,[127] we can read in a source from that date that in Dalmatia 'the Morlacchi, like Montenegrins, may vie with the Americans in this odious practice.'[128]

This rule is illustrated even more clearly by reports about the relief of physiological needs. Since in the seventeenth century it was still decent to speak about it, an English traveller could frankly inform his readers how during a night journey in an open coach he passed water over the side to avoid inconveniencing the rest of the company by making them wait while he alighted, thus delaying their journey.[129] In sixteenth- and seventeenth-century travel reports we can encounter detailed descriptions (given as illustrations of the meticulous cleanliness of the Turks!) of how the Turks used to 'make water like women' and afterwards washed their hands, and how they reviled a Christian if they saw him 'pissing against a wall, and sometimes striking him.'[130] A member of the Royal Academy of Sciences and chief botanist of the French king informed his readers at length of a curious story relating to this subject:

> When they make Water, they squat down like Women, for fear some Drops of Urine should fall into their Breeches. To prevent this Evil, they squeeze the part very carefully, and rub the Head of it against the Wall; and one may see the Stones worn in several Places by this Custom. To make themselves sport, the Christians smeer the Stones sometimes with Indian Pepper, and the Root call'd Calfs-foot, or some other hot Plants, which frequently causes an Inflammation in such as happen to use the Stone. As the Pain is very smart, the poor Turks commonly run for a Cure to those very Christian Surgeons, who were the Authors of all the Mischief: they never fail to tell them it is a very dangerous Case, and that they should be oblig'd perhaps to make an Amputation: the Turks, on the contrary, protest and swear they have had no Communication with any sort of Woman that could be suspected. In short, they wrap up the suffering Part in a Linnen dipp'd in Oxicrat, tinctur'd with a little Bole-Armenic; and this they sell them as a great Specifick for this kind of Mischief.[131]

TWO

Ladies with Greasy Fingers

Food and table manners were recorded at length in most of the accounts of Eastern travel, providing a particularly remarkable picture of the differences between Eastern and Western ways of life that stimulated, rather than satisfied, their readers' imagination. Thus, when a *sofra*, an octagonal or hexagonal table, was set up before which diners had to squat 'like tailors' for their meal, many Westerners found this manner of eating 'not a little incommodious.'[1] Moreover, napkins were not laid on the table, but were spread by servants on their masters' knees. The servants stood behind their masters to cut their meat, 'for 'tis beneath the Turkish Grandeur to do any thing for themselves.'[2] There were no plates either and everybody ate with their fingers. The bill of fare seemed another violation of all Western rules. Dishes were brought in covered and put down in the middle of the table, one at a time, and removed when they were empty. One dish followed another 'in the most heterogeneous manner,' the savoury following the sweet and the stew preceding the custard – proof that 'gastronomy was no science in the East.'[3]

A Venetian diplomat of the first half of the sixteenth century, Benedetto Ramberti, regarded the Turks as entirely lacking in table manners. His opinion that they ate 'like animals'[4] was shared by many authors of later periods, who claimed that their diet was 'far from luxurious, and little differing from that which ordinary persons content themselves with,'[5] and 'so nastily and ill season'd, that a Man needed to have been prepar'd by a Month's Famine

Turks of quality at dinner, late 17th century

to swallow one single Morsel.'[6] On the tables of the wealthier classes the courses numbered twenty or thirty but, as reported by Jean Du Mont at the end of the seventeenth century, the Turks could not be 'accus'd of Luxury in Eating; for a Hen boil'd with Rice, Coriander-Seed, and Sugar, is the best Dish that comes before a man of 20000 Livres a Year, and 'tis they call Pilo. The rest of the Meal is made up with a Dish of Fish, and some Sweet-Meats, in which there is always more Honey than Sugar.'[7] When travels widened their horizons, travellers saw with their own eyes that except in the French Embassy in Istanbul 'they know not what *Good Eating;* no, not if you were to go to the further end of Japan.'[8]

In the nineteenth and early twentieth centuries, Westerners were fully aware of the fact that habit is always superior to taste, but they still stuck to the opinion that there was only one way in which course should follow course and only one set of appliances which should be used at meals. The multiplicity of courses that followed each other 'with increasing lusciousness' and the fact that they were eaten with the fingers amounted to convincing testimony 'to the uncivilised condition of the Turk.'[9] This is how landscape painter Edward Lear described his dinner at the three-tailed pasha in Shköder in the middle of the nineteenth century:

> I counted up thirty-seven dishes, served, as is the custom in Turkey, one by one in succession, and then I grew tired of reckoning (supposing that perhaps the feast was going on all day) though I think there were twelve or fourteen more. But nothing was so surprising as the strange jumble of irrelevant food offered: lamb, honey, fish, fruit; baked, boiled, stewed, fried; vegetable, animal; fresh, salt, pickled; solid; oil, pepper; fluid; sweet, sour; hot, cold – in strange variety, though the ingredients were often very good. Nor was there any order in the course according to European notions – the richest pastry came immediately after dressed fish and was succeeded by beef, honey, and cakes; pears and peaches; crabs, ham, boiled mutton, chocolate cakes, garlic, and fowl; cheese, rice, soup, strawberries, salmon – trout, and cauliflowers – it was the very chaos of a dinner![10]

However noteworthy, the food enjoyed by the Balkan people and their table manners were so unpleasant and unpalatable to some Westerners as to appear responsible for other unpleasant elements of Balkan culture. Thus, the French consul in Travnik at the beginning of the nineteenth century attributed the cruelty of the people to their peculiar food and eating habits:

> When a Bosnian gets out of bed, he starts his day with a tumbler of slivovitz. Shortly before lunch, he drinks at least two more, which he tempers with sweets. To extinguish the intolerable burning in his stomach caused by the drinks, he devours his onion and chopped turnip slops without any bread; followed by disgusting sauerkraut and tough dried lamb. Copious amounts of bean soup are served after this; and the meal is concluded with yet another slivovitz.[11]

The Immutability of Oriental Customs

In the sixteenth and seventeenth centuries Western travellers made no mention of people in the East eating without forks; they only noted that they

Interior of a house in Bosnia, late 19th century

boiled their meat till it was very tender, because knives were never used at meals.[12] Among my sources, the first to miss them was Dr John Covel who noted in his diary on 27 July 1675 that Easterners 'had no such finicallnesse as knives or forkes onely the weapons the nature gave us, our hands and teeth.'[13] This fact implies that Westerners had not missed forks before because they themselves were not yet accustomed to eating with these weapons.

In the late seventeenth century, Western travellers saw the absence of knives and forks as proof that the people of the East were, as Thomas Smith put it in 1678, 'strangers to luxury and high feeding.'[14] Then, till the 1820s, they regarded it as an exotic curiosity, although some of them already found it troublesome to use their fingers for forks.[15] On some more formal occasions, in deference to Western customs, knives and forks were placed before Europeans, 'which however they thought proper to dispense with as much as possible.'[16] But by the end of the eighteenth century, Westerners found the practice of tearing off pieces of meat with the fingers to be a 'barbarous operation.'[17] Eventually, the people of the West came to regard this mode of eating as another proof 'of the immutability of oriental customs: it was thus the disciples supped when Judas was designated by the circumstance of his "dipping" with our Saviour in the dish.'[18]

When eating in the Eastern style, or, in the words of Sir John Finch's record of his embassy, using but 'the implements provided by Nature,'[19] people helped themselves with two fingers and the thumb of the right hand, assisted by a piece of bread; the left hand was never used. Well-mannered persons kept to their own particular part of the meal and refrained from excursions into their neighbours' choice morsels. However, it was considered quite polite for the host, with gushing hospitality, or perhaps for 'the black fingers' of an attentive slave, to tear asunder the fibres of mutton or fowl for his guests. From the nineteenth century on such friendly attentions by their hosts were not perceived as such by Westerners, who found them 'insuperably offensive and disgusting to European feelings.'[20] Thus a British doctor recalled a lunch he had eaten in Istanbul in 1824:

> There are neither knives nor forks, nor plates, nor drinking glasses, nor chairs, nor tables; one common dish appears at a time, and perhaps fifty are brought in succession. The prejudice against greasy fingers, at first, made it rather monstrous to see delicate ladies plunging their hands into reeking dishes, tearing a leg of mutton piecemeal, or tugging at the wing of an obdurate fowl.[21]

The prejudice against greasy fingers was so strong that the great majority of Westerners completely failed to notice the ritual significance of eating and drinking peculiar to the Eastern world. Eating and drinking were not merely acts of satisfying basic physical needs but constituted a kind of sacrament of brotherhood full of symbolic meanings. When a host broke off a piece of meat with his fingers and passed it to his guest, he was not just giving him the piece of meat; he had performed an *ikram* to him (an act of honour and regard). By that act he had pledged to protect his guest with every drop of his blood and to prevent any evil befalling him on his territory. For that space of time they were brothers.[22]

Western tastes and appliances were first introduced by the Greek nobility of Constantinople, among whom European customs became increasingly fashionable from the late eighteenth century. Then, reportedly, in some well-to-do families nothing was wanting but practice, and European cutlery remained for a while 'rather hindrances than auxiliaries to most of those who have adopted them.'[23] Baron de Tott described seeing a woman pick up olives in her fingers and then pricking them with her fork to eat them *à la française*.[24] In the 1830s the use of chairs and tables, knives and forks was becoming general among the Ottoman nobility: Sultan Mahmut exchanged the old-fashioned stool and tray for a chair and table. But not everyone followed the fashion; according to Western authors, many people in Turkey still preferred to eat *à la turca,* with their fingers.[25] At least, Westerners expected them to do so. When Turkish banqueters aboard a British ship at anchor in Istanbul in the mid-nineteenth century were given knives and cutlasses, forks and tomahawks, spoons and sponges, they 'laid aside their gravity, and dispensed for that night with the orthodox use of their fingers,' and their British hosts 'feared that sundry manslaughters would have taken place in consequence of their awkwardness with those "accursed contrivances," knives and forks.'[26]

In the Western narration of the Other any novelty travellers met during their Balkan journey was usually ridiculed as too 'Balkan' or else dismissed as not 'Balkan' enough. Thus many of them reported that people of the higher classes in Istanbul and other larger Balkan towns only used plates, knives, forks and glasses when 'Europeans' were present 'as a proof of civilisation.'[27] But as soon as they were alone at the table or among close friends, it was supposed that they went back to using their fingers.[28] Hence, not even those used to this 'symbol of civilisation'[29] were considered civilised in the European sense. 'Europeanised Turks,' who learned to eat with forks, wore the new uniforms tailored in the European style and socialised with non-Muslims, were seen by many Europeans as representing either 'that kind of human creature which is the closest to an animal species of all living things,'[30] or 'the real animal concealed bellow the European cloak.'[31] According to some authors, Western attempts to improve the Turks recalled the old story of trying to wash the negro white: 'He never was, or will be, or can be anything but a barbarian.'[32]

During the nineteenth century various European customs were adopted in some of the principal houses of Istanbul. In most, tables and chairs replaced dinner trays and in some a complete European dinner service might even be found. Tables furnished with cloths and forks and knives were used as a sign of prestige by distinguished individuals on special occasions.[33] With this change of custom, however, Westerners developed an appetite for the old ways of eating. When provided with knives and forks European style, they asked their hosts as a favour to permit them to dine with them in the Eastern fashion, which they now found charming 'by its novelty.' So they used their fingers, even if without great effect[34] and 'to the amusement of the numerous spectators, who gathered round to see how awkward Franks were at eating.'[35] Eventually, towards the end of the nineteenth century, individual reports began to appear stating that there was nothing 'in the least nasty in dispensing with knives and forks, when one's fingers, or rather one's right forefinger and thumb, are kept as scrupulously clean as a well-bred Turk's.'[36] As a final point, in the twentieth century, when the use of forks was already as common in the Near East as it was in the West and had entirely lost its former significance as a status symbol, individual travellers looked forward to the opportunity of eating with their fingers, which was 'not so unpleasant as it would seem.'[37] Some travellers' joyous expectations occasionally turned to chagrin when they found that Albanians, for instance, contrary to their expectations, ate with knives and forks.[38]

Observers' Work Is Never Done

Observers' work is never done, however. At the beginning of the twentieth century, travellers to the Near East were confronted with another previously unknown 'terrible choice' between eating several 'large courses without any drink and the unspeakable qualms of sharing the vessel with your companions,' as 'at a Turkish meal' only one glass was provided for all the guests.[39] In the civilising process, which, according to Norbert Elias, is characterised by casting a veil over certain activities, the carving of meat was relegated to the kitchen.[40] Meat as a single joint ceased to appear on the table; instead it was presented in carved slices, which gradually blurred the close association with the animal. This process was taken furthest in Britain: the English language has completely different words for animals and their meat. Travellers used to this dissociation between an animal and its meat were in danger of finding themselves in severe distress when faced with the facts.

The carving of an animal, as Elias shows, was once an integral part of social life in the West. Then, after the seventeenth century, the spectacle became increasingly distasteful. When, for instance, an Albanian innkipper killed a sheep for his English guests, he butchered the animal in front of them. His Western guests, however, were less delighted by the process than he anticipated, and induced him 'with difficulty' to conduct his activities a few metres away. They were quite disturbed by being 'regaled with the spectacle of cutting up the carcass, hung on a branch of the tree in front of the door.'[41] The public nature of the cooking arrangements, which was a feature of many Balkan eating-houses, had the advantage of making a menu unnecessary. Foreigners could see for themselves what food was available just as easily as natives and could indicate the dish of their choice by simply pointing to it. But for people who were not accustomed to watching the butchering of animals, or as some of them put it, seeing their 'to-morrow's dinner in the raw state,' was the scene that put to the test the strongest of stomachs. It was

perceived as a 'revolting sight' which brought some of them 'to the verge
of vegetarianism.' Since the Balkans was essentially a meat-eating land, they
realised that it was not a suitable place to begin experiments in a vegetable diet
and they were therefore obliged to stifle their 'better instincts and carry on for
the nonce in the old carnivorous way.'[42]

THREE

Breast-feeding Prejudice

In the age when as-yet-undiscovered, unknown lands were generally assumed to exist, many naturalists took part in voyages to extend the borders of European empires throughout the world. Their task was to explain the new discoveries and the possibilities they offered to the home country. These voyages extended not only the horizons of their native states but also the frontiers of knowledge: for day by day new species of flora and fauna were discovered. Of all the knowledge obtained from the new discoveries, the most radical was perhaps the recognition of relativity. Perspective had changed. Notions once believed to be universal turned out to be contingent on place:

> All preconceived notions and beliefs concerning cosmography, history, politics and society were made ridiculous by the new discoveries. The world had been opened up by the fanatical self-confidence of visionaries, and had proved to be wilder than their wildest fancies. New kingdoms were to be had for the taking.[1]

In the eighteenth century it was believed that only knowledge could bring happiness. It is not surprising, then, that in the seventeenth and eighteenth centuries natural history was held in high esteem and was regarded as the most interesting and comprehensive of all the sciences, embracing 'all objects which the universe displays to us.'[2] Naturalists set themselves the important

Alberto Fortis observing the waterfalls of Velika Gubavica

goal of sweeping away the prejudices which had for so long disguised the real nature of the world, causing common errors to be taken as undeniable truth. In their writings scholars focused increasingly on method; in the year 1749 Georges Louis Le Clerc de Buffon published both his eminent *Natural History* and an essay *How to study natural history*.

Abbot Alberto Fortis (1741–1803) lived and worked in this intellectual climate. In the 1770s, he travelled several times in the service of the *Serenissima* and of private patrons to Venetian Dalmatia. In his time, Fortis was considered Italy's foremost naturalist and later he was seen as a talented journalist and polymath. Today he is known principally for his travel writing. His *Viaggio in Dalmazia* (1774), in particular, presents a picture of the conditions, natural products, history, costumes and popular traditions of the region. It includes a long and detailed chapter on the Morlaks, their way of life, their manners, costumes, rites, songs and so on. In European literature the book was received as an 'epochal revelation of that near primitive world and its beautiful and original poetry which nobody had written down.'[3]

In his letters from Dalmatia, a country 'far from Italian politeness,'[4] Fortis did not report only on natural phenomena and curiosities. Even his first book, meant as a mineralogical study, was in fact a unique monograph on the islands of Cres and Lošinj and their inhabitants. Later, from being a researcher on fossils and minerals, plants and insects, ancient inscriptions and antiquities Fortis became a keen naturalist and reformer. He did not dedicate a special chapter to the theoretical questions of natural history, but he often returned to them in his writings, in which he declared the aim of natural history to be observation of the structure of mountains, the composition of waters, the constitution of animals and other natural phenomena 'without the spirit of prejudice' and 'with the sole view to investigate the truth.'[5] He included a significant amount of anthropological data in his works, although this was not among his declared objectives. This was no accident: he was following the established praxis of contemporary naturalists and the methodology of Buffon, who argued that man should be included within the scope of natural history since human beings are part of nature.[6]

Hairy Fish

In the Age of Enlightenment it was believed that the scholar's principal duty was not to succumb to prejudice and not to be misled by any authority if empirical facts led to conclusions different from those stated in books. As Fortis wrote in a letter to John Strange, the assertions of reputable writers on points of physical facts were 'frequently false and erroneous.' However, neither the authority of the few nor the volume of the many could induce him to make hasty assertions on things he had not examined with his own eyes.[7] Indeed, his observations led him to different conclusions from those of many distinguished naturalists: he found Linnaeus to be mistaken on certain points, he opposed de Réaumur on others and he argued with de Tournefort, to mention but a few examples.[8] He was even less ready to put blind trust in laymen: 'Many other things were related to me concerning the fossil history of Bosnia, but I think it improper to mention them upon the simple report of others. I know by experience that in facts of natural history a prudent incredulity is very requisite.'[9] Consequently, he urged other naturalists to take the same precautions as he always did before asserting a fact to be true on the allegation of another: he said they should go to the place in question themselves or at least threaten to go, whatever difficulties might intervene: 'that is how the lies are revealed.'[10]

Fortis himself was not prepared to assert any fact on the basis of mere hearsay. For instance, he was not prepared to believe the inhabitants in the area around the Krin Lakes when they claimed that a hairy species lived in these waters, although some of them appeared very serious in their descriptions, adding that these fish keep to the bottom so it was very difficult to catch any without poisoning the waters. However, Fortis was not disposed to believe physical extravagancies unless he saw them; he therefore suspended his belief in the hairy fish because he had not seen them.[11]

It was not always easy to follow such strict principles: it required a great

deal of energy and any result was by no means a foregone conclusion. Fortis
had been travelling through a country where science was little cultivated and
natural history scarcely known, even by name. It was difficult to find anyone
to direct him on his way and his only means of obtaining knowledge of useful
or strange phenomena was to discover them himself. Thus he often wandered
over vast deserts and craggy mountains in the hope of finding something
interesting but was often disappointed.[12] But he was well aware that the
shortest distance between two points is not always a straight line:

> Whoever might pretend to judge of this at distance would act
> imprudently and run the risk of giving some ridiculous explanation;
> as is too often the case even with the greatest naturalists, when they
> undertake to unfold some strange phenomenon upon a superficial
> inspection or according to the accounts of others: like that good man
> who wrote the natural history of the Swiss Alps without ever travelling
> to observe them.[13]

Fortis himself illustrates how misleading this method can be with an example
from the first volume of *Illyricum Sacrum* by Father Daniele Farlati where the
reader is told that the Arkanđeo pass is extremely dangerous because it is
where the Neretva and Cetina rivers meet the Krka from different directions.
In reality, the mouth of the Neretva lies at least 130 kilometres away and the
river flows so slowly towards the sea that it is tidal for over 20 kilometres
upstream.[14] By ignorance we make mistakes and by making mistakes we learn:
this was Fortis's motto. Hence, the reader can follow him as he walk along
the coast, climbs mountains, descends into underground cave and travels by
boat. Wherever he went, curiosity followed. Breaking new ground, he often
made his rowers pause so that he could attentively examine 'the strange
modifications of calcareous matter disposed there in a manner quite different
from the laws which the masters of nature use to prescribe in elaborate
discourses on stratifications without once stirring out of their study.'[15]

Before field observations had become routine, naturalists were greatly
preoccupied with extraordinary phenomena and miracles, often resorting to
theology. By the second half of the eighteenth century such an approach had
already become a thing of the past. Fortis himself shared the negative attitude
to it. He was of the opinion that exact observations of ordinary things which
had been little examined by the majority of writers were more interesting to
a true naturalist than more extraordinary and unusual phenomena.[16] He was
angry because museums of curios in the Venetian Republic had purchased
exotic shells at high prices but had no shells whatsoever from their own sea.
According to Fortis, this did the museums no credit and was also an insult

to a country which produced as many natural curiosities as any other. These objects should be the first choice of collectors and would do them credit, when seen by learned travellers.[17]

Work on extraordinary and apparently inexplicable phenomena was fraught with difficulties of all kinds, according to Fortis. The best method for a person to adopt when analysing them for the first time was to describe simply but with the most scrupulous and exact precision everything he had seen. Everyone was then free to explain the phenomena their own way, according either to the systems of others or to a new hypothesis formed for the specific case. Fortis explicitly stated that he was not willing to place himself among those who, in discussing a point of natural history, either gave too much scope to an inflamed or prejudiced imagination or implicitly followed the 'unphilosophical doctrines of the thirteenth century.'[18] He believed it was wrong to call on religion for assistance in formulating a hypothesis or to endeavour to contradict the observations of respected naturalists of the time by arbitrary interpretation of sacred texts. For the enlightened abbot, religion never benefited on such occasions: 'witness the abjuration of Galileo which does so much dishonour to Italy.'[19]

Fortis regarded his research as a contribution to development and progress as he understood them. To achieve so great a goal was only possible, he felt, with scrupulous and accurate observation, that is, the empirical method. The advantages of the new method, which was so much emphasised in the Age of Enlightenment, were universal and obvious. The prevailing sense was no longer one of human helplessness at the mercy of destiny. Science constantly widened the horizons and increased human powers. In the words of Samuel Johnson, knowledge is 'more than equivalent to force.'[20]

But the empirical method produced not only these advantages but also certain pitfalls. Observation is always subjective and therefore incomplete or even incorrect; it can also contain *unseen errors*. What appears more obvious than the journey of the sun across the sky? It is therefore not surprising that Fortis faced great difficulties in trying, for instance, to solve the question of the so-called gradual elevation of the waters in Venice.[21] The difficulties inherent in the empirical method were even greater when he used it to explain certain phenomena which he had not been able to observe himself but which were attested by data obtained from his informants and borne out by his own prior knowledge or expectations. When, for instance, he was told that a shower of anchovies had once fallen in the heart of Bosnia 'to the greatest terror and contrition of those poor Turks,' a fact which accords with data already collected by Pliny in his *Natural History*, he tried to find an explanation by reference to some typhoon or hurricane 'of which there are many examples.'[22]

These methods proved the least reliable when explaining cultural phenomena, for here the subjective role of the observer is vital. Such questions can only be treated from a perspective of awareness of a certain cultural context. Cultural phenomena are for the most part not precisely replicable or irreversible, and therefore they usually need to be treated on the basis of multiple observations. With insufficient knowledge of the Croatian language, he had to rely on interpreters, and this also hindered him in collecting cultural data.[23] Fortis's approach was further inhibited by cultural bias. On his journey through Cres and Lošinj, he observed that the people there were generally filthy.[24] During his visit he noted ignorance and superstition among the villagers of Cres and Lošinj. By contrast, Sir Gardner Wilkinson, who merely passed both islands on a steamboat, saw the situation quite differently:

> The Venetians even purposely avoided every measure that could enrich, or better the condition of the people, in order, more easily, to rule Dalmatia, while they supplied their army from its hardy peasantry; and, however, incredible it may appear, the Venetian Senate openly interfered to prevent the establishment of schools in that country. Printing was also forbidden there; and the Venetians severely punished one of their people, for having dared to establish a press in the independent city of Ragusa.[25]

He was also able to see the causes of the situation: 'When under the Venetians it had about 5000 inhabitants, and the revenues of Cherso and the neighbouring Ossero were 1273 ducats, of which 630 were paid in duties to the Republic.'[26]

Fortis had a very sceptical attitude to systems and theories which reminded him of 'unripe fruits that would soon rot.' He was persuaded that future systems and theories would be of the same quality unless sufficient observations were made.[27] According to him, theorists of systems concerning the formation of mountains did not, in general, pay enough attention to the effects of water. Those with a gift for mathematics simply took fright at the boundless extent of time needed for erosion. Their observations strongly disagreed with the Bible and teachings of the church which were based on the assumption that the world was created in six days and that plant and animal species were created in isolation from each other and from human. These elements, according to the church, took place about 6,000 years previously.[28] This point of view was ultimately rejected only when James Hutton presented his *Theory of the Earth* in 1785 (published in 1788).

While travelling in Dalmatia, Fortis had an opportunity to become familiar with local oral traditions and folk beliefs. He came across many remarkable and interesting examples of folk poetry, of which he became an enthusiast. But he was much upset by the 'abuse of tradition' and could not accept the role of the clergy in keeping the people ignorant. Thus, he was deeply disgusted by a friar who, he was given to hope, might provide him with useful information but who instead told 'the most foolish fables that can enter into a brain vitiated by superstition' about children crying in ravines and fairies dancing in caverns.[29] In the appendix to the English edition of his *Travels to Dalmatia* he enumerates examples of superstitious customs among 'those poor ignorant islanders' of Pag. These customs, he alleges, were to a large extent kept alive by the friars 'for their own interest' and sometimes even 'for more criminal ends.'[30]

Advantages and Deficiencies of the Empirical Methods

In accordance with the concepts of the Age of Enlightenment, science was not studied merely for science's sake. Scholars abandoned the investigation of the original principles of essence and existence; instead of looking for original causes, they tried to discover which means could achieve which effect. This change in approach led to the invention of an abundance of material goods, this being the object towards which the most advanced sciences tended. Fortis complained that natural history in the Venetian Republic was 'still despised and derided by many as a useless study notwithstanding the improvements of the age and the examples of the other polite nations of Europe.'[31] He himself wanted to contribute to 'national advantage' through his research 'by pointing out the places which want cultivation and the advancement of natural science by describing the production of nature.'

> Besides these objects, I thought it my duty also to rectify the mistakes which authors who have written about this country have fallen into; and I have consulted the convenience of travellers by indicating popular reports which I found to be false. Nor have I omitted to mention the remains of ancient settlements, though that belongs rather to the antiquary than to the naturalist. I have, indeed, more readily taken notice of them as they give a juster idea of Dalmatia than we have generally entertained; for if it were that horrid country which it is often represented to be, so many Roman colonies would not have been planted in it.[32]

At the beginning of *Viaggio in Dalmazia* Fortis wrote that his noble patrons could be pleased if the published work brought no other profit than that of replacing the marble sold by foreigners 'at an exorbitant price' to the city of Venice, where the quantity of marble used every year was considerable, with Dalmatian marble which, he adds in parentheses, had been used by the Romans to make their most precious statues as well as for buildings, at a trifling cost.[33] And, if his zealous research into nature, the current state of lakes, swamps and rivers and possible new discoveries should bring other benefits to the national wealth, trade and arts, the generous patrons of his travels should have the undeniable right to be called great patriots; he himself would enjoy the satisfaction of being a useful subject, which should be the ambition of every nobleman rather than fame as a great scholar and scientist.[34] This is why fishing was one of the principal objects of his observations along the coast of Dalmatia, for 'any improvement or any expansion of this activity becomes a source of national economy and interest.'[35] He wished it was in his power 'to declare war against the northern fishes which invade our Italy as the men used to do in barbarous ages' and thought himself happy could he 'arm the fishermen of the Adriatic against these foreign intruders.'[36]

But, since fishing was not flourishing and catches of fish not rich enough, he blamed lazy fishermen. He was especially angry with fishermen from the village of Zloselo (Evil Village), present-day Pirovac, near Šibenik: 'Yet notwithstanding the great plenty and variety of... fish, the lazy Zlosellian neglects every means of profiting by them: he is contented if he can find provision for the day and often devours without bread or any sort of sauce all the fish he has caught.'[37]

In his introduction to the chapter on the manners and customs of the Morlaks, Fortis disproves the rumours portraying them as a savage people. His contemporary Carlo Gozzi, despite knowing Fortis's work well, in his memoirs published in Venice 1793, called them barbarians and anthropophagi and, in general, unruly and abject people.[38] Town and country dwellers of the Dalmatian coast told many terrible stories about the cruelty of the Morlaks, their plunder and cattle thieving. They described them as a fierce people, unreasonable, devoid of humanity and capable of any crime. In Dubrovnik the word 'Morlak' remained a curse as late as the nineteenth century, 'just as in Scotland a hundred years ago every Highlander, in the eyes of Lowlander, was a cateran and a robber.'[39]

According to Fortis, if the Morlaks had ever displayed such characteristics, it was either long ago or, if there were more recent examples, they were the responsibility of a few individuals, not of the group as a whole. Fortis now thought it his duty to write what he had personally observed of their customs and behaviour and thereby make some 'apology' for a people who had welcomed him and treated him with so much humanity. Travellers, he observed, often exaggerate the dangers and difficulties they face in remote lands. He felt far removed from 'that kind of charlatanism' and he wanted to report only what he had seen himself, not what he had merely heard: *non audita sed visa scribo*.[40] Much of Fortis's travel writing proves him a sober and accurate observer. But some of the phenomena he describes he could not have seen himself and he had to trust to the accounts of informants. Not all his descriptions, therefore, result from work following his declared principles.

Fortis spent most of his time in Dalmatia in towns.[41] The townspeople were educated in Italian culture so that 'all the genteel people of both sexes speak good Italian.'[42] Fortis explicitly stated that the citizens of Zadar were as polite 'as could only be wished in any respected Italian town.' But when he left the towns, he met 'with ignorance and distrust of the backward people in the country so poorly inhabited and far from Italian politeness.'[43] This appears to be the main reason for his opinion of the village people of Dalmatia whom he found generally 'lazy and malicious.' He infers that this was because they were 'too much protected by the laws and put on an equality with their masters.' In his view, subordination was 'absolutely necessary to render these maritime people happy; and in some cases, even forcible and violent methods would prove very useful to rouse them from their habitual indolence.'[44]

The French painter Louis François Cassas, who was familiar with Fortis's work, writing about his journey through Istria and Dalmatia in 1783, portrayed the inhabitants of Zloselo in even darker hues, claiming: 'If we were to describe these people as savages, it would be an insult to the human race; for they have neither the candour, the affecting simplicity, the pride, nor the independence, of that character. Savages are the first link of the chain of human nature: these people almost appear to be the last of some other.'[45]

This, of course, was not the reason why fishing in Dalmatia was in decline. The reason was the heavy duties imposed on salt by the Venetian government, not the personal characteristics of the fishermen, who were prevented from following a lucrative trade by the artificially high price of salt, imposed by the government in a country where the coasts were rich in fish and where the occupation would have been beneficial to the people and the government.[46] Sir Gardner Wilkinson ascertained that the Venetian government could have improved fishing and increased revenues and trade by a few alterations in their fiscal system, 'had they understood the principles of political economy, and relieved the island from injudicious duties on salt.'[47] But they did not and, as a result, it simply did not pay the fishermen to catch more fish than necessary for their daily needs, since salt was so expensive that they could not afford to use it to preserve the surplus.[48] Preserving fish requires one part salt to two parts fish by weight. According to calculations by historian Mijo Marković, a barrel of 60 kilograms of salted fish would have had to command a very good price, since its one-third salt content would have been equivalent in price to three cows or an ox.[49]

Presumptuous Thieves

The uncritical nature of such descriptions shows that they could not have been the result of observation. The descriptions, therefore, indicate the social prejudices of townspeople and noblemen rather than the true situation. The same kind of social mistrust can also be identified in the stories of the Morlaks' great propensity to thievery. Of all the stories of bold and clever tricks he was told in Dalmatia, Fortis found the following especially characteristic. A poor man bought a kettle in a fair. He put it down while he was talking to an acquaintance he had met. As he was talking a thief grabbed the kettle and put it on his head without leaving the place. When the owner realised his loss, he asked the thief standing nearby with the kettle on his head if he had seen anybody stealing his kettle. The thief responded he had not been looking and added that the owner of the kettle should have taken the same precaution as he himself had in order to protect his kettle. 'But despite of those frauds,' adds Fortis, 'a foreigner can travel those parts safely and expect to be hospitably welcomed.'[50]

Cassas used the same motif to prove the shamelessness of Morlak thieves, the only difference being that the stolen item was ennobled from a common kettle to a sabre. In Cassas's version, a traveller resting at the foot of a hill was relieved of his sabre, lest it should incommode him. Two Morlaks approached him and while one of them engaged him in conversation, the other adroitly purloined the sabre and then very calmly joined in the conversation. When the traveller found out that his sabre had been stolen, the thief answered, 'Why did not you take the same precaution as I do? I always keep mine in my hand.'[51]

Cassas claimed that 'similar examples of roguery might be cited without number.' This was true for the readers of a British architect who, together with picturesque views of the antiquities of Pula and Istria, recorded a similar story of a traveller resting under a tree who laid aside his sabre to be more comfortable. Then two Morlaks came up to him and while one talked to the traveller, the other neatly drew the sabre from its scabbard, fastened it to his side and then coolly joined in the conversation. 'Some one has stolen my sabre,' exclaimed the owner, after a fruitless search. 'That is unfortunate,' replied the thief, 'but why do you not manage as I do? I always keep mine in my hand.'[52]

In the mid-nineteenth century Sir Gardner Wilkinson, who was familiar with these reports from Dalmatia, had no doubts that in 'the good old times,' the Morlaks 'were remarkable for their dexterous, and impudent, thefts; which were effected with an effrontery, as extraordinary as it was amusing.' He goes on to explain how after entering into conversation with a man, they would wait till he turned away. They then took something that belonged to him, hid it for a moment and then, bringing it out, asked the owner if he did not think it very good and handsome. On the man saying he had lost something very like it or that he believed it to be the same, the thief would simply observe that he himself always took care of his goods by not allowing them to go out of his own hands and that he recommended taking the same precaution.[53]

Not until the beginning of the twentieth century was it turned out that the story believed by Fortis and many after him as the literal truth was only a joke. Mrs Durham, describing her travels throughout the Balkans, noted how the Albanians loved jokes, particularly tales of a successful swindle. As an illustration she recounted the story of a man who bought a donkey at a bazaar and led it away. Two thieves followed him. One slipped the halter from donkey and went off with the animal. The other put the halter on his own head and followed the man. When the first thief had had time to escape with the donkey, the second began to pull and groan. The astonished man looked back, and found the donkey gone and a man in its place. 'Where is my donkey?' he asked. 'Alas!' cried the thief. 'I am that luckless being. A wicked magician turned me into a donkey for fifteen years. The time has just come to an end. I have nothing, and know not where to go.' The kind man then released him and even gave him some money.[54]

Fortis is significant for how seldom such accounts occur in his writings. But he was no exception to the rule that anthropology says as much about the teller as the told. In his account of the Morlaks, Fortis relies heavily on the conception of the 'good savage.'[55] He therefore selected in his writing the elements of their way of life which confirmed those expectations. In his letters he gives an account of a world so near (geographically) and yet so far (culturally):

> Innocence and natural liberty of pastoral ages are still preserved among the Morlaks or at least many traces remain in the places farther distant from our settlements. Pure cordiality of sentiments is not restrained by other regards and displays itself without any distinction of circumstances. A beautiful Morlak girl meets a man from her village and kisses him naturally, free of any evil intentions. I have seen all the women and girls, the youth and old men from different villages kissing when they meet at the church for a holiday. I had an impression all

Il Vajvoda Pervan di Coccorich.

Vojvoda Pervan

that world was one big family. Later I have met with the custom over a hundred times on the road and at the fairs of the littoral towns, where Morlaks came to sell their goods. During the holidays and public feasts hands are allowed many liberties, which would be perceived as indecent with us; but the Morlaks do not think the same way. If scolded, they would respond it was 'only an insignificant joke.'[56]

Fortis was also amazed by the fact that the Morlaks revered friendship almost as if it were a religion. He himself was present at a ceremony whereby two young women were made *posestrimas* (ritual sisters) in the church of Perušić; he thus had an opportunity to witness with his own eyes 'that delicacy of sentiments can lodge in minds not formed or rather not corrupted by society which we call civilised.'[57]

The best proof of how completely Fortis's descriptions harmonised with the predominant taste of his time is the fact that *Viaggio in Dalmazia* was translated into German, French and English within four years of its publication. The chapter on the customs and manners of the Morlaks was published several times in different languages and thus became a bestseller in European intellectual circles. It gave Europe a 'primitive' world on its own doorstep: now there were savages not only in Africa, Asia and America, but next door too. Fortis's book was the inspiration for the novel *Les Morlaques* (1788) by Giustiniana de Wynne, Comtesse des Ursinis et Rosenberg, the mysterious Mademoiselle X.C.V., lady-love of Casanova in Padua. The novel has now sunk into oblivion but in its time it was praised by Cesarotti, Goethe and Madame de Staël and launched what could be called Morlakomania.[58]

Breasts Down to the Navel

Fortis devotes a section of his work on the Morlaks to their upbringing of children. First we learn that newborn Morlak babies were immediately washed in cold water. Then, according to Fortis, neonates 'thus carelessly treated in their tenderest moments' were wrapped in miserable rags in which they remained for three or four months under the same ungentle management. When that period elapsed, they were set at liberty and left to crawl about their cottage and in front of the door till they learned to walk upright by themselves. During this time, and thanks to this treatment, they acquired 'that singular degree of strength and health' with which the Morlaks were allegedly endowed, making them able 'without the least inconvenience to expose their naked breast to the severest frost and snow.' An infant would be allowed to suck its mother's milk while she had any or till she became pregnant again; if that did not happen for three, four or even six years, a child would continue all that time to receive nourishment from the breast. To this he adds: 'The prodigious length of the breasts of the Morlak women is somewhat extraordinary; for it is very certain that they can give the teat to their children over their shoulders or under their arms.'[59]

This fragment came in for severe criticism from Ivan Lovrić. Brought up in a different culture from that of Fortis, Lovrić wholly internalised the most important Morlak value, namely the emphasis on male toughness. According to Lovrić, childrearing among the Morlaks, 'which to the polite nations appears strange and barbarous,' in fact was very close to the state of nature. This tough treatment in infancy gave the Morlaks the health and strength which were seldom found in civilised and beautiful towns despite all the care children received there. Morlak children spent the first five or six months of their lives wrapped in sackcloth, then they were left to crawl on the floor of their hut until they gradually learned to walk, 'from nature which is their only guide.' Only then could they be seen roaming the fields. 'For even if one sees a child crawling in the field on all fours even before he has learned to crawl upright, one should not jump to the conclusion that all children roam in this manner. This is the same as if, upon seeing a boy crawl amidst oxen, we would conclude that all boys crawl amidst oxen.'[60]

The persuasive nature of Lovrić's argument is illustrated most clearly by the following passage from the work of the British consul-general at Dubrovnik, also a member of the Royal Academy, from the middle of the nineteenth century:

> The Morlack himself is the greatest curiosity in the whole land: he is inured to a hardy life from infancy, the new-born children being allowed to be in its swaddling clothes and to cry or be quiet at discretion, while the mother attends to the household offices regardless of the infantine humours which are a source of such disquiet to the civilised matrons of the towns. There is no set time of weaning, the milk being continued to the next pregnancy; and if none succeed, the child may suck for several years. As the children grow up, they are allowed to gambol on the floor of the hut, and to find their legs and learn to walk by themselves; in short, the Morlack principle is to allow the man to grow as the beast of the forest, strong, healthy, and savage, averse from every labour, and untamed by any discipline.[61]

Lovrić also disagreed with Fortis about the duration of lactation and the size of the Morlak women's breasts. He also mentioned that, for the Morlaks, the practice of giving children to wet nurses, which was generally followed by the wealthier classes in Venice, was worse than bestial since animals feed their own young with their own milk.[62] But this did not mean that the breasts of Morlak women were of any extreme size. They were similar to the breasts of most women of other European nations and were 'never so long that they could breast-feed their children from the back over the shoulder or beneath the armpit.' According to Lovrić,

Fanciulla nobile di Coccorich.   *Fanciulla del Kotàr.*

Two Morlak women (by Fortis, 1774)

this opinion is a tale invented by strangers and I would never think that a naturalist such as Fortis would accept it. It is true that Juvenal persuades us that with Meroe a child suckled a breast bigger than the baby, (majorem infante mamillam) and I gladly believe it, but our Morlak women are not of that kind.[63]

In his answer to Lovrić's observations, Fortis[64] did not raise the question of childrearing among the Morlaks; we may conclude that they agreed that humans were more robust and more active when living a simple rural life, that they consequently enjoyed more stable health and lived longer than amidst the luxuries and unhealthy employments of great towns. But Fortis did insist that what he had written about the large breasts of the Morlak women was accurate. In order to sex-up his case, he claimed on top of that that they had 'large and loathsome breasts because he [Fortis] had seen that and because many honest people incapable of making a fool of anybody confirmed that; I can assume that Croatian women, the Vlach and Gypsy women from Banat have the same defect.'[65] Whereas previously he had written that he had heard this, he now maintained he had seen it.

Since neither Lovrić's observations nor Fortis's affirmations can be either proved or disproved, it could be useful to ask where Fortis could possibly have seen what he claimed to have seen. This is a difficult question, almost impossible to answer unless we also ask *why* he saw what he claimed he did. As far as we can gather from the drawings of Morlak women in *Viaggio in Dalmazia*, they wore costumes buttoned up to the neck, whatever the season. Moreover, this same book informs us that it was customary for Morlak women to keep out of sight when strangers were in the house.[66] We also know that Fortis never went to Banat. It seems to me that all these facts justify the conclusion that Fortis could not have observed what he claimed he did during his travels in Dalmatia.

In the second half of the eighteenth century scholars dedicated much attention to practices surrounding lactation among women 'savages' and to the length of their breasts. Buffon's *Natural History* records, for instance, that Samoyed women's 'breasts are of such length that children are able to receive the nipple, which is of a jet black, over the mother's shoulder.'[67]

Fortis twice explicitly compared the inhabitants of Dalmatia to the Hottentots. First, in the chapter on the manners and customs of the Morlaks, he claimed that in general they had little notion of domestic economy: 'they resemble in this particularity the Hottentots and readily consume in a week as much as would be sufficient for several months whenever any occasion of merriment presents itself.'[68] Then he adds that on Rab the islanders live 'a way of life differing little from that of the Hottentots.'[69]

Almost a century later the British consul-general in Dubrovnik wrote more explicitly:

> When a festival comes round, pigs and poultry are roasted, or a sheep killed; and they eat to repletion, and drink brandy to inebriation. The Morlack is generally in misery from his dissipations and anticipations of income; but if a Saint's-day comes round, although he has scarce bread to eat, a feast must be provided with the profusion and extravagance of the East, rather than the reasonable hospitality of Europe.[70]

With these passages in mind, I examined reports of travellers from the seventeenth and eighteenth centuries on Hottentots. Olbert Dapper, the Dutch author of the oldest description I came across, wrote that married Hottentot women had exceedingly big bosoms, 'so big that their breasts, which hang loose and uncovered, can be passed back over the shoulder to suckle the children whom as a rule they carry there.'[71] Similar descriptions of a mother's breast being pushed up over her shoulder so that the baby could suckle while on her back were given by several later writers.[72] Thus, two years after Dapper's book came out, a book on Africa by an English traveller gave almost the same description: 'The Married Women are so great Breasted, that they can give them into the Mouthes of their Children to Suck behind over their Shoulders, where they commonly carry them.'[73] About two centuries later Gustav Fritsch, a German student of Hottentot anatomy, concluded that Hottentot women were easily able to throw their breasts over their shoulders to nurse the babies carried on their backs, or, if they were sitting, pass them under their shoulders.[74] The image of the Hottentot woman with extraordinarily large breasts was very popular among Europeans. On 20 June 1754, *The Connoisseur* published a detailed description of such a woman in 'the Hottentot tale' under the title *Tquassouw and Knoninquaiha*. Tquassouw, the son of Kqvussomo, the story goes,

> arrived just at the instant, when the enraged animal was about to fasten on a Virgin, and aiming a poisoned arrow at his breast laid him dead at her feet. The Virgin threw herself on the ground, and covered her head with dust, to thank her deliverer; but when she rose, the Prince was dazzled with her charms. He was struck with the glossy hue of her complexion, which shone like the jetty down of the Black Hog of Hessaqua: he was ravished with the purest gristle of her nose; and his eyes dwelt with admiration on the flaccid beauties of her breasts, which descended to her navel.

The German philosopher Gotthold Ephraïm Lessing ensured that even highbrow readers were acquainted with the tale, citing it *in extenso* in his essay on aesthetics.[75] Of course, this was just a construction of the Hottentot woman's body.[76] But why was it so important? What was its purpose? The antithesis of European mores and European beauty was blackness, and the archetype of blackness, the lowest exemplum of mankind in the great chain of being, was the Hottentot. For Europeans, the Hottentots were the ultimate savages; the Iroquois were beautiful in comparison.[77] As Gui Tachard put it: 'The South point of Africa is no less remote from Europe, than the manners of its inhabitants are different from ours.'[78]

The very fact that Fortis was not disposed to believe in the existence of hairy fish because he had not seen them, but was disposed to believe what he was told about the prodigious length of the Morlak women's breasts, indicates that there is more in this than meets the eye. Traditionally, women's breasts were perceived as the essential symbol of womanhood.[79] Even a perfunctory survey of the seventeenth- and eighteenth-century literature reveals that breasts of exceptional size were an inseparable, integral part of the image of so-called (female) savages. In an essay arguing that the Pygmies of the Ancients were a sort of ape, not of the human race, Edward Tyson, the father of modern anatomy, gave a detailed description of a Pygmy. Even though the Pygmy he had bought was a male, and he himself had never seen a female, he nevertheless expressed no doubt that they had such large breasts 'that no Woman's are larger.'[80] At that time the Western ideal of female beauty demanded small, high breasts.[81] Whereas the breasts of Turkish women were 'at full liberty under their Vest, without any restraint of Stays or Bodice,' being 'just as Nature made them,' contemporary European women used to wear 'Machines of Iron and Whalebone to correct Nature.'[82]

The 'lacing' of women's garments began around the eleventh or twelfth century, with the discovery of body 'form' among aristocratic women. In Europe, by the fourteenth century a kind of corset had become obligatory in upper-class dress.[83] During the sixteenth and seventeenth centuries in Spain the breasts of young girls in the early stages of puberty were covered with leaden plates, with the result that many Spanish ladies actually had a concave outline. Undue and unhealthy constriction of the breasts was found not only among townspeople but also among the peasants of certain districts in Central Europe. In Upper Swabia, for instance, tight clothing and bodices caused complete functional atrophy of the breasts, so that only remnants of the nipples were left and women could not suckle their babies, causing high infant mortality.[84] A similar custom was also known in Dalmatia, where some women had a 'strange fancy of making themselves appear flat breasted.'[85]

Lemuel Gulliver in his fourth book of travels into various remote nations of the world, gives this description of Yahoos: 'Their Dugs hung between their Fore-feet, and often reached almost to the Ground as they walked.' Even though Gulliver describes the Yahoos as the most disagreeable animals he ever beheld in all his travels and the ones against which he conceived the strongest antipathy,[86] they are people. The idea of human quadrupeds seems strange nowadays, but it was not so in the eighteenth century when Jean-Jacques Rousseau was able to produce 'several Instances of human quadrupeds'[87] and Buffon stated that Europeans compared the Negroes of the island of Gorée and the Cap Verde coast to horses.[88] A closer look shows that the Yahoos, that 'race of brutes,' are remarkably like Fortis's Morlaks, whereas the Houyhnhnms resemble Venetians. If, according to Gulliver, 'the Yahoos appear to be the most unteachable of all Animals, their Capacities never reaching higher than to draw or carry Burthens,'[89] on the other hand 'these Noble Houyhnhnms are endowed by Nature with a general Disposition to all Virtues, and have no Conceptions or Ideas of what is Evil in a Rational Creature, so their grand Maxim is to cultivate Reason, and to be wholly governed by it.'[90] Or, as Buffon put it,

Rudolf Valentino (published by Biasutti)

the most stupid man is able to manage the most acute animal; he governs it, and renders it subservient to his purposes; and this, not so much on account of his strength or skill as by the superiority of his nature, and from his being possessed of reason, which enables him to form a rational system of action and method, by which he compels the animals to obey him.[91]

A slightly different question was exercising scholars of the time, namely, by what means 'were Europeans thus powerful? or why, since they can so easily visit Asia and Africa for trade or conquest, cannot the Asiaticks and Africans invade their coasts, plant colonies in their ports, and give laws to their natural princes? The same wind that carries them back would bring us thither.'[92] The Abyssinian Prince Rasselas was taught by his teacher that Europeans were more powerful because they were wiser: 'Knowledge will always predominate over ignorance, as man governs the others animals.'[93] To adapt this question to our case, it would sound something like this: Why did the Morlaks not conquer and annex Venice, since they were regularly reported to be stronger and more courageous than the Venetians?[94]

In many of its aspects the conduct of the Venetians was determined by a very specific policy. Paolo Sarpi even proposed in the Venetian Senate that in order effectively to keep the Dalmatians in subjection, everything should be done to render them poor and ignorant, because the 'Queen of the Adriatic'

Typical Slovenes (published by Biasutti)

Typical Croats (published by Biasutti)

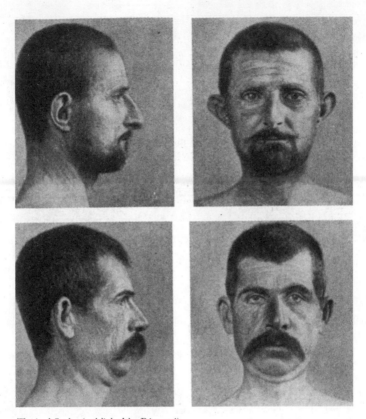

Typical Serbs (published by Biasutti)

needed the province of Dalmatia not for scholars but for soldiers. Every artifice was employed to prevent the establishment of schools so that those who wished to have their sons educated were obliged to send them to Italy or to be satisfied with the instruction provided by the clergy. By keeping the people in ignorance and poverty, the Venetians hoped more easily to govern the country. Rich landowners were also discouraged. Whenever a piece of land was recovered from the Ottomans by the Venetians, instead of being restored to its original owners it was appropriated by the state.[95]

The forging of racial stereotypes and notions of savagery was vital to the colonialist worldview. Thus, explorers discovering and conquering new lands were not explorers and plunderers, but bearers of culture and executors of God's will. Europeans defined themselves as civilised and therefore had to find 'barbarians' (as they called those with a different way of life, a different worldview or different norms and values) in newly discovered countries. The empirical method invented as an efficient tool to do away with prejudice turned into its own mirror image. The rise of science during the Age of Enlightenment, which introduced ideas of relativity to the world, thus also helped to elevate European culture to the level of the absolute, its validity based on proven facts. Pre-existing prejudices were thus not actually repudiated but simply assimilated into the new context of 'reason.'

Fortis's travel writing was received with considerable interest and attracted great attention. It strongly influenced West Europeans' knowledge of the lands on the eastern coast of the Adriatic. His work was translated many times and gave rise to a new school of European *belle-lettres*. But Dalmatia nevertheless remained 'an unknown, romantic country.'[96] In the nineteenth century Zadar, and Dalmatia generally, were known in the Austro-Hungarian army as the 'Siberia of Austria'[97] or 'Austrian Albania,'[98] and travellers to Dalmatia in the same century called its inhabitants 'the wildest people of Europe.'[99] At the beginning of the twentieth century they were described as 'a people still happily primitive, still unashamed to be picturesque,' and their country as a land 'where three quarters of the blessings of civilization are blessedly unknown.'[100] An Italian lady, commented to the author of a book on the birth of Yugoslavia that the Yugoslavs were 'very wild and black.' And when saying so 'her beautiful lips looked as if they could scarcely bring themselves to pronounce the name.'[101] An Italian anthropologist of the age of Mussolini outdid all others by presenting a photograph of Rudolfo Valentino as typifying the *pugliese* branch of the Mediterranean race[102] and contrasting it to photographs of prisoners of war showing 'typical' Serbs, Montenegrins and other South Slavs.[103]

FOUR

Men with Tails

He who would seek may find in the Balkans not only ladies with greasy fingers but stranger beings as well. Those zealous enough were even able to find men with tails. We have the most detailed account of them in a book written by Philip Thornton who travelled to the Balkans a number of times in the 1930s, visiting several countries on each occasion. On his travels, he encountered many interesting people and customs, then known in the West only from books. His more or less bizarre adventures on his Balkan travels included a close encounter with a man with a tail. He described it as follows:

> We sat and drank coffee and ate plates of sweets, listening to the Turkish musicians who played in one corner of the room. I noticed the Doctor [Dr Stanislav Mladović] kept staring about, watching every new arrival and whispering to the waiter about somebody called Nazir. 'Perhaps I shall not be able to show you the surprise, Mr Thornton, it is not always easy to arrange things as one wishes.' Scarcely were the words out of his mouth when he jumped up, crossed the room and disappeared into the kitchen, calling back, 'Wait – I have seen him.'
>
> I looked at Hassanović, he just shook his head mutely. He had no idea what it was all about. The Doctor reappeared in the doorway and beckoned us to follow him into the kitchen. 'Here is a man with a tail,' said the Doctor triumphantly, placing his hand affectionately on the shoulders of a fine looking young Albanian who in no way appeared to be disconcerted by this astonishing revelation.

I remember once having heard of a clan of Ghegs who lived near Peć and were noted for having produced tailed men. That I was to see one such man seemed too fantastic and I laughed at the Doctor's apparent joke. But it was not a joke.

'Do you mean to tell me this man has a tail – a real tail like a cat or a dog?'

'Not only have I seen and examined this man's tail but I shall ask him if he will permit you to feel it beneath his clothes,' retorted the Doctor with considerable heat.

He spoke to the Albanian who had no objections to my placing a hand at the base of his spine, where to my mingled horror and astonishment I felt hard boy thing that grew from the base of his spine, and as the Doctor had said, moved about beneath his clothes like a finger.

'You are convinced?'

'I am convinced, and possibly bewitched as well,' I answered.[1]

When Thornton returned home and sat down at his desk to describe his adventures, the pleasant atmosphere of the smoke-filled Balkan coffee house had faded away and he became doubtful, for after all he was an educated gentleman. He continued his description:

For months I wondered, if the whole thing had been a trick, and the only people to whom the story was divulged greeted me with humiliating derision. I was clearly drunk or the victim of a hallucination. One day in a dirty Edinburgh second-hand bookshop I found a book written a long time ago by a German scientist called Hahn. On page 163 of his *Albanische Studien* he says:

'This belief is more than popular superstition. One of my *cavasses* at Yanina, maintained that in his part of the country tailed men of this sort were not uncommon, and that he himself had a tailed cousin, whom in his youth he had often pulled by this gift of nature when bathing. A much more trustworthy man, Theodoris, related to me that in his detachment there was for several years a short-sized broad shouldered man of a very fair complexion, called Captain Jannaki. He was reputed to have a tail. In order to convince themselves of this, once he was asleep in the middle of the day, six of them fell upon him at once, for he was uncommonly strong. He himself had taken part in the ocular inspection, and he distinctly remembers having seen a goat-like tail about four fingers breadth long, covered on the outside with short red bristles.'

> I am glad that Herr Hahn wrote about this curious *lusus naturae*, it is pleasanter to be laughed at with somebody else who can share my side of the joke.[2]

Thornton concludes the story about his close encounter with a caudal man by rationalising his discovery. He attributes it to a coffee-house prank or an alcohol-induced hallucination, so that it is not clear to the reader what, in fact, Thornton's opinion is of the human tail described in his record of this unusual adventure in a Sarajevo coffee house. Was it nothing but a prank, or did he really encounter a man with a tail? The story creates a mixed impression, as if the author became afraid of his discovery because of its bizarre character, although for some reason he did not want to disown it. But why does he cite von Hahn as saying that 'This belief is more than popular superstition'? Because it really was?

The Satyr Islands

Since it is impossible to reach any definite conclusion about the existence of caudal men from Thornton's account, we must turn to the von Hahn book quoted above. Johann Georg von Hahn was an imperial-royal consul in eastern Greece and one of the most competent experts on Albanian culture and history. In his celebrated *Albanische Studien*, published in 1854, he discusses men with tails in the chapter on Albania's folk heritage and heroes. He suggests these were of two kinds, those with a goat's tail and those with a small horse's tail, both reputed for being extremely strong men of stocky stature and excellent hikers. According to von Hahn, 'a few years ago' a man had died who could walk astonishing distances in a day and had obviously not been bothered by the fact that he sometimes had to hold his tail to avoid getting it dirty. He also states that such people lived not only in southern Albania (in northern Albania they were unknown), but could frequently be found in Greece and Asia Minor as well. For instance, the infamous brigand Koutowunisios, who came from Langkadia in Peloponnese, was said to have a tail. Later on in the text, it becomes evident that von Hahn was convinced that there was 'something' in these tales. He wrote: 'All my efforts to see such an individual have failed and all the Turkish army doctors reject the matter as a fairy-tale, since in all their years of examining recruits from all parts of the country, they have never seen such a trick of nature.' And then he added:

> According to certain sources, Buffon, in his *Natural History*, mentions that tailed men live in Albania. It suffices me to know that in southern

Albania people still undoubtedly believe in the existence of human beings similar to those often depicted in Hellenic art. Nevertheless, in Albania I could not find out anything about people possessing the body of a horse or the hooves of a goat.

According to von Hahn, the existence of caudal men was recorded in the work of a distinguished eighteenth-century naturalist and member of academies in Paris, London and Berlin Georges Louis Le Clerc, Baron de Buffon, a man to whom even Jean-Jacques Rousseau bowed in respect. The English translation of Buffon's *Natural History*, contains the following passage on men with tails:

> In Formosa Struys declares, that he actually saw a man with a tail, above a foot long, and covered with a reddish hair, not unlike that of an ox; and, that this man assured him, if it was a blemish to have tail, it was a blemish which proceeded from the climate, all the natives of the southern part of the island having tails like himself.
>
> I know not whether we ought to give entire credit to what Struys relates of the inhabitants of Formosa. The last fact appears to be highly doubtful, or at least exaggerated, and different from what other travellers have said, with respect to these men with tails. It is even different from the account of Ptolemy, whom I have already quoted, and from that of Mark Paul, in his geographical description, printed at Paris in 1556. From the latter we learn that, in the kingdom of Lambry, there are mountaineers who have tails of the length of the hand. Struys seems to rest upon the authority of Mark Paul, as Gemelli Careri does upon that of Ptolemy; though the tail he mentions to have seen is widely different in its dimensions from the tails of the Blacks of Manilla, of the inhabitants of Lambry, and other places, as described by writers in general.[3]

It is possible to surmise from the above that the famous naturalist himself believed in the existence of men with tails and so did other eighteenth-century naturalists. Carolus Linnaeus, for instance, even classified them in his *Systema naturis* as a separate species:

> The tailed SATYR, hairy, bearded, with a manlike body, gesticulating much, very fallacious, is a species of monkey, if ever one has been seen. The *tailed men*, of whom more recent travellers tell much, are of the same genus.[4]

Satyri altera fpecies.

Aldrovandi's satyr

Accounts of men with tails go back to Greek and Roman authors. According to Claudius Ptolomaeus' *Geographike*, for instance, there were three Satyr Islands, inhabited by people who were said 'to have tails such as they picture satyrs with.'[5]

Towards the end of the twelfth century the term *caudatus* emerged as an epithet of reproach insinuating that Englishmen were, in one particular, not as other men. For centuries Frenchmen and Scots believed, or professed to, that Englishmen possessed tails – the lack of which forms one of several characteristics of superiority distinguishing human beings from beasts.[6] Indeed, in the mid-sixteenth century, the Bishop of Ossory even complained:

> That an Englysh man now cannot travayle in an other lande by waye of marchandyce or anye other honest occupyenge, but yt ys most contumelyouslye throwne in hys tethe, that al English men have tailes.[7]

Homme à queue vu à la Mecque, en 1842.

Man with tail as seen in Mecca, 1842

Later, the illustrious Venetian traveller Marco Polo informed the West about the faraway kingdom of Lambri, populated with 'men with tails, a span in length, like those of dogs, but not covered with hair.'[8] Since Polo's information was subsequently verified by other travellers,[9] and *Wunderkammern* accorded a warm welcome to caudal man no matter what form he might assume,[10] far and near men with tails produced many offspring who were very much alive and kicking. Uncertainty regarding men with tails emerged only at the close of the eighteenth century, when not all who learned of them were any longer prepared to vouch for the veracity of their existence. They did give the reports some benefit of the doubt, however.[11] It took the nineteenth century to bring categorical denials of the tale of caudal people. *Homo caudatus* might now have vanished into the dim obscurity of bygone times if it had not been that some travellers learned from Arab slave traders and from various African peoples about Niam-Niams, men with tails.[12] Furthermore, Louis Ducouret alias Hadji Abd-El-Hamid-Bey averred that he had personally seen a Niam-Niam with a tail in Mecca in 1842.[13] His book, to which the novelist Alexandre Dumas contributed a biographical sketch of the author, 'so rich in its charming simplicity, had, exactly at the right moment, raised a small memorial which contributed to its preservation.'[14] According to

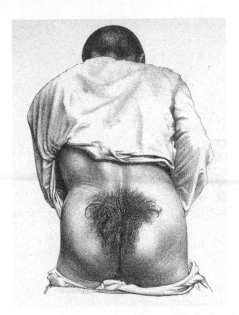
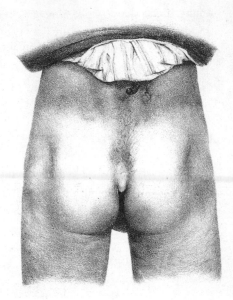

Men with tails from the collection of the Berlin Anthropological Society

Dumas, Ducouret was in the process of convincing the *Académie des Sciences* of the existence in remote parts of Africa of monsters intermediate between monkeys and humans, who had language like humans and tails like monkeys.[15] In 1863 another famous French novelist, Jules Verne, intervened, claiming that 'it is now known that these tails belonged to the skins of the beasts with which they are clothed.'[16] Still, not all were convinced. Only five years after Verne's book was published, the medical doctor Johann Paul Gleisberg published a treatise in which he claimed that 'in the present a tailed Negro race in Abyssinia was met.'[17]

Late nineteenh-century explorers who made their way into the heart of Africa to see with their own eyes the 'naked truth of naked people' were unable to confirm the reports of caudal people.[18] Charles Chaillé Long, for instance, dismissed them altogether as a 'mythical category' of those 'who have yielded to Munchausenism, in endeavouring to attach the caudal appendage to the Niam-Niam people.'[19] What was believed in Europe about non-Europeans, however, was not yet wholly disbelieved as an existing fact. Some remained faithful to their belief in the existence of men with tails, arguing that their existence was so well vouched for 'that we cannot disbelieve it or even doubt of it without rejecting all human testimony and resolving to believe nothing but what we have seen.'[20] Thus, although seriously harmed, men with tails outlived even the nineteenth century's assaults on their integrity. During the 1870s studious members of the Berlin Anthropological

Society succeeded in collecting several photographs of 'tail formation.'[21] On 20 October 1895 British daily papers announced a Frenchman's discovery of a tailed man in Africa.[22] And in 1920 the former Yuzbashi of the Imperial Ottoman Naval College, H. H. Johnson, published a story that he had heard from an 'extremely handsome *divorcée*.' She told him that,

> when a little girl, – not so long ago – she went with her mother to visit a family where the nurse was from the Niam-niam. Hide-and-seek was the nursery game that evening, and my informant was offered a temporary shelter under the nurse's makeshift petticoat. Taking this coign of vantage, she was frightened by the nurse's tail, and scrambled out.[23]

Since his informant was 'too handsome to lie,' he added with some irony, he believed her 'absolutely, more especially as she but confirms what we all knew already of Central Africans.'[24]

What, then, is the truth about men with tails in Albania: have they some foundation in truth, or were they just one more variation of the old travellers' tradition of buying rumours and selling them as facts?

Our quest for an answer to these questions now moves on to a book on Albanians and the great powers by Vladan Đorđević, a Serbian politician (prime minister from 1897 to 1900), a member of the Serbian Academy of Sciences and a distinguished author. In this book, Đorđević characterised Albanians as bloodthirsty, stunted, animal-like individuals, so invincibly ignorant that they 'could not tell sugar from snow.' These 'modern Troglodytes' reminded him of 'prehumans, who slept in the trees, to which they were fastened by their tails.' Over the millennia, the human tail had withered away, but 'among the Albanians there seem to have been humans with tails as late as the nineteenth century.'[25] It should be pointed out that Đorđević did not himself invent any of these (quite stark) claims. Actually he merely rewrote the data about men with tails from the above-mentioned books by Consul von Hahn and the Viennese newspaper editor Paul Siebertz.[26] The information that the Albanians could not tell sugar from snow was recorded by Ivan Jastrebov in his monograph on Old Serbia and Albania, where he claims that during his travels among the tribes of Albania he often encountered people who mistook sugar, which he took in his tea, for snow.[27]

The fact that Jastrebov served as Russian consul in Prizren for many years and was knowledgeable about the situation in the region at the end of the nineteenth century gives additional weight to his claims. Nevertheless, doubt is cast on his reliability by a passage from a travel book by H. A. Brown, a late nineteenth century British traveller, who met three 'Europeans' in

Prizren – a Russian consul he called Astraboff, an Austrian vice-consul and Austrian bookmaker – and who stated that the consuls rarely went outside their own doors and still more rarely outside the town.[28] During his travels in the Albanian hills, Brown was served coffee without sugar, according to the Albanian custom, in every house he stopped at. But when he was among the Mirdite, his guide told the landlord that Brown drank coffee with sugar. Since there was none in the house, the landlord, hoping that there would be some in a house a quarter of an hour's walk away, immediately dispatched a messenger to get it. 'In about half an hour the messenger appeared, covered with snow, and shivering with cold, but bringing a handful of coarse sugar.'[29] However, when it stopped snowing on the way from Mirdite to Lume, Brown's guide Frana, waving his hand at the snow-clad mountains, cried: 'Good-bye, good-bye Mirdite sugar!'[30]

Our story about men with tails is thus not merely an invention; rather, it is a story about how individual groups, nations or cultures perceive others. As they construct the social world, people try to determine which construct is best suited to give a certain event a meaning. At the same time, they define their experiences and generalise them in communication with others, so giving them a certain permanence. Different periods, different social groups and different individuals recognise different constructs as suitable for their purposes, according to their various expectations and interests. Construction is therefore an endless process of giving meaning to the world. It reflects religious, ethical, political and other conceptions, in the context of which interpretations and evaluations are made, and what is important, unimportant, sensible or absurd is defined. These constructs tell us nothing about the groups of people they describe, but they are precious sources of knowledge about the group that constructed them, since what a group of people imagine about others is as a rule the mirror image of how they see themselves.

What do all these Balkan caudal men signify? What purpose did they serve and in what way? Some light may be thrown on these questions by the following passage from my book *Non cogito ergo sum* (1994). Prisoners on Goli Otok and other concentration camps for so-called Imformbureau agents still 'under investigation' were identified by tails made of old rags tied to their backs. The length of the tail indicated the charges against them. In order to make the tails as authentic as possible, occasionally a real bovine, sheep's or pig's tail was used. These stigmatised prisoners were called *reponja* (taily), a term of abuse also used during the beating they received on the way to and from work.[31]

It follows that men with tails were a cultural construct used by those in power to degrade certain individuals to the level of animals: they were good for work if forced to it, but were otherwise assumed to have no intelligence.

Though an obvious cultural construct, their 'animal' nature implied the need for them to be reformed or civilised so that they could become human beings again. As we have seen, a stick was a useful means of achieving this lofty aim.

The Serbian Sea

However, our story of men with tails as a construct of racists and chauvinists does not end here. It plays a prominent role in a book by the sociologist Peter Gay published in 1993. In his study of hatred, Gay quoted Vladan Đorđević, 'a Serbian politician and expert in public health,' to illustrate how racists had been 'letting their imaginations roam… for decades.'[32] But the sociologist Gay failed to notice that Đorđević, whom he cited as an example of an extreme racist, had not concocted this story himself. Furthermore, he clearly did not waste much time reading Đorđević's actual book – he does not even always spell his name properly – and he completely overlooked the fact that the story in question was more than 2,000 years old and, although based on pure hearsay, had been very successful in catching the people's fancy. By ignoring a story that drags such a long tail after it and pointing the finger at Đorđević, Gay not only exculpated Đorđević's informants and their predecessors, but also stultified his own arguments.

In order to understand properly why Đorđević (re)wrote the old story – a question to which Gay paid no attention in his study – it is of vital importance to know whom he was trying to address with it. Đorđević was an experienced politician and well aware of the fact that, no matter how powerful his argument, it would not take hold of the public mind if it did not strike some deeper chord. In the same year in which he sought to represent Albanians as modern troglodytes, he publicly acknowledged himself to be 'a grateful student of the German school and friend of my dear Vienna,'[33] and explained that he 'firmly believed in the big slogans of European politics.'[34] In that case it was not so weird if he calculated that arguments already recognised by the German-speaking public as trustworthy would be sufficiently powerful to persuade them. The more so since he was rather pleased with them.

Serbia aspired to get a window on the sea through northern Albania because the coast of Dalmatia was closed to it. Until 1878 Serbian enthusiasts for the Serbian cause hoped to annex those districts of European Turkey inhabited by sizeable Serbian minorities. Thus, on 16 September 1876, Serbian Prince Milan was proclaimed by his army 'King of Serbia and Bosnia.'[35] By annexing Kosovo and Bosnia-Herzegovina, Serbia would have a long border with Montenegro and the two Serb states might ultimately unite, thus realising the dream of a Greater Serbia. But at the Berlin Congress in 1878 the European powers granted Austria-Hungary the mandate to occupy Bosnia-Herzegovina and consequently the entry of Serbian forces into those areas would have meant war with the Dual Monarchy. Serbia tried to find some other means of achieving its 'justifiable claim' to have its own access to the sea.[36] Soon the Serbian chauvinists, who were anxious to get possession of the Albanian Adriatic coast, started a propaganda campaign aimed at re-establishing Tsar Dušan's empire.[37] For this purpose they used both the methods and the ideology of European colonialism. As Serbia's plans coincided with the interests of Germany, Chancellor Bismarck, with his brutal disregard of facts which did not suit him, asserted at the Berlin Congress that there was no Albanian nationality.[38] In compliance with this viewpoint, Western correspondents on the spot reported that the Albanians were an absolutely uncompromising people who gave and expected no quarter, so that 'in the hospitals they bite the doctors who try to help them.'[39] When a British traveller in Podgorica asked Dr Fox, who had lived for years in Serbia, 'as near to Albania as the average business man to his office,' what he knew of the Albanians, he explained that 'Albanians were the scum of the Balkans, descendants of bandits driven out of the other Balkan countries; a bad lot, morally and physically.'[40]

Albanians were not to have a state of their own on the grounds that they hated all forms of government and were incapable of managing their own affairs.[41] This argument was used for the first time by Austria-Hungary and Germany to counter the British proposal made in 1880 for the establishment of an independent Albania. Later, this viewpoint was embraced by Serbian politicians. The prime minister of Serbia, Nikola Pašić, for instance, claimed that 'it will be in the interest of neither the Albanians nor of Europe to insist on having an autonomous Albania, for the Albanians are neither ready, nor worthy of autonomy; they have no men to rule the country. Albania, if autonomous, will always be a cause of disturbance in the Balkans.'[42] Against this background Đorđević rewrote the tale of caudal people, using 'arguments' borrowed mainly from Austrian authors, to prove the Albanians' inability to govern themselves. It was published in Serbian and also German in an attempt to be accessible to readers in the West.

Balkan statesmen had learned from long experience of the great European powers that nothing succeeds like self-help, that a *fait accompli* was worth more than a reasoned argument.[43] So when an opportunity presented itself, Serbian forces occupied the port of Durrës in northern Albania in December 1912:

> When from the last lines of hills the soldiers saw the sea, all recognized the solemnity of the moment in the history of their race. The door

of national freedom lay open to them. There was the open sea across which Serbia could join without hindrance in the commerce and the civilization of the world. In perfect order they marched to the beach at Durazzo. The Serbian tricolour was planted in the water, and as the red, blue, and white fluttered out on the breeze a threefold shout was raised of 'Živelo srpsko more' ('Three cheers for *the Serbian sea*').[44]

However, the Serbs failed in their attempt to ignore the Albanians and to represent Shköder, Durrës and the plains around them as Slav, on the grounds that the Serbian tsars had held them then and now. This failure was chiefly due to Austria-Hungary's assertion of its own interests and not to any love for historical justice on the part of Europe: Austria-Hungary simply wanted to block Serbia's access to the sea.[45] Consequently, not only was Serbia forced to withdraw its troops from northern Albania, with its 'arguments' refuted, in addition certain Western experts denounced Serbian authors as 'extreme racists,' although where they were actually at fault was in their enthusiastic wish to construct the Serbs as 'real Europeans' and to represent them as such to the world.

FIVE

Eyes that Cannot See

In the countries which were once part of the Ottoman Empire, frescoes and icons in Orthodox churches often bear the painted images of saints whose eyes have been gouged out. This fact was often reported by travellers to the Balkans in the nineteenth and early twentieth centuries, including such well-informed writers as the French consul-general at the court of the vizier of Epirus, Ali Pasha,[1] the first Russian consul in Sarajevo,[2] an Anglican cleric,[3] the Russian consul in Prizren,[4] a Russian archaeologist,[5] an Austrian archaeologist[6] and several British travellers.[7] In every case the culprits were said to be Turks or Albanians, that is Muslims, their motive being iconoclasm and/or barbarism. The phenomenon would appear to be typically Balkan, arousing astonishment and consternation in the reader:

> The figures of saints which form the subject of several frescoes have suffered from the Turks, who fired pistols at them, and were also at the trouble to poke out their eyes. This latter injury evinced so much of the malice of deliberate insult, that it riled the Serbians more than wholesale destructions which might be supposed to have taken place in the confusion and heat of assault. Besides, the desecrated forms remain on the church wall, so that their injury can never be forgotten; and their marred faces meeting the upturned eyes of the worshippers, seem ever to cry out for retribution. In the Principality of Serbia, where some ruined churches have been rebuilt, these blinded pictures are left

Der Großwesir
bei der Armee.

Turkish vizier

unrestored. An old bishop said to us, 'We still need them — they are the
archives of centuries of oppression and our people must not lose sight
of them so long as the oppressor still keeps foot on Serbian land.[8]

The Eyes of Princess Simonida

The phenomenon was used in the 1980s in the Serbian propaganda war against the Albanians in Kosovo. The Belgrade-based magazine *Duga* published a special issue in July 1989 with the image of Simonida of Gračanica on the front page with 'the front page poem' added. The poem was written by the former Serbian consul in Pristina, Milan Rakić, at the beginning of the twentieth century and is dedicated to the fresco of the Byzantine Princess Simonida in the monastery of Gračanica near Pristina, Kosovo:

Iskopaše ti oči, lepa sliko!
Večeri jedne, na kamenoj ploči
Znajući da ga tad ne vidi niko
Arbanas ji nožem izbo oči!

(They gouged out your eyes, lovely picture!
One evening, on a stone slab
Knowing that then nobody could see him
An Albanian put out her eyes!)

At first glance this seems to be perfectly clear and simple but a closer look reveals an underlying methodological issue: how the prejudices and biases of the viewer influence the differences between what is seen and what is 'seen,' that is understood.

According to Richard Burton, in the East blinding was a common practice, especially in the case of junior princes not required as heirs. At about the same time in western Europe the operation was performed with a heated metal basin – the well-known *bacinare* (used by Ariosto) – as happened to Pier delle Vigne.[9] In his history, Mauro Orbini of Dubrovnik enumerated many cases of this punishment, each time inflicted on persons who would have been powerful pretenders to the throne had they been left with all their faculties.[10] Sometimes the blinded person was also castrated.[11] As maintained by Albanian oral tradition, Lekë Dukagjin, the famous law-giver, blinded his brothers Pal and Kocka.[12] The International Commission to Inquire into the Causes and Conduct of the Balkan Wars in 1912 and 1913 quoted an extract from a Greek soldier's letter documenting that putting out the eyes of living persons was practised as late the beginning of the twentieth century.[13]

In the oral tradition about the ruins of the castle of Zvečan, recorded by a British traveller, King Stefan Dečanski, son of Milutin, the founder of Gračanica, was strangled there in 1336. Stefan was Milutin's eldest son, but the young Byzantine princess, his second wife, bore him another son and plotted to make him the heir. In a fight that ensued Stefan was captured and his stepmother prevailed upon his father to cast him into prison, where, to make matters sure, she had him blinded with red-hot irons. After many years the tale spread that he had been miraculously cured and was not blind at all. He came to the throne with a great reputation for piety and built many churches, notably the very beautiful white and pink marble church of Dečani.[14] The blinding of a competitor, then, signified his disqualification: the one who had lost his eyesight had thus also lost the ability to reign, for a ruler had to 'see more' than his subjects as among the blind a one-eyed man is king. In many cultures an eye denotes intellectual perception: it knows because it sees.[15] According to the words Orbini attributed to King Asen, the evidence of one eyewitness is more reliable than that of ten based on hearsay, for the one who saw draws on his own experience, not the testimony of the others.[16]

In the paintings of saints, the eyes gouged out by the 'Turks' (unbelievers) would thus prove their weakness and worthlessness, their disqualification. But in the cases cited by Orbini the people punished in this manner were exclusively male. To put out the eyes of a woman would have no purpose at all, for in a patriarchal society women were disqualified as rulers by their gender. An assault on the dignity of a woman was therefore aimed at other parts of her anatomy, her breasts and/or pudenda.[17]

Similarly inadequate is the specification of the time when the event must have taken place, 'an evening when the culprit knew that nobody had seen him,' which in itself is merely a qualification of an act as a crime. For, as the proverb goes, 'The night is a cloak for sinners.' However, such a qualification of the act further impugns the theories of Muslim iconoclasm as the cause of this vandalism. Had it really been the motive of his act, the culprit would not have hidden himself: to prove the impotence of idols requires the presence of an audience. Grand Vizier Sinan Pasha, for instance, ordered the body of the Serbian national saint, St Sava, to be brought from Mileševo monastery in Herzegovina to Vračar near Belgrade and he had it burnt on a pyre *publicly* on 9 May 1594.[18]

Reports of painted images with gouged-out eyes do not as a rule include details about the causes and the time of the vandalism. Austrian archaeologist and traveller Felix Kanitz does, however, state that the monastery of Suvodol in Serbia 'had been the site of a battle between the Serbs and the Turks. The Turks robbed the monastery and took out their rage on the otherwise unremarkable frescoes of its church, carving out the eyes of saints with the tips of their sharp daggers.'[19] But, as an editorial footnote to the Serbian translation of his work maintains, 'historical sources do not mention a battle by the Suvodol monastery in 1810.'[20]

Orthodox monasteries in general, and the frescos inside them in particular, are considered a symbol of Serbian culture; violence against them would be an act of barbarism. The barbarity of the culprit would be attested by the fact that he used a knife (a symbol of violence) in *mala fide* to deface a 'lovely picture' (a symbol of culture). And yet even this interpretation does not suffice as a full explanation of the phenomenon in question: the view of sacred objects as primarily cultural monuments acquired a meaning only within the framework defined by Nietzsche's pronouncement of God's death, for here the artistic artefacts lose their previous sacred substance. We have ceased to believe in their magical power and do not kneel before them any more; they merely represent a source of aesthetic pleasure: 'The statues set up are now corpses in stone whence the animating soul has flown, while the hymns of praise are words from which all belief has gone.'[21] Or, it in the words of an English traveller who visited Orthodox monasteries on Mt Athos in 1837:

> It is difficult to conceive how any one, even in the dark ages, can have been simple enough to look upon these quaint and absurd paintings with feelings of religious awe; but some of the monks of the Holy Mountain do so even now, and were evidently scandalised when they saw me smile.[22]

Infernal Torment Dante Never Knew

In the nineteenth century in the Balkans, roads in the Western sense of the term did not exist, and when travellers reached Zemun on the Austrian border they found themselves 'at the end of this wheel-going Europe.'[23] The very use of wheeled carriages was almost unknown in the Ottoman Empire until the end of the eighteenth century. A kind of cart was used in Istanbul and a few other places, mostly for women to travel in. In this vast empire, for centuries, all the merchandise was carried by horses, mules or camels.[24] The roads were 'heaven-made,' meaning 'the hand of man had had little to do with them,' almost till the end of the nineteenth century.[25] Or, as a British traveller to Albania complained, 'If Dante had ever found himself on a large and ancient Culderim, with three feet of water and two of mud on each side, night coming down and three miles to do, he would have added another torment to the Inferno.'[26]

The culture of the wheel only started to advance through the Slavic countries of European Turkey in the second half of the nineteenth century, at which time there were only two carriages in Sarajevo, one belonging to the vizier of Bosnia and the other to the Austrian consul. But they only kept

Carriage on an Austrian stamp

them to enhance their authority and prestige. When travelling about the city, they had to alight from the carriage and go on foot when a turning had to be negotiated. Out of town it was possible to travel only in one direction one hour's distance.[27]

Inevitably, 'the light of reason' could only advance at a snail's pace along such roads. So, in the first part of the twentieth century, Western visitors to European Turkey encountered examples of extreme superstition. The main reason for this state of affairs was the poor education of Orthodox priests, a direct result of the system by which people were elected for church offices. The election of the patriarch of Byzantium cost thousands of ducats: half for the Ottoman government, half for the pashas and eunuchs. In order to collect enough money, noble families from Phanar formed a kind of joint stock companies. 'This encouraged baksheesh which had returned with profit. How? According to the same system. Dioceses were sold at auctions, the costs of bishops were reimbursed by the priests, and these in turn wronged the whole religious folk.'[28] When a priest was ordained, he was not asked what he knew but, rather, how much money he could offer.[29] The custom was already established in the seventeenth century,[30] and various posts were on sale even at the beginning of the twentieth century.[31] The priest of the commune was obliged to contribute to the support of the bishop, the bishop to that of the high dignitaries and these to the patriarch. In order to provide funds for all these wants and demands they often resorted to charlatanism. Absurd stories were circulated of the miracles wrought at some celebrated shrine, of the sudden appearance of the Virgin, or saints and angels, diseases cured by the power of relics, the marvellous effects of particular amulets, the necessity of making pilgrimages and processions to this or that holy place, all of which was regarded as a legitimate source of wealth for the clergy.[32]

Although illness did not always denote punishment from God, for their recovery believers mainly trusted in Him who was considered the primordial cause of all good and evil.[33] The ill undertook pilgrimages to monasteries, to the ruins of old churches or to springs which they believed possessed healing powers, giving the priest abundant alms in order to read prayers over them. This continued well into the twentieth century. In the monastery of Suvodol, Kanitz reported almost stepping on a girl who lay unconscious in front of the portal. She had been brought there by her mother 'so the monk could exorcise her of the devil that tortured her!'[34]

At the end of the nineteenth century travellers Georgina Mackenzie and Adeline Irby were told by a vicar that in sickness Muslims often asked for the prayers of priests, 'apparently by way of spell.' They were told how once a *hodja* came to him and besought him to breathe on him and give him a blessing as a means of curing some disease. The priest objected, arguing that since the *hodja* had not faith the blessing would do him no good. 'Never mind,' exclaimed the *hodja*, 'only bless me; faith or no faith, it can do me no harm.' The priest laughed heartily at his 'stupidity' but the story made the travellers 'somewhat suspicious that he should have found fault only with lack of faith, instead of frankly stating that neither blessing nor breathing of his could avail to cure disease.'[35]

If reports of images with damaged eyes leave the cause and time of their despoliation unclear, the connection between churches in which travellers saw these frescos and supernatural healing is much more apparent. A Venetian diplomat and traveller from the first half of the sixteenth century reported that not only Christians but also Muslims and Jews made pilgrimages for their health to the monastery of Mileševo in Herzegovina where Gil'ferding saw the damaged frescos.[36] That this practice continued into the middle of the nineteenth century is attested by Consul Gil'ferding, who saw Muslim men and women in the monastery when he visited it.[37]

Before being superseded by pills, various powders played an important role in medicine.[38] Especially cherished were those from sacred places. As recorded by Evliya Çelebi, there were eighty doctors for eye diseases in Istanbul.

> Their eldest patron was a Jewess of the time of Moses, who was directed by God to apply to her for relief for his sore eyes. The woman took dust from under the right eye of Moses and put it into his eye, by which means he was cured. She exercised the profession of an oculist during two hundred years. The patron of the oculist in the Prophet's

time, who was girded by Selmán, the Persian, is buried at Isfahán, and the dust of his tomb is reckoned a specific against sore eyes.[39]

According to information gathered in Bosnia-Herzegovina in the first half of the twentieth century by Vejsil Ćurčić,[40] there were 'exceptionally many cases in which people scraped dust from different monuments and used it in medicine, even when this involved statues from pagan times.' Ćurčić's information testifies to this practice mainly in places with a predominantly Muslim population, while in some Catholic areas it had already been abandoned and the people knew nothing of it, 'this probably being the result of the influence of Catholic priests.'

A book of prescriptions entitled *Domaći liekar* (Home Healer), written in 1868 by Fra Nikolić from Široki Brijeg in Bosnia-Herzegovina, gives as his instruction no. 66 the following remedy for 'eyes that feel pain': 'If they are hurting, take three points of a knife of white stone (vitriola-pulveres senci depurati) and half a litre of water, insert into the water from the knife and mix it into an oily substance, take a clean rag, soak it in that water and put over the eye three times daily and you will get well.'[41] Nikolić's instruction does not specify where the requisite white stone should come from, but it was self-evident that for this purpose powder acquired from sacred places, from tombstones and relics, was regarded as more effective.[42] Folk medicine in the Balkans ascribed especially high curative powers to the painted images of saints.[43] 'The people attributed miraculously curative power to frescos and icons. A part of the specific damage seen on frescos in the first layer is a result of these superstitions. The blind used to scrape colour and plaster from the eyes of painted saints, the lame from the feet and the disabled persons from the hands, etc.'[44]

More educated Catholic priests certainly played an important part in the disappearance of this custom, which, I presume, has still not entirely died out. Not only simple folk but also members of the local intelligentsia went to a Polish healer from Kalisz, who recommended powder scraped from a church as a cure for epilepsy as recently as at the beginning of the twentieth century.[45] In the Dobrepolje Valley (Slovenia) in the first half of the twentieth century, a traditional cure for epilepsy in young children consisted of a few splinters taken from the back of the statue of St Valentine in the local church. Mothers who believed in the great healing power of the statue would ask the sexton to cut a few slivers of wood from it for their sick children, with the result that this statue in the church of St Florian in Ponikve was all 'cut up.'[46]

The data supplied by Oskar Kolberg and Anton Mrkun are important here because they come from localities which had not been reached by the 'Turks' and, even more, because they tell us how people gained possession of

Marko Kraljević

the necessary powder: through the sexton, for an unconsecrated hand should not touch that which was considered sacred. Handling the sacred requires an intermediary with the necessary power or knowledge to neutralise any potential dangers. In the early days this function was carried out by priests, but when they refused to perform it or even condemned it as superstitious and backward, people in need turned to their sextons, who had fewer scruples. Archaeologist Kondakov recorded that in the church of St Nicholas the Miraculous in Thessaloníki he had found many frescos which were the victims of Turkish barbarism, 'but they suffer even more from barbarous treatment by the lower clergy.'[47]

The Material Basis of Superstition

That careless handling of sacred objects can be dangerous is well known and some authors tell interesting stories of what it can lead to. Thus two Englishwomen told a story that they heard during their visit to the monastery of Dečani. Muslims had decided to take over the church as a mosque. Their *hodja* bowed before the door in prayer, but the statue of a monster fell and crushed his head, 'thus giving the misbelievers a lesson which has lasted them till now.'[48] Such traditions were very popular and many stories circulated hinting at what had happened to this or that individual who tried to damage or rob a church. One of the oldest was recorded in 1675 by French traveller de la Guilletiere. During his visit to the mosque on the Acropolis, his janissary showed him a picture of the Virgin Mary in which one of the eyes had been shot out with a musket bullet by a 'Turk.' The story was remembered by both Muslims and Christians. The Muslims, who were 'keen on exaggeration,' told him that the sacrilege was punished miraculously: the bullet rebounded upon the malefactor and blew out his brains. The Christians, whose testimony he found more credible, merely claimed that the perpetrator had immediately lost the use of his right arm and remained disabled ever after.[49] A similar story was recorded more than two centuries later by Felix Kanitz. In his story a robber, an Albanian, shot at the image of the dragon slayer, shouting to those present: 'See how I'll kill your St George!' But the bullet rebounded from the wall and knocked him over.[50]

It is certain that such stories were mainly disseminated by Orthodox priests 'for their own benefit.' That they knew how to make good use of them is evident from Gil'ferding's report that the Albanian population living near the monastery of St Marko in Kosovo Polje believed that the theft of any of its property or any other desecration of the monastery would result in severe punishment – the inevitable insanity of the culprit.[51] Belief in the sacredness of everything owned by the church was so strong that throughout Albania deserted churches often stand in thick woods, 'as some superstition prevents even the Moslems from cutting wood near them.'[52] This belief was common throughout the Ottoman Empire and it was rare 'to find a poor Turk who does not feel that the Christian Churches have some kind of thaumaturgical power, and this probably did much to save them.'[53]

Such stories, and the beliefs they created, do not mean that Muslims inflicted no damage whatsoever on Christian objects: if that were so, the stories would have not exist. Bernard Randolph, for instance, recorded that during his visit to the Peloponnese in the 1680s he had heard how the local pasha publicly set fire to a sacred picture of the Holy Virgin, known as La Madonna Spiglia, in a monastery:

> There was another Picture of the Virgin Mary, which did many Miracles; and every Year great numbers of Greeks flock'd from all parts to pay their Devotions to it. The Basha of the Morea having notice, went to see the Ceremony, telling the Priests he was desirous to see some Miracle; they telling him it had done many, he ordered one of his Men to bring him another Picture out of any House, which being

brought, he asked the priests what difference there was betwixt those two Pictures, they answered, that, that Picture which was in the Church was a most Sacred thing. But the Bassha caused a Fire to be made, and both Pictures to be put into it, saying, he would Worship that which escaped the Fire; but both were burnt, and the Bassha laughing at the Superstition, went his way.[54]

Such actions, however, were the exceptions rather than the rule and violated the Islamic spirit of tolerance. Even those who used the actual desecration of Christian sacred objects as an anti Turkish propaganda were well aware of this. It became notorious that most, if not all, of the Bulgarian bishops and their lay secretaries were involved more or less directly and more or less voluntarily in the rebellious activities of the Macedonian Committee. The Ottomans knew this very well, but they never dared do more than place a bishop under a courteous and temporary version of house arrest.[55] When a Russian war correspondent, Leon Trotsky, travelled from Tetovo to Veles in Macedonia during the Balkan Wars, he had an opportunity to observe the landscape, which had been turned 'into a wilderness.' All the villages he visited near Kičevo had been burned by the Ottomans: only the churches still stood amid the ashes.

> As a rule the Turks don't touch churches – churches, priests, or women. Two officials of our former consulate in Skoplje told me an interesting thing. When our government was arming for the *komitadjis* in Old Serbia, the revolvers and cartridges that passed through the consulate were handed over to priests and women – and nearly all of them reached their destination. The Turks don't search women or priests – nor, of course, the Albanian kochaks or the Ottomanized Serbs (they're the worst of the lot), or the real Ottomans, the Turks themselves: They undoubtedly possess some elements of chivalry.[56]

Sacred objects desecrated by someone who remained unpunished usually lost their former significance. But travellers report a firm faith in the supernatural power of the frescos with gouged-out eyes. An account of the evil destiny which befell the culprit would thus have been an indispensable element of the story had these desecrations been carried out by an unconsecrated hand. The lack of this element in itself confirms, first, that these actions were not meant to desecrate and, second, that they were carried out by persons who were in possession of the necessary power and knowledge, that is the Orthodox priests themselves (who thus obtained a potent 'drug').

If the travellers had pieced together the individual elements of the story of the blinded images, the indictment of 'Turkish' iconoclasm and/or barbarity would have turned out to be a mere construct. However, Western travellers did not ask such questions. The one exception was Grace Ellison:

> All over South Serbia I was shown superb frescoes minus the eyes, 'the work of the barbarous Turk' explained my guides. But this I could not believe. That the Turk should hack down statues (Cromwell did the same), that he should fling buckets of stucco or cement at the beautiful frescoes, I could also understand: but that he could climb up 7,000 feet, and with a small knife carefully remove the eyes of the Saints from the frescoes in the monasteries is not within the realm of possibility. He is much too lazy!
>
> The real explanation I believe is the one given me by a monk at the monasteries. The eyes were removed, he told me, by the Serbs themselves as a cure for eye trouble. The eyes of the Saints were cut out, ground down to powder, and made into a lotion which, when applied to the eyes, made miraculous cures! Such is the healing power of Faith![57]

My own fieldwork fully confirms her theory. During my visit to Visoki Dečani in March 1991, I asked a caloyer what had happened to the eyes of several frescos in the church. They were gouged out, he explained, because 'someone wanted to do harm.' My next question was: Why had 'someone' gouged out only the eyes although they were four or five metres high and hard to reach, and not a single nose or ear? Well, he said, some people believed this was a remedy for eye trouble.

The story of 'Turkish barbarity' was just an element in the struggle of the Balkan people to define themselves as Europeans, that is civilised people. They wanted to modernise themselves, so they struggled to board the Occidental bandwagon, fully determined not to return to the Orient, which for them had become synonymous with yesterday, with backwardness. They chose to view their point of departure from the perspective of orientalists, not Orientals, as students and critics of the Orient, not as part of it. This reversal in outlook used the 'Turks' as an explanation and excuse for all shortcomings in the Balkans, blaming them for the mere loss of an umbrella, let alone for any violation or damage done to churches.[58]

Predictably, Christian churches and monasteries in Serbia, Greece and elsewhere were the main stage for this psychodrama. 'In every church and monastic chapel in Servia,' a British traveller to 'the Poor Man's Paradise' reported, 'your cicerone always takes a pride in pointing out the traces of

Turkish vandalism: here a gouged eye in a fresco, there a bullet-mark, and there wholesale destruction or desecration.'[59]

Many similar stories could be heard throughout the Balkans and only rarely did they meet with disbelief from their Western listeners. The following is an example:

> I expose elsewhere the false story that was widely believed of the Greek wounded having been burnt alive in the church at Rizomylou on Friday, the 30th. This was wholly untrue. There were no wounded in the church, and the sacred edifice was standing and uninjured, except that some trifling damage had been done to the interior. The altar had been overturned and some twenty pictures of saints pulled down. It is very likely that this was done by Greek irregulars in order to invent an outrage, for elsewhere the churches were treated by the Turkish soldiers with great respect.[60]

Many of these stories were pure inventions, fabricated with a view to exposing 'Turkish barbarity.' If this or that fact contradicted them, a procrustean bed was always there to accommodate it. For instance, an Orthodox priest wrote a book on the Serbs in Bačka, maintaining among other things that Filip Višnjić, the famous folk singer from the Serbian revolution, was blind because the Turks had gouged out his eyes when he was a child, although Višnjić himself told Vuk Karadžić that he lost his eyesight because of a childhood disease.[61]

It is strange but noteworthy that Western travellers took such stories at face value, regardless of all their contradictions. They travelled to distant countries to see unknown lands, but once there they often turned a blind eye to what they saw, because they were prepared to 'see' only what they believed they would see. In our case, they blinded themselves to the contradictions in the stories of the blind eyes they were looking at, so as to avoid seeing facts which might contradict their belief in the indisputable superiority of Christianity over Islam in every respect. Only when communism was overthrown did the scapegoat change its name. When I asked a monk in the monastery of Jovan Bigorski (Macedonia) in November 2000 who had gouged out the eyes of the saints in paintings in the monastery, he explained laconically: 'Communists.'

Gusle player

SIX

The Romantic Charm of Freedom

The age of romanticism played an important role in the development of anthropology, for it was then that interest both in ancient societies and cultures and in the languages, customs and way of life of unknown and distant peoples began to flourish. A yearning for personal freedom, unshackled by social or material reality, drove the romantics in search of unknown countries and ancient times where people supposedly lived in peace and happiness in a world unspoilt by civilisation. In the romantic period the attention of the West focused especially on Montenegro, or the Black Mountain, which alone, from the latter half of the fifteenth century, 'rose, like Ararat, amid the overwhelming floods of Islamism.'[1] Montenegro's rugged mountains had not only constituted an impregnable fortress for its own people but also offered a safe haven for oppressed Christians from neighbouring nations; the aspirations and hopes for Balkan freedom had been fostered in the austerity of its grim highlands.[2] On the other hand, squeezed between Turkey and Austria-Hungary, the mountains of Montenegro constituted an insurmountable obstacle to the advance of civilisation. So Montenegro was cut off from Europe, 'from Western education and arts, no less than from Western ills, weakness of spirit and body: here syphilis is unknown.'[3]

Exaggerated Romance or Actual History

Western visitors to this diminutive highland principality, surrounded on three sides by Ottoman provinces, were inspired by the people's sustained struggle for Christianity and freedom against the efforts of the Ottoman Porte and by their heroic resistance to armies greater in number than their entire population, enabling them to stand 'a free and Christian people in the midst of countries which have long succumbed to the rule of an Infidel Power.'[4]

It was generally believed in the West that the history of Montenegro was quite the most wonderful in the world:

> To study carefully the whole history of the land from the days of the Great Dushan down to the Treaty of Berlin thirty-two years ago is more like reading a rather exaggerated romance than actual history. It seems incredible that a race so small in numbers, so inferior in sinews of war, should have been able to withstand even for half a century the almost overwhelming resources of a foe that had all but conquered Europe and, moreover, was at the zenith of its power; but that they should have withstood that mighty foe for nearly five centuries is nigh beyond belief.[5]

Vladimir Bronevsky, a Russian naval officer and the author of the first travel book on Montenegro, was enraptured with his experience. During his three-day stay there he was 'transported into a new world' where he met his predecessors 'from the ninth and tenth centuries.' The short visit enabled him to examine 'the simple life of the time of Patriarchs' and made acquaintance with 'Ilja Muromec, Dobriny and other heroes of our distant past.' He was mesmerized as if at Sparta, 'a republic in the literal meaning of the word, a fatherland of equality and real freedom where custom takes the place of law, manliness protects on freedom, the sword of revenge thwarts injustice' and his admiration was excited with 'the sublime spirit, the pride and courage of these people whose name fills all their neighbours with fear.'[6]

Two years after Bronevsky's notes were published, travel accounts by the governor and commander of French troops in Kotor (1807–13) appeared. In the 1810s Vialla de Sommières travelled across Montenegro and met many of its inhabitants. Although an independent Montenegro was a potential obstacle to the dissemination of French influence in the Balkans, he wrote sympathetically about its people, previously described to him 'as little better than barbarians and cannibals.'[7] Although a great number of works in various European languages were published in the nineteenth century on the subject of Montenegro, very little was known about this tiny principality and its highlanders, and that little was quite frequently incorrect. Montenegrins had usually been represented as wild, savage, bloodthirsty, thieving scoundrels.[8] So, when Gustav Rasch set off on his journey to Montenegro in 1872, many educated Berliners felt he was a 'dead man' or, at the best, would return from his dangerous journey without his ears or nose.[9] During the nineteenth century in Kotor 'Montenegrin' was still an insult, like 'Morlak' in Dalmatia.[10]

Occasionally, Prince Nikola of Montenegro himself ridiculed such prejudices, as when he received an unnamed British traveller in 1873. Speaking in French, Nikola congratulated him on his courage for having ventured so far into the country, not on account of the state of the roads 'for all English are good mountaineers,' but on account of the bad name the country had in Europe. 'Don't you know,' he said, laughing, '*que nous sommes des ogres, et que nous mangeons les enfants*,' however, you should try how we cook them if you will dine here to-night at eight.'[11]

Nationality and Liberty

In the age of the romantics the idea of liberty was particularly attractive for the Balkan peoples who did not have their own states. In the first half of the nineteenth century the people of Greece were obsessed by the ideas of *genos* and *elentheria* (people, freedom),[12] and Slavs, it seemed to some, had 'but one idea – to think and talk of nothing but their eternal nationality and freedom.'[13] In the Balkans in general, and in Montenegro in particular, politics, freedom and nationality made important topics of conversation.[14] As noted by Vialla de Sommières,[15] the Montenegrin people liked to boast of being 'the freest in the world.' Like his predecessors, Prince Nikola greatly extolled the independence of character and love of freedom of his people, declaring: 'The Austrians and Russians were slaves, the Montenegrines free men who would not tolerate arbitrary or despotic rule. They were all equal.'[16]

In the second half of the nineteenth century a poetic story was invented in Montenegro, which claimed that its people were the aristocracy of the Slavs. The story gained much popularity with Western authors and inspired Prime Minister Gladstone to call Montenegro 'the beach on which were thrown up the remnants of Balkan freedom.' British diplomat William Miller, who was well-travelled in European Turkey, even claimed that the inhabitants of Montenegro were all 'descendent from the aristocracy of ancient Servia, and a believer in the doctrine of heredity may detect in their exquisite manner a proof of their aristocratic lineage.'[17] As the story went, after the great defeat in Kosovo Polje in 1389 when the Ottomans destroyed the Serbian Empire, a mere handful of Serbian nobles emigrated to Montenegro, where these 'children of freedom' could alone defy their enemies during five centuries of unremitting warfare. Rather than exist in the fertile valleys under a conqueror's yoke, those old-world heroes made their homes in barren mountains.[18] Although the story found many hearing ears, it was nothing but an invented tradition which purpose was to intensify the Montenegrins' patriotism in support of Prince Nikola's dream of restoring the old Serbian Empire.[19] According to Miss Durham, the oft-repeated tale that Montenegro had been founded by refugees from Kosovo was but a myth, for, lineally, the Montenegrins were Bosnians, Herzegovinians and Albanians rather than Serbs of Serbia.[20] Her assertion is further substantiated by the historical fact that, for a long time, Montenegro served as a safe haven for any inhabitant of neighbouring countries who fell foul of the Ottoman authorities or the local *agas* or beys.[21]

The Petrified Ocean

Rugged, barren, defiant mountains, rocky and desolate, a fierce-seeming country of stone dwellings, utterly bare on all sides, looked 'like a petrified ocean, its waves rising literally "mountains high."'[22] To give explanation of the Montenegro's rocky landscape, its visitors often retold a native legend in one of its numerous versions. When God finished making the world he realised that it needed stones. He took a big bag of stones to scatter all over the world. Whilst he was in Montenegro the bag split and out fell the stones, pell-mell, and there they have remained ever since.[23]

For visitors from abroad, the first view of the land came as a shock, as if by penetrating into Montenegro they had ceased to live in their century and were 'transformed into a witness of the creation of the world.'[24] The next instant filled almost every one of them with respect and admiration for these heroic highlanders who preferred freedom in this wilderness to slavery in abundant lands. George Bernard Shaw once stated that Montenegrins must all have been philosophers to love these barren rocks as they did.[25] Their descriptions of the Montenegrins were for the most part admiring but were occasionally spiced with a decided flavour of derision:

> My first impulse on arriving in the main street of Tsetinie was to burst out laughing. It is the meanest capital in the whole civilized or uncivilized world; and the village of the most petty Rajah, or chief, in India, is in every way superior to this small collection of Montenegrin cabins, resembling the dirty out-houses of an English farmyard, or what are called the downs of an Indian bungalow. The thatched huts

are altogether out of proportion to the big men who inhabit them; and an armed peasant, who in his natural state might be considered a very respectable person, is made extremely ridiculous when called the Minister of War, the Secretary of State for Foreign Affairs, the Archbishop, the Minister of the Interior; or by some other title which, borrowed from civilized countries, is here lampooned in a manner that becomes infinitely more diverting because the holders of such exalted dignities, unconscious of their drollery, and inflated with an idea of their own importance, are firmly persuaded of their equality with any other high officers of state in Europe.[26]

Notwithstanding the great poverty and need in which the Montenegrins lived, visitors from abroad found them a proud and dignified people since they were free or, at least, were made out to be so by travel guides to this remote country:

> They [Montenegrins] are, as a rule, extremely poor. Their thatched huts resemble stables rather than the dwellings of human beings. Yet the men are remarkably dignified in their bearing, and they customarily carry quite an arsenal of weapons in their girdles, while the women, though often beautiful, perform most of the menial tasks and soon lose their good looks. At places the traveller encounters quite a Homeric state of society, where war and poetry are the sole pursuits, and where a hero is seen seated in presence of the blind minstrel who extols his exploits in war or his last 'ceta' or predatory expedition to the twang of the one-stringed 'gusla.'[27]

Western travellers' yearning for an elementary, just and hospitable world was the reason why they bought these guide-books and followed their itineraries in search of proud elementary men who were prepared to live in utmost poverty just as long as they were free. A British traveller, for instance, was firmly assured that 'every Briton's heart must warm to this little land if he had but read its history.'[28] Those who actually went there were recompensed as the Montenegrin love of liberty and sense of honour made them feel 'more at home in this far corner of Europe than in any other foreign land.'[29] However, as Prince Nikola occasionally complained, they looked upon Montenegrins 'only from a picturesque point of view,' for he sensed that they would really like to keep them 'like a sort of menagerie of wild beasts,' to be looked at occasionally for their amusement value.[30]

But the travellers' yearnings to see survivals of distant times mattered more than the natives' feelings, and Westerners were happy to observe this archaic picture even in the middle of the twentieth century:

> The Montenegrin people made the impression upon us of a most
> attractive nation. Even the poorest of them, and that means most
> people, have a quiet dignity in bearing and a reserve in manner which
> is to some extent shared by all European peasantry and especially by
> those who live in the mountains. But the Montenegrin, however poorly
> clad, looks as though he were always conscious of the way in which his
> people maintained themselves against the Turk throughout history.[31]

Baptism of Muslims on Christmas Eve

Montenegrins were very proud of their fearlessness in battle and considered
themselves the finest heroes. In their opinion, other nations were more
or less feminised, with the sole exception of the Albanians.[32] The highest
ambition and dearest wish of the Montenegrins was to die in battle to the
sound of gunfire, with the smell of gunpowder and blood in their nostrils.
As death upon a sick-bed was considered unworthy of a man, people would
say contemptuously: 'Go wretch, you dishonour your family; you will die in
your bed!'[33] Heroism filled a large space in the minds of Montenegrins, who
were brought up on tales of the cool daring and extraordinary pluck of their
forebears. 'Be a brave boy, like Miloš Obilić,' mothers used to say if their
little boys were crying.[34] To be thought a 'great hero' was the height of male
ambition. Their old enemies, the 'Turks,' saw the Montenegrins in a somewhat
different light, however. Osman Pasha Resulbegović used to compare them to
snakes: 'They are like snakes; when you catch them, they whimper; but when
you let them go, they whistle.'[35]

That Montenegrins were a proud and dignified people was attributed to
the absolute equality prevailing in their country. Many Westerners were of
the opinion that nowhere in the world did there exist such complete equality
as in Montenegro. This image, however, was just another fruit of romantic
idealisation, for in Montenegro equality was a privilege reserved exclusively
for people who professed Orthodox Christianity. In this respect Montenegro
was the true antithesis of the religious tolerance of the Ottoman Empire, for
all Montenegrins professed but one religion and their homeland offered no
place to any other.[36] The massacre of Muslims that allegedly took place at
the beginning of the eighteenth century represented a defining moment in
Montenegrin identity. As the myth (often repeated with approval by Western
authors) has it, on Christmas Eve 1702 (or some years later, depending on
the source) an armed band rushed from one Muslim house to another in

Montenegro and slaughtered all the inhabitants who refused to be baptised. Next morning the land was 'cleansed' and ceased to stink of Mohamed,' the murderers went to church in Cetinje, where the people assembled to announce 'Montenegro is free!' – their arms 'bloody to the shoulders,' in the words of a song commemorating the event.[37]

The Christmas massacre has played an important role in the mythology of Montenegrin independence. Such was the renown of this real or fictitious Christmas Eve that it was enthusiastically cited during the Balkan Wars of 1912–13 as an example to be followed by Montenegrin soldiers, and baptism was actually periodically enforced 'with hideous cruelty.'[38] Janko Vukotić, the secretary of the Montenegrin prince, did not conceal the Montenegrins' hope of getting rid of all Muslims and resettling their lands. When he informed Miss Durham that they had killed every man of the Rugova tribe, she expressed her indignantion. He then cried: 'But they are beasts, savage animals. We have done very well.'[39]

Indeed, by the nineteenth century such deeds no longer received indiscriminate approval from Western authors, but many of them found extenuating circumstances in that the victims were Muslims: 'If we must condemn that fatal night, in which death or baptism was offered to the Moslems of Montenegro, let us at least admire that constant love of independence, and that firm adherence to their own faith, which form so noble a contrast to the ignominious renegation of Christianity by the degenerate nobles of Bosnia and Albania.'[40]

In contrast to their usual disdain and contempt for the poor and powerless, Western attitudes towards Montenegrins were respectful on account of their feeling for honour and dignity. Two British teachers who, upon hearing uniformed Montenegrins sing on a Christmas morning, could only say that the words of the old Serbian ballad of the late nineteenth century were still as true as in the time of Ivan Crnojević: 'The Latins are rich, they have gold and silver, and the skill of workmen; but the Serbs have the proud and princely bearing, and the glad, fearless eyes of heroes.'[41] The Montenegrin bards, however, had borrowed the ethical ideal contained in these words from their mortal enemies, the Turks. They, too, were sensible of the fact that making money was their weak-point. Or, as a *vali* told a British diplomat: 'All Christians, big and small, like making money. We Turks don't know how to make money; we only know how to take it.'[42]

The Stronger and the Weaker Sex

Western travellers paid a great deal of attention to the ancient manners

Herzegovinians on their way to market

and customs that regulated gender behaviour in Montenegro and that had
survived in the inaccessible mountains of this warlike and freedom-loving
people where the distinctions between the stronger and the weaker sex were
not yet as confused as they had become in the civilised world. Domination
by the husband and total dependence by the wife supposedly defined the
relationship between couples, 'as it did once in Sparta.'[43] In Montenegro, war
and raids were the employment of men, their tools were their rifle and *khanjar*
with which they defended the honour of their homeland in the battlefield;
they left other forms of work to the weaker sex, as manual labour was
considered degrading to heroes.[44]

   If the history of Montenegrin men was rich in stories of unremitting
warfare and daring brigands' raids, the history of Montenegrin women can be

reduced to one of unrelenting labour and suffering. In Montenegro, even in the twentieth century the very word 'woman' was used as a term of insult. A man who had been deprived of his weapons as a punishment was shamed by his comrades calling him a woman.[45] Women were burdened with agricultural as well as domestic labour. In addition, they span and wove and took goods to market. Reportedly, the sight of a Montenegrin man striding unencumbered up a mountain road followed by his heavily laden womenfolk was not uncommon.[46] Some authors even claim that a common saying in Montenegro could have been '*le nostre donne sono le nostre mule*' (in Italian!).[47] Not all those who reported such scenes actually saw them in Montenegro; some had come across them in older travel reports or in tall stories.[48] This seems to be true of the above-mentioned saying. Reverend Henry Tozer illustrated the place occupied by the female sex in these parts by a story he had heard some years before in Corfu from the late Sir Henry Ward. As Sir Henry was riding into the country one day he overtook a man who had laden his wife with a very heavy bundle of faggots. He remonstrated with him, saying: 'Really, my good man, it is too bad that you should load your wife in that way; what she is carrying is a mule's burden.' 'Yes, your Excellency,' the man replied, 'what you say is quite true, it *is* a mule's burden: but then, you see Providence has not provided us with mules, and He *has* provided us with women.'[49]

Such reports, then, indicated the very low level civilisation had reached in Montenegro and at the same time also convey a certain nostalgia for the times when male supremacy was unchallenged in the West, when Western women too had to listen – indeed did listen – to their husbands without arguing, as Montenegrin women did.[50] Montenegrin women, reportedly, expected if not desired a little severity. A certain British traveller, for instance, mentioned a Montenegrin girl who married a foreigner. She became quite melancholy because he did not beat her. 'For if he did not beat her, when she knew she deserved it, it could only be, she thought, because he was indifferent to her.'[51]

Montenegrin society was split between *ljudi* (men) and *žene* (women), honour and respect being reserved exclusively for the former. Even in old age women could not command respect in their society as men did. Old age was just an excuse for still heavier drudgery. Women's most important role was to be mothers of sons: in accordance with Turkish custom, the Montenegrins counted people by the number of rifles they represented. When a boy was born, there was no end of exultation for the house became stronger by one gun. After the age of ten males carried a loaded rifle with them at all times and never laid it aside, even while cultivating their fields or tending their sheep.[52]

Visitors from abroad looked in vain for female beauty in Montenegro. The women there were 'very muscular and strong' and their beauty was usually soon exhausted by 'laborious, and unfeminine, occupations.'[53] Allegedly, those who were handsome in their younger years were, even at thirty, 'very old and repulsive; the terms "tender," "beautiful" and "weaker" sex do not suit them.'[54] At any rate, except for the princess, they did not find Montenegrin women beautiful. This confirmed them in their opinion that feminine beauty was the product of civilisation.[55] On the other hand, foreign visitors were constantly overwhelmed with admiration for those 'fearless fighters of gigantic stature.'[56] Colonel Egor Kovalevski, for instance, described them as 'a real tribe of Athletes,' adding that 'they know how to wear their arms and their dandyish garb, which shows the manliness of their stature, – everything in them defeats a European, a child of illness and luxury.'[57]

Interestingly, the warlike aspect of the Montenegrins did not disturb Western travellers, at least not as much as that of the Albanians did.[58] If a Montenegrin kept his arms on him at all times, they saw this as a sign of heroism. Upon seeing all men in Cetinje wearing arms, Aleksandr Amfiteatrov described the place approvingly as 'neither a town nor a village, but a military camp,' its inhabitants being all 'beautiful young men.'[59] But when the same traveller saw the Albanians, who like the Montenegrins never laid aside their arms, he saw them very differently: 'He is sitting at home, like a frightened wolf, with his arms on his knees.'[60]

The stronger and the weaker sex in Montenegro ate their meals separately. Almost until the beginning of the twentieth century women were not allowed to sit down with the men; they had to stand. They never went to the coffee houses frequented by their husbands.[61] Nor it was becoming for a Montenegrin to go for a walk with his wife, even to church, or to appear with her in public. This would set his friends laughing 'as if an Austrian minister had gone for a walk with his female cook.'[62]

The Montenegrins would reckon it a shameful liberty for a woman to call her husband by his name in public during the first year of their marriage; a wife would even have scruples about doing so when they were alone. Similarly, a husband would avoid mentioning his wife; and if he could not avoid speaking of her, he would apologise, saying, '*Da prostite, moja žena*' ('With your pardon, my wife'), the same expression used after mentioning a pig, an ass or the like.[63]

As a Czech author put it, 'Sexual love, which the good Lord gave us as a prop for poor poets and novelists, is unknown to Montenegrin women.'[64] At night a husband had to creep secretly to his wife's bedside because it was not becoming for him to be seen doing it. According to Vuk Karadžić, old traditions forbade newlyweds to sleep together during the first year of marriage. The bride slept with her mother-in-law and the groom with the

Albanesen in Verfolgung des Feindes

Albanians chasing their enemies

livestock. Montenegrin brides were so modest that they did not want to sleep with their husbands. Sometimes the mother of the bride had to come and talk her into submitting to the duties of her new life. Then she lay between her son-in-law and daughter; when she noticed that the bride had fallen asleep, she left the newlyweds alone together.[65] The reason for such modesty, some authors explained, was that people lived in houses without separate rooms, so the newlyweds had to have their bed amidst other members of their family. However, couples in other countries living in similar circumstances did not cultivate such modesty, but it was found among Muslims, although they lived in bigger houses. Muslims considered it a sign of good breeding to avoid 'all indecent haste' when going to bed. For this reason, in some Muslim countries the bridegroom did not consummate the marriage for seven nights out of respect for, first, his father, second, his mother, third, his brother, and so forth.[66]

A Montenegrin wife never mourned for her husband; it was not the custom. She cut off her hair as a sign of mourning only at her brother's death. To lament her husband was a burning shame; the only greater shame was if a fiancée lamented her intended.[67] For their part, men bore their pain stoically.[68] Similar rules of decency prevailed in Albania, where men were likewise not allowed to shed tears.[69]

The inferior position of women in Montenegrin society was symbolically expressed in a custom by which they had to salute their husbands and guests by kissing their hands and the hem of their tunics. In the nineteenth century, when a guest arrived, a woman of the household took off his shoes and washed his feet.[70] In the first half of the nineteenth century in Greece, newly married women also practised this custom towards strangers who came to their house; it would have been deemed irreligious and inhospitable to neglect it.[71]

Montenegrin customary law knew no punishment for women except capital punishment if a woman murdered her husband. Otherwise, her husband and parents were responsible for any transgression on her part and had to pay fines for her. A Montenegrin man would cut off his wife's nose or kill her if he caught her in a gross transgression. Capital punishment for a woman under customary law was by stoning, for it was considered shameful to use arms against those who could not take up arms in their own defence. According to an old custom, the father had to cast the first stone and the whole community followed his example until the woman was killed and buried under stones. Medaković recorded in 1860 that no one he spoke to could recollect this punishment having been carried out.[72] According to the entry in the *Encyclopaedia of Social Sciences*, in Greece stoning was a capital punishment for slaves; free people, condemned to death, were compelled to drink poison (s.v. Capital Punishment).

Since Montenegrins attached great importance to their honour, they did not practise corporal punishment. Nobody was permitted to hit a man, let alone beat him; if someone was hit, he could kill his attacker immediately, without being brought before a court or anybody else: 'Although a poor man, yet no stick for his body could grow in the forest. All Montenegrins were always and everywhere equal; they all fought for honour and integrity. Hence it appears that they were all noblemen, because no one wanted to suffer ignoble corporal punishment.'[73]

When Prince Danilo tried to introduce law and order into the country in 1855, he prescribed birching as a punishment for stealing. Montenegrins received the novelty with little understanding. As recounted by E. F. Knight, corporal punishment was a most dreadful verdict, unimaginable for a hero: 'A whipped Montenegrin is worse than dead – disgraced – outraged – an outcast on the earth. Many who have been condemned to the whipping have been known to fall down at the Prince's feet and pray to him for mercy – for death – death with torture, rather than the great infamy.'[74] In his memoirs from the Balkans, Martin Gjurgjević gave an account about an incident that took place after the war of 1876 in Vučji dol. A Montenegrin found a pistol and discharged all the cartridges, despite the strict ban on shooting. He was punished with a stick. After the verdict was announced, some *perjaniks* went into the woods for sticks. They broke off several twigs with leaves, as big 'as the biggest dove's feather.' The condemned person lay down and began to lament because of the strokes. Although they were not painful, the man was reproachful that he was given the rod.[75]

The image of Montenegrin male heroes in such accounts received some embellishment, however, for the same notion that it was honourable to be killed with a bullet and shameful to be beaten or hanged, was also common among to the Albanians and other Balkan peoples.[76]

Photogenic Knights

The majority of people on the eastern coast of the Adriatic Sea professed Christianity, although according to Consul Pouqueville their sole object of worship was in fact independence.[77] In this respect Montenegro was in no way different from other Christian districts ruled by the Ottomans who 'with a tolerance at that date rare' always recognised the religion of their subject countries and left the affairs of the Christians to their own ecclesiastics. To the Ottomans, the Montenegrin and Albanian highlanders, ruled by their own bishops, were simply insubordinate tribes against whom they sent punitive expeditions when taxes were in arrears and raids became intolerable.[78] The geography of the land had always prevented more effective conquest by the Ottomans: in Montenegro and Albania a small army was defeated and a large one starved.[79] Even in the *vilayet* of Shköder the subjection of its inhabitants was merely nominal. There was an Ottoman vizier, some troops and a customhouse, but otherwise Ottoman law and institutions were not recognised. There was no conscription, though Albanians were often employed as volunteers. No taxes were paid except the tithe, and that only occasionally, and more as a friendly act than a debt which could have been claimed by law. Above all, an Albanian could not be tried for capital offences by Ottoman law but had to be handed over to his tribe to be judged according to its particular customs.[80]

In the eyes of Western travellers, the fact that Montenegro was ruled 'by the only remaining militant bishop who led his courageous mountaineers in wars and victories' rendered it 'one of the most interesting countries in the world.'[81] In their view, Vladika Peter I (reigned 1785–1830) had realised the ideal of the Homeric king.[82] He enjoyed the high esteem of his people, although the pomp of his equipages was reduced to a single mule and a modest dwelling. The convent in which he resided was a building of moderate size, remarkable only for being surrounded by a thick wall with loopholes,

Vladika Peter Petrović II

which gave it the appearance of a small fortress.[83] His nephew and successor Peter II (1813–51) beatified him and Montenegrins were very proud of their saint because 'The Saint Peter who is in Rome renounced Christ three times; our Saint Peter who is in Cetinje never renounced Him!'[84]

The Montenegrins were no less proud of Vladika Peter II for his shooting prowess: he could hit a lemon thrown into the air by one of his attendants. Such dexterity may appear a singular accomplishment for a bishop, but it enhanced the confidence he enjoyed among his flock[85] who appreciated martial arts. Likewise, the Ottomans were proud of their Sultan Mahmut as 'indisputably the best and strongest shot in his dominions.'[86] Vladika Peter II, however, surpassed him, being 'perhaps the tallest and the most beautiful man in Montenegro, and Montenegrins perhaps do not lag in height behind any people in Europe.'[87]

The successor of Vladika Peter II, Prince Danilo (1851–60), was educated in the West and tried to introduce Western ideas and civilisation to his country. As stated by William Carr, he was of the opinion 'that the position of his "island of barbarism in a sea of civilization" was an anachronism, and that the time of necessary change was at hand.'[88]

The last of the Montenegrin chieftains of the Petrović dynasty was Nikola; proclaimed the prince of Montenegro in 1860 he elevated his title of prince into king fifty years later. Travellers described him as 'the last of the old kings of legends and romance,' in Europe at least.[89] He was also a 'wonderful pistol shot' and, it was said, could shoot a cigarette from a man's mouth at twelve paces.[90] King Nikola was unique in his time in that he governed and maintained his state without levying taxes. Other Balkan countries allowed foreign powers to manipulate their policies; Nikola manipulated those foreign powers. He would go to Russia asking for money to defend his country against Austria-Hungary, the following year Austria-Hungary would subscribe to defend Montenegro against Russia.[91] King Nikola was allied by marriage to half the crowned heads of Europe and his ten pretty daughters were in great demand as consorts: one became queen of Italy, another queen of Serbia. When foreigners commented on the country's lack of exports, Nikola always answered: 'Sir, you forget – my daughters!'[92]

Before the marriage of Princess Jelena of Montenegro and the future king of Italy in 1896, the European public knew little about the highland principality. The name of Montenegro was perhaps less familiar to the European public than that of Monaco and only a little more than that of San Marino.[93] At the end of the nineteenth century well-educated people in London's drawing rooms asked a British diplomat whether Cetinje was the capital of Bulgaria and whether Montenegrins were black. Montenegro became famous in Europe only after the marriages of Nikola's daughters.

Italian journalists flocked to Montenegro, German photographers found the king and his people very artistic models, 'and tourists from all lands discovered, to their surprise, that the Near East is not quite so dangerous as many European capitals.' So, paradoxically, the marriages of the prince's daughters did 'more for the country than all the brave deeds of this nation of warriors.'[94] And even the prince himself was renowned less by his valiant deeds than as 'European father-in-law.'[95] This fame did not last for long: during the First World War, a British traveller was told an amusing story of two wounded Tommies who were talking about the retreat from Serbia. One said to the other, 'Oh! I know all about Albania. Them's Albinos there, people wot 'ave white hair and pink eyes, and who marry the Montenegro folks, who're niggers, and their kids are called Dalmatian, cos they're spotted black and white.'[96] In the 1930s, however, a British captain was asked quite seriously whether the natives were 'Mountain Niggers.'[97]

Prison as a Yardstick

A great majority of Westerners took the Montenegrin love of freedom for granted. I only came across two examples of it being questioned. A French doctor remarked on the subject: 'Often I ask myself, "*Qu'est-ce que c'est que la liberté monténégrine?*"' Cannot any one be independent who chooses to dwell on the top of the rock? I avow, that rather than cultivate such liberty, I would a thousand times be subject to the Turk.' This comment, which really expressed the impossibility of freedom in poverty and isolation, was rejected 'with considerable irritation' by a Bosnian who was present and rebuked the speaker, remarking that Montenegro was nevertheless preferable. Life there might involve privations, he argued, but the Christian subjects of the Ottomans 'must be content to bear cruelties, insult, shame.'[98]

In the West in the eighteenth century, prison as a means by which society dealt with criminal behaviour was a relatively permeable institution, effecting incomplete captivity. Only during the nineteenth century were prisoners fully segregated from society as a punishment behind the closed walls of the penitentiary. In the Ottoman Empire, too, at the beginning of the eighteenth century, there were 'very few, and those weak Prisons; for the Justice or Injustice of the Sentence, which condemns a Criminal of any kind, is so speedily inflicted, that there frequently are now but fourteen Hours between the Crime and Execution; so that any Place will hold the Guilty, since… an escape from Justice is esteem'd impracticable.'[99]

The first prison in Montenegro was built by Vladika Peter II in the capital in the first half of the nineteenth century. Later, another one, for 'more serious

Turkish zaptiehs

criminals,' was opened on the island in the Lake of Skadar.[100] At the beginning of the twentieth century a new prison was built in Cetinje which had no doors or bars between the inmates and the outside world. The inmates had to be in their cells at night, but during the day they were allowed to communicate with the outside world. On festivals they were even allowed to leave the prison to dance with their friends. According to the sources, prisoners never escaped, for escape would have meant flight to a foreign land and loss of honour in their own. The theory of setting a thief to catch a thief was practised here most literally and methodically. If a prisoner did in fact escape, all the others inmates were set free to hunt their shameless comrade high and low over their native mountains; they would return at whatever time had been appointed, with or without the fugitive.[101] More than by the fact of their imprisonment, prisoners are said to have felt disgraced by being deprived of their arms: to a Montenegrin this was a degradation equivalent to prison uniform or branding elsewhere.[102] The truth is that prisoners had 15–kilograms weights chained to their feet. But why let a small detail spoil a romantic story?[103]

Prisoners in Montenegro were detained without the benefit of being fed at government expense. During their confinement they all depended on family and friends for their food. In a poor country like Montenegro this ensured that captivity would not become a resource for the improvident or the lazy.[104] The authorities in the Ottoman Empire took similar precautions, for prisoners there relied on their families for everything except bread and water, or alms begged from passers-by. However, they could talk as much as they pleased, played cards, sung and did all kinds of work for their own amusement or profit.[105] These precautions taken by the authorities show that there was a reverse side to the coin: they were afraid that many of these freedom-loving people would be prepared to commit any transgression in order to be imprisoned, if this would guarantee them their daily bread.

SEVEN

Passionate About Head-hunting

In the nineteenth century the Balkans became a promised land for hunters of bizarre phenomena like severed heads. Western travellers homed in on this custom, treating the existence of such trophies in the Balkans as symbolic of a clear-cut division between civilised and barbarian lifestyles, evidence 'of the naivety of the Homeric age'[1] or proof that in the Balkans 'but a century ago much of the population was as wild as the Red Indians of the same date.'[2]

Sir Austen Layard, for instance, famous in later life for the discovery of Nineveh and its remains, gave the following cameo of his stay in Cetinje in 1839:

> [A] number of gory heads with their long tufts of hair waving in the wind, the trophies of a recent raid upon the neighbouring Turks. It was a hideous and disgusting sight which first greeted the traveller on his arrival at the residence of the Priest-Prince. Our guides, however, pointed to it with exultation. They had all, as it was the duty of the warlike inhabitants of the Black Mountains, taken part in raids upon the Mussulmans and in the border wars, which were constantly taking place, and had their stories to relate of slaughtered Turks and bloody spoils, such as those exposed on the round tower.[3]

The *vladika* of Montenegro gave a reception for Sir Austen while he was in Cetinje, in a fort decorated with 'Turkish' heads. To illustrate the difference between civilisation and the lack of it, Sir Austen described how the *vladika* had procured a billiard table (a symbol of civilisation) from Trieste on which they played several games; on one occasion, a loud noise of shouting and gunfire was heard from without. It came from a party of Montenegrin warriors who had triumphantly returned from a successful raid into the Ottoman territory of Shköder. They carried several of their victims' heads in a cloth held up between them. Covered with gore, these heads were described in his account as 'a hideous and ghastly spectacle.' However, they were duly deposited at the feet of the *vladika* and then added to those already on display on the round tower near the convent.[4]

The West must have had a short memory and forgotten its own practices of a few generations earlier 'when it, too, was young.' In the early centuries of the modern era London Bridge was an attraction for tourists who came to see the criminals' heads on show there, stuck on the points of spears.[5] In England, the public display of severed heads continued until the second half of the eighteenth century, when passers-by paid sixpence for the privilege of viewing them. The heads of the Cato Street conspirators were severed from their dead bodies as late as the year 1820.[6] A seventeenth-century prisoner in Newgate wrote:

> I saw the heads when they were brought up to be boiled. The Hangman fetched them in a dirty dust basket, out of some by-place; and, setting them down among the felons, he and they made sport with them. They took them by the hair, flouting, jeering, and laughing at them; and then, giving them some ill-names, boxed them on the ears and cheeks. Which done, the Hangman put them into his kettle, and parboiled them with Bay-Salt and Cummin-Seed – that to keep them from putrefaction, and this to keep off the fowls from seizing them.[7]

The First Reports

A detailed report on the custom of severing and displaying heads in Montenegro was written by Vladimir Bronevsky who visited the country at the beginning of the nineteenth century. Bronevsky regarded the people of Montenegro as brave and reliable allies of Russia in its wars against the Ottoman Empire. So, in his eyes the practice of severing (Turkish) heads was conclusive proof of Montenegrin heroism: 'A Montenegrin never sues for mercy and whenever one of them is severely wounded, and it is impossible to save him from the enemy, his own comrades cut off his head.'[8]

Some years later, Vialla de Sommières visited Montenegro. He viewed

War with the Turks in the late 17th century (Baron Valvasor, 1689)

this custom with less compassion, paying full attention to details instead. According to him, the Montenegrins cut off the heads of captured robbers and 'Turks.' His travel book described a journey he took with a group of Montenegrins, during which they encountered a group of Muslims. The Montenegrins darted forward and the 'Turks' retired abruptly in great disorder, leaving one of their party dead and two wounded. The latter were immediately seized and decapitated; their heads were brought in triumph to the French officer. This spectacle was not a pleasant one for him, causing him 'many painful sensations' and making him 'more than once regret having undertaken this journey.'[9] Yet it was not so unpleasant as to make him change his plans to visit and see as much of this strange land as possible. During his journey, he came across further examples of the practice. He saw the greatest number of severed heads during his stay in the monastery of St Vasil where the 'horrible spectacle' of vast numbers of 'Turkish' heads fixed upon staves could be seen on the hills in every direction for two or three leagues.[10]

In the spring of 1838 Frederick August, king of Saxony, visited Vladika Peter II of Montenegro while making a botanical tour. Frederick August was less delicate than the French officer and expressed his wish to see 'a souvenir of the valour of the Montenegrins,' namely the embalmed head of Mahmud Pasha of Shköder. The Montenegrins had been formally incorporated into the *pashalik* of Mahmud Pasha under the peace treaty between Emperor Leopold II and the Sublime Porte of 1791, but they refused obedience and tribute, provoking the pasha to attack Montenegro with fire and sword in 1796. Vladika Peter I fought in the thick of the battle, a cross in one hand and a sword in the other, as he urged his people against the invaders. The Montenegrins were victorious and slaughtered many enemies. They even seized the pasha himself, cut off his head and preserved it as a token of their victory. It was taken to the monastery of Cetinje, together with his sword and turban, where it was 'religiously kept' in a special walnut chest of fine workmanship.[11]

When Sir Gardner Wilkinson visited Montenegro in 1844 he did not see the head of Mahmud Pasha – or at least he did not mention it – although he paid close attention to the heads on the round tower above Cetinje. He inspected them down to the smallest detail:

> On a rock, immediately above the convent, is a round tower, pierced with embrasures, but without cannon; on which I counted the heads of twenty Turks, fixed upon stakes, round the parapet, the trophies of Montenegrin victory; and below, scattered upon the rock, were the fragments of other skulls, which had fallen to pieces by time; a strange spectacle in a Christian country, in Europe, and in the immediately vicinity of a convent and a bishop's palace. It would be in vain to expect that, in such a condition, the features could be well preserved, or to look for the Turkish physiognomy, in these heads, many of which have been exposed for years in this position, but the face of one young man was remarkable; and the contraction of the upper lip, exposing a row of white teeth, conveyed an expression of horror, which seemed that he had suffered much, either from fright or pain, at the moment of death.[12]

Bowling with Heads

Until the middle of the nineteenth century, the Montenegrins severed the heads of enemies killed or wounded in battle and kept them as a sign of their heroism, even if they had to endanger their lives to do so. The severing of heads was a sign of triumph over a contemptible foe and a means of achieving personal renown within the Montenegrin community. The importance of a victory or a defeat was expressed in the number of heads taken. If someone was considered a *dobar junak* (great hero), the number of heads he had taken would be cited as evidence. Folk songs celebrating heroes tell of the heads of their enemies being severed in battle or brought home from raids into neighbouring territories. This custom provided Montenegrin society, which did not have hereditary rank, with a system of social prestige.[13] Allegedly, up to the twentieth century old men enjoyed telling tales of the heads they and their friends had taken. In a monastery near Danilovgrad, a local doctor and young monk proudly showed Miss Durham the tomb of Bajo Radović

Telling stories of heroic deeds on the border

on which was a carving showing his weapons and medals and an epitaph recording that he had fallen in a battle with the 'Turks' in 1876 after hewing off fifteen enemy heads. As the doctor explained, when King Nikola rode by, he reined in his horse, lifted his cap and prayed: 'God give thee salvation, Bajo. Fifteen heads to one sword – *O Thou dobar junak!*'[14]

Grand Vojvoda Mirko, father of King Nikola, wrote the poem 'A Monument to Heroism,' describing the exploits of Montenegrin heroes in their battles with the 'Turks.' The tale of nearly every fight ends with a list of booty taken, heads included. In 'Vengeance for Father Radosav,' for instance, Mirko sings that to avenge the death off one priest, the Montenegrins cut off thirty-three heads and impaled them on stakes. They mounted the stakes where 'Turkish' women in the town could see them and understand they were a monument to Radosav. Even more heads were taken in the wars. In the battle of Kolašin in 1858 1,000 heads were said to have been taken, and at Nikšić in 1862 the tally was given as 3,700.[15]

The Montenegrins brought home human heads not only from the battlefield but also from raids into neighbouring Muslim territories. They would give the heads to the *vladika*, who would reward them. Heads, including those of women and children, were then usually added to the heap before the *vladika's* house or fixed on poles on the Kula or round tower above Cetinje, or on houses or trees nearby.[16] Montenegrins likewise cut off the heads of French soldiers regardless of rank, when they were neighbours in the beginning of the nineteenth century.[17] According to the French commander at Dubrovnik, 'many French soldiers, including General Delgorgeus,' had fallen victim 'to this barbarous practice.' During the siege of Hercegnovi 'instances of singular atrocity occurred,' when some

> Montenegrines, in a fit of intoxication, amused themselves by playing at nine-pins with the heads of some Frenchmen, and, at the same time, directing insulting language towards them. 'See, see,' said they every moment, 'how roundly these Frenchmen's head roll;' – a cruel irony on the imputed levity of the French nation.[18]

A more prudent British diplomat from the end of the nineteenth century was of the opinion that the story of Montenegrins bowling the heads of French soldiers while remarking on the levity of their enemies was 'probably an invention.'[19]

There were rules for the taking of heads. If in a fight two Montenegrins wounded the same man, the head belonged to the one who had drawn the first blood. Bitter disputes arose over this question and Miss Durham was told of cases in which two men fought almost to the death on the very battlefield where their enemy's corpse had fallen.[20] Conforming to their code of military honour, the Montenegrins would rather take the heads of their fallen comrades than let them fall into the enemy's hands. This was to ensure that their comrades were buried 'as humans.' When two *pobratims* (sworn brethren) went to war, it was the duty of each to cut off and carry away the head of the other if slain, to prevent it falling into the hands of the enemy. The head even had to be cut off if a man was fatally wounded or so badly hurt that he could not be carried from the field and might be taken by the enemy. According to tradition, this often happened.[21]

Bronevsky gave an account of how a Montenegrin warrior entreated a Russian officer who had fallen during a retreat from a battle to let him cut off his head to prevent it falling into enemy hands, for all those taken prisoner were regarded as dead. He recorded that the Montenegrins carried their wounded comrades from the battlefield, 'and, be it said to their honour, they acted in the same manner by their allies the Russian officers and soldiers.' So, when at the attack of Klobuk a small detachment of Russian troops was obliged to retreat, 'an officer of stout build and no longer young,' fell to the ground, exhausted. On seeing this, a Montenegrin ran immediately to him with his *khanjar* in hand, saying, 'You are very brave and must want me to cut off your head. Say a prayer and make the sign of the Cross.' The officer, horrified by the proposition, made himself stand and rejoined his comrades with the assistance of the friendly Montenegrin.[22]

Any Montenegrin who fell in action without his head being severed and taken away did not quite count as dead. An individual whose head had been reclaimed in exchange for several enemies' heads was considered a fortunate man.[23] If the head of a man killed in action was taken by the enemy, his relatives made great efforts to recover it for burial with his body. Grim tales were told on both sides of the Montenegrin border of women who made the dangerous journey across the border at night to bring back their husband's or brother's head from the pole on which it was rotting.[24]

Heads in Bags

Some authors went beyond merely reporting the custom of severing head in Montenegro and expounded theories about how the victors carried the trophies. Miss Durham suggested that, 'according to popular belief,' the long lock of hair that most people wore served 'as a handle to carry home the head when severed,' as a 'head, it seems, can be carried only by the ear, or by inserting a finger in the mouth.'[25] Her theory was based on stories she came across among the Slavs, Albanians and Turks. All the Balkan peoples had retained the ancient Homeric custom of shaving the front part of their head, leaving only a lock on top or patches of hair at the sides.[26] According to the popular explanation Miss Durham heard in Montenegro, clean-shaven heads could only be carried by a hand in the mouth. Since even in death, a Christian would object to a Muslim hand in his mouth and a Muslim, with equal justice, would object to the hand of an unclean *giaour*, a convenient handle was left.[27]

In fact those who succeeded in cutting off an enemy's head carried it in a bag, if necessary for three or four days, together with their allowance of stale bread and onion. While satisfying their hunger, they emptied the bag completely. They then put the head in front of them, and looked at it and talked to it while eating, thus treating the enemy as a friend.[28] As was the custom in the heroic ages, the *khanjar* was used not only for defence but also as a knife at meals.[29]

The Strength of Custom

Western observers had a very different take on these heads from the Montenegrins. Sir Austen Layard could not conceal his disgust at what he had witnessed with the *vladika* and expressed his astonishment that someone with his desire to civilise his people 'permitted them to commit acts so

revolting to humanity and so much opposed to the feelings and habits of all
Christian nations.' The *vladika* readily admitted that the practice of severing
and exposing the heads of the slain was 'shocking and barbarous,' but added
that it was 'an ancient custom of the Montenegrins in their struggles with
the Turks, the secular and blood-thirsty enemies of their race and their faith,
and who also practised the same loathsome habit.' He was compelled 'to
tolerate, if not to countenance, this barbarous practice which he condemned
on every account, because it was necessary to maintain the warlike spirit of
his people.' Montenegrins were in a state of continual enmity with their
neighbours. They were few in number and unless always prepared to defend
their mountain strongholds they would soon be conquered and exterminated
by the Ottomans or the Austrians. The *vladika* declared that there was nothing
he dreaded more than a long peace. As soon as the Montenegrins could
sleep soundly and abandon their state of continual warfare, they would be
conquered. It would thus be unwise on his part to make any attempt 'for the
present' to put a stop to a practice that encouraged his people in their hatred
of the 'Turks' and their determination to perish rather than allow the Muslims
to obtain a foothold in their mountains.[30]

When, a few years later, Sir Gardner Wilkinson tried to persuade the *vladika*
to abolish the custom, he replied, that he could not do so on the grounds
of Montenegrin security; his people must not be the first to abandon the
usage. Their foes would mistake their humane intentions for fear and would
respond by increasing their harassment. 'Our making any propositions of the
kind would almost be tantamount to an invitation to invade our territory.'[31]
After that he tried to persuade the vizier of Mostar, Ali Pasha Rizvanbegović,
who agreed that nothing would be more desirable, but 'all attempts hitherto
made had been fruitless, and there was no trusting to a reconciliation with
Montenegro.'[32]

Nevertheless, in 1853, Prince Danilo ordered all heads exhibited in Cetinje
to be removed. He forbade his warriors to salt and preserve the heads of
enemies killed in battle. The immediate cause for his order was the semi-
official visit of a Russian colonel after Omar Pasha's expedition in the spring
of 1853. The Russian colonel argued that this example of domestic manners
was not calculated to raise the Montenegrins in the estimation of all other
nations of Christendom in the nineteenth century. He finally succeeded in
persuading them to stop cutting off the heads of their prisoners by proposing
to pay them a ducat for every prisoner instead.[33] However, 'custom carried
more weight than his word'[34] and it did not completely die out. If nobody
practised it, there would have been no need to sanction it and, as visitors to
Cetinje were informed in 1875, a Montenegrin was serving a short prison
sentence for decapitating a dead Muslim at Podgorica.[35] The practice had to

be prohibited again by Prince Nikola.[36] In 1876 he even forbade his warriors
to cut off their enemies' noses and ears, and ordered that instead they should
bring back fezzes, rifles or swords as proof of valour in battle and entitlement
to reward. He advised them to capture and bring back alive as many noblemen
as possible.[37]

Although Prince Nikola was unyielding in his prohibition of the practice
and went in person to any place where 'Turkish' heads were said to be
exhibited, during their stay in Montenegro Miss Mackenzie and Miss Irby
reportedly saw three heads dangling on an apple tree.[38] Travellers could
see with their own eyes the 'astonishing number' of men living near the
Montenegrin border who had been victims of the Montenegrin custom of
cutting off the noses of their Muslim neighbours.[39] When a Muslim soldier
fell wounded on the field of battle, he cried to his Christian foes: 'Cut my
throat rather than mutilate me!' But 'No,' said the Christians; 'we prefer to cut
off, and carry away with us as a trophy, your nose and upper lip.'[40]

Prince Nikola's order was respected where the Montenegrins were
victorious in battle. But when their enemies drove them into a corner, the old
ghosts could be heard urging the Montenegrins to go take heads.[41] Sometimes
the Ottoman soldiers' inhumane treatment of their prisoners acted as a
spur.[42] Many heads were cut off in the battles that took place in 1876–7, but
due to anti-Turkish prejudice Europe was not prepared to believe eyewitness
testimony on the practice:

> Poor Canon McColl was jeered at and discredited when he came from
> the seat of war and said he had seen heads on stakes and that the
> heads were those of Turks. Gladstone had represented the Balkan
> Christians as something like angels – never having lived among them
> – and Canon was completely disbelieved. But the truth will out. About
> twenty-five years afterwards I was at the Grand Hotel at Cetinje. An
> English parson and his wife arrived and talked with some Montenegrin
> officials who were dining there, spoke French, and wore nice frock-
> coats. They talked of Turks, and the reverend gentleman mentioned
> Canon McColl's foolish blunder. 'Of course, no one believed him.'
> 'But why not?' asked Miouskovitch (afterwards Minister of Foreign
> Affairs), completely puzzled, 'in a war naturally one sees decapitated
> heads.' Then, seeing the horror on the other's face, he added hastily:
> 'But when one teaches children to put cigarettes in the mouths – no,
> that is a bit too strong (c'est un peu fort, ça).' For one moment the Balkans
> were unveiled.[43]

An Enemy's Nose for a Wife

The Montenegrins finally succeeded in making their regular troops abandon the custom of decapitating dead enemies. But irregular insurgent bands and Albanians who sometimes joined the Montenegrin forces kept up the custom of cutting off dead enemies' noses instead of their heads.[44] According to reports by correspondents in Bosnia-Herzegovina at the time of the uprising in Trebinje in 1875, the Montenegrins and rebels in Herzegovina cut off over 800 'Turkish' noses in a single battle.[45] A German war correspondent, Albin Kutschbach, reported that some 'Turkish' heads were cut off as well.[46]

The custom remained in force until they made war in small groups. Long-range rifles turned out to be the most efficient weapon for doing away with it, for in the time a soldier took to cut off a head he could reload and fire his rifle twenty times. Severed heads were also an inconvenient encumbrance. A man carrying two or three of them could no longer fight: the heads stopped him running and using weapons.[47] According to Miss Durham, the last heads to be cut off were those of three Montenegrins killed in a border fight in August 1912.[48]

If the Montenegrins yielded slowly and unwillingly in the matter of severing the heads of dead foes, their princes had more success in abolishing a no less cruel custom, namely cutting off the nose of a living foe. Occasionally a man whose hands were not free would seize his enemy's nose in his teeth and try to bite it off, as, for young men, success in battle seems to have been a prerequisite for marriage.[49] A Montenegrin gendarme once told his story:

> 'Then came war and I went to fight the Turks in Herzegovina (1876). We fought almost to Mostar. But I was ashamed in the eyes of my comrades, for I had not taken a head. Others younger than I had taken heads and sent them home to their mothers, and I, never an one. I swore in the next fight to take one or die. I fixed my eyes on a Turk and slashed at him with my handzhar, but he fired his pistol and caught me there' – he showed a deep scar on his right forearm – 'the handzhar fell from my hand. I snatched my pistol with my left hand, but as I fired he sliced me with his knife and the pistol fell, too.' (He showed two fingers of his left hand stiff and contracted.) 'Both my hands were useless, but I saw nothing but that Turk's head. I must have it. I flew at him like a wolf and fixed my teeth in his nose. God! how I bit into him! And I knew nothing more till I woke up in the Russian field-lazaret. There was a Russian nun; she told me my sworn brother, Joko Shtepitch, had brought me in – God rest his soul. He shot the Turk through the head. My teeth were locked in the Turk's nose as we fell together. Joko

severed it with his knife. He knew I had sworn to take a head, and that now I should not have another chance. With us, you know, a nose count as a head. He could not carry me and the head too, so he thrust the nose into my breeches pocket. I found it there and it did me more good than all the doctor's stuff...'[50]

Some authors were of the opinion that the custom of severing noses developed for the practical reason that it was inconvenient to carry a head.[51] Others stated that this was an ancient and widespread form of corporal punishment, described by Homer and Strabo, especially for slaves and women.[52] So, when a certain Greek named Stridia Bey made his offer to obtain principality of Wallachia, the sultan told him that he was 'too proud and aspiring' and therefore ordered the tips of his nose and ears to be cut off in order 'to clip the wings of his ambition.'[53] According to some reports in the nineteenth century the Montenegrins and other Balkan men still used to cut off their wife's nose if she was caught 'in a heavier sin.'[54] In case of a wife's adultery, a husband could, if he pleased, cut off her nose and, as Miss Durham wrote, he 'not infrequently did so.'[55]

When war was declared in October 1912, Kovačević, professor of modern languages at Podgorica, predicted gleefully that there would be baskets full of 'Turkish' noses. When Miss Durham commented that such conduct would disgust all Europe, he flew into a rage and declared that the severing of noses was a national custom and 'Turks' were not human beings: 'It is our old national custom, how can a soldier prove his heroism to his commander if he does not bring in noses? Of course we shall cut noses; we always have.'[56] And so they did, repeatedly.[57] Miss Durham herself saw nine victims who survived, with the nasal bone hacked right through and the whole upper lip removed. Her Montenegrin patients all boasted of the noses they had taken and they wanted to recover so as to take more. They told her with shouts of laughter that they had not left a nose on a corpse between Berane and Peć and had also mutilated living victims, saying as they did so: 'Go home and show your wife how pretty you are.'[58]

Authors with strong sympathies for the freedom-loving Montenegrins attributed the custom to the nation's allies rather than the Montenegrins themselves. Two English women travellers reported that the determined severity of their rulers really seemed to have ended this barbarism in Montenegro itself; every foreign agent they asked was of the opinion that no noseless patients had been seen or authenticated at Shköder; but they believed that some had been seen at Dubrovnik and on board steamers for Corfu. They said there seemed to be some truth in the highlanders' assertion 'that those mutilated suffer at the hands of the Herzegovinian insurgents, whose barbarities the Prince of Montenegro cannot control, and who, being Turkish rayahs, behave as such.'[59]

Some of the authors who acknowledged that the practice was once common among the Montenegrins claimed that their motives for it were 'not altogether bad.' The Montenegrins were Christians 'and by nature of a gentle disposition.' They felt scruples about taking the life of their prisoners. They did not wish the 'Turks' to boast that they had discomfited a Montenegrin, hence they put this mark upon 'Turkish' faces so that all might know they were vanquished men. They also added that the barbarous custom had been abolished and more civil practices adopted in its stead.[60]

The Wine of Honour

The custom perceived by nineteenth-century travellers as a particularly Balkan barbarism has, in fact, a very long tradition. In Europe, head-hunting as a proof of prowess was far older than the Ottoman invasions and there is clear evidence of it as far back as Mesolithic times. Taking part in head hunts was a rite of passage into adulthood and readiness for marriage. The practice is well documented among Indo-European peoples such as the Scythians. According to Herodotus, Book IV. 64–6, Scythians drank the blood of the first man they killed. They took the heads of all those they had slain in battle to the king in order to be rewarded with a share of the booty. They then scalped the heads and kept the skin as a napkin, attaching it to their horse's bridle. The more scalps a man had, the better he was judged to be. Once a year each provincial governor would brew a bowl of wine for those Scythians who had slain enemies. Those who had slain more than one enemy received two cups and drank them both, while those who had killed no one sat dishonoured without a taste.

Before the Ottomans occupied the area, there were frequent clashes between Bulgarians and Byzantines during which many enemy heads were taken. Under their Khan Krumm Bulgarians overran Thrace and twice appeared under the walls of Constantinople, and defeated and killed two emperors in succession (Nicephorus and Michael), and made 'one of the immortal legends of the Balkans by converting the skull of Nicephorus into a drinking cup.'[61]

As regards common charge of cruelty and barbarity levelled at the Turks, it is interesting to note some of the Christian practices recorded in documents and pamphlets of the sixteenth century. The Hungarian historian Isthuanfy described how the Croatian nobleman Miklos Zrinyi killed Johann Katzianer in 1539, cut off his head and sent it to Emperor Ferdinand II in Vienna.[62]

The pamphlet *Les tree excellente... entre faicte à Rome*, published in Lyon in 1572, on the battle in Lepanto which took place that year, describes a statue of a gladiator on the Campidoglio: in his right hand is a bare sword and in his left, the head of 'Seliman Othman.'[63] It was noted with complacency that at the victory at Győr the head of the Ottoman governor was placed on a pike in a conspicuous place and that at the recapture of 'Albe-regale' a number of Muslim leaders were killed and their heads exchanged for several Christian prisoners. In victorious battles with the Ottomans in 1598, one encounter netted '72 heads of Turks,' another '18 Turkish heads.'[64] In the sixteenth and seventeenth centuries, when Austrian soldiers drove back the Ottoman enemy, they used to cut the heads off dead bodies on the battlefield and stick them on a stake in triumph. They also used to cut off the heads of Ottoman soldiers found dead on the battlefield after falling in retreat and would impale them on stakes as a sign of triumph. At one time in Croatia and other frontier lands no one was allowed to wear a feather in his cap until he killed a 'Turk' and brought home his head.[65] Baron Valvasor described seeing how the people of Senj, Vlachs and Uskoks, cut off Turkish heads, lifted them up and let the warm blood dribble into their mouths 'in a barbarian way with a great lust.'[66]

In the seventeenth century, not only Austrian but also Venetian soldiers kept Ottoman heads as a sign of triumph. In a letter about the war between the Venetians and Ottomans, the Earl of Castlemaine described how successful Captain Thomas Middleton had been in the service of the Republic of Venice. When he safely reached port on the island of Crete, he presented there to 'the General a whole Tun of salted Heads of those he killed in their often boarding.'[67]

Enemies' heads were also used as a deterrent. As described in a much read and quoted book on the history of the Turks from their nation's beginning to the rise of the Ottoman dynasty, Sinan Pasha, who laid siege to the town of Komarno in 1594 with a large army and a large fleet of ships, sent five Turks into the city, to find out if the governor could be induced to surrender rather than hold out to the last. The governor, having heard them 'until they had discharged their whole trecherie,' had four of them beheaded and their heads set upon long pikes on one of the bulwarks where the pasha could see them. The fifth he sent back to the pasha to tell him that although he had found 'one in Rab to serue his turne, he was much deceiued, if in him hee thought to finde Countie *Hardeck*, and that hee wished rather to die the Emperors faithfull seruant in the bloud of the Turks, than to betray the city committed to his charge.'[68]

This practice was even more common in the Ottoman Empire. In the seventeenth century it was customary for the heads of highwaymen to be displayed on town walls, spiked on the end of a lance. In the sixteenth and seventeenth centuries, travellers saw such heads in several towns in European Turkey.[69] During his visit to the island of Crete an English traveller, Bernard Randolph, saw before the gate 'a half moon built of earth about 20 foot high; at each end is a small Pyramid of mortar and sculls, which are the sculls of Christians, who were slain before the place in the year 1666.'[70] This practice remained current till the beginning of the twentieth century. When a thief was killed his head was cut off and presented to the governor of the district who remunerated the act with a fixed price. In order to deprive their enemies of this reward and save the bodies of their friends from this insult, members of raiding parties would cut off and take away the heads of their companions as soon as they fell in battle.[71] Near Missolonghi in Greece, where the romantic idol of literary Europe Lord Byron died, the bodies of several hundreds Greek patriots which had been left unburied were placed in heaps and burnt in order to prevent infection after the fall of the town to the victorious Turks on 23 April 1826.[72]

Unmissable Sights for Travellers to the Orient

For travellers looking for blood the main entrance to the sultan's court, the so-called Sublime Porte, was a sight not to be missed. It was not garlanded with 6,000 severed heads, as depicted by the French poet Victor Hugo.[73] Reality was less fantastic than fiction, but the severed heads of rebels, or rather the scalps – the skulls and bones were removed and the skin stuffed with hay, a *yafta* affixed to it, giving the reason for the decapitation – were occasionally exhibited in the niches in both sides of the wall. The heads of pashas or other great men beheaded by order of the sultan were exhibited between the first and second gates of the seraglio. Usually they were exposed to public view for only a few hours, but when the government wanted to make an impression on the people they were left for three or four days. Sometimes the heads of prominent people were displayed, for instance the heads of the whole *divan* of ministers under Sultan Selim III after his death, the head of Kislar Aga being placed on a silver dish on account of his great dignity. When wars ended, the noses, ears and lips of foes were nailed to the walls of the court for public view. These displays of noses and ears were a common occurrence during the Greek revolution in the 1820s, when many sacks of noses and ears were sent to the sultan as proof positive of the success of actions against the Greek patriots at Missolonghi.[74] From the 1830s onwards, however, these items were only rarely to be seen, but none the less extensively reported.[75]

Reverend Robert Walsh took pains to describe thoroughly 'the display of Oriental usage which has remained unchanged from the earliest times' that he witnessed on 24 February 1822 when he saw the severed head of the legendary Ali Pasha Tepeleni who for many years had fascinated Europe. On 5 February 1822 at the age of 82, he was beheaded upon the sultan's order by Mohammed Pasha of the Peleponnese. Ali Pasha's head was then sent in a box to the sultan and displayed on a dish on a pillar in the first court of the seraglio.[76]

As Ali was a Pasha, his head was treated with the respect due to his rank. Instead of being exhibited in the common way at the gate, it was placed on a dish, on a low marble pillar, between the first and second gates of the Seraglio; where exactly resembled John the Baptist's head in a charger. Over it hung a yafta, or paper containing his accusations, like that which was placed over malefactors on the cross; and beside it stood a bostangee, with a wand in his hand. The dish was surrounded by a small circle of people, who, when I approached, made way for me; and the bostangee touching the dish with his wand, it turned round, that I might have a distinct view of the head in every position; while the people looked on with the most imperturbable gravity, without evincing any more emotion than if they were looking at the stone pillar on which it stood.

The head was merely a scalpt – that is, the cranium and brains were abstracted from the flesh, and their place supplied with a stuffing of other materials; but the operation, which the Turks are very dexterous in performing, was executed with such skill and neatness, that the external form and features were as perfect, and the expression more vivid, than if the head not been detached from the body. The countenance was pallid but plump; not collapsed, but full, and expressive of character. It was large and comely, evidently belonging to a portly man of a commanding presence; it had the appearance of openness and good humour – covering, as I thought, under a smooth exterior, and ferocious and faithless heart. The top of the head was bald, giving the full contour to a remarkable ample forehead. On the crown, however, was a large tuft of grey hair hanging down for some length behind, after the manner of the modern Albanians, and the ancient Greeks of the same country, the Karakomaontes Ahaloi. On his chin was a remarkable handsome beard of silver grey, about six inches long.[77]

Such trophies were unmissable attractions for Western visitors to the City of Césars and some of them were visibly disappointed if there was no

Head of Ali Pasha on a silver plate

opportunity to see any.[78] When Ali Pasha's head was on public display, a Greek merchant of Constantinople offered 'a large sum of money' to purchase the head and dish and send them to be exhibited in London, as the fortunes of Ali Pasha aroused much interest there.[79]

Heads of famous figures in Ottoman political and military history were much in demand in other parts of Europe as well. The Viennese, for instance, pretended that they had in their possession the head of Grand Vizier Kara Mustafa, the commander-in-chief of the Ottoman troops who unsuccessfully besieged Vienna in 1683; in fact his head had been taken to Istanbul and exposed there to the public view in a manner similar to that of Ali Pasha.[80] According to data supplied by an Austrian historian, Karl August Schimmer, Kara Mustafa's head met with some further adventures. The sultan returned it to Belgrade to be deposited in a mosque there. It was discovered after the surrender of that city to the Christians and sent by them to Bishop Kollonitsch. The prelate arranged for the grisly remains of the man who had threatened to send his head on a lance's point to the sultan to be dispatched to the arsenal of Vienna, 'where it still keeps its place among the other trophies of a long struggle of race and religion.'[81]

Human heads were regarded as precious trophies among Ottoman soldiers in the sixteenth and seventeenth centuries. Soldiers forced their captives to take the heads of their dead enemies and stuff them with grass. On the morning of an expedition, they solemnly stuck the heads on poles and carried them at the head of the column. Heads were salted and, with other trophies of war (trumpets, flags and crosses), wrapped in woollen bags and taken to the sultan's court. They were victoriously paraded through the streets of Istanbul before they were presented to the sultan who rewarded the bearers.[82] The government fixed a price on enemy heads which it paid from the treasury. The usual custom after a military engagement was that as

Grand Vizier Kara Mustafa after the defeat outside Vienna in 1683

the grand vizier returned to his tent the soldiers lined his path with severed heads.[83] Janissaries and other Ottoman soldiers used to wear 'various kinds of Feathers on their Heads... and other strange marks, to shew how many Christians they had killed.'[84]

In the arsenal of the castle of Turjak in Slovenia, Baron Valvasor saw a wooden chest with 'inestimable valuables' hidden in it, including two pieces of skin peeled off human skulls and stuffed from the inside. The heads belonged to Herbart von Auersberg and Friedrich von Weixelberg who were both killed in a battle with the Ottomans near Budački in 1575. The heads were cut off, the skin tanned and sent to the sultan's court. From there, the lords of Turjak ransomed them for 'a substantial reward' and brought them back home, to be held 'in eternal memory.'[85]

In preparation for an expedition to Montenegro in 1768, the pasha of Shköder issued a proclamation forbidding the sale of wheat and gunpowder to the Montenegrins under pain of death. In order to arouse in his people the spirit for a fight against the Montenegrins, he promised payment for each Montenegrin head.[86] Some of these heads, impaled on stakes, adorned the walls of Ottoman towns as token of victory. At the beginning of the nineteenth century Sultan Selim put an end to this custom, but as late as 1877 Ottoman soldiers and irregulars beheaded many wounded prisoners who fell into their hands, or cut off their noses or ears. For that very reason, the Russians made it a point of honour to remove from the field not only their wounded but also their dead.[87] When hostilities against the Russians began in

Insurgents after a successful attack

1828, a new Ottoman cavalry division surprised and captured an outpost of about 400 men, and cut off their ears and sent them as trophies to the capital. Instead of showing the satisfaction usually expressed on such occasions, the sultan condemned the custom, insisted that it should be abandoned, and gave orders that in future prisoners should not be maltreated but should be taken in safety to Istanbul. The orders from Istanbul explicitly required officers to repress the mutilation of corpses under the threat of death. However, some reports claimed that Ottoman soldiers did not reckon their victory complete if they could not desecrate their foe's bodies. According to some sources, once the custom had been forbidden, difficulties were experienced in obtaining recruits.[88]

During the nineteenth-century upheavals, Ottoman soldiers and irregulars used the severing of heads, noses and ears as means of terrorising insubordinate Balkan peoples. Such methods were employed through the second half of the nineteenth century to aggravate the terror of killings and the burning of villages, robbery and rape.[89]

In some provinces the custom survived until the beginning of the twentieth century. Albanians in the Ottoman army suppressing insurrection in Bulgaria were allegedly seen displaying 'pickled women's breasts and ears' as trophies on their way home.[90] During the insurrection in Bulgaria, 'blood shed in streams and pyramids made from 1,000 human heads were rising into heights of infected air.'[91] At the end of the nineteenth and beginning of the twentieth centuries Ottoman troops paraded in triumph with the heads of *komitadjis* on their bayonets. At the beginning of the twentieth century a photographer in Bitola took many pictures of Ottoman soldiers and officers standing behind tables on which lay the battered heads of Bulgarians and other 'brigands.'[92]

And the Ottoman troops who attacked a Montenegrin village in August 1912 decapitated several villagers and took their heads as trophies.[93] In Rugovo in 1913, a Montenegrin from the tribe of Vasojevići was killed during a raid. The Rugovians took his head to Peć where the people spent an entire day venting their derision on it. Finally it was given to children to play with as a ball, then, when night fell it was thrown on a rubbish heap in the Serbian quarter. The next day the Serbs decided to bury the head. For the Ottoman government the only problem in all this was that a photographer took a picture of this funeral: he was condemned to fifteen years' imprisonment for his audacity.[94]

As victors in the First World War in 1918, Serbian soldiers in northern Albania robbed Bariaktar Kollowozi. They shot him, but he survived. Kollowozi swore vengeance, assembled his neighbours together, and with their help killed sixty Serbs. They took two captives 'who were not worth a bullet' and cut off their heads, 'Serbian style.'[95]

Bosnian soldiers who resisted the Austro-Hungarian occupation of Bosnia-Herzegovina in 1878 allegedly also cut off many heads.[96] A Czech author who took part in this expedition, Edmund Chaura, was scandalised by 'the Bosnian cannibals' who in Vranduk on 18 August 1878 stuck several heads of Austrian soldiers on poles:

> We stood in full battle dress against the ignoble cannibal enemy and it is no exaggeration to say that the Zulus, Bagurus, Niam-Niams, Bechuans, Hottentots and similar South African bands behaved more chivalrously towards European travellers than the Bosnian Turks did towards us. I always recollect with dismay the peoples of the Balkans, where the foot of the civilised European has not trod for decades, how the Turks, 'native lords,' probably rule down there![97]

The 'Turkish' atrocities must have made a deep impression on the Austrians. The famous war correspondent John Reed, who visited the town of Šabac in Serbia during the First World War, testified in his book to the existence of hundreds of reports, affidavits and photographs, giving victims' names, ages and addresses and details of the horrible things the Austrians had done to them. Among other things, he saw a picture 'showing more than a hundred women and children chained together, their heads struck off and lying in a separate heap.'[98]

It Is Hard to Get to Heaven with Only One Leg

For long, the Turks did not perform operations or consent to amputation even if loss of life was otherwise certain to follow. In the Ottoman army permission had to be obtained from headquarters for each amputation, and could only be issued after an investigation. According to Western authors, the reason for this regulation lay in the belief, widespread among Muslims, that those who arrive at heaven's gate without a limb or otherwise mutilated are kept waiting for a long time before being allowed in to enjoy the pleasures promised by the Prophet.[99]

Strong reluctance to lose a limb, even when survival was at stake, was widespread all over European Turkey. People insisted on keeping limbs that were mere black and offensive stumps of suffering. As reported by two British nurses, the Serbs had a superstition that if a man went to his grave with one leg, he would rise on the day of judgement and exist for all eternity with only one leg.[100] War correspondent Frank Fox reported that Bulgarian soldiers in the Balkan Wars also had very strong feelings against amputation and if they understood that this was intended they sometimes begged to be 'killed instead.'[101] From this point of view decapitation seems an extremely severe punishment. Perhaps this explains why in wars between Christians and Muslims so many mutilated corpses were left on the battlefield.

Four Eyes See More Than Two

In the nineteenth century Western authors were reserved on the Montenegrin custom of severing and exhibiting human heads in public. They also spoke in defence of those who treated their enemies in this uncivilised fashion, calling readers' attention to the fact that it was 'very easy for us, enjoying all the good things of civilisation, to rebuke the Montenegrins for returning in kind to their pitiless enemies those very cruelties which they suffered themselves at their hands.'[102] Others quoted the following anecdote to illustrate how short was the memory of the West. When Marshal Marmont reproached Vladika Peter for this horrible custom practised by his people, the reply was that there was nothing remotely surprising in it. What did surprise the *vladika* was that the French should have beheaded their lawful king. Perhaps, he went on, the Montenegrins had learned their barbarous practice from the French, but only beheaded their oppressors, not their prince or fellow countrymen.[103]

For their part, the Montenegrins in the nineteenth century were bitterly unhappy with the reputation they enjoyed around the world. The five words 'The Montenegrins are severing heads!' turned most of the world press against them. The Montenegrins felt that Westerners arbitrarily proclaimed the custom a barbarity and then on this basis constructed endless horror stories making them out to be a truly barbarous people. It was easy to do so, wrote Ljubomir Nenadović, as Montenegro was unknown and 'its enemies took more trouble to find out about it and write about it than its friends did.' Thus 'nobody' came to Montenegro's defence 'to say and prove what was later said and proved: that the Montenegrins are no barbarians, but that Montenegro is a Thermopylae, a bulwark against barbarism; that they are not inhumane, but opponents of inhumanity.' This prejudice would only change if the Slav nation awoke to glory and extol its own.[104] The secretary of the Montenegrin prince was enraged with the 'irrational *lacman* [scornful term for a stranger] press' that heaped infamies and barbarities on Montenegro's name. He was indignant that no one called it a barbarity that

> even today in England there exists a law by which man can be put in prison and left without food until he dies of hunger; in Prussia even today there is a law by which a living man can be stretched out on the floor and then slowly have his bones broken under a heavy wheel, starting from the feet then moving to the head, until he dies from these torments.

He was persuaded not only that criticism of Montenegrins on account of their alleged barbarity was absolutely unjustified but also that the precise opposite was true:

> When have you heard that Montenegrins do as the English did, fasten their captives in front of the cannon's mouth, and then pull the trigger? The Montenegrins were never inhumane with their enemies. They never tortured the captive Turk, not even to a small degree, they never beat him, they never gouged out his eyes, they never hanged him! Never! – In what death is there more beauty and poetry than that described like this: 'He swung his sword and cut off his head?'[105]

Serb Spiridon Gopčević shared this opinion. Moreover, he contended that severing heads was not a Slavic custom, 'but Asiatic-Turkish.'[106] Or as a German author put it:

> The atrocities of which the Montenegrins are guilty can for the most part be attributed to the Turks, perhaps the wildest and cruellest people who ever invaded Europe. They introduced the custom of severing heads and raised it to a cult. Who could blame the Montenegrins if they took over the habit simply in retaliation![107]

Others claimed that it was not an act of barbarity at all, but an act of compassion when practised by Montenegrins: 'What should they do with the wounded? It was impossible to carry them, since they had hardly enough men to carry away their own wounded, and where should they have taken them? To Montenegro?'[108]

The Montenegrins were described with passionate eloquence by many Western authors as a nation of heroes endowed with every virtue (and vice) of the heroic age, who had with unsurpassed bravery resisted every attempt of the Ottoman hordes to subdue them. Some would persuade their readers that they were the finest people in Europe, exaggerating the virtues of the noble Montenegrins in contrast to the 'unspeakable Turk.' A correspondent of the *Times*, William James Stillman, left Cetinje with the feeling of having broadened his own horizons by the discovery of 'a people of the old heroic type – a survival of the Homeric age, doubtless with heroic vices which also survive elsewhere, but with some virtues which hardly survive larger civilization.' He thought that few Englishmen could resist this impression and most would entertain a wish that Montenegro 'might be preserved intact and unchanged by civilization as a study of what mankind has once been.'[109]

Of course, all this grand exaggeration was accompanied by a great deal of ignorance of the real conditions and history of the people and spiced with some desire to conceal and pervert the facts for political reasons. Thus, according to Charles Pelerin, due to testimonies such as those described above, 'when civilisation expanded into Africa and Asia and was already stretching towards the Far East,' Turkey should have been excluded from the European nations 'in the interests of civilisation,' while the Montenegrin heroes deserved support 'in the name of liberty.'[110]

The Montenegrins and their love of freedom were most admired by Slavic authors, who extolled and praised them as Slavic Spartans.[111] They were ready not only to overlook many of their characteristics that others saw as evil, but rather to make them out to be virtues. Egor Kovalevski who spent four months in Montenegro in the middle of the nineteenth century was enthusiastic about its inhabitants, found it odd that

> the sources of the Nile had seen travellers from strange and remote countries, but Morača, a part of Europe, remained for them *terra incognita* and arouses no curiosity: it is not even marked on maps. But in Morača there are up to 1,200 young soldiers, and what soldiers! Each of them has a score of five, six, even twenty Turkish heads.[112]

Kula in Cetinje, mid-19th century

Tower of the Skulls

When the marriage of the king of Italy to Princess Jelena of Montenegro was announced in 1896, many Italian reporters visited her country to see their future queen. Not surprisingly, they also dwelt on the 'barbarous custom' of decapitating dead or wounded enemies and on the Kula of Cetinje.[113] Since the facts were not romantic enough, they adorned them with motifs worthy of Oriental fiction. In their reports, the round tower was poetically called the Tower of the Skulls and described as a curious 'historical monument.'[114] However, some of them felt that Montenegro's valiant history needed yet more embellishment and attributed a singular background to the 'Tower of the Skulls' in Cetinje, associating it with 'epic battles in 1690 between a handful of Montenegrin heroes and the Turks.' The latter, it was alleged, 'after a ferocious combat, conquered the tower, decapitated the dead and flung down the heads on the floor to intimidate the heroic defenders of Czernagora who still survived.'[115]

This description evokes not the real Kula in Cetinje, but the Ćele-Kula (Tower of Skulls, in Turkish) in Niš, singled out by certain travellers as an 'object of absorbing interest.'[116] This was literally a tower composed of 1,024 human skulls, commemorating the Turkish victory over the Serbs near Niš in 1809. A romantic story was told of the Ćele-Kula. Stefan Sinđelić, commander of

a brave little band, after stoutly defending an outpost near Nisch was defeated by overwhelming odds, and sooner than surrender exploded the powder magazine, killing himself, his gallant followers, and an even greater number of the enemy. The Pasha, infuriated at the loss of his men, resolved to punish the Christian population by collecting the heads of their vanquished ones, and erecting this ghastly monument.[117]

This monument was gruesome enough when the French poet Alphonse de Lamartine saw it in summer 1833 during his stay in the last Ottoman town of his Eastern tour. The skulls which were cemented together by lime and sand were by then already bare of flesh and bleached by sun and rain, but the effect was still quite grim since 'there might perhaps be about fifteen or twenty thousand of them; some of them still had their hair attached to them, waving like mosses and lichens in the gusts of wind; the mountain breeze blew strong and cool, and reverberating among the innumerable cavities of the heads, faces, and skulls, made them give forth plaintive and melancholy sounds.' Or so this famous member of the French Academy wrote in his recollections of the East. To add some local colour to this horrific picture he observed: 'the boy that held the bridles of the two horses, was playing with the bits of skulls that had fallen in the dust at the base of the tower.'[118]

De Lamartine's marvellous description of 'a large white tower standing in the midst of the plain, and as brilliant as if built of Parian marble,' as a reminder to Serbian children of 'the value of a country's independence, by showing them what a price their fathers have paid for it,' attracted many Western travellers to Niš. Upon seeing the tower, some visitors were astonished 'to find it merely the size of a large dovecote!'[119] but others magnified what they saw and portrayed it as 'an immense conical mound formed of twenty thousand human skulls'[120] or as 'a good specimen of oriental architecture,' 'of pyramidical shape' and 'made up of thirty thousand sculls which were contributed by the rebellious Servians.'[121]

However, by 1840 only half of the skulls remained and by 1860 they had almost disappeared: only one remained in its place, too deeply embedded in the mud cement for easy extraction. Some had been removed by locals or eaten away by time, others bought by foreign travellers and taken away.[122] A similar fate befell the heaps of bodies at the 'bastion of Greek freedom,' Missolonghi, which were soon reduced 'to a half-dozen sorry specimens, quite unworthy of the brains which once grew big with Platonic thought, and throbbed with the pulses of Attic fire.'[123] Philip James Green, for instance, who was one of the first Westerners to visit the place, preserved merely some of the teeth from the skull of Markos Botsaris (1790–1823), a hero of the Greek War of Independence, because he was uncomfortable with the idea of being seen by Turks carrying a whole skull.[124] But many others did take away a whole skull for their private collections.[125] The author of *The Spirit of the East*, David Urquhart, who visited the place a decade later, was luckier. There were no Turks there any more, so he could select from the heap 'one beautifully formed skull, which bore the traces of four wounds,' and remained for long 'a very cumbersome companion' of his.[126] Like many fellow poets in his time, Lord Byron kept a skull about him, but this skull was useful as well as ornamental – he drank beer out of it.[127]

No museum of any repute was considered complete without a collection of skulls although in premodern museums they were exhibited not for anthropological purposes but as common simples of pharmacopoeia. A man's skull was a specific for curing 'the Falling Sickness, and indeed… most Diseases of the Head,' as chief druggist to the French King Louis XIV, Pierre Pomet, put it.[128] According to the experts, these curative powers were attributed only to skulls which had never been buried, in particular those of persons who had died violent deaths.[129] Skulls which were traded were generally those of criminals and in the old days of hanging were always in plentiful supply. Furthermore, Pierre Pomet claimed that English pharmacists generally used to obtain their skulls from Ireland, a country famous for them ever since the Irish Massacre.[130] At the beginning of the eighteenth century it was recorded by Michael Bernhard Valentini that the Germans got their supply from the last Turkish war.[131]

In the eyes of Western travellers in the nineteenth century and later, the custom of severing the heads of enemies slain in battle was seen a powerful symbol of barbarity, a sign that marked a clear division between the Balkan people with great predisposition to atrocities and the civilised West. As we have seen, in the sixteenth and seventeenth centuries such a division had been unknown. The first to notice it was the French officer who was obviously not an ardent supporter of the reign of terror after 1789 when hundreds of enemies of the revolution were publicly guillotined. British travellers became aware of this only after the practice of beheading convicts was abolished in their own country. However, after the practice acquired its new meaning, not all Balkan peoples were judged by the same standard and the stereotyped 'Turk' – savage and bloodthirsty, swooping down upon innocent Christians and massacring them indiscriminately – was emphasised above all others in Western narration. There was a saying 'that the Turk has a mild nature, when he is not cutting off heads.'[132] Montenegrins' password to the Westerners' heart were their steadfast belief in Christianity and continuous warfare with their Muslim neighbours. They could not point, like the Greeks, to a great past, and they could not boast that their ancestors gave rise to 'our arts and civilisation.'[133] Thus, they found correspondingly less favour in the Westerners' eyes. Atrocities committed by the 'Greek heroes' against 'Turkish ferocious beasts'[134] were given less publicity although during the Greek Revolution in the 1820s hundreds of 'Turks' were beheaded.[135] Moreover, if the 'Turks' cut off heads, this was considered an indication of their barbarism, but when Kolokotronis and other brigands discovered 'the latest and most approved method of uniting the heads of Turks to canine bodies, and those of dogs to the trunks of Mussulmen,' they were praised as 'the glorious heroes of Grecian independence.'[136] This attitude made it easy to overlook the detail whereby atrocities in the Ottoman Empire became more common during the nationalist upheavals of the nineteenth century; this shows that they were not endemic and that Europeanisation was one of their causes.[137] Moreover, this attitude effectively kept from their sight any doubts about their own keen interest, indeed fascination, as observers and collectors, in this 'barbarous custom.'

EIGHT

Where Paradise Was but a Sip of Hellish Brew Away

Black as the Devil

The history of coffee has been written many times and rewritten almost as many to accomodate readers' ever-changing tastes. Europe's first printed evidence of interest in coffee appears in a chapter on the manners and customs of the city of Aleppo written by the German doctor of medicine and botanist Leonhard Rauwolf in 1582. He described *chaube* as 'almost as black as ink and very good in illness, chiefly that of the stomach.'[1] But despite this recommendation as 'very good in illness,' people in the West did not immediately become enthusiastic coffee lovers. At the beginning of the seventeenth century, Lord Bacon, for instance, mentioned coffee and coffee houses in Turkey in a way that showed that both were then regarded as exotic in Western Europe.[2]

In accordance with the fact that it was their essential function to record and relate the bizarre, the new, the different and the unknown, Western travellers of the seventeenth century offered quite a lot of information about this exotic beverage, its popularity among the people of the East and how they enjoyed it.[3] But they described it as a singularly repellent beverage. Sir Thomas Herbert, for instance, who encountered coffee during his visit to

Coffee on its way out of Yemen (by Rauwolf)

Persia in the 1620s depicted it as 'a drink brewed out of the Stygian Lake, blacke, thicke and bitter.'[4] No wonder, then, that in England coffee at first met with violent opposition and charges of being a 'hell-drink' or 'hell-poison'[5] or 'a poison which God made black that it might bear the devil's own colour.'[6]

Coffee conquered the mountains and hills of the Balkans long before it reached the rest of Europe. When travellers came across the beverage and its related social customs, it was regarded as an amusing Turkish vagary by many of them. Poullet, a French traveller from the middle of the seventeenth century, who came across it on his way from Dubrovnik to Sarajevo with a caravan of Greek, Armenian and Turkish merchants, described his impressions as follows:

> They are waiting to be served coffee, which is prepared from some small beans which grow in Egypt, roasted in an oven, ground into powder and cooked in water. Even someone generally highly adept would be in doubt as to which was worse in this hotchpotch – its blackness or the bitter taste. All the relish of this beverage is in observing the grimaces and pouts which are necessarily made while drinking it, considering that it has no effect if it does not burn; and in the attempt to ease its bitter taste it is sipped, withholding the breath and accompanied with such gurgling that, compounded with everything else, Scaramouche, if he could prepare a Turkish feast as he prepares the stone feast, would gain one skill more than he ever achieved with all his tricks.[7]

However, if authors of the seventeenth century made faces over the black and bitter beverage, their successors in the next century had a complete change of mind. In the second half of the eighteenth century in the West, coffee became synonymous with enlightenment. When this change took place, Englishmen, Frenchmen and Italians began competing for the honour of being the first to introduce coffee to Europe and made rival claims for Oxford, Marseille and Venice as the site of the first coffee house in Europe. *La Grande Encyclopédie* (1886) claims that the first coffee house was opened in Marseille in 1654; according to the *Encyclopaedia Britannica* (14th edition), the first coffee house in the British Isles was established in Oxford two years earlier than that in Marseille; and the *Enciclopedia italiana* and *Dizionario enciclopedico italiano* (1955) claim that the first coffee house opened in Venice around 1640. The book *All About Coffee* contains a slightly different piece of information, namely, that the first coffee house in Italy was opened only in 1645 but, it adds, convincing confirmation is lacking.[8] According to yet another author on the history of coffee, Edward Forbes Robinson, coffee was probably sold in Italy even before 1638, though only in apothecaries' shops as a medicine.[9]

Whatever the case, in the eighteenth century coffee eventually gained popularity among high society in the West. When it became fashionable, attempts were made to give it a sacred association. Diderot and d'Alembert, the editors of the *Encyclopédie*, seem to have toyed with the notion that at least one Hellene had known of coffee, namely Helen of Troy. They referred to the passage in Homer's *Odyssey* which mentions a magic draught: in this episode in the fourth book Telemachus, son of Odysseus, searching for his lost father, is sitting at Menelaus's table. The company are weeping and no one can stop the lamentations. Then Helen, daughter of Zeus, changed their thoughts by casting a drug into their wine:

> a drug to lull all pain and anger, and bring forgetfulness of every sorrow. Whoso should drink a draught of it when it is mingled in the bowl, on that day he would let no tear fall down his cheeks, not though his mother and his father died, not though men slew his brother or dead son with the sword before his face, and his own eyes beheld it.

Diderot and d'Alembert got this idea from Pietro della Valle, an Italian traveller who visited Turkey, Egypt, Palestine, Persia and India, his journeys lasting from 1614 to 1626, and who supposed that Helen's drug might have been a mixture of wine and coffee. George Paschius, however, in his treatise on the new discoveries made since the time of the ancients, which was printed in Leipzig in 1700, declared that coffee was among the gifts which Abigail brought to David to appease his anger against Nabal, as noted in the Bible.[10]

Sarajevo.
U turskoj kafani
H. Avelot &
J. de la Nézière,
1894.

Sarajevo.
In a Turkish café
H. Avelot &
J. de la Nézière,
1894.

Coffee house in Sarajevo, early 20th century

Serving coffee to a guest

Coffee and Cigarettes for People with Nerves of Steel

The sixteenth century was the period of great expansion of the Ottoman Empire and wherever its armies went, coffee, later branded as the 'Turkish national poison,'[11] was among their supplies. As most of the Balkans was conquered by the Ottomans, coffee and the coffee houses spread quickly in this region. According to the *Encyclopaedia of the Lexicographical Institute* in Zagreb, the first coffee house in Belgrade was open by 1522, exactly sixty years before the Rauwolf's book was published. The Turkish historian Ibrahim-i Peçevi reported that he stayed in Sarajevo in the year 1000 of the hegira (which began on 19 October 1591) and visited a 'well-equipped coffee house' there.[12] Coffee houses soon became very popular with the Muslims of the Balkans. In the 1660s, for instance, there were 'seven well-furnished coffee houses' in Ohrid; in Bitola, a town of 'around three thousand small and large houses,' lovers of coffee could refresh themselves in no less than forty coffee houses; and in Radovište, which was at that time but 'a small *kasaba*,' there were two coffee houses.[13]

After the Turks had left most of European Turkey, coffee houses remained very popular and played an important role in the social life and culture of the local urbanites. The number of these institutions in the Balkans was quite fabulous. The author of a book on the life and customs of the Muslims of Bosnia-Herzegovina at the beginning of the twentieth century Antun Hangi estimated that 'almost every tenth, twentieth Muslim house was a *kahva*.'[14] In the city of Sarajevo they were even more common: at the beginning of the twentieth century 'every fourth house' was said to be a coffee house.[15]

Nevertheless, coffee reached the less wealthy classes and some parts of the Balkans only in the nineteenth century. In Montenegro, for instance, it was 'completely unknown' at the beginning of the nineteenth century.[16] However, in the second half of that century a cup of coffee was already an inevitable part of 'the never failing hospitality of leisurely Eastern life' throughout the Balkans. Coffee was chiefly valued for its ceremonial function in tendering hospitality and it always made its appearance during a visit, whether social or diplomatic. On the other hand, those who outstayed their welcome were served the so-called *sikter*-coffee (be-off-with-you-coffee).[17]

A French traveller in Bosnia-Herzegovina in the middle of the nineteenth century reported that the poorest Muslims could live on stale bread, wild fruit and vegetables, but they had to drink 'several' cups of coffee a day.[18] Austrian officer Johann Rośkiewicz was more precise, specifying that many Bosnians drank between fifteen and twenty cups of coffee a day.[19] Antun Hangi cited *hodja* in Livno who drank between fifty and 100 cups of coffee almost every night during Ramadan and smoked as many cigarettes.[20] Others heard of men whose daily allowance was between 100 and 200 cups of coffee and 100 cigarettes.[21] In the early days the quality of the coffee was not always very good. Medaković, for instance, described the *kahvecibaşi* of the *vladika* of Montenegro who was too lazy to make coffee for a lot of people, so he simply poured warm water into the remains of an old pot of coffee, declaring that it made no difference whether they were given real coffee or warm water because they did 'not know what good coffee is like.'[22]

Antun Hangi speculated that 'our modern man, who continually suffers from a nervous disposition, should die or go mad if he had such quantities of caffeine and nicotine.' The Muslims of Bosnia began to drink coffee at the age of two or three and then continued to do so with the same appetite every day of their lives. As soon as they had said their morning prayer in the mosque or at home they went to the nearest coffee house to have a cup of coffee and smoke *narghile* before going to work. In the evening, too, they stepped in to have a chat with their neighbours and hear the news of the day. According to an old custom, only married men who had had their first child could frequent a coffee house. It was not becoming for younger men to join the society of older men and interfere in their talk. The main customers of coffee houses were Muslim landowners who had people to work for them.

Workshop in the bazaar

They did not drink alcohol and existential problems did not bother them, so they lived peacefully and happily with 'what God gave them.' Therefore, as Hangi concluded, it was no wonder, that their nerves were 'of steel' and that coffee and tobacco could do them 'no harm.'[23]

It was in the nineteenth century in the West that coffee came to be viewed primarily as a stimulant. The industrial era demanded, in theory at least, a twenty-four-hour working day. This could be achieved with the help of coffee which in the West at that time was consumed freely by the working class.[24] From this point of view, however, drinking coffee just for pleasure seemed more an abuse than a proper use of it. Western authors detested in particular the habit of frequenting coffee houses on a daily basis, which they saw as a sign of laziness or even hostility towards work. It was beyond their comprehension that people would rather live happily with a cup of coffee and a *chibouk* than work in order to have more. This is why the Austro-Hungarian administration took great pains to stop people sitting about idly in coffee

Coffee house in Tešanj (Bosnia), late 19th century

houses talking politics, which it considered a 'psychic stimulant to the laziness of the Balkan people,' and to motivate them 'from the laziness of their limbs and skilfulness of their mouths towards serious peasant work.'[25]

Balkan Coffee Houses

Coffee houses in European Turkey were typically situated in picturesque places near water or above it. Another popular locality was on a hill which afforded a good view on all sides. These were especially frequented during summer when patrons could sit with their coffee and *chibouk*, watching the beauties of nature. According to some Western travellers, the coffee house was the single most important embellishment of the life of the Balkan people, allowing them to 'enjoying a foretaste of Paradise.'[26]

A typical 'Turkish coffee house' was 'most unpretentious, and by no means very inviting in appearance.'[27] Coffee houses in European Turkey were furnished with reed mats, rugs and cushions. The one article of furniture in these places was usually a set of wooden benches surrounding the room, on which the visitors sat cross-legged, smoking. In one corner there was a somewhat finer and higher cushion, the place of any distinguished *aga* or bey who patronised the coffee house. At night benches or carpets served as beds. Such accommodation was free, the 'Open Sesame!' being the purchase of a cup of coffee. Travellers, too, availed themselves of this kind of accommodation, but those of the twentieth century found in them many unpleasant room mates accompanied by a range of distasteful smells, many times impelling them to end their night's rest as early as possible.[28]

In the nineteenth century the furniture was still predominantly Oriental, but occasionally Western, meaning that tables and chairs were added to the wooden benches and mats. Coffee houses of the European type with billiard tables became fashionable only in the last quarter of the nineteenth century, in the period of intensive 'Europeanisation' of Balkan towns. At that time the people of the East were no longer satisfied with their invention and perfected it by borrowing from 'the more civilised nations.'[29] However, these improvements were not without their imperfections, for 'French institutions were copied by Turkey with much the same success as would attend the efforts of a Parisian to make a cup of good Turkish coffee in the Turkish fashion.'[30]

Until the first half of the twentieth century the inhabitants of the Balkans enjoyed their coffee rather 'differently from in Europe.' Coffee made in the 'Turkish fashion' was boiling hot, thick and without sugar or milk. When Sultan Mahmud, in the 1830s, at an audience for Western diplomats offered his guests coffee with sugar, the gesture was understood as a sign of 'extraordinary approximation of a Turk to European propensities.'[31] But within a few years coffee houses in larger towns served the drink already sugared or presented sugar with it. According to a seventeenth-century Arab physician (1659), to drink it with milk was 'an error,' which could cause leprosy. This notion prevailed till the beginning of the twentieth century, the admixture of milk being considered 'an unheard-of sacrilege.'[32] Ante Messner-Sporšić described in detail the trouble he had on his journey in various Eastern towns in the 1930s. When he ordered coffee with milk in the largest coffee house in Varna, the director of the coffee house herself, who had been abroad and supposedly understood what he wanted, was sent for. He explained his requirements to her in detail, with the result that she brought him a teacup of watery black coffee and, separately, in a small cup, a tiny amount of milk.[33]

Coffee Houses in the Imperial City

The first *kahvehanes* in the City of Delight were established by two private individuals from Syria, Hakam from Aleppo and Shams from Damascus.

Each opened a large shop in the Tahtalkale district and began to purvey coffee. Allegedly, they both made their fortune by introducing the habit to the Ottoman capital. Shams is said to have returned to Damascus after only three years with a profit of 5,000 gold pieces. People assembled in the coffee houses of Istanbul in the sixteenth century in such numbers that there was no room 'even to stand let alone to sit.' The coffee houses were so popular that they soon attracted civil servants, *kadis*, professors and many others. The new institution was soon called *mekteb-i irfan* (school of the cultured). Coffee itself soon came to be called 'the milk of chess-players and of thinkers.'[34]

The two main Turkish sources give dates differing by more than ten years for the opening of the first coffee houses in Istanbul. The historian Ibrahim-i Peçevi, a native of Bosnia, writing around 1635, says that in the capital city, and the Ottoman lands in general, coffee and coffee houses did not exist until 1555. The second Turkish source on coffee is the famous cosmography entitled *Gihan-numa*, the work of the historian and geographer Mustafa ben Abd Allah Haji Khalifa, known also as Katib Çelebi. In 1656 he wrote a work on various controversial issues of his time; in the sixth chapter, which is on coffee, we learn that the drink found its way to Ottoman lands in 950 of the hegira, which began on 6 June 1543.[35] Some authors estimate, however, that it can be justifiably presumed that the Ottomans were acquainted with coffee even earlier. When Sultan Selim I conquered Syria, Palestine, Egypt and the Arabian Peninsula including Yemen in 1517, his army, recruited from all parts of the Ottoman Empire, stayed in Arab lands for two years. Even if pilgrims to the Muslim holy places had not taken that miraculous beverage home with them, it is unlikely that the immense army overlooked it during these campaigns.[36] But whatever the case may be, a French royal geographer of the mid-sixteenth century, Nicolay de Dauphinoys, did not mention coffee when he itemised the beverages then in use in the Orient;[37] neither did Bartholomeus Georgieuiz, although he devoted a special chapter of his book, published in 1570, to the diversity of drinks of the inhabitants of Istanbul.

When coffee arrived in the capital city of the Ottoman Empire, it was accompanied by disturbances, outbursts of religious superstition, political hatred and interference by the civil authorities; and yet, in spite of it all, coffee attained new honour and fame. Among the servants of the upper classes were the so-called *kahveci*, whose special task was the preparation of coffee, and at court special officers (*kahvecibaşi*) were commissioned to prepare the beverage for the sultan. According to Hazim Šabanović, in Bosnia these officers were mentioned for the first time in 1611, but in all probability they were first appointed in 1592 when coffee was introduced to the country.[38]

Coffee houses encouraged conviviality. People went to them to chat and gossip and be entertained. In the relaxing atmosphere of leisure the art of

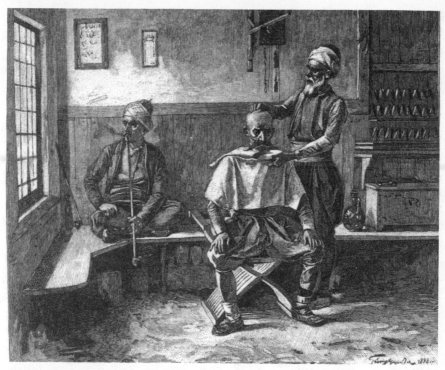

Turkish barbershop

conversation thrived even more than it did on the carpets of the mosque. Some talked of literature, and poets submitted their most recent works to the verdict of their acquaintances. However, quite often the talk was of a light, frivolous kind,[39] but it was not the custom to speak of women: 'it would be as improper to ask a Turk, how his wife did, as with us it would be to desire to see our neighbour's wife naked; so contrary are their customs to ours.'[40] Games were another vital part of coffee-house life, chess and backgammon being the most popular. It is unclear whether card games, so often seen in modern coffee houses, were common in early times. They are not mentioned in early sources and it is possible that they were introduced later from Europe. Seventeenth- and eighteenth-century travellers said the Muslims 'never' played cards or dice, or any game of hazard, thinking them to be sinful,[41] but at the beginning of the twentieth century a common saying in the Balkans was: 'He is a Moslem, but almost a Christian: he drinks and gambles.'[42] Women never entered Eastern coffee houses: social norms of the day envisaged them as a world strictly for men.[43]

The coffee houses increased rapidly in number and it looked as if they had become part of society. Then, around 1570, religious circles began to lament that the mosques were empty and desolate while the coffee houses were crowded. The bigoted *ulema* preached sermons against coffee and coffee houses, proclaiming that going to a coffee house was an even worse sin than going to a tavern. Religious fanatics argued that since Mohammed had not known about coffee and thus could not have drunk it, it must be an abomination for his followers to do so; on this account, it should be forbidden (*haram*), like wine. Some warned that coffee was burned to charcoal before being made into a drink, and the Koran specifically forbade the use of charcoal, placing it among unsanitary foods. A celebrated *mufty*, Abou Essad, issued *fatwa* against it, under the singular pretext that 'all matter consumable or carbonised by fire ought to be proscribed by the true faith.'[44]

But, as Haji Khalifa wrote, all the prohibitions, all the moralising against coffee were to no avail. The public followed the strict principle that rules are there to be broken. Coffee drinking had become firmly established and its consumption continued to be widespread, but in private instead of in public. Some became so addicted to it that they were prepared to pay with their lives for the pleasure of drinking coffee. Civil officers, deciding it was useless to try to suppress the custom, winked at violations of the law and, for a consideration, permitted the private sale of coffee. Thus many 'speak-easies' sprang up – places where coffee might be consumed or bought behind closed doors in backrooms. Gradually, coffee houses opened on every street, now with singers and dancers who attracted pleasure-seeking patrons from all walks of life: 'from the sultan to the cowherd,' as Haji Khalifa put it. People virtually gave up work, so that the economy and commerce all but halted. Many opponents of coffee publicly called for the sultan to forbid it. Indeed, in 1633 Sultan Murat IV, on the pretext of preventing the disastrous fires that sometimes started in coffee houses, ordered them to be pulled down and banned coffee itself.[45] According to traveller Jean Du Mont, Murat IV had a daily custom of walking in disguise through the capital city, so that he could see for himself how much care was being taken to implement the law; 'and he seldom or never walk'd the Rounds without leaving some headless Monuments of his Justice.'[46]

As time passed, coffee houses were sometimes permitted in Istanbul and then forbidden again. The main reason why the authorities worried about coffee houses was that 'These men who drink only Water and Coffee, enter into discourses of State Matters, censure the actions and pass Characters on the Grandees and great Officers.'[47] This was why Grand Vizier Mehmet Köprülü again suppressed coffee houses in Istanbul in 1656, without regard for the considerable loss of revenue to him personally. He did allow taverns, however. Later, iron-handed Köprülü, having assured himself that coffee houses were no longer a menace to his policies, permitted free consumption of coffee. While the ban was effective, however, it was in no uncertain fashion: for a first violation the punishment was a cudgelling, for a second the offender was put into a leather bag which was sewn up and thrown into the Bosporus.[48]

The *firman* of Sultan Murat IV also applied to coffee houses in the interior of his realm. When it came to his ears that some coffee houses still remained open in Edirne, he sent his *bostancibaşi* there with orders to destroy all of them and hang their owners. The officer carried out the instructions and promptly had all coffee houses burnt down. All those he caught selling coffee in violation of the sultan's ban were hanged without mercy. But, except in Istanbul and Edirne, coffee houses stayed open in spite of the *firman*; the edict was not even followed in the suburbs of Istanbul where certain coffee houses catered mainly to sailors.[49] Jean de la Roque, for instance, found them wherever he went on his travels in the Levant, even in the smallest country towns, and particularly in the city of Damascus.[50] In European Turkey, apparently, coffee houses never closed down.

After the coffee houses in Istanbul were closed down, the inhabitants continued to drink coffee despite threats of severe punishment. Vendors of the beverage appeared in the marketplaces with large copper vessels which they heated over fires. Antoine Galland wrote that when he visited Istanbul, there was no house in the city, rich or poor, Turkish or Jewish, Greek or Armenian, where coffee was not drunk at least twice a day. Many people drank it more often, for it became the custom to offer it to visitors and it was considered rude if they refused it. Twenty cups a day per person was not an uncommon average. Galland also observed that families in Istanbul spend as much on coffee as was spent on wine in Paris, and that it was as common for beggars to ask for money to buy coffee, as it was in Europe for them to ask for money for wine or beer.[51] In the Ottoman Empire at one time, a man getting married would promise never to let his wife go without coffee and to do so was considered a legitimate cause for divorce.[52]

'Houses of evil deeds,' as *ulema* called coffee houses, were prohibited once again during the reign of Sultan Ahmad. However, edicts issued in this period were not strictly enforced and still less obeyed. Coffee houses were soon reopened and the 'tasteless,' as the opponents of coffee and tobacco were called, accepted defeat.[53] And, according to Western authors, the taste of the Ottomans did not change much. Their wants were simple: a wife or two (more for those who could afford them), bread, tobacco, coffee and time to think. 'It is so easy to be happy, if you are a Turk,' many people in the West believed.[54]

Coffee-house Politics

One of the main topics of coffee-house conversation was politics. As described by the French consul in Travnik Amédée Chaumette des Fossés, what happened in a coffee house near the vizier's *konak* had an important influence on the governor's decisions. The coffee house was visited two or three times a day by the *eski-agas* and other distinguished janissaries who debated the news that reached Travnik from different parts of the province. After these discussions they often went together to the vizier's *divan* (council) and presented some petition, which he usually granted.[55] After Abdurahman, the vizier of Bosnia, quelled a rebellion of janissaries in 1827, his next move was to close down the coffee houses as 'meeting-places of insurgents and hotbeds of seditions.'[56] In the first half of the nineteenth century, the Ottoman police kept coffee houses under surveillance and, in many instances, the *kahvecis* served as paid spies.[57]

Felix Kanitz in Serbia in the second half of the nineteenth century, after the country had become independent, found that ministers, high officials and officers often discussed the affairs of the town and the state while smoking a *chibouk* and drinking coffee, entirely in the Ottoman style, 'as in those times the entire court had a very Oriental character.'[58]

Many Western authors looked upon such 'coffee-house politics' with great contempt. Johann de Asboth, for instance, expressed his negative attitude in the following passage:

> Thanks to the Caravansaray, the Tsharshija is not only the centre of the city, but also of all the country gossip. It is the forum, the exchange, and also occupies the position of the press. European politics are arranged in the coffee-houses of the Tsharshija. It is here that old spectacled Hadshi-Ahmed-Aga explains – a Turkish newspaper held upside down in his hand the while – to his astonished audience what the six kings are doing: the white Czar of Moscow, the German Czar in Vienna, the King of England, the King of France, and the King of Spain, and finally that poor sixth, who shivers in the far North in eternal gloom and cold. How they went to Stamboul to beseech the Sultan to permit them to make short work of the Russian Czar, as he would no longer pay the tribute; for of course he is not worthy that the Sultan should deal personally with him. In vain, however, did the other kings petition: the Sultan would force even the Muscovite to unite. It was thus that the Conference at Constantinople was restrained, and thus a great war arose; only to the Viennese Czar, because he is such an excellent man, the Sultan entrusted the office of bringing order into Bosnia, where

Turkish rebel in Novi Pazar, 1878

the rajah were constantly revolting, for they were really not worthy to have the Sultan negotiate with them in person. The Muscovite was foolhardy enough to march as far as Constantinople; he was, however, at last obliged to retire ignominiously if he did not wish to be entirely crushed. He certainly relied too much upon the long-suffering of the Sultan, for perhaps he had not even yet paid over the tribute money. But the Sultan would yet settle matters with in when his patience was exhausted. In the meantime he could wait all the more easily, because he had even now hardly room in his cellars for his piles of gold.[59]

This Hungarian parliamentarian remained so aloof from coffee-house political discussions that during an official tour of Bosnia-Herzegovina he apparently did not even venture into any of these establishments to hear for himself what the customers were actually talking about. He used poetic licence instead and retold the fragment from the *Illyrian Letters* by the *Manchester Guardian* correspondent Arthur John Evans where he described how Tahir-Beg Kulenović, a great Bosnian landowner and commander of the irregulars, informed his subjects about the mandate by which the European powers allowed Austria-Hungary to occupy Bosnia-Herzegovina in the name of the sultan:

The Beg informed the assembled people that the 'Emperor of Emperors, King of Kings, Prince of Princes, and Lord of all the Earth unto the Sky' had called together the seven subject kings of Europe – (who was the seventh?) – to Stamboul, there to signify to them his sovereign will and pleasure as to the disturbers of the peace in his dominions, and more especially those rayah dogs who had fled from their lawful lords and masters; that he had bidden the Swabian Czar (the Emperor of Austria) to slay all those rayah dogs who refused to return; that the Swabian Czar had promised to do his bidding; and that, furthermore, condign justice should be executed on those who did return for having presumed to leave their lawful lords and masters.[60]

Cannon Balls in Tune with National Music

The coffee houses would hum with social, political and religious debate while hired musicians and dancers entertained the customers with music that was 'rather Eastern, rather melancholy.'[61] The ubiquitousness of music in coffee houses did not, however, meet with universal approval. On the contrary, it is clear from some of the moral treatises written against the coffee houses that the music contributed significantly to the odour of debauchery that made the places so repugnant to the pious. The Prophet himself had much to say about music, very little of it favourable. Coffee-house performers and performances exacerbated many people's disapproval. In some of the coffee houses in the early sixteenth century, the music was provided by female singers, often demurely screened off from the company. Though unseen, these female performers made the coffee houses seem – and in fact be – places where sexual desire and sexual proclivities could find expression. Some coffee houses indeed appear to have accommodated a variety of sexual tastes. In the city, which was also known as 'The Gate of Delight,'[62] till the nineteenth century coffee houses were patronised by customers who gazed 'on the graceless dances of boys dressed in female habits.'[63] The boys, who were generally 'very thin and shrill,' sometimes accompanied their songs 'with a heavy languishing movement – a caricature of the graceful dance of the Harem.'[64] George Sandys, writing of Istanbul in the early seventeenth century, implies a bit more about the role of these youths, mentioning that 'many of the Coffamen keeping beautifull boyes, who serve as stales to procure them customers.'[65] Since the word 'stale' in English may denote 'a prostitute of the lowest class,' Ralph Hattox interprets this passage by the poet Sandys as meaning that the role of these boys went beyond that of waiter.[66]

In the Muslim world dancing was for long regarded as 'unbecoming the

Bosnian dancer

dignity of man.'[67] According to Westerners, the people of the East could take no pleasure in any occupation more active than smoking with the possible exception of riding. Easterners were, allegedly, much surprised that wealthy people in Europe should make themselves hot and tired by dancing, instead of doing as they did and paying other people to dance for them.[68] Both male and female dancers could be hired, but only the latter were admitted into harems or private parties; in public places, women's dances were usually performed by boys dressed in women's clothes. When ladies were among the spectators, the dancers observed a certain degree of decency which was dispensed with for all-male audiences.[69]

The female dancers were young women who belonged to a separate, despised section of the lower class, who intermarried only among themselves. Their parents were usually furriers. They were accompanied by a man who played the *semenge*, and sometimes by an old woman who played the tambourine, and may have supervised their conduct. When dancing they would throw up their veils and leave them to float on their shoulders. Their costume consisted of a petticoat reaching scarcely below the knee, open behind and attached to a broad belt with two large buttons. They were valued neither for the elegance of their steps nor for the grace of their bearing, but nevertheless they gave infinite pleasure to their public 'by such talents as they possess(ed).' As for their virtues, they were notorious for going wherever they were well paid.[70] Two French travellers from the seventeenth century gave fairly similar descriptions of them, adding that for a few aspers they would 'put their Bodies into a Thousand obscene Postures, which the most shameless Strumpets in *Europe* wou'd hardly be persuaded to imitate.'[71]

In the Balkans in the twentieth century prostitutes were usually Gypsy or foreign women, and many of them served in coffee houses.[72]

Rebecca West estimated that in the mid-twentieth century, any sizeable village in Macedonia would have at least one coffee house where a girl sang and music was played. In the town of Skopje, with less than 70,000 inhabitants, there were 'many such.' She described in fascinating detail the performance of a dancer in Sarajevo:

> A stout and clad in sequinned pink muslin trousers and brassiere was studying on a platform revolving her stomach in time to the music of piano and violin, and as we entered she changed her subject matter and began to revolve her large firm breasts in opposite directions. This gave an effect of hard, mechanical magic; it was as two cannon-balls were rolling away from each other but were for ever kept contingent by some invisible power of attraction.[73]

Although they often waxed indignant at oriental dancing, Western travellers were fascinated by the performances. A Croatian traveller in Istanbul in the 1930s, for instance, investigated some 'plain and loathsome' coffee houses and amusement places where he came across 'not the simple village people who enjoy themselves, but the harsh townsfolk who have lost their natural human affection and take pleasure in ribaldry and lowly voluptuousness, which they enjoy so much the more as it becomes more vulgar.' In one such place, called Oriental Varieté, a drum was beaten and a flute whistled 'some Asian tunes' while a woman danced. The performance went on inside wide-open doors, so that it could be seen from outside as well. He stood across the street and spent some time observing the scene inside the doors and watching the faces of the spectators which were 'like those of a starved wolf when it sees a sheep!'[74]

Peace of Mind and Locke's Maxim

Few travellers to the Near East failed to notice and describe the tranquil enjoyment shown by people sitting in front of a tiny cup full of thick black coffee. Such descriptions recur time and again in the work of authors of the nineteenth and early twentieth centuries when European thought construed an image of the Oriental as a sensual and lazy being 'doing nothing, and wanting to do nothing,' whose only delight was to sit day after day in a coffee house sipping his coffee, smoking his pipe and fiddling with the beads of the *tesbeh,* thus 'passing much time that might better be devoted to his own improvement and to the regeneration of his country.' For many Westerners such an attitude was 'animal rather than human.'[75]

Unlike industrious Westerners, Easterners were thought to be able to sit for hours, lost in reverie and enjoyment, the main characteristic of which was the absence of thought. William Loftus described how he met the pasha of Baghdad sitting on the edge of a high bank overlooking the river, 'with that expression of utter stolidity,' which, according to him, characterised Turkish features. He asked a grave old Turkish gentleman what he was thinking about, and his answer was: 'By Allah! what should I think of? Nothing.'[76] Baron de Laveleye described the state of mind which was supposedly characteristic of Muslims as absolute enjoyment of the *dolce far niente.* According to him, Muslims absorbed in their *kayf* enjoyed the here and now, were content with the leisure given them by Allah and did not think of the morrow. Their 'vague fixed eyes' showed 'a dreamy, almost ecstatic state,' for they were 'at the gate of Paradise.'[77]

Doctor Richard Robert Madden who was not satisfied with mere

Taking kayf

description of that state of mind tried to find an adequate explanation of its causes. His understanding was that 'the reveries in which the Turk passes the greater part of his time' constituted an argument against the theory that 'thought is coeval with existence, and only ceases with its termination.' He asked the Turks repeatedly what they had been thinking of during these reveries and they all gave him the same reply as the pasha of Baghdad, being unable to recall a single idea which had occupied their minds. Madden concluded that this was a peculiarity of the Turkish character, and was closely connected with their moral condition. From this presumption and from Locke's maxim that 'the soul only thinks when the senses have furnished it with ideas to think on,' he came to the conclusion that 'of all people, the Turks receive the fewest impressions by the senses, and consequently have the fewest ideas.' Their apathy, which he found to be 'partly constitutional, and partly the effect of their doctrine of predestination,' was also seen as helping to paralyse reflection. Thus in their reveries either they ceased to think or their minds became 'as mirrors, which receive images, but retain none.' The opinion of Locke, that the soul of a waking man is never without thought because this is the condition of being awake, was 'contradicted by the waking somnambulism' of Muslims.[78]

It was of no account if in reality the Turks worked hard, and were active and athletic, or if the stereotype Turk stretched out on a sofa and yawning between innumerable cups of coffee and countless pipes of tobacco was 'as unknown in the Balkan as the conventional Rayah, passive, pious, and patriotic.'[79] Even though the *tesbeh* did not differ much from the rosaries used by the Christians of the area, in the eyes of Western authors they were like chalk and cheese. If the *tesbeh*, with a pipe and a cup of coffee, evoked an image of the utter indolence of the 'Turks,' a rosary in 'Greek' hands was testimony of their activity:

> Activity is as characteristic with them as indolence with the Turks. Whatever they may have in hand, whether it be business or amusement, they do it with all their might; and when their hands find nothing else to do, they employ them with indefatigable diligence in twirling and counting their rosaries.[80]

Richard Burton, the renowned British Orientalist, analysed the Arab's *kayf* as 'the savouring of animal existence; the passive enjoyment of mere sense; the pleasant languor, the dreamy tranquillity, the airy castle-building, which in Asia stand in lieu of the vigorous, intensive, passionate life of Europe.' This state of mind was supposed to be the result of an impressionable, excitable nature and extreme nervous sensibility, which were said to indicate 'a voluptuousness unknown to northern regions, where happiness is placed in the exertion of mental and physical powers.'[81]

Western authors believed that the Arabic *kayf* baffles all translation into European languages, quoting the Italian *dolce far niente* as the closest approximation. For English-speaking authors 'indolence' and 'idleness' were the nearest, but they have a pejorative meaning. They believed that English has no equivalent because 'busy anxious England has not allowed one to be invented.'[82] The Turks adopted the untranslatable Arabic word as *kef*. According to Rastko Močnik,[83] for the same reason the word enjoyed an eminent career in the Balkans: from the modern Greek *kefi* and the Tsintsar *chefe* to the Slavic *keif, kef, ćeif, ćef*. Obviously, the Balkan peoples of the past found it worthwhile to adopt the culture of this state of mind together with the term denoting it. Long before Albert Smith or Richard Burton, Vuk Karadžić knew how *kayf* should be translated into European: *libido*.[84]

Bosnian beys

After liberation from the Ottoman occupation the Balkans went through
tremendous changes in the process of 'Europeanisation.' Wide-ranging
though this may have been, it has not always reached very deep. In their
hearts the people cherished customs whose origins were rooted in the
Ottoman past. And coffee and coffee houses were certainly a legacy of the
Ottoman past which the Balkan people accepted and preserved. 'Best of all is
to be a "*gazda*" (head of a large household family community),' explained an
informant to Miss Durham, 'then you tell all the others what to do, and you
may spend your leisure elegantly in a *kafana*.'[85]

First sugar and then milk, once detested, now gradually found their
way into the Balkan coffee houses which increasingly resembled their
counterparts in the West, with tables and chairs, newspapers and billiard
tables. For Baron de Laveleye these were the symbols of the future, signalling
'activity in production; improvidence or insanity in consumption.'[86] However,
in the twentieth century, when the Balkan coffee house with its black and
bitter coffee was rapidly disappearing, it became an attractive destination for
many Western travellers in search of the Balkan spirit and, in the words of
a British journalist, anxious 'to see the Mohammedans as they really were.'[87]

By now, many travellers had learned to appreciate a cup of Turkish coffee as 'the most delectable beverage that can be well imagined.'[88] In the first half of the twentieth century, some of them even claimed that one could get a better coffee in the worst coffee house in the Balkans than in the finest European hotel or café. British correspondent from the Balkans Paul Edmonds who travelled through 'the land of the eagle' after it had become an independent state claimed that even in a 'poverty-stricken and remote hovel' in Albania he had tasted better coffee 'than you could obtain in a first-class London hotel.'[89] German traveller Franz Zedtwitz, too, was overwhelmed by enthusiasm when speaking about Turkish coffee, 'the incomparable coffee' made in an open copper coffeepot on a charcoal fire 'according to a marvellous recipe' and served in tiny cups, 'with all the sweetness of heavens in them.' People sipped it with deliberation until only one finger of grounds remained in the tiny cup. 'The pleasure costs about six *pfennings* and one can become addicted to it body and soul, *Turska kava*, Turkish coffee!'[90]

NINE

A True Comedy of Errors

In the Balkans geography has often been smaller than political aspirations and it has not been uncommon for the name of a Balkan country to be larger than its territory. Since the dream of every emerging Balkan state had been the conquest of the Golden City, all of them had at one time or another laid claim to Macedonia and had kept emissaries there to win the favour of the population. This watch on the inheritance of the 'Sick Man of Europe' and hopes for the realisation of 'great national ideas,' in the shape of Greater Greece, Greater Bulgaria, Greater Serbia, Greater Romania and Greater Albania, were essential elements in the transformation of Macedonia, from the second half of the nineteenth century on, into an arena of political and cultural contention between Balkan states which regarded it as their promised land. It was as if the hopeful sons were called in as physicians to the bedside of the sick man. If Macedonia were double its actual size, it would still not have been big enough to accommodate the conflicting claims of its neighbouring states, born out of Ottoman decline:

> In fact, Macedonia is the *sentina gentium* of Europe, the barrier between East and West, civilisation and barbarism, education and ignorance; a very mosaic of peoples, creeds, and tongues; the most prosperous district of a decaying empire, and therefore the coveted of all. And thus it happens that the phrase 'Macedonian Question' has become a generic term for all the problems connected with Turkey in Europe.[1]

A Macédoine

Macedonia owes its name to the ancient kingdom of Macedonia (or Makédon). In the fourth century BC it ruled Greece and conquered lands as far to the east as the Indus River, thus establishing a short-lived empire that ushered in the Hellenistic Age. Although this kingdom seems to have been largely Greek-speaking, the Athenian opponent of Makédon, Demosthenes, in his patriotic speeches described Philip of Macedon as a 'barbarian.'[2] The relationship between Macedonians and Greeks was defined by a modern Greek historian as follows:

> The root *mac-* is Greek and means *high* or *long*, consequently, *Macedonia* means highland and *Macedon* highlander... According to Hesiod, the father of the Macedonians was Macedon, who was a cousin of Helen's sons, Dorus, Xuthus (Ion's father) and Aeolus. Therefore, Macedon's descendants were cousins of the Dorians, the Ionians, and the Aeolians, the three main Greek tribes... Furthermore, according to Hellanicus, Macedon's father was Aeolus, which indicates a close connection between Macedonians and the Aeolians.[3]

The invasion of the Balkans by Slavs in the sixth and seventh centuries AD substantially changed the ethnic composition of Macedonia. The area fell under the sway of the Ottoman Empire in the late fourteenth century and was subsequently colonised by a significant number of Muslims (Slavs, Albanians and Turks). After the Balkan states gained their independence in 1878, Macedonia received its final wave of (Muslim) immigrants who came either of their own free will because they found the idea of living under Western conditions intolerable, or because they were the victims of Christian intolerance and injustice.[4] They were to be found in all parts of the country, especially in the larger towns and many of the villages in the plain, but they were on the whole outnumbered by Christians who usually inhabited mountainous and less fertile parts of the country.[5]

In Western eyes, the Ottoman idea of government was always simply to take tribute and secure the paramount position of Muslims. Once these goals were achieved, they did not interfere with the ways and customs of their subjects, but treated them with a contemptuous toleration. Thus, according to Western authors, Ottoman rule contributed much to the survival of centuries-old traditions by perpetuating and preserving as if in 'a vast ethnographic museum' the different peoples who lived in south-eastern Europe during the last years of the Byzantine Empire.[6] The diversity of the population of

Statue of Alexander the Great. (Naples.)

Alexander the Great

Macedonia in the nineteenth century was so well known that it inspired the French expression *Macédoine,* meaning a salad of mixed fruits or vegetables.[7]

Sons of Alexander the Great

Memories of the golden age, especially the time of Alexander the Great, survived the period of Ottoman occupation, for even the Turks had a high opinion of this conqueror.[8] The memory of Alexander's valiant deeds was further revived in the nineteenth century when rival Balkan historians with their modern historical consciousness, combining their science with their nationalism, battled over classical and mediaeval history, each claiming the famous conqueror as the forefather of his own Balkan people. The Greeks invoked the famous Macedonian kings, proudly claiming that they were Macedonians, 'children of Alexander the Great.'[9] The Bulgarian historians, no less patriotic, responded by including the kings of ancient Macedon in the list of the 'Tsars of Bulgaria,' who, having conquered the whole of Greece, extended the Bulgarian Empire as far as India.[10] The Albanians, in their turn, agreed that Philip of Macedon and his son Alexander, like all the

Macedonians, were not Greeks at all, for in their tradition Alexander's mother Olympias was an Albanian woman. Therefore, it was the Albanians who were 'the soldiers of Alexander the Great, who conquered the whole known world of his day.'[11] Some Serbian authors, too, claimed both Macedonian kings as predecessors of the Serbs.[12] Lastly, but with no less enthusiasm, the Macedonians wanted the great conqueror for themselves, the 'descendants of Alexander the Great.'[13]

To prove their possession of ancient Macedon, Balkan nationalists sometimes tampered with history by installing or removing historical monuments that confirmed or refuted their thesis.[14]

When the national consciousness of the Balkan peoples began to crystallise during the nineteenth century, the European powers found that drawing international frontiers along strategic or economic lines could not easily be reconciled with ethnic considerations. While Macedonia was under Ottoman dominion its entire Slav population regarded itself and was regarded by the world as Bulgarian.[15] Then, following the Balkan Wars, the Balkan allies took Macedonia away from the Ottoman Empire and divided it unequally among themselves, drawing arbitrary boundaries through its territory regardless of the ethnic identification of its people. Macedonians were subjected to more or less violent campaigns of assimilation and denationalisation whose goals were to deprive them of their identity and convince them that they were actually 'Slavophone Greeks,' 'South Serbs' or 'Bulgarians.'

Balkan Geography and Statistics

For decades, Macedonia was a political problem rather than a geographical entity. For convenience, at the beginning of the twentieth century Western authors made the boundaries of Macedonia coincide with three *vilayets* of the Ottoman Empire (Skopje, Bitola and Thessaloníki).[16] However, this satisfied neither the Greeks, nor the Bulgarians nor the Serbs. The majority of Greek authors preferred 'historical Macedonia.' This was the most restricted delimitation of Macedonia, including only the two southern *vilayets*. The Bulgarians favoured 'geographical Macedonia,' which left out certain districts in the west where the population was overwhelmingly Islamised and a corner in the south-west which was exclusively Hellene. The Serbs proclaimed that the Skopje region in the north-west was not part of Macedonia at all, but of Old Serbia.[17]

Indeed, there was no consensus as to the exact borders of Macedonia, nor was this the only point of disagreement. The interested parties were at even greater variance over the size and ethnicity of the population, each exaggerating the number of its own members and diminishing the claims of the other nationalities. In the war of words, as in every war, in the exchange of killer facts, the first casualty was truth. Thus, Turkish experts produced maps coloured red as far as Vienna and population censuses listing more Muslims in European Turkey than there were inhabitants.[18] Balkan nationalists soon began to do the same thing and each nation concerned could supply a shoal of facts to prove its own claims and its rivals' mendacity. They did not worry much about the accuracy of the figures, which they took with deadly seriousness, however. Thus the numbers given tell their own story, quite an amusing one for outside observers. The Serb Spiridon Gopčević,[19] the Greek Cleanthes Nicolaides[20] and the Bulgarian Vasil Kŭncov[21] reported a total of, respectively, 2,880,420, 1,825,482 and 2,258,224 and inhabitants of Macedonia, comprising

	Gopčević	Nicolaides	Kŭncov
Turks	231,400	620,491	499,204
Bulgarians	57,600	427,544	1,181,336
Serbs	2,048,320	9,831	700
Greeks	201,140	647,384	228,702
Albanians	165,620	NONE	128,711
Vlachs	74,465	18,769	80,267

Thus the Bulgarians, the Greeks and the Serbs drew up population statistics for Macedonia, reflecting their authors' patriotism more than reality, to support their respective aspirations to expand their national territory. Each figure they gave was different and they only agree on one which was conspicuous by its absence: there were no Macedonians in Macedonia.

The Greek statistics were particularly remarkable. In Macedonia the word 'Greek' had an ecclesiastical rather than ethnic connotation: allegiance to the Greek Patriarchate or the Bulgarian Exarchate was accepted as a criterion for Greek or Bulgarian ethnicity. Some Greek nationalists even claimed the Serbian communities of Macedonia as Greek because the Serbs had no autocephalous Church. The Greeks also claimed the Vlachian communities, the Orthodox Albanians and the Bulgarians who did not adhere to the Bulgarian Exarchate: these they called Albanophone, Bulgarophone or Vlachophone Greeks.[22]

In Ohrid during the summer of 1861 the secretary of the Constantinople

Synod issued a pamphlet reviewing the history of the Bulgarians' relationship with the Greek church and showing the groundlessness of their demands and grievances. The writer argued that the Bulgarians made up only a small part of the population of western Macedonia and that many of them were Bulgarian-speaking Greeks. He even asserted that the physical appearance and customs of the Bulgarians in those parts proved them to be of Greek, not Bulgarian, origin.[23] Even now Greek authors are adamant that at the beginning of the twentieth century Hellenism overwhelmingly prevailed in Macedonia and the Macedonians were Greek. They cite as their trump card the official Ottoman statistics of 1905 compiled by Hilmi Pasha for the *vilayets* of Thessaloníki and Bitola, listing 678,910 'Greeks' (adherents of the Patriarchate) and 385,729 'Bulgarians' (adherents of the Exarchate). More specifically, in the *vilayet* Thessaloníki these were 395,222 'Greeks' to 207,073 'Bulgarians,' and in that of Bitola 283,683 'Greeks' to 178,412 'Bulgarians.'[24] Even in 1973, the Institute for Balkan Studies in Thessaloníki issued a publication which states that 'the Vlach-speakers are Greek, as are the other inhabitants of Macedonia, whatever their language.' The author cites a petition submitted to the French government in 1903 by the inhabitants of the Bitola region, stating that, 'We speak Greek, Vlach, Albanian, and Bulgarian, but nevertheless we are all Greeks, and we refuse to allow this to be questioned.'[25]

The Ottoman Empire only carried out censuses in relation to military service, counting Muslims liable to conscription and Christians who were liable not to conscription but to a special tax instead. In 1881 the Rumelian government issued detailed statistics giving Macedonia a total of 1,863,382 inhabitants, comprising 1,251,385 Slavs, 463,839 Muslims and only 57,480 Greeks.[26] A Greek ethnographic map of Macedonia, however, showed many districts coloured blue (the Greek colour) although not a single Greek was to be found there. Dr Cleanthes Nicolaides even gave Kosovo the Greek name of *Kossyphopéidon*.[27] Although even the most favourable statistics for the Greeks gave them only one-tenth of the population, Athens asserted that Greeks predominated in Macedonia. At the end of the nineteenth century, for instance, Professor Saripolos, a correspondent of the French Institute, quoted the following figures as reliable: 500,000 Greeks, 100,000 Slavs and 40,000 Jews. Some influential inhabitants of Thessaloníki sent an address to the Patriarch and the Ottoman government in the name of 800,000 'Greeks' living in the province, a figure produced from the returns given by the ecclesiastical authorities counting all members of the Greek church as Greeks. According to this definition Bosnia would have more 'Greeks' than Catholics amongst its Christians.[28]

Greek propagandists worked hard to influence the international community in the demarcation of Greece's borders. They produced statistics to prove their claims to the lands inhabited by Slavs, supporting them with the theory of their 'ethnocratic pre-eminence.' According to this theory, the Greeks were nobler than the Macedonian Slavs who ought to submit to them, being 'devoid of culture, barbarians, with incoherent speech, coarse, slave.'[29] As a person of rank from Athens put it in a letter to Baron de Laveleye:

> You are mistaken about the Bulgarians; they are barbarians, and such they will remain. They are of Tartar race, and consequently not readily civilized. Christianity itself is not enough to soften them. They have some good qualities, but they are those of beasts of burden, including the instinct to store like the animals. Whilst I am writing to you I have half a score of Bulgarian masons working at the house which I have given to my daughter Athené as dowry; they work well, but are stupid.[30]

A further argument was put forward by the Greek ambassador in London in 1885. He argued that as the land had formerly belonged to the Hellenes, its present occupation by Bulgarians did not justify its being assigned to them because the right of the Greeks was imprescriptible. The Belgian baron refuted this argument as follows:

> It would therefore follow that New Holland, New Zealand, Tasmania, having been discovered by the Dutch, ought to belong to Holland, because these countries have Dutch names. The English have colonized them, but that gives them no right of possession. It is difficult to discuss such theories, and distressing even to have to notice them.[31]

During the 1780s, Catherine the Great devised her 'Greek project,' intended to replace the crescent on the dome of St Sophia with a cross and to restore Byzantine Empire with a Russian prince on the throne. Her second grandson was named Constantine to mark him for the role. In preparation, Greeks were brought to nurse him, so that he could suck in the Greek language with his milk.[32] The plan fell through, but the ambition remained.

When nationalism spread from western Europe to the Balkans in the nineteenth century, the Greeks were the first to come under its influence and claim their freedom as a nation.[33] The abolition of the Serbian Patriarchate in Peć and the Bulgarian Archbishopric in Ohrid, in 1766 and 1767 respectively, left all of Macedonia under the jurisdiction of the Patriarchate of Constantinople. This meant the Greek liturgy was celebrated in churches and Greek education was given in schools. Thus the people of Macedonia were subjected to an unchallenged process of Hellenisation. They might have become completely Hellenised, had not the noble Greek prelates and teachers looked down on the poor and miserable peasants of Macedonia, speaking of them as 'animals,'[34] 'barbarians,' 'beast of burdens'[35] or 'wearers of sheep skins'[36] who spoke unintelligible Slavic dialects and were unworthy of their efforts to teach them to read and write: 'it was humiliating for a lover of the muses to dwell in a barbarian world.'[37] As a consequence, they remained largely untouched by Greek culture.[38]

Neighbouring independent states also cast covetous eyes on Macedonia and tried to prove that part or all of it was theirs by natural rights. The Bulgarians claimed Macedonia as 'the cradle of the Bulgarian nation for which a river of blood has been given.' Bulgarian patriots maintained that when and how the Bulgarians reached Macedonia did not matter; all that mattered was that a majority of the population yearned for union with the mother country, that Macedonia 'weeps like a child for its mother' and would not be satisfied to live under any rule other than that of Bulgaria. The other Balkan states have of course never accepted or admitted Bulgaria's claim to Macedonia.[39] The Greeks considered Macedonia theirs for historical reasons although in the classical age the claim of Macedonians to enter the sacred circle of Hellas was received with some jealousy and the kings of Macedon were required to prove their Greek descent before being granted the privilege of competing in the Olympic Games. But Macedonia was indispensable to the realisation of 'the great Hellenic idea.' The Serbs, in their turn, had attempted to prove to the world that Macedonia should belong to Serbia alone on the grounds that it was the ancient centre of the empire of Tsar Dušan. Its own pretensions towards Macedonia, 'on ethnographic grounds,' advocated even Romania because of a number of Vlachs who lived there. The Albanians used the same basis for a similar claim to the territory.[40] After Austria-Hungary received the mandate to occupy Bosnia-Herzegovina in 1878, it, too, soon turned a jealous gaze on Macedonia and the port of Thessaloníki.[41]

In such circumstances it came as no surprise that the Macedonian question became a problem of international magnitude 'that nobody could solve' or that the land itself was destined 'almost inevitably in future to become one of the great battlefields of Eastern Europe.'[42] A British observer who travelled in Serbia, Bulgaria, Montenegro, Albania, Romania and Macedonia at the start of the twentieth century, and made a thorough investigation of the question, came to the conclusion that, 'The Macedonian question is the burning question of to-day, and one that can only be solved in one way – by a fierce and bloody war.'[43]

The Megale *Idea*

When Greece became free, its inhabitants considered the process of emancipation only half complete as they aspired to the annexation of a much larger portion of Ottoman territory. Many of the ruling and political class dreamed of Greek reunion and repossession of Byzantium.[44] The king of Greece had the same title, *Basileus*, as the Byzantine emperor, and the first son of King George was christened Constantine to give a dramatic flourish to his recovery of the throne lost in 1453.[45] This was the so-called *megale idea*: the redemption of 'unredeemed' Greeks and their unification. In consequence the Greek state adopted an aggressive policy, aimed at the 'liberation' of Macedonia, Epirus, Thrace and Crete, 'the adored daughters of Greece' who were 'ever looking to the mother to free them from the Turkish yoke.'[46]

Since propaganda did not bear the expected fruits, Greece from the south and, to a lesser extent, Serbia from the north launched armed bands into Macedonia to 'liberate the land of Alexander of Bulgarians,' with the result that a proselytising war was carried on for national and political ascendancy. The Greeks, Serbs, Bulgarians and Romanians all endeavoured to increase the number of their compatriots by means of churches and schools, financed largely by the respective governments. The schoolmasters vied with each other in offering inducements to attend their school, so much so that parents could sometimes not only have their children clothed and educated for nothing, but could also make an income out of them, for instead of paying for their schooling they received a fee. Occasionally, the national leaders even resorted to killing village leaders and forcing the local people to declare Greek or Serbian nationality. Greek priests were forced upon Bulgarian villages and Greek schools multiplied all over the country. When these territories were occupied by the Greek army during the Balkan Wars, they gave the unhappy people twenty-four hours to renounce their nationality and proclaim themselves Greek although they did not understand the most common Greek words, such as *kalispera* (good evening). Bulgarian schools were closed and unless the teachers undertook to teach in Greek, they were exiled or imprisoned. Bulgarian priests were given the choice of death or conversion to the Greek church. The Greek army entered villages where no one spoke their language. 'Don't speak Bulgarian: we are in Greece,' cried the officers, 'and anyone who speaks Bulgarian shall be off to Bulgaria.' Refusal to comply meant death or flight. 'What a shame,' cried the Greek gendarmes at Gorno Kufalovo on 25 March 1912. 'We have freed you. The voice of Alexander the Great calls to you from the tomb; do you not hear it? You sleep on and go on calling yourself Bulgarians!'[47]

The ethnic structure of the inhabitants of Greek Macedonia changed dramatically after 1918 as a result of the upheaval of the First World War and Greece's disastrous campaign in Asia Minor: the number of Greeks increased while that of almost all the other nationalities decreased due to the settlement of about 640,000 'Asiatic Greeks' after the Greek defeat in 1922, followed by the emigration in 1923–4 of 348,000 Muslims. During the wars and immediately after them many Slavs were killed or forced to flee; the same fate befell the Turks, the Albanians and to some extent the Kutsovlachs.

Nationality and Religion

After the conquest of Byzantium in 1453 the Ottomans did not attempt to impose their state institutions on their new subjects or to assimilate the Christian populations they had conquered. Though despised and humiliated, the *rayah* continued to enjoy a certain degree of autonomy. The rulers of the conquered peoples were replaced by representatives of their religious organisations. Sultan Mehmet II, conqueror of Byzantium, conferred upon the Patriarch of Constantinople the title of *milletbaşi* (chief of the nation) and allowed its Orthodox citizens to retain some of their churches and free exercise of their religion. Besides, he entrusted to the Patriarch the administration of the spiritual and secular needs of his flock. In this way, the clergy formed a body of functionaries invested with broad administrative and judicial powers. All cases involving marriage, divorce and inheritance were tried before an episcopal court and in matters of a civil nature Christians did not have to go to Ottoman tribunals. Every religious community was entrusted with the collection of taxes from its members and their payment into the state exchequer. The same prerogatives were also granted to the Bulgarian patriarchs of Tŭrnovo and Ohrid, as representatives of the Bulgarian nation.

In the Ottoman Empire there was no visible dividing line between secular and religious law. The Ottoman state divided its subjects according to their religion into *millets* or 'communities, consisting of a lay and an ecclesiastical council, which dealt with the internal affairs of the people. These *millets* or 'church nations,' as a Turkish professor of Western literature translates it,[48] were the only subdivisions recognised by the state. The diverse Muslim elements (Slavs, Albanians and Turks) had no community of ethnicity. They spoke their own languages in their homes, Turkish being an acquired tongue. But they were Muslims and all were 'Turks' in a political sense: they belonged to the dominant caste, they were the declared rulers of the 'infidels' and were bound together by a shared interest since they formed the minority exploiting the subject peoples and living off the various informal tributes paid by the Christian majority.

Millet-i-Rum (*Rum* is a Turkish corruption of *Romaios*, or Romans, as the Byzantines called themselves; a name used by all until the revolution of the 1820s) was all that remained of the Eastern Empire. Under bishops and patriarchs it carried on the life of the Byzantine court and preserved the Greek nationality with the Greek form of Christianity. The entire Christian zone within the Balkan Peninsula had been termed 'Rumi *vilayets*' (Greek districts) by the Turks. Until the mid-nineteenth century the Ottomans regarded Orthodox Christianity as 'Roman,' *i.e.* the same as the Graeco-Byzantine faith. Whoever was not a 'Turk' was a *Rumi* or 'Greek,' a designation which was applied to Albanians, Bulgarians, Macedonians, Serbs, Vlachs and Greeks, and only implied a recognition of the authority of the Patriarch of Constantinople.[49] Thus, John Morritt of Rokeby, wrote in his letters in the 1790s that since leaving Hermanstadt in Transylvania he had been travelling 'in a Greek country.'[50] And Francis Hervé in Plovdiv and Sofia in the 1830s 'could not hear of any person having become regular inhabitants of those places, independent of the natives, Turks and Greeks.'[51]

Until the beginning of the twentieth century it was commonly supposed 'throughout Europe' that the Slavs of Macedonia and even Bulgaria were Greeks and every educated person coming from those countries called himself a Greek as a matter of course.[52] They affected to be Greeks as *Bugar* (Bulgarian) was a term of contempt: the people were known as *honthrokefalos* (stupid, thickheaded) and the Bulgarian language was supposed to be, 'as their very name tells, "vulgar," boorish.' Some of them even adopted the Greek language, as fluency in Greek was considered a sign of an educated person.[53] Thus 'Greek' denoted a 'member of the Orthodox Church' or 'townsman' because townspeople were 'Greeks' and villagers were 'barbarians.'[54] Or, as a member of the Parnassus Philological Society put it, 'For the Slav it is promotion to become a Greek, as it is promotion for the Hindu to become a Briton.'[55]

Religion was the basis for these divisions; language and ethnological theories played merely a secondary part. A Bulgarian could become a Turk whenever he pleased by embracing Islam, as a Greek could become a Bulgarian by joining the Exarchate. One man might have entered the Romanian fold and his brother the Serbian. The system lasted in its entirety until the beginning of the twentieth century, when there were still towns in Albania with no civil court where the Koran was the only source of law. At the beginning of the twentieth century this system was abolished amid extensive reforms of the political system in Turkey and a code based on the Napoleonic model was introduced instead. At the beginning of the twentieth century, however, the idea of nationality was so new to the Turks that they still confused it with religion. Orthodox Albanians, Bulgarians, Serbs and Vlachs who had not joined the 'schismatic' Bulgarian church were still classified in the census under the comprehensive title 'Rum.'[56]

The rationale for this state of affairs was the system of government. Ottoman law was a religious code which could not be imposed on unbelievers, who could not be recruited into the army. The true believers, the followers of the Prophet, were declared rulers of the *giaours* (infidels). These purely theocratic principles of state organisation formed the basis of the Ottoman Empire. However, owing to the peculiarity of this policy, the Christians in the Ottoman Empire enjoyed relative independence and were able to preserve their nationality, language and customs. These exceptional historical circumstances also explain why, for these Christians, patriotism was transformed into attachment to their religious communities and national church. Contemporary Western authors found this concept of nationality extraordinary, and wondered that in the Balkans race and language were not factors in nationality, which was decided by which church a person belonged to. 'It is much as though a London-born Roman Catholic were called and counted an Irishman, or a Presbyterian in New York, though his ancestors came from Germany, were called and counted a Scotsman.'[57]

A new spirit of national consciousness awoke among the peoples of the millets with the attempt to create civil laws to replace religious ones. They had to reorganise themselves on national lines if they were hold their own at all in modern international politics because nationality was the contemporary basis of Western states and, owing to the ascendancy of the West in the world, the relations of non-Western peoples to each other and to Western powers had to approximate to the forms which the Western world took for granted. However, according to Arnold Toynbee, this principle of nationality in politics was taken for granted in the western Europe simply because it had grown naturally out of their special conditions, not because it was of universal application.[58]

The Descendants of the French Crusaders

Thus, till the beginning of the twentieth century the Slavic people in Macedonia developed no clear consciousness of nationality: those who did not belong to their local community were strangers. Vasil Vodovozov reported that many people simply could not understand the concept of nationality and explained: 'I am an Orthodox, I was an Exarchist, but now I am a Serb.' Only when directly asked again whether they were Bulgarians or Serbs, might they answer: 'I was a Bulgarian, now I am a Serb.'[59] The vital element of their identity was their Christianity and when asked about their nationality, until well into the nineteenth century, they declared themselves as *rayah, kaur,* as the Muslims used to call them, or as Bulgarians, Christians.[60] The Russian consul in Bitola, Rostkovski, for instance, in spite of his seven-year stay in Macedonia, used the 'Turkish' method and divided the inhabitants of Macedonia into Slavic Patriarchists, Slavic Exarchists and Slavic Muslims, because he could not decide whether they were Bulgarians or Serbs. Aleksandr Amfiteatrov, who spent three years there, came to the conclusion that the Macedonians themselves did not know what they were. So he called them a 'nation without national consciousness.'[61]

On account of specific conditions in Macedonia at the end of the nineteenth and beginning of the twentieth centuries, national affinities were decided on political grounds. In Macedonia there was Bulgarian, Greek, Serbian and Romanian propaganda, each with its own ideals and aspirations. It was the object of each party to make as many converts as possible. If propaganda alone was not sufficient, these attempts to reorganise the political map of Macedonia on European lines were carried out by more procrustean methods of expropriation, eviction and hostile interference with worship and the use of the mother-tongue. The business of targeting communities was expensive and did not always yield profit proportionate to the outlay, and the little Balkan states whose resources were as meagre as their ambitions were great would hardly have been able to stake their claims without monetary aid from one of the interested powers.[62]

If at the beginning of the twentieth century the people of Macedonia were constant in their Orthodoxy, according to Western writers, they were correspondingly inconstant in their national affinities. Allegedly, it was quite possible for a Slavic village in Macedonia to be one thing in the presence of a Serbian consul and another in the presence of Bulgarian agent.[63] When Petr Rittih asked peasants in Skopska Crna Gora if they were Serbs, they answered in the affirmative. But when he immediately asked them if they were Bulgarians, the answer was in the affirmative again.[64] When he put the same question to the peasants of Bašino Selo near Veles one-half told him that they were Serbs and the other half that they were Bulgarians.[65] Some researchers were able to find cases where one brother claimed to be a Bulgarian and the other a Serb. In addition, some people claimed to be Greeks, although they could not speak the Greek language.[66] In Bitola, for instance, in 1905, the three Talevtchiné brothers, Stevan, Nikola and Dimitrie, notable merchants, were respectively Bulgarian, Romanian and Greek.[67] Since nationality was by no means immutable in this part of the world, but changed according to conviction, individuals and even whole communities that were Greek yesterday might become Bulgarian today and perhaps Serb tomorrow.[68]

For Western authors of that period, who understood nationality not as a cultural construction but as a kind of natural category, as a 'pure blood,'[69] meaning something permanent, innate and immutable, such a situation was unprecedented. They commented with sublime contempt that nationality in the Balkans was 'a variable quantity, largely depending on considerations with which sentiment, blood, or language have little or nothing to do.'[70] Their opinion of the patriotism of the inhabitants of Macedonia was just as low. In the Balkans, they claimed, patriotism was purse-deep. For instance, a French consul declared that with a fund of a million francs he would undertake to make all Macedonia French. He would preach that the Macedonians were the descendants of the French crusaders who conquered Thessaloníki in the twelfth century and the francs would do the rest. However, Henry Noel Brailsford who quoted this statement immediately added that the Greeks disposed of ample funds but had lost Macedonia.[71]

Where choice is free it will every now and then be governed by personal interest. As reported by some authors, money played an important role in determining the national consciousness of the people. Allegedly a Serbian consul once mentioned to a certain 'Serb' that they had quite a lot of money and the time had come to do something for free for the fatherland, in the name of patriotism. The answer was: 'Oh, Mr Consul!… it'll be very unpleasant for you, since when I get money from you, my patriotism says that I am a Serb, but as soon as my pocket is empty it begins to assure me that I am a Bulgarian.'[72]

The truth is that, on the whole, the Macedonians have shown remarkable steadfastness in the face of corruption and terrorism.

The Bulgarian Threat

Bulgarian patriotism which from 1770 had been so far crushed by the Greek clergy as to make the people forget their identity and regard themselves as Greek was reawakened during the second half of the nineteenth century. There were Bulgarian enthusiasts who, inspired by the traditions of the doubtful glories of a somewhat hypothetical past, looked forward to the day when a Bulgarian empire might be re-established, including all of Macedonia, with Constantinople as its capital.[73] In 1893 the Internal Macedonian Revolutionary Organisation was founded with the aim of liberating Macedonia from the Ottoman occupation under the motto 'Macedonia for the Macedonians.' In practice, the *komitadjis* (the armed members of IMRO) pursued a policy of extermination of Greek and Serbian teachers and clergy and terrorising the Slav villagers who still adhered to the Patriarchate. Before the creation of the Exarchate, when there was only one Orthodox Church in European Turkey, the Greek clerics strove to destroy the Bulgarian language, banning its use in schools and churches. When the new church was established the Patriarch of Constantinople responded to the *firman* by excommunicating all adherents of the Exarchate. Many Bulgarians were afraid to leave the old church and remained faithful to the Patriarchate – and the Greek community.[74]

The Bulgarians claims on Macedonia were based on the fact that in the eleventh century King Samuel had briefly occupied it and, in consequence, the population of Macedonia had been Bulgarianised and was almost exclusively Bulgarian. Bulgaria became increasingly involved in Macedonia in the 1870s when the Bulgarian church seceded from the Patriarchate in Constantinople and laid claim to the villages of several provinces of Thrace and Macedonia. At the beginning of the twentieth century the Exarchate in Macedonia held jurisdiction over seven dioceses (Skopje, Ohrid, Debar, Bitola, Veles, Nevrokop and Strumica).[75] Religion became the symbol of ethnicity: Greeks belonged with the Patriarchate and Bulgarians with the Exarchate. The Bulgarian Church started a process of enforced Bulgarisation of the country, persecuting Greek teachers and priests and replacing them with Bulgarians.[76] The so-called Bulgarian threat produced a serious response in Greece, which, in 1895, began to send armed bands to Macedonia to resist the enforced Bulgarisation by waging guerrilla war on the Bulgarians and Serbs. The Greeks hoped eventually to win a section of the country, although its inhabitants could not speak Greek. The most effective guerrilla group was the *Ethnike Hetairia* (National Society), whose troops became active in Macedonia during the Cretan revolution but, despite its initial successes, the defeat of Greece in the Graeco-Turkish war of 1897 was a major blow to the 'Greeks' of Macedonia who temporarily lost the support of the Greek state.[77]

Greater Serbia

When, after 1878, the Serbs were obliged to seek their Greater Serbia elsewhere they turned towards the south and conceived the idea of a Serbian Macedonia with Thessaloníki as its seaport. For the previous century Serbian scientists and political leaders had recognised that Macedonia had a Bulgarian ethnic physiognomy and even in the treaties of the Balkan Alliance that preceded the war of 1912 Serbia recognised Macedonia as Bulgarian.[78] However, at the end of the nineteenth century some nationalists began to promulgate a new truth: that Macedonia was and always had been a Serbian land.[79] They cited evidence from geography, ethnology, philology and history. In the beginning, the Serbs themselves derided their overzealous scientists, but eventually Macedonian fever seized the Serbian intelligentsia and even important scholars such as Stojan Novaković and Jovan Cvijić had either to remain silent or to compromise their integrity by inventing new arguments for Serbian character of Macedonia. The Macedonians were defined as 'an amorphous mass of people,' with no specific sense of nationality but with a predisposition to assimilate with Serbs or Bulgarians.[80] Ingenious philological and historical arguments were devised by patriots to prove that those 'who speak such a pure Serbian language and observe *slava*, cannot be Bulgarian.' To substantiate the assertion that Macedonian Slavs were Serbs, it was even claimed that the ethnic name *Bugar* was Serbian, not Bulgarian.[81]

In Serbian schools the children were taught the geography of not only Old Serbia 'but of all the Serbian lands, *in order of their redemption* – first Macedonia, then Dalmatia, Bosnia, Herzegovina, Croatia, Banat, and Batchka!'[82] Schools in the Balkans taught their pupils not merely the usual subjects but also the crucial issue of their nationality. Thus schools in Macedonia became 'factories of *kannonen futter*.'[83]

Secret societies were founded in the major Serbian towns to propagate the idea that Macedonia belonged to Serbia. In addition Serbian schools were established and the Serbian language was disseminated in the north-west of Macedonia. By the end of the nineteenth century the Serbs had more than 200 schools in Macedonia and a Serb bishop was appointed at Skopje under the auspices of the Patriarchate of Constantinople. Ambitious Serbian nationalists also sent *komitadjis* there to fight Bulgarian influence. According to Francesca Wilson, they discharged their duties with great fervour. One of their leaders, the schoolteacher Stefanović, told her: 'We had no wine – our wine was the blood of the Bulgarians.'[84]

As a result of the two Balkan Wars of 1912–13, Serbia gained Kosovo and northern and central Macedonia. The campaign medal referred to the 1389 battle, bearing the inscription 'Kosovo Avenged,' but this military success left Serbia with the task of assimilating a heterogeneous population, which included a high proportion of Muslim Albanians as well as many Orthodox Slavs, many of whom still looked to Bulgaria. The Serbian government declared that 'the level of culture' was not sufficiently high among the Macedonians and their 'state consciousness' was not sufficiently developed to permit the immediate granting of full political rights.[85] Intensive Serbianisation took place in the part of Macedonia under Serbian authority, aimed first of all against the Bulgarian Exarchate and Bulgarian schools in the country. The Serbian authority also forcibly modified Macedonian surnames by adding to them the Serbian suffix –*ić*.[86]

If the Ottoman Empire acknowledged the Macedonians as Bulgarians and Greece acknowledged them at least as Slav-speaking people, Serbia denied that they had any Bulgarian identity whatsoever and banned any outward expression of such a thing. The people of Macedonia were not allowed to commemorate the brothers Miladinov, which they had been allowed to do even during the Ottoman occupation.[87] Stoyan Christowe recorded how a Serbian king had used his hands to help to deprive the Bulgarian population of their nationality. In 1912, during the First Balkan War, King Alexander of Yugoslavia, then crown prince, stopped a little girl in a street in Prilep and bending over her, asking her her nationality. The little girl said: 'Bulgarian.' Alexander, later called the Unifier, slapped her face with his royal palm.[88]

After Serbia annexed the counties of Niš, Pirot and Vranje (with a Bulgarian-speaking population) in 1878, the authorities carried out an agrarian reform, introduced Serbian schools and subordinated the Church to the Metropolitan of Belgrade. In fact, Serbia did the same here as it did later in Macedonia. The result was that in the space of less than twenty years the people forgot their Bulgarian identity and began to feel themselves to be Serbian. When Vasil Vodovozov visited these counties in 1894 there were no signs of national or religious discontent, for the 'uncompromising Bulgarian elements who in any case constituted but an unimportant part of the population' had moved away; the remaining Slavs had already become reconciled to the fact that they were 'Serbs.'[89] Their success in this process led the Serbian authorities to expect similar results in Macedonia where the existing differences between the 'Serbs' and the 'Bulgarians' were 'almost entirely a matter of education.' People there had 'duplicate religions, similar ideas, identical customs.' According to observations of Frederick Moore, the peasants of Macedonia dressed alike, and only the partisans and propagandists were distinguishable by their attire: 'A European cut of clothes is worn by those who attend the Bulgarian gymnasium, while a military jacket attests the adherents of the rival school.'[90]

As reported by correspondent Aredern Hulme-Beaman in the *Standard*, at the start of the process of Serbianisation of Macedonia the Serbian element was practically non-existent.[91] Within a short time this had been changed dramatically. However, the Macedonian people were not as straightforwardly Serbianised as those of Niš and other formerly Bulgarian places. A few years later, during a visit to Bitola the Serbian assistant minister of education, Dr Stevanović, tried to find out how far the idea of Serbian nationality had been disseminated. With this in mind, he asked pupils he met on their way to the school about their nationality. They answered that they were Macedonians. In response to further questions, he found out that their parents were Slavs. Only one out of five said that he was a Serb; when asked what his father was, he answered: 'A Tsintsar.'[92]

For Macedonians the concept of being Yugoslav held much more appeal

This part of Macedonia fell under Serbian occupation (Yugoslavia) in 1913.

In 1944 the Macedonian freedom fighters created it's Macedonian Republic that enjoys limited freedom, but falls short from being totally independent.

This part of Macedonia is occupied by the dictatorial puppet regime of Bulgaria.

This part of Macedonia is under the Greek terror of occupation since 1913.

Map of Macedonia

than the concept of being Serb. Fran Tućan travelled through Macedonia soon after the establishment of the State of the South Slavs following the First World War. The people he met there who were 'unusually hospitable, but in their statements very reserved.' They were partisans of national unity, 'which is not odd at all, for Yugoslavism is here an idea that gathers together, unites, that calms passions and raises faith in the future of the nation.' As a man from Kavadarci explained to him, the Serbs, Croats and Slovenes were 'old men at their last gasp, as a powerful, strong Yugoslav is being born.'[93]

After the Second World War Bulgaria dropped the Macedonian question as far as Greece was concerned. After the Greek Civil War and the departure of the Slav minority from Greece the Macedonian question only affected Bulgaria in relation to Yugoslavia, mainly because of the de-Bulgarisation of the population of Yugoslav Macedonia on one side and denial of the existence of a Macedonian minority in Pirin Macedonia on the other. But in neighbouring states of Macedonia the existence of a Macedonian nation continued to be denied. Since the Second World War the Bulgarian Academy of Sciences has published a large number of documents to demonstrate that Macedonian nationality was an artificial construct and that the people of Yugoslav Macedonia are Bulgarian. Even today some Greek authors believe that the Macedonians are Greek.[94] The very existence of the Macedonian nation was denied by many Westerners as well, perhaps most explicitly by John Foster Fraser who claimed that, 'You will find Bulgarians and Turks who call themselves Macedonians, you find Greek Macedonians, there are Servian Macedonians, and it is possible to find Roumanian Macedonians. You will not, however, find a single Christian Macedonian who is not a Servian, a Bulgarian, a Greek, or a Roumanian.'[95]

Notwithstanding the long oppression the inhabitants of Macedonia have endured and the propaganda persuading them they were not who they thought they were, at the end of the nineteenth century the Slavs of Macedonia used the name Macedonian as a term of self-designation in contrasts with other categories of national identity, such as 'Serbian,' 'Bulgarian' and 'Greek.' Gorgi Pulevski in his trilingual dictionary defined *narod* (nation) as a group of people of the same origin, who speak the same language, who live together and share the same customs, songs and festivals; he states, 'Thus the Macedonians are a nation and our homeland is Macedonia.'[96] According to Krste Misirkov, at the end of the nineteenth century the national awareness of Macedonian Slavs was 'very widespread and clear.'[97] As other authors noted, they openly declared that they were not Bulgarians or Serbs, but Macedonians.[98] Thus, the Father Superior of the monastery of Lešok near Tetovo, Father Jezekiel, proclaimed himself 'a pure-bred Macedonian'[99] and a teacher from Ohrid declared: 'I am not a Bulgarian, nor a Greek, nor a Tsintsar; I am a pure Macedonian, as were Philip and Alexander of Macedon and Aristotle the Philosopher.'[100] Individual representatives of local intelligence also insisted that the Macedonian dialect, though related to Bulgarian and Serbian, was not identical to them and that the Macedonians were a separate nation of Slavic origin.[101]

Western authors paid much attention to Macedonia at the end of the nineteenth and beginning of the twentieth centuries on account of its explosive and murky political situation. Many wrote about it, still more toured it determined to look under every stone they chanced to pass on their way. They grasped the countless ins and outs of the Macedonian question and its deep historical roots. They became profoundly aware of the highly complicated political and ethnological situation due to the many different and conflicting interests at stake. But the single fact that the Macedonians lived in Macedonia somehow escaped their notice, although occasionally they did notice that Macedonian Slavs were neither Bulgarians nor Serbs.[102] Macedonians were conspicuous by their absence in their writings:

> Converse with a Roumanian consul, say at Monastir. 'True, these people talk Bulgarian or Greek,' he says; 'but they are really Roumanian, though they don't know it. Therefore, when Macedonia is freed from the Turk, its natural and proper ruler is Roumania.' Interview a Servian. 'Before the coming of the Turks,' says he, 'the Servian Empire stretched south

to the sea.' Seek the views of a Bulgarian. 'It is obvious,' he tells you, 'that practically all Macedonia is filled with Bulgarians. They speak Bulgarian, and are adherents of the Bulgarian Church. Many people who speak Greek and are Orthodox have been coerced; but they are Bulgarian. Macedonia is the rightful heritage of Bulgaria.' 'Nothing of the kind,' retorts the Greek; 'the Bulgarians are schismatics, and are not even entitled to the name Christian. They compel villages by threats to renounce the Orthodox Church, and then they are reckoned Bulgarian. Bah on the butchers![103]

It did not make much difference whether this was so because of their taking side with one of the Balkan states or whether it was just too difficult for them, accustomed as they were to connect space and number with greatness, to suppress the feeling of contempt suggested by the small number of the people of Macedonia in comparison with the greatness of Balkan empires and their pretensions. It was of no consequence what people thought and said:

> In truth, the difficulty of the situation is not surprising when it is remembered that, since the Empire of Philip, Macedonia has been subject to Greeks, Servians, Bulgarians and Turks. The peasant, therefore, may well be excused if he has lost count of his true ancestry. And thus it happens that such words as 'race,' 'nationality,' 'lineage,' or whatever be the expression most suited to differentiate between a Macedonian and the rest of the Balkan world, have lost their savour, with the result that the peasant is ready to adopt any nationality as his own, provided the arguments sufficiently plausible are advanced in the process of conversion.[104]

Because the Ottoman Empire had laid great stress upon religious difference, nationality had been considered secondary and less important. When the notion of nationality developed in western Europe as a substantial element of human identity, even more important than religious difference, it ran into major obstacles in the Balkans. It might never have found its way there, had it not been sponsored by the European powers. For circumstantial reasons consciousness of a specific national identity was the least developed among the Slavic population of Macedonia. The neighbouring Balkan states tried to turn this situation to their advantage, each anxious to enlarge its own national territory. Bulgaria, Greece and Serbia were particularly anxious to enforce their territorial claims, maintaining that the people of Macedonia were really Bulgarians, Greeks or Serbs. However, none of them ever really succeeded in assimilating the people of Macedonia whom they subdued by fair means or foul. But their success in representing the people of Macedonia to Western observers as a people without national consciousness was quite another story. According to George Frederick Abbott who found the stories invented by Balkan propagandists more interesting than reality, in one and the same Macedonian household one could occasionally come across 'representatives of all the branches of the human family,' that is, a father claiming Serbian descent, his son swearing that only Bulgarian blood flowed in *his* veins, while the daughters, if allowed to speak, would be equally positive of their descent from Helen of Troy or Catherine of Russia or Aphrodite of Melos. The old mother was generally content to express her national convictions in the declaration that she was a Christian. After presenting this vivid picture of total confusion as reflecting actual reality, he gave his diagnosis:

> A true comedy of errors in which no one knows who is who, but everybody instinctively feels that everybody is somebody else. Verily no country ever was in such sore need of a herald's office, or of a lunatic asylum, as Macedonia. It may be described as a region peopled with new-born souls wandering in quest of a body, and losing themselves in the search.[105]

TEN

A Bridge Between Barbarity
and Civilisation

A Stone Arch Above a Torrent

The stone bridge of Mostar was arguably one of the most famous achievements of the Golden Age of Ottoman architecture and, for some, 'the greatest and most beautiful monument, not only of Mostar, but of all the Balkans,'[1] if not 'one of the most beautiful bridges in the world.'[2] It was built in 1566 according to the plans of Mimar Haireddin, a court architect and a pupil of the famous Hodja Mimar Sinan, the greatest Ottoman architect.[3] This beautiful bridge spanned the Neretva at the narrowest point of a deep and rocky canyon where the river's foaming waters flow through a veritable labyrinth of rocks. It consisted of a single arch with an elevation of 17.85 metres at its highest point (19 metres including the parapet); the full width from one side to the other was 27.34 metres; the bridge was 4.56 metres across. These proportions gave the colossal structure its graceful lightness.[4] At both ends of the Old Bridge there still stand towers which once housed a garrison of 160 men who guarded the bridge day and night. The local people used to call these towers and the Old Bridge the Castle. The tower on the left bank of the river was known as Herceguša and the one on the right bank as Halebinka or Ćehovina. In the nineteenth century the Herceguša tower served as a powder store and the Halebinka as a city dungeon.[5]

Old Bridge in Mostar

In sixteenth- and seventeenth-century documents the bridge is called
the Bridge of Sultan Suleiman. Later it was referred to as the Great Bridge
and, more recently, it became known as the Old Bridge.[6] Its dimensions,
construction, shape and setting made it a unique monument of its kind.
The only similar bridge is one on the Vojusha river in the town of Konica in
north-west Greece near the Albanian border, 'which is as like the Old Bridge
as a twin is like his brother, except that it has no towers.'[7]

Its fame attracted many travellers, among them viziers and dignitaries from
all the Ottoman territories. Everyone who saw the bridge was overwhelmed
by its beauty and the boldness of its construction. In his poem dedicated to
the town of his birth, the Turkish poet Dervish Pasha Bajezidagić (1552–
1603), a famous general and adviser to Sultan Murat III and vizier of Bosnia,
compared it to the vault of heaven, full of moving stars, but he claimed that
the beauty of the bridge was beyond the beauty of the skies.[8] Evliya Çelebi,
who visited Mostar in 1664, declared that although he had travelled widely
and visited 'sixteen kingdoms,' he had never seen 'a bridge so high.'[9] An
unknown Arabic traveller is quoted as saying, 'I have travelled far and have
stopped in awe at the doors of Mostar, for I have noticed minarets, slender as
voices at prayer, and a bridge over the water as the moon in the sky.'[10]

Before the Ottomans took Mostar, it had a wooden bridge mentioned for the first time in a letter from Dubrovnik dated 3 April 1452.[11] The first information on the mediaeval bridge of Mostar dates from a time when the stone bridge had already been in use for a century. Haji Khalifa, who also wrote about Rumelia and Bosnia at the beginning of the seventeenth century, described this bridge, which according to him was built in 974 of the hegira, as 'suspended from chains' and 'swaying to such an extent that people feared for their lives in crossing it.'[12]

It is known from existing sources that the wooden bridge became unusable in the middle of the sixteenth century. The citizens of Mostar then asked Sultan Suleiman the Magnificent to authorise the building of a better, more substantial bridge across the Neretva. The request was granted and the bridge was built in 1566. The date of its construction is confirmed by two inscriptions cut into the bridge. The first one reads:

> The soul of Sultan Mehmet should be glad,
> For it has left such a work of men's hands.
> And an homage also to Suleiman,
> Who ruled when the bridge was being finished.
> By the efforts of the nazir the bridge was built
> And the chronogram was written: '*qudret kemeri.*'
> The year 974.[13]

Evliya Çelebi noted not the whole inscription but only the chronogram: *qudret kemeri* (The Arch of God Almighty), which was inscribed into the middle of the arch.[14] If the numerical values of the letters are added together, in accordance with a sophisticated Arabic custom, the sum gives the year of the construction of the bridge, that is the year 974 of the hegira: $q = 100 + d = 4 + r = 200 + t = 400 + k = 20 + m = 40 + r = 200 + j = 10$.[15]

Over time alternative accounts of the building of the bridge developed. According to Haji Khalifa, at the request of the inhabitants Sultan Suleiman sent Mimar Sinan with instructions to build a stone bridge. But after the architect had seen the place, he declared the task to be impossible, so the plan to build the bridge was abandoned. Later on, however, a local carpenter declared himself willing to take responsibility for the task, and the single-arch stone bridge was built. Everyone said, 'the bridge is a masterpiece, which puts to shame all the architects in the world.'[16]

In the village of Podporim along the old Mostar road leading to Konjic there stands a carved stone trough, although there is no sign of any well or spring there. The story was that the builder of the bridge pledged to forfeit his head if the bridge collapsed. When the bridge was completed, he could

Muslim woman from Mostar

not bring himself to witness the removal of the scaffolding but fled from
Mostar and waited until this was done. Excited and impatient for news, so the
story went, the builder distractedly drilled a hole in a stone by hitting it with a
hammer and thus carved out the trough. People used the rainwater in it as a
medicine at least until the beginning of the twentieth century.[17]

   Another tradition was told by the Muslims of Mostar. Sultan Suleiman
heard of the exceptional beauty of a woman named Mara Lehovkinja and
he swore he would kiss her, dead or alive. He embarked on a long siege
of the town of Promin, of which Mara's husband was king. When Mara's
husband realised that Suleiman's troops were about to break into the town,
he beheaded his wife and had her head and body thrown into the deep river,
so that Suleiman could not keep his word. But in order to do so and save the

Immuring a woman

throne, Sultan Suleiman offered a large reward to anyone who would take the castle and find Mara's body. A certain Huso from Mostar brought her head to the sultan from the depths of the river and a certain Ahmo from Višegrad brought him her body. Having kissed the dead Mara, the sultan summoned Huso and Ahmo, and asked them what reward they wanted for their service. Each of them asked him to build a bridge as their reward: one on the Neretva river in Mostar and the other on the Drina river in the town of Višegrad. The sultan kept his promise and had the bridges built.[18]

According to the Orthodox tradition, the architect Rade, who had been sold into slavery, regained his freedom from the Turks by means of this bridge. For a long time his work was in vain: what he built during the day, the river would wash away during the night. The bridge always collapsed until, on the advice of Vila, the fairy of the mountain forest, he walled up a pair of lovers, Stoja and Stojan, alive in the foundations.[19]

One frequently encounters similar traditions and motifs associated with the building of castles and bridges in the Balkans.[20] One of the best known is probably the story about the building of the citadel of Shköder;[21] another tells of the building of the bridge in Višegrad which collapsed repeatedly for seven years until the architect Mitra was advised by his fairy to wall up Stoja and Ostoja into the bridge.[22] The tradition was so strong that at the beginning of 1870 the inhabitants of Trebinje stole a child's corpse in the Dubrovnik area and had it walled up in the foundation of the bridge over the river Trebinjčica.[23] In one of the Ionian islands, Zákinthos, another tale, also from the second half of the nineteenth century, is told: there the people believed they had to sacrifice a Muslim or a Jew when an important bridge was being built.[24]

Roman Bridges from the Nineteenth Century

A story which circulated in the nineteenth century among foreign visitors to Mostar associated the construction of the Old Bridge with conquerors prior to the Ottomans. First, Consul Chaumette des Fossés attributed the building of the Old Bridge to the Greeks of the Eastern Empire, maintaining that they built the bridge in Višegrad in the twelfth century and that the Old Bridge of Mostar also dated from the same period.[25] Later on, it was believed that the bridge must be Roman, as such a tall and solid single-arch bridge made out of big blocks, spanning such a wide and turbulent river with such steep banks, bore all the hallmarks of Roman architecture;[26] in consequence, several attempts were made to find a Roman *municipium*, Mondertium or Matrix, in its environs.[27]

The first author to name the Romans as the builders of the bridge was French officer Charles Pertusier.[28] His view had many supporters, among them experts on Bosnia-Herzegovina. Most of them believed that either Trajan or Hadrian had ordered the bridge's construction;[29] others thought it was Emperor Anthony[30] or Justinian[31] or even Julius Caesar.[32] These assumptions were based on the belief that the Romans had built the bridge there because the Roman road to Pannonia was thought to lead that way. Some authors even calculated the exact date of the construction of the Old Bridge, putting it at 98 BC.[33]

But if the site of Mostar seemed so favourable that in the nineteenth century it was regarded as the one obvious crossing point over the Neretva, it was not always so. In the seventeenth century, for instance, Quiclet on his way from Dubrovnik to Sarajevo did not go through Mostar and in his travel report he stated that there were several wooden and stone bridges over the Neretva.[34]

The Roman origin of the bridge was even upheld by experts like the famous English Egyptologist and traveller Sir Gardner Wilkinson who argued:

The tradition pretends, that the towers are on Roman substructions, and that the one on the eastern side is the most ancient.

The building of the bridge is attributed to Trajan, or, according to some, to Hadrian; and reports speak of an inscription, that once existed upon it, with the name of one of those emperors. The Turks attribute its erection to Suleyman, the Magnificent; but the Vizir, in answer to my question respecting the date, said that 'though they claim it as a work of that Sultan, the truth is, it was there long before his time, and was probably built by the Pagans.' The Turk entirely concealed the original masonry, not a block is to be seen of Roman time, and the smallness of the stones, the torus under the parapet, and the spandril projecting slightly over the arch, give it all the appearance of Turkish. But the grandeur of the work, the form of the arch, and tradition, all favour its Roman origin; and the fact of the town being called Mostar, shows that an 'old bridge' already existed there, where it received that name; and Mostar was a city long before the Turkish invasion of the country.[35]

What is especially remarkable about this theory is the fact that all those authors who accepted it were acquainted with the tradition that dates the building of the bridge to Sultan Suleiman's reign.[36] The tradition was substantiated by two inscriptions on the bridge itself that were 'unquestionably Turkish, even though difficult to decipher.'[37] But as usual prejudice was too strong to overcome. So, people chose to dismiss the inscriptions as references merely to repairs made during the Ottoman era, not to the building of the bridge.[38] Some even accused the Ottomans of having deliberately removed the original (Roman) inscriptions and substituted Turkish ones to conceal the real authorship of the bridge.[39]

In the sixteenth and seventeenth centuries the Ottoman Empire was perceived as possessing unlimited power; its army was 'the very terror of Europe,' which made 'the most distant Christian monarchs to tremble in their capitals,'[40] for it seemed that 'they may probably obtain and conserve a far larger Empire, and even all Europe, unto the Western Ocean.'[41] Even England, though surrounded by sea, shared the sense of danger and horror which Ottoman enormities inspired.[42] At that time European authors had no doubts about the abilities of Ottoman architects to erect bridges, for instance.[43] As for the Old Bridge, a French traveller of the seventeenth century, Poullet, described the bridge of Mostar as 'hardier, without comparison, and wider than the Ponte Realto in Venice, although the latter is esteemed a marvel.'[44]

But, if the Ottoman Empire was once a great power, its strength began to wane after the defeat of Kara Mustafa's army in Vienna in 1683. By the

The outgoing Turk (a cartoon from a Slovenian newspaper, 1912)

beginning of the nineteenth century some authors were already predicting great changes: history was moving quickly and 'before a half century be elapsed the sword may retake what the sword has gained, and Christian rites once more be celebrated within the walls of St. Sophia.'[45] The empire which once upon a time had been considered the greatest power in the world[46] was thus becoming a 'dying lion,' which 'after a few violent convulsions would never rise again.'[47] Then people in the West began to ask another question about the Turk: 'Is this the man that made earth tremble, that did shake kingdoms; that made the world as a wilderness, and destroyed the cities thereof?'[48]

At the same time, perspectives on Ottoman civilisation and culture also changed. In the mid-nineteenth century the Ottoman Empire was considered 'still the same Oriental monarchy as it had been in the fourteenth century.'[49] For the authors of the second half of the nineteenth century it was axiomatic that the Turks were simply 'Asiatic barbarians in Europe.'[50] Parallel with this perception of the Ottoman Empire as a diminished and barbaric power were wide-ranging doubts about Ottoman ability in the fields of culture and architecture, particularly about their ability to construct bridges. Some thought that during the long period of Turkish nationhood, the Turks had never gone beyond a certain stage in house architecture, and that the mosques in Istanbul (apart from their minarets) were 'always copies of Santa Sophia with trifling variations, and have no claim to originality.'[51] At any rate, during this period, the majority of stone bridges in the Ottoman Empire were considered to be the work of 'ancient Romans or Greeks of the Byzantine Empire or even Bulgarians.'[52] By the beginning of the twentieth century it was common knowledge that the 'Turks cannot build a road, or make a bridge.'[53]

This underestimation and devaluation of Ottoman abilities culminated with the publication of images of Dalmatia and Herzegovina by the painter Charlotte de Lazen. In her rambles along the eastern Adriatic coast she was especially attracted to Mostar and its stone bridge, which she described as a remnant of Roman civilisation amidst Turkish barbarity:

> Its famous bridge with a single arch that spans two riverbanks and rises in the midst of Turkish barbarity is a marvellous remnant of Roman civilisation. Unfortunately, history offers no reliable information on that remarkable monument. In general it is attributed to Emperor Trajan, or by others to Hadrian; according to tradition, it used to have an inscription with the name of one of the Emperors.
>
> Two towers, covered with ivy, guard access to the bridge and it is possible to block the passage on the right bank if necessary. The foundations of the towers are said to have originated in Roman times.
>
> On both pillars of the bridge are inscriptions in Turkish, one of them from the year 1087 of the hegira or 1659 of the Christian era, probably referring to repairs done at that time.
>
> In the opinion of Turkish people the construction of the bridge of Mostar is attributed to Suleyman II. But the primitive masonry, though in great part recovered by repairs, does not permit further speculation about its origin.
>
> The form of arch, the grandeur of the style, hardness and levity of proportions point to ancient tradition.[54]

Similarly, Western authors, unwilling to believe that Indians could have built the magnificent buildings of pre-Columbian America, long attributed these architectural achievements to the Egyptians. At the end of the seventeenth century Francesco Gemelli Careri, for instance, noted down that they were thought to have been built by people from the island of Atlantis; as evidence he cited a passage from Plato stating that the inhabitants of this island originated in Egypt, where pyramids are traditional, and a passage from Aristotle stating that the Carthaginians had sailed to an island very distant from the Pillars of Hercules where many of them settled. 'If this be true, it is not to be looked upon as any wonder, that the Mexicans should raise pyramids after the Egyptian manner...'[55]

As regards Bosnia, certain nineteenth-century authors maintained that the town of Jajce had been built by an Italian architect in imitation of the Neapolitan Castello del Uovo (although no old building similar to any in Jajce could be seen in the Naples area in the middle of the nineteenth century).[56]

Doubts on the Roman origins of the Old Bridge were first expressed in the 1850s in the travel account of Ida von Reinsberg-Düringsfeld who, mentioning the bridge of Mostar, says that 'history mislabels it as Roman.'[57] But in notes added to her book by her husband Baron Otto, the reader is once again informed that the bridge was built by either Trajan or Hadrian.[58]

The myth that the Old Bridge was Roman was convincingly dispatched by a German consul-general, Dr Otto Blau, who claimed that nothing about it was reminiscent of Roman architecture: 'From an architectural point of view, the whole bridge is of one piece and style, even the stones of the lowest layer that can be reached show no sign of an older foundation. Neither the bridge nor its surroundings contain any inscriptions, sculptures or other remnants of the Roman art.'[59]

One of the most famous English archaeologists, Arthur John Evans, published a book at the same time as Dr Blau. He paid no attention to details like these and was still able to claim that the bridge was built by the Romans and not by the Turks:

> According to the tradition, this was the work of the Emperor Trajan, whose engineering triumphs in Eastern Europe have taken a strong hold on the South-Sclavonic imagination. Others refer its creation to Hadrian, and the Turks, not wishing to leave the credit of such an architectural masterpiece to Infidel Emperors, claim the whole for their Sultan, Suleiman the Magnificent. He and other Turkish rulers have certainly greatly restored and altered the work, insomuch that Sir Gardner Wilkinson declares that none of the original Roman masonry has been left on the exterior, but he was the less convinced of its Roman origin; and anyone who has seen it will agree with Sir Gardner that the grandeur of the work, and the form of the arch, as well as the tradition, attest its Roman origin.[60]

When at the end of the nineteenth century it became impossible to resist the evidence that the bridge was of Ottoman origin, some authors, unable to accept this fact, still tried to justify the tradition of its Roman origin: 'Though now proved to be of Turkish origin, dating from the time of Suleiman II. (1566), it is not unlikely that a Roman bridge preceded it on the same site, and so gave the rise to the tradition that this one is of Roman constitution.'[61] Even though they had to accept that it had been built on the sultan's command in 1566, some still maintained that it must have been built either by Dalmatio-Italian architects[62] or by stonemasons from Dubrovnik.[63]

Bridge over the Drina at Višegrad (1530)

Bridge over the Drina at Višegrad (1878)

It is noteworthy that this viewpoint influenced even the local people's opinion of who had built the bridge: 'Disregarding the judgement of the experts concerning the era of the construction of the bridge, I would conclude that it certainly must have been built before the conquest of Herzegovina; which nation had built it, I leave to the technicians to decide.'[64] Fra Grga Martić of Herzegovina expressed the dilemma in a poem:

> Who built the bridge of Mostar?
> Everybody asks, who passes by it.
> Some say: all-knowing Romans,
> Some, that it was built by Turks.[65]

In any case, the dilemma of who its builders were remained unsolved at the beginning of the twentieth century. In the West the Old Bridge continued to be known as *Römerbrücke* (Roman bridge), although its Ottoman origin had been proved.[66] The *Narodna enciklopedija srpsko-hrvatska-slovenačka* (Serbo-Croat-Slovenian Encyclopaedia) maintained in the 1920s that 'the stone bridge over the Neretva in Mostar is believed to be of Roman workmanship, as is confirmed by the style of the construction.'[67]

The bridge over the river Drina at Višegrad and the Kameni most (Stone Bridge) at Skopje provide two other instances of a similar misattribution. A photograph of the bridge at Višegrad in a book published by a German traveller, Louis Matzhold, in 1936 has the caption 'Old Roman bridge over the Drina.'[68] A picture of Višegrad Castle in a travel account by Benedikt Kuripešic contains a representation of the bridge over the Drina from the first half of the sixteenth century, but with a completely different shape from the legendary bridge over that river.[69] After the incorporation of the town of Skopje into Serbia, some attributed its attractive Stone Bridge to Tsar Dušan,[70] while others asserted it was much older and attributed it to the Romans:

> A magnificent stone bridge, a wonderful piece of work by a Roman architect, still connects the right bank of the Vardar river with the left bank. For two thousand years this bridge has served man, and continues to do so today. An honourable monument left behind by the ancient Romans... What would a European have created from this town, if the Asian barbarian had not by accident stormed into our land![71]

The Importance of Identity

The first foundations of Mostar were laid round the original wooden bridge on the left bank of the Neretva. In the mid-fifteenth century a small settlement was built, mentioned for the first time in a letter dated 3 April 1452. The letter says, *inter alia*, that Vladislav Hercegović made war on his father Herzeg Stjepan and conquered the town of Blagaj and two towers on the bridge over the Neretva ('duo castelli al ponte de Neretua').[72] Because the old wooden bridge was an unstable construction, dangerous to cross, the town with its *çarşi* (marketplace) and *mahallas* (residential districts) developed almost exclusively on the left bank of the river. Although the bridge had been constructed to meet the needs of regional traffic (the Ottoman troops crossed it when conquering western Herzegovina and Dalmatia), its existence determined the gradual concentration of the population. A town called Most, Mostići or Mostari, in which the Ottoman governor had his residence, was already in existence at the end of the fifteenth century. The first mention of Mostar's present name dates back to the year 1469. The sources from that year mention *nahiya* Mostar and, in Turkish, Köprühisar (Tower on the Bridge). The census of 1477 noted that Mostar had nineteen houses (families) and one single inhabitant at the time. Due to its favourable location at the crossroads of regional communications, the town quickly evolved into the economic, cultural and political centre of Herzegovina during the Ottoman era. It overtook Blagaj, which had been the capital of Hum, and by the first decades of Ottoman rule had entirely supplanted it.[73] Prior to that it used to be '*şehir* Blagaj and *kasaba* Mostar.'[74]

The close link between the town of Mostar and the Old Bridge is reflected in the way its inhabitants connected their names. Çelebi had already documented that the name Mostar was supposed to mean *Köprüli-şehir* (Town with a Bridge).[75] By the nineteenth century the inhabitants of Mostar reportedly believed that the name of the town itself was merely a shorter form of *Most-star* (Old Bridge).[76] Furthermore, writers who argued that the bridge was Roman in origin referred to this tradition, claiming that 'the very name of the town would imply the existence of a bridge in very early days.'[77] Certain historians have therefore assumed that the bridge was first built because the Romans had a settlement there, Pons vetus (Old Bridge). It was then assumed that when the Slavs arrived there they translated the name into their idiom and made it *Most-star*, Mostar.[78]

The first person to cast doubt on this etymological derivation of Mostar from Most-star was the Russian linguist Aleksandr Gil'ferding, on the grounds that it does not comply with the normal patterns of Slavonic languages. He assumed that a settlement had developed around the Old Bridge, that its inhabitants had started to call themselves Mostari (just like the Blatari of Blato or the Drvari of Drvo) and that the settlement had eventually developed into a town.[79]

These linguistic arguments against the derivation of the Mostar from Stari most can be supplemented by a historical argument: the name Mostar is older than Stari most, which dates back only to the eighteenth century, that is three centuries after Mostar already had its present name. Besides, till the year 1884 Stari most was the only bridge in Mostar. But, in spite of the problem created by this etymology, the development of Mostar was nevertheless closely related to its Old Bridge:

> Although the existence of a Roman place name Pons vetus is yet to be proved definitively and the derivation of the name of the town from Most-star must be discredited as inappropriate according to the rules of the Slavic languages (the name would have been Starimost), it is nevertheless possible to derive the name of the town from the presence of an old bridge, which was certainly the core of the original settlement (actually Mostari, plural 'die Brückner,' just like Mostari near Bjelovar in Croatia).[80]

According to the most recent research, the name Mostar is derived from 'bridge keepers' (*mostari,* guardians of the bridge); its inhabitants became known as Mostari. According to Ivan Milićević, the keeper of the bridge (*most*) was known as the *mostar*, just as the keeper of the gates (*vrata*) was known as the *vratar*, the keeper of the road (*cesta*) *cestar* and the keeper of the cattle (*govedo*) *govedar*; Mostar's name thus follows a general Slavonic linguistic pattern.[81] There are some other theories on the origin of the name Mostar. Some purport that Mostar got its name from the towers of the bridge, popularly known as *mostare*.[82] Others derive its name from *most-tara* (tower on the left bank), *most-ar* (from most + ahar; the janissary's *ahar*, stable, was on the right bank near the bridge) or from *mostarina* (a toll for crossing the bridge), omitting the ending –ina.[83]

In any case, the Old Bridge became the symbol of Mostar and so closely identified with the town that one was unimaginable without the other: 'Mostar without the bridge would not be what she is. She would be a body, congruent and beautiful, good-hearted, but with no soul or mind.'[84] Until its destruction, the citizens of Mostar believed that the Old Bridge was inextricably linked with the very name of the town.[85]

The deliberate destruction of this unique cultural monument in 1993 amounts to the deliberate destruction of a symbol of the Muslim presence in Herzegovina and a brutal attempt to change the fundamental identity of the town. If earlier observers were reluctant to recognise the contributions of the Ottomans to Bosnian culture and erased the Ottoman past by attributing the bridge's construction to other cultures, the Croat forces went one step further by obliterating the bridge itself. The Old Bridge with its towers was what the town was famous for. This treasure of Ottoman cultural heritage encapsulated its identity. It was to Mostar what Notre Dame is to Paris, the Kremlin to Moscow or Hagia Sophia to Istanbul.[86] As long as the Old Bridge spanned the Neretva, it was Mostar itself. It was impossible to imagine the town either as the Greater Serbian Aleksinac (after the Serbian poet Aleksa Šantić, born in Mostar) or as the Greater Croatian Herceg-Stjepan Grad (after Herzeg Stjepan). The men who destroyed the Old Bridge did not have it alone within their sights but aimed to destroy its symbolic value and meaning: they aimed to destroy the most important monument of Mostar's cultural history and to destroy the possibility of communication between the citizens on the two sides of the river, the Bosniaks (Muslims) on the left bank and the Croats (Catholics) on the right.

ELEVEN

Little Parises and Large Bucharests

The final chapter of our journey takes us on a guided tour through various towns and cities of the 'savage'[1] or 'wild'[2] Europe. The tour starts some 300 years ago in the Hungarian capital, passes through the turbulent history and geography of Romania, Bulgaria, Greece, Albania, Serbia, Montenegro and Macedonia, and ends in Bosnia-Herzegovina. Our principal guides are west Europeans who travelled in the Balkan Peninsula between the seventeenth century and the present day, some of them connoisseurs of the Balkans, and all of them rich in personal experience.

The Eastern Queen with a Dirty Face

The centuries of Ottoman occupation left an imprint not just on the history of the Balkans but also on the people and their culture, and this was probably most clearly visible in the appearance of Balkan towns. Sir Edwin Pears wrote:

> Under the Turkish rule, Constantinople has become the most retrograde capital in Europe. Under such rule, Athens, Bucharest, Belgrade, and Sofia, eighty years ago, were mere collections of mud huts, occupied

Distant prospect of Istanbul, late 17th century

by dejected and poverty-stricken people. Since their inhabitants got rid of Turkish oppression these villages have rapidly grown into towns, have adopted the appliances of civilization, and are all making good progress. The first two, which have enjoyed freedom for a longer time than the others, are now well-built and well-governed cities with bright, intelligent, and progressive populations, and Sofia will soon run them close. To pass from any of these towns to Constantinople is to pass from a civilized to a barbarous city.[3]

The degeneracy which, according to Western travellers, was the main characteristic of Balkan towns was generally attributed to the physical and intellectual decay of the Ottoman ruling class 'who neither plant nor sow, build nor repair,'[4] and to the spiritual and intellectual decay entailed by the Islamic religion's hostility to and unfitness for cultural development.[5] Little wonder that a Serbian author at the end of the nineteenth century appealed to European readers that Islam 'should be uprooted in the interest of culture.'[6]

When Captain Henry Austell visited Istanbul in 1586, he found that 'the great and most stately Citie of Constantinople,' with its superb location and great and sumptuous mosques, was 'to be preferred before all the Cities of Europe.'[7] However, this perspective soon changed. When, early in the seventeenth century, the English poet George Sandys visited the Levant, he found its aspect very promising from afar, but his expectations were much deceived when he entered the city: 'But to say something of Constantinople in generall: I thinke there is not in the world an obiect that promiseth so much a farre off to the beholders, and entered, so deceiueth the expectation. The best of their priuate buildings, inferior to the more contemptible sort of

Bosanski Brod

ours.'[8] After that period, to Western eyes, most Ottoman towns in the Balkans appeared more or less unattractive, despite having a certain charm when first seen from afar, the mosques, minarets and numerous domes intermingling with cypresses and fruit trees to create a fabulous spectacle.[9] When distance had ceased to lend enchantment to the view, most travellers were almost as disappointed at the close-up view as they were delighted with the long shot of Istanbul, the 'Queen of Cities.'[10] In the mid-nineteenth century Théophile Gautier, for instance, explained to his readers that the lovely mirage which had enwrapped the city when seen from the sea, rapidly disappeared upon entering it. 'The paradise was changed into a cloacae,' he avows.[11]

As for 'squalid architecture and filthy dressing,' in the eyes of Western travellers 'all Turkish towns were similar.'[12] Everywhere they have been observing low houses that were built for the most part of wood, nowhere they could perceive a hint of style or any suggestion that a man could be judged by the cleanliness of the house he lived in. In building the towns the natural topography was allowed to remain unaltered; while this made them more picturesque in onlookers' eyes, it was a permanent obstacle to business because the streets were too narrow or too steep and the pavements too rough for transportation, as they had been in many European cities several centuries before.[13] This is how a French traveller from the late seventeenth century described the streets of Istanbul:

the Houses are generally of Wood, and the Streets so narrow, that in the greatest part of 'em two loaded Horses cannot go a-breast. But this is not the greatest inconvenience of their manner of Building; for their Houses jut out so far near the Top, that in several places one may step from one Window to another, and cross the Street without going from his Chamber. This Contrivance of their Houses does not proceed from want of Room, for the City is full of Gardens, and large Courts that are perfectly useless.[14]

That he described the streets of Istanbul with an inspired precision was attested by a British military officer, Peter Henry Bruce, who visited the city a quarter of a century later. According to this account, the sight remained almost unchanged:

the houses are generally built of wood, and the streets so narrow, that in most of them, two loaded horse cannot go a-breast; and the houses project so much at the upper parts, that in many places one may with ease step out of the window of one house into the window of another on the opposite side of the street: this capital error in building the city does not seem to have proceeded from want of room, for it abounds in gardens and large squares and courts.[15]

This point of view underwent a substantial change only at the beginning of the twentieth century. The towns still looked as though nothing was finished and nothing repaired, but the perspective altered: 'A Turkish town in Europe is a Byzantine town; that is to say, it is a scene from the Middle Ages magically preserved to our own days. We are in Fairyland, we are in *The Arabian Nights*, and the wicked djinn has cast a spell upon the land. Let us walk on tiptoe, lest we disturb the enchanted slumber of the Sleeping Beauty of the Wood.'[16]

Many travellers tried to find an acceptable explanation for such a state of affairs. Some imagined that as the ancestors of the Turkish population were a military people, trained in camps and used to camp discipline, they did not care to build great houses, but looked upon their towns only as temporary settlements to be vacated at short notice. The Turks, it was assumed, believed it was a sign of pride to covet sumptuous houses; their argument would be that humans, frail creatures, should not seek any kind of immortality by building everlasting habitations in this life, when they are mere pilgrims on this earth who should use their dwellings as travellers do their inns, merely to be secure from thieves, cold, heat and rain.[17] This theory was refuted by the fact that not only the Turks but also the Greeks, the Jews and the Armenians shunned any architectural display. According to Lady Montague the true explanation was much more prosaic. At the death of its master, every house was at the sultan's disposal and therefore no man cared to take on a great expense from which he was not sure his family would benefit. All they wanted to do was to build a house that would last their lifetime and they were indifferent as to whether it would fall down the year after.[18] Others argued that the Ottomans did not dare to make a display of wealth, because in a country where all men were slaves except one wealth was a dangerous thing. If someone was so fortunate as to accumulate a large sum of money, his first care was to conceal it from view; it would be troublesome and dangerous for him to have a fine house. To save himself problems, the chief dragoman of the Sublime Porte at the beginning of the nineteenth century had his large house painted three different colours in order to make it look like three different houses, so that no one passing by would be struck by its size.[19] The final result was that while the interiors might teem with 'all the luxury that vanity could prompt and money procure,' their external appearance was 'a picture of abject meanness.'[20]

Whatever the reason, the fact remained that all over the Ottoman Empire, wherever Western travellers went it was hard to find a stately home, whatever the wealth of the inhabitants; most people lived in huts or cottages, and while the nobles favoured handsome orchards, gardens and bath houses, their houses had no gatehouses or porches, no courtyards or anything magnificent or worthy of admiration, however large the family. According to nineteenth-century travel reports, this situation changed little. Neatness might be the elegance of poverty, but, supposedly, throughout the Ottoman Empire people despised such a homely ornament. When a building fell into decay, it was first allowed to go from bad to worse, and eventually it was abandoned with little sense of loss.[21]

Not only the external appearance but also the interior of houses all over European Turkey was arranged in the Eastern style, without tables or chairs, without fork and knives, and without mirrors or painted images on the walls. The only decoration might be one or two *yaftes* (illuminated texts).

Balkan cities and towns seemed even more dreary to Western travellers in the nineteenth century for their lack of such urban institutions as museums and theatres, parks and pleasure gardens. There were neither promenades nor 'society' in the European sense; there were only all-male coffee houses.[22] The idea of the seclusion of women survived until the Second World War in the sense that women had to cover their faces when they went out and were not allowed to frequent places of entertainment; this rendered society 'dull and uniform.' Education was available only to men; a woman skilled in reading and writing was spoken of as a prodigy. The focus of social life was the coffee house, where men of leisure assembled to drink coffee and smoke tobacco.[23] The only exception was the capital of Romania, which, in the first half of the

Muslim women

nineteenth century, became notorious as 'the Mecca of pleasure lovers,'[24] on account of its women's reputation being 'as bad as that of Venetians.'[25]

This short survey of Balkan towns clearly shows that their importance has little to do with their achievements in town planning or architecture. It lies more in their production of an environment in which the spirit of the age was manifested. There is no history without a place, and no place without a history. All towns have a history and some of them have a mythology; Balkans towns have histories and mythologies which are often deliberately interwoven. As Peter Ustinov[26] once remarked, Oedipus has long departed, but his complex remains. Achilles has left us his heel; Aphrodite, aphrodisiacs.

Muslim men

Mosques and Minarets

Our imaginary tour begins in the company of Frederic Kregwitz, whom the
Roman Emperor Rudolph II sent to Istanbul with rich presents in the year
1591 as ambassador extraordinary to Sultan Murat III. As Baron Wratislaw
noted in his diary, the legation paid a visit to a Christian church while in the
Hungarian capital.[27] Those Westerners who visited that city in the 1660s
did not think it the fairest in the world, as Sultan Suleiman had in his time,
but they saw a large number of mosques there, their minarets dominating
Buda, and numerous caravanserais and *hammams* (bath houses).[28] Visitors
to the same city in the late eighteenth century could observe huge changes
in its appearance, following the departure of the Ottomans from Hungary:
hammams were the only visible remnant of the Ottoman occupation, as the
mosques had been pulled down.[29] But a few decades later, in the town on the
banks of the Danube which was once 'composed in great part of mere huts,
without lamps, pavement, or any other of the comforts of civilized life,' a
visitor could see 'a range of buildings, which would be admired for the beauty
of their architecture even in the meridian of London, or Paris.'[30] The only
mementoes of Ottoman prowess to be seen in the mid-nineteenth century
were a number of granite balls displayed in the bastion which then served
more peaceful purposes.[31]

Joining James Creagh on his journey through Hungary, Serbia, Bosnia-

Herzegovina, Dalmatia, Montenegro and northern Albania in the summer of 1875, we call Mohacs, a small town in southern Hungary, which at that time still resembled 'more an Asiatic than a European town.'[32]

Before departing for Romania, let us make a short excursion to Croatia, where visitors to Osijek, like the famous Turkish 'globetrotter' of the 1660s, Evliya Çelebi, could count as many as 'sixty-six Muslim houses of prayer.'[33] Companions of the English family who travelled through Imotski at the beginning of the twentieth century would have been able to see for themselves that 'the mosques and Moslem houses had long been replaced by Christian buildings.'[34]

Of course, at this stage it would be premature to draw any conclusions from this – it is better to resume our journey. Bidding farewell to Hungary, we make our next stop at the beginning of nineteenth century in Timişoara, a Romanian town with the reputation of being 'quite French.' Timişoara was taken by Prince Eugene of Savoy for Emperor Charles VI in the year 1716, at which time it was 'miserably built on the Turkish plan.' After being ceded to the Germans, it was totally remodelled and strongly fortified upon 'modern principles;'[35] that is, during the process the town centre entirely disappeared. Even the stone mosques disappeared – two of them were demolished immediately after the conquest and replaced by the modern Franciscan church and the Bishop's Seminary. When in the mid-nineteenth century a member of the Royal Geographical Society of London, who was also British consul-general at Dubrovnik, searched Timişoara and its environs for monuments of the Ottoman period, the only signs of the former masters of Hungary were a tombstone embedded in the wall of an edifice and a small suburb which still bore the Arabic name of Mahala.[36] As described by Andrew Archibald Paton, not only the architecture but the appearance of the inhabitants had changed: 'After the victories of Eugene down fell the minarets of Temisvar and up rose the architecture of the age of Charles VI. The peruke, the cocked hat and the shaven chin took the place of the turban, the bald pate and the bushy beard.'[37]

According to travellers who visited the capital of Romania at the end of the eighteenth century, Bucharest was 'nothing more than a collection of villages, without regularity or plan.' The streets were narrow and paved with planks of wood which were badly fastened and much decayed, so that walking was rendered infinitely tedious. Near the centre of the town there were many rows of open shops, bazaars built according to 'the Turkish plan.'[38] In the 1820s Bucharest was 'the point of union where European and Oriental habits meet; half the inhabitants wear hats and coats, the other half calpacs and pelisses.'[39] With this 'strange mixture of Oriental and European costumes and manners,' it was 'a very interesting place to the picturesque traveller.'[40]

There were some large and handsome buildings in Bucharest, but these were erected 'with true Turkish inconsistency,' and wretched huts and booths were generally to be seen in their immediate neighbourhood, 'prodigal splendour, and squalid misery, jostling each other in all directions.'[41]

In the course of the nineteenth century new ideas prevailed and the French language became universally spoken. French manners and toilettes, French furniture and decorations became the fashion, showing a surprising degree 'of taste and civilisation in an Eastern town so isolated from the rest of the world.' The Europeanised inhabitants of Bucharest forgot their nationality and adopted both the pleasures and the manners of the West. Soon the city became known as 'the little Paris of the East.'[42] After Bucharest became the capital of independent Romania in 1878, its inhabitants achieved a miraculous transformation in its appearance. During renovation works in the second half of the nineteenth century immense changes were made to its layout and architecture, creating a 'city of light,' startling in its beauty, style and brilliance.[43] In the first half of the twentieth century, the streets of Bucharest were thronged with soldiers 'all wearing elaborate uniforms, not one of which remotely resembles another, except for the one common characteristic of dirt.' The women seen walking with the soldiers, or walking together, had little to recommend them. 'They were all of the same type: profusely and coarsely painted and dressed in ill-fitting copies of Parisian clothes.' But those who still wore the traditional costumes were a pleasure to behold:

> What a delightful contrast was the other half of people! The peasants in national costume were not ashamed to mix with the rich, degenerate, and supercilious town dwellers. It was quite a relief to see these magnificent specimens of manhood, with wide-brimmed black hats, embroidered smocks, and bare feet, shoulder to shoulder with effete and painted army officers. And peasant women in their gorgeous multi-coloured dresses formed a refreshing comparison with the cheap and gaudy representatives of the Rumanian bourgeoisie.[44]

In such picturesque company foreign visitors to the newly built Bucharest rarely noticed that it only contained one mosque.[45]

Moving southward, we find history repeating itself many times over. In the seventeenth century Sofia had many mosques, most notably the great mosque in the centre of the town and another in the south, with a magnificent college attached to it; Sofia also had many stately *hans* or caravanserais and exquisite *hammams*.[46] When Bulgaria was constituted as an autonomous principality in 1878 Sofia was portayed as a 'little Constantinople,'[47] but in just a few years it 'almost entirely lost its Eastern aspect.'[48] The 'Turks' folded their tents

Gabrovo (Bulgaria), mid-19th century

'like Arabs and as silently stole away.' They left for other regions still under the sway of the Crescent, only slight traces of their empire remaining. The mosques were demolished to make room for modern buildings or were converted to secular uses as prisons, markets, warehouses or arsenals. At the end of the nineteenth century only one mosque was still in use in the capital, and a few years later it was turned into an archaeological museum. Then, the squalor was swept away. The old houses, never more than two storeys high, overhanging narrow, ill-smelling passages, disappeared as though swept away by fire to make way for bricks and mortar. If in 1878 Sofia was 'a squalid Turkish town' of 11,000 inhabitants, twenty years later it had been almost entirely rebuilt and had paved streets, 'European' buildings and a population of nearly 60,000 souls. Broad new streets and avenues were traversed by a system of electric trams and the whole city had electric lighting. The mosques were pulled down immediately after the liberation. The *muezzins* ceased to call from the minarets; instead church bells summoned the faithful to prayer.[49] The inhabitants were proud of what they had achieved in rebuilding Sofia, and foreign visitors readily acknowledged that the results were so glittering that Istanbul now looked like 'almost an antithesis of Sofia.'[50]

The same thing happened in with most other Bulgarian towns, although as they were smaller than Sofia the results were less noticeable.[51] Western visitors only lamented the fact that part of the Balkans remained under Ottoman control and therefore unchanged.[52]

Our first stop in Greece is Thessaloníki, where in the seventeenth century geographer Haji Khalifa identified 'ten larger or smaller mosques.'[53] On 15 June 1788 Gentleman Bisani counted 'above forty mosques.'[54] At the beginning of the twentieth century, the style of building in Thessaloníki was still 'entirely Turkish.' Until 1918 there were many mosques, worthy of note for their size and antiquity and their numerous elegant minarets, and many other examples of Ottoman architecture contributing to the magnificent aspect of the city. Visitors to Thessaloníki in this period report that no attention was paid to town's cleanliness or convenience, so that dead rats and offal of every kind were left to rot in the blazing sun. They also report that the exterior of the houses was designed to conceal all indication of wealth.[55] Indeed, at the close of the nineteenth century Thessaloníki had 'that unmistakably Eastern look which modern Athens lacks and modern Belgrade has lost.'[56] However, a substantial change in its appearance had already begun and the town was rapidly taking on a new character:

> Near the quay, where are the big hotels and boulevards and the syrup-sippings and the horse tramcars, is a touch of Europe. Within the town the streets are narrow and covered: the bazaars are gloomy and Oriental and smelly – the more Oriental the more smelly. There is the aroma of the East.[57]

In 1914 the hilly districts on the outskirts of the town were still 'uncontaminatedly Turkish,' with their roughly paved narrow streets, jalousied windows and veiled women, with Turks and peasants sitting cross-legged in the shade over their coffee. The Greeks, however, were ashamed of this part of the town and planned a new, improved layout for the city. The Eski mosque was eventually restored as a museum but the other mosques were abandoned to the ravages of time or converted into Orthodox churches.[58]

However, Thessaloníki was not only 'a dirty town,' it was also 'full of Jews.'[59] As remarked by Colmar von Goltz, in the 1890s there were 120,000 inhabitants in Thessaloníki, and 'among them 130,000 Jews.'[60] The Turks could only be seen and the Greeks both seen and heard, but the Jews impinged on the Westerners' 'sense of smell as well.'[61] So it remained until the Second World War when the Germans 'cleansed' Thessaloníki by transporting almost the entire Jewish community to Auschwitz.[62]

Art Lovers on the Acropolis

Visitors to Athens in the seventeenth century would have seen more than 100

Athens, early 19th century

churches in and around the town (most of which were originally temples) but only five mosques.[63] In spite of the prevalence of churches, the external appearance of Athens was Oriental, its multitude of flat roofs interspersed with lofty minarets, cypresses, ruins, single columns and domed mosques. Athens retained its Oriental look until the first half of the nineteenth century, when like other towns in Greece it presented 'a mere cluster of shabby houses, without steeple, or spire, or prominent feature.'[64] After 1834, when the seat of Greek government was transferred to Athens, the walls built round the city during the Ottoman period were pulled down so that the new Hellenic capital could spread. Several streets were opened, levelled and widened, and new buildings sprang up throughout the city. In the phrase of an Anglican priest, the city of Pericles was then 'like the young phoenix of Greece, rising afresh from its parents.'[65] Foreign visitors could purchase a map of Athens showing squares, fountains, theatres and public gardens, but these only existed on paper. By the mid-nineteenth century, however, the Turkish part of Athens had disappeared. Soon all the mosques had either been pulled down or were being used as warehouses.[66] By the second half of the nineteenth century, instead of historic Athens, a modern 'French' town or 'south-German town' of about 50,000 inhabitants could be seen.[67]

Naturally, any trip to Athens must include a visit to the Acropolis, 'ever admired and imitated, and never equalled in beauty,' as Christopher Wordsworth wrote of it.[68] Nowadays, visitors from around the globe flock

The Acropolis

to Athens in their thousands to see the world's most famous ruins, the
Acropolis. However, to see it in its full magnificence visitors would have had
to go before the end of the seventeenth century, in the company of someone
like Francis Vernon[69] or Sir George Wheler,[70] when the temple of Minerva
and the Rotunda were completely intact. They would have been well advised
to take three *okes* or so of coffee with them to bribe the Ottoman authorities
for permission to visit the Acropolis. The more curious of them would have
had some difficulty in making exact measurements of it because the castle of
Athens, in which it stands, served as an Ottoman garrison, and the Ottomans
were 'jealous, and brutishly barbarous' if they noticed anyone measuring it.
Nevertheless, Francis Vernon was able to give exact figures of this and other
Athenian monuments.

   Paganism survived for a long time in Athens, and eventually relinquished
its sacred edifices unharmed to a new religion. Temples to Theseus and the
Virgin Goddess were rededicated to St George and the Virgin Mother. Under
the Ottomans, who took the citadel in 1445, it was converted again, this time
into a mosque. In the conversion the communion table was removed, but a
mosaic picture of the Virgin Mary on the ceiling above the altar, which the
Greeks had added to the temple, escaped destruction until the mid-eighteenth
century on account of a tradition that when a Turk fired a musket at it his
hand immediately withered. A mosque built in the centre of the temple of
Minerva was used as a barracks by Bavarian troops in the 1820s. To take their
revenge on the Muslims its new inmates occasionally endeavoured to force

their horses to defile it. In the 1830s it was converted into a repository for the relics brought to light in the excavations of the Acropolis.[71]

The last and most deplorable episode was carried out in 'a civilised polite age' by a people renowned for patronage of the arts. In 1676, when Sir George Wheler visited Athens, the Parthenon was almost intact: the only dilapidation he noticed was that the statues had fallen from the eastern pediment. On 28 September 1687, however, the Venetian Doge Francesco Morosini laid siege to the Acropolis. His soldiers fired red-hot cannon at the Propylæa and the temple of Minerva. A cannonball destroyed the roof of the temple, ignited some barrels of gunpowder and destroyed for ever what time had spared. After the town fell, Morosini exercised the rights of conquest. Intending to beautify Venice with the spoils of Athens, he attempted to have a group of figures representing Minerva in her triumphal chariot removed from the pediment of the Parthenon. However, the figures were dashed to pieces when the ropes on which they were being lowered broke.[72]

Later, another modern visitor, inspired by love of the arts, finished off the work of destruction which the Venetians had begun. Those parts of the frieze which had survived the explosion, the statues on the pediments and all the metopes remaining on the south side of the temple, were removed by the British ambassador to Greece, Lord Elgin, in 1802. Lord Elgin declared his intention to carry off the little Caryatids of the Erectheum and the metopes of the Parthenon. Allegedly, all the Athenians, including the Turks, lamented the destruction thus committed, and loudly and openly blamed their sovereign for having granted permission for it. The whole scheme was so unpopular in Athens that workers had to be paid more than their usual wages to be persuaded to take part in it.[73]

The damage done to the building in the operation provoked huge debate, some people arguing that European travellers, 'who should have appeared here only as admiring pilgrims, have expressed their veneration in detaching fragments, and transporting them to their ambitious cabinets;' foremost among the guilty was 'stone-monger,' 'marble-dealer' or even 'marble-stealer' Lord Elgin, who had contributed to the destruction of that which 'Goth, and Turk, and Time had spared.' But certain others, mainly British authors, congratulated Lord Elgin for seizing these unrivalled specimens of ancient sculpture and preserving them from further violence and decay, in the safe custody of the British Museum, which thus became, in the words of Adolf Michaelis, 'the most distinguished museum of antiquities in the world, and with the secure prospect of always remaining such.'[74]

The British captain and traveller Edmund Spencer used the following words to reject any 'anti-British' argument by those who doubted that the British Museum was a better place for the work of Phidias and his pupils than its birthplace:

Much has been said and written by foreigners, indeed now and then by some of our countrymen, not very favourable to the character of Lord Elgin and the British Government, for having deprived Athens of so many beautiful works of Grecian art. Those who are so ready to censure, ought to remember that at the date of their removal the Turks were masters of the country, who, in conformity with their Mahometan prejudices regard every representation of the human form divine, as a violation of the second commandment. If therefore Lord Elgin had not removed them, it is highly probable that Turkish bigotry would have destroyed these incomparable friezes. Again, even assuming that Turkish moderation had spared these treasures of art, can it be supposed in the deadly struggle that subsequently took place between the Turks and the Greeks, that either party would have paused to spare any crumbling buildings that stood in their way. With this consideration in view, every admirer of the matchless works of immortal Greece ought to feel deeply indebted to his Lordship, who, in preserving these beautiful friezes, conferred a benefit upon the artist of every country.[75]

Several times in the second half of the nineteenth century representations were made to the British government to restore the Elgin marbles, but they met with the following response: 'When you show yourselves capable of appreciating and taking care of what you still have, England may consent to restore to you the priceless treasures she is now taking charge of, and which are a legacy left to the whole civilised world, and not to one particular people.'[76]

Western art lovers were busy not only in the Acropolis. At the beginning of the nineteenth century a group of British travellers in Mistra in the Peleponnese came across several broken fragments of elegant fluted columns that may once have belonged to a temple to Ceres. Near these relics was a defaced inscription. Allegedly, it was defaced 'by two Frenchmen, who, because they could not read it themselves, chipped it off out of spite to the British travellers.'[77]

Dante and Boccaccio in Albanian Towns

Our last stop before reaching parts of the former Yugoslavia which was also once under Ottoman occupation is Albania and its cities of Tirana and Shköder. Albania became an independent monarchy in 1913, and a process of 'Europeanisation' started there in the 1920s. Tirana was not a particularly impressive place and Western visitors looking round Skanderbeg Square felt themselves 'less in the centre of a capital than in a temporarily and quite accidentally abandoned building site.'[78] Its chief claim to artistic fame was its mosques, which were all beautiful examples of old Byzantine architecture and decoration. The streets were of rough cobbles and most of the houses were single-storeyed. The shops were the wooden boxes 'that could be expected in this part of the world,' and their proprietors sat, Turkish fashion, waiting for custom.[79] In Tirana in 1989 I saw only one mosque, which had long before been converted into a museum.

According to visitors to Shköder in the nineteenth and early twentieth centuries, entering it, despite its numerous mosques, they never seemed to reach 'any town at all.'[80] In short, Shköder was 'a delight to the hunter of the bizarre, but a nightmare to the lover of hygiene, presenting as it does one vast, ever changing panorama of almost grotesque characters. Its Turkish population is perhaps the most picturesque and atrociously dirty on the face of the globe.'[81] But this picture changed completely when Albania became independent in 1913. Visitors to Shköder in the 1930s could admire 'quite a modern town,'[82] though not yet modernised to the same extent as Belgrade and Sofia. But it was already clearly apparent that 'the old life will pass away to be replaced by a bastard civilization which will form a thin veneer over the true manners and customs of the people, just as it does in the other Balkan capitals.'[83]

Europe and Asia Face to Face

Our first stop in former Yugoslavia is Belgrade. Until 1867, when the Ottoman garrison left the fortress of Belgrade, it was 'an Oriental town,'[84] so much so that 'it did not require much stretch of imagination to suppose oneself suddenly set down in the East, or transported to the scenes of one of the tales of the "Arabian Nights."'[85]

In the seventeenth century, visitors to Belgrade could count 100 mosques, ten *hammams*, many *hans*, two *bezestans* and a *caravanserai*.[86] With its domes and minarets and the Turkish flag waving from the fortress, its appearance was as Eastern as its language. It fully deserved its sublime name *Dar al-Jihad* (City of the Holy War or Abode of War for Faith).[87] Visiting Belgrade at the beginning of October 1841, a famous Russian linguist Izmail Sreznevsky was disappointed that among all the mosques he could locate only one church.[88] In 1886, however, Belgrade was already enthusiastically being called the 'Serbian Paris.'[89] Its Europeanisation started in 1718 when the Treaty of Požarevac was signed after Prince Eugene's brilliant victories of the previous year which included the capture of Belgrade. The treaty gave Austria not only the whole of Hungary, but also most of Serbia and Wallachia (now Romania). It was during this period that the French-style Lange Gasse of Belgrade rose amid the swelling domes and pointed minarets.[90] This period, however, did not last for long. In 1812 the Ottomans reconquered Belgrade, and the pace of change eased for a short time. After the departure of the Ottoman garrison, 'Belgrade as the capital... made the largest strides towards claiming its place amongst the civilised centres of Europe.'[91] Some travellers at the time asserted that no city in Europe was making more rapid progress than Belgrade. Within a few years the town had been almost entirely rebuilt, rapidly assuming 'a European character.' The picturesque Turkish and distinctly Serbian houses gave way to the style of Vienna or Pest. The streets were laid out in straight lines crossing each other at right angles; electric trams sped along them. The roads were paved with stone, lit by electricity and lined on both sides with houses several storeys high, the ground floor given over to shops in which goods familiar to Europeans were displayed in large windows. The low single-storey houses, tiny shops and Turkish coffee houses lost ground day by day.[92]

The Serbs used to boast of being the finest of the Balkan peoples; their pride spurred them to make Serbia a modern European state.[93] The Serbs constantly drew the attention of their European visitors to the enormous improvements made since Ottoman times. If those travellers looked for landmarks of local history, they looked in vain. The citadel, two mosques, a few fountains with Turkish inscriptions and a ruined arch called the Gate of Istanbul were the only physical reminders of Muslim domination left at the beginning of the twentieth century. The treaty of evacuation had stipulated that Belgrade's many mosques and cemeteries should be respected but this did not happen. The mosques were closed or used for the vilest purposes; and in the place that was considered sacred by the 'Turks,' their temples were defiled and desecrated by their former subject people.[94] Of Belgrade's many mosques in 1887 an Austrian archaeologist could find only one, and that in a dilapidated state, marking a 'pathetic outpost of a retreating civilisation.' In fact, another mosque, with a chimney, was being used as a gas-store for the National Theatre.[95] Only rarely did European travellers express regret for the destruction of the mosques or suggest that the Serbian government ought to preserve them as signposts of history and architectural jewels.[96]

In the centre of the old part of the city was a large desolate square, which in the mid-nineteenth century had marked the boundary between the Crescent and the Cross; later it was where the daily market was held. This piece of ground was formerly the city's largest Muslim cemetery. In 1868, when the Ottomans left, several metres of soil were removed from some areas to level the ground and paving stones were laid in across it. In 1880 a fountain with an obelisk was erected in the middle of the square in honour of the crown prince.[97] Some 'ultra-patriotic' Serbs levelled to the ground the tomb of Kara Mustafa.[98] Many Turkish families who owned property in Belgrade and had lived there for several generations were summarily evicted from their homes. Nobody spoke up for them and they could find no sympathy in Europe for the simple reason that the Serbs were Christians, the Turks were not.[99]

In Belgrade, as in the other towns mentioned above, 'the retreating Turk' left little behind; in the words of Grace Ellison: 'Venice and Rome have left monuments of exquisite beauty; Austria has left railways: Turkey left destruction and mosques.'[100]

Niš was annexed by Serbia in 1878. Though on the direct route from Paris to Istanbul, the town had remained largely unchanged for three centuries, with its mosques, minarets and wooden dwellings. The municipality now destroyed them to make wide streets and build new stone houses in the Western style. The level of many streets was raised, often bringing them to three metres in depth, which meant that many old houses found themselves below street level and lost their value. The owners had two alternatives: to sell their property at a rock-bottom price or to rebuild their house. They were also faced with the obligation to pave the walkway and one half of the roadway in front of their house.[101] Within a period of less than ten years everything was transformed and had taken on a Western look. 'The victorious sway of the Occident' over Niš transformed its appearance in a few years. Mosques, minarets and winding roads were replaced by squares and straight streets; a new church bloated with cupolas proclaimed its orthodoxy. Two slim minarets alone testified to its Muslim past.[102]

Scenes from the Thousand and One Nights

Podgorica was ceded to Montenegro by the Treaty of Berlin in 1878. Soon after, a new town began to rise on the opposite bank of the river and the market was transferred there. However, even at the beginning of the twentieth century visitors could observe the same 'Turkish life' as that 'in full swing' in Bosnia-Herzegovina.[103] The situation changed little until the Second World War; to visitors in the late 1920s 'it still gave the impression of having more mosques than churches.'[104] This changed during the 'construction of socialism' after 1945.

The Montenegrins conquered Nikšić in 1877, and twenty-five years later 'a tumbledown mosque and some dozen Mohammedan Albanian families' were, as a British woman traveller described it, 'the only traces left in Nikshitje of the Asiatic invader.'[105]

Our first stop in the Republic of Macedonia is the capital, Skopje. In the second half of the seventeenth century, visitors there could see 'a great number of Moshea's or Turkish Churches,'[106] and this panorama remained more or less unchanged till the Balkan Wars. The Ottoman town of Üsküb was a picturesque but sprawling, muddy place.[107] After the Ottomans left, it was apparent to close observers of the Turkish quarter of Üsküb in the 1930s that it was 'an eyesore, and will have to go when the building fever spreads.' Since it was impossible to construct the 'first-class up-to-date town' that Skopje was striving to become, with this 'destitute relation sitting on the front door step' and the 'open sewers of the prehistoric sanitation of Turkish homes,' whole districts of the town were fated to vanish during 'an acute attack of building fever.' Buildings of classical beauty, suited to the local climate and tradition, gradually gave way to a Western architectural style bereft of character. New houses, streets, shops, a fine theatre, a town hall and a military club, trams and many schools appeared with extraordinary rapidity.[108] The local people would explain their zeal for change by saying, for instance: 'We have wasted 500 years and we are now going to make up for lost time.'[109]

The new city of Skopje grew in a manner characteristic of the Balkans: without any regard for the cultural and artistic values of the defeated past. The results of this effort to catch up with Europe as quickly as possible were not always the most desirable:

> It regrettably happened that the Yugoslavs, in their joy at turning out the Turks and becoming masters of Macedonia, pulled down the beautiful mosque that had stood for three centuries in this commanding position, and replaced it by an Officers' Club which is one of the most hideous buildings in the whole of Europe. It is built of turnip-coloured cement and looks like a cross between a fish-kettle and a mausoleum, say the tomb of a very large cod.[110]

Acting in accordance with the mandate given by the European powers, Austria-Hungary occupied Bosnia-Herzegovina in 1878. Although Sarajevo's beautiful setting remained, the city soon lost its appearance of the pre-Austrian epoch, when the people of Bosnia proudly called it 'the Damascus of the North.'[111] In those days the river ran unchecked between its natural banks. On the right bank, set far back, were many houses, each with a garden down to the riverside, making Sarajevo look like one huge garden. They were mostly not laid out in straight lines or crescents on the European model; 'Oriental freedom' reigned, 'intolerant of all monotony.'[112] After the occupation, all this changed. Stone quays were built on either bank of the

Počitelj (Herzegovina), late 19th century

Miljacka river's course through the town, giving it the straight and unpleasant look of a canal. The Ottoman gardens that luxuriated on the right bank were all swept away and replaced by a row of modern buildings. In short, Sarajevo was an Ottoman town, tinkered with and altered to make it look something like of a conventional European city. Before the First World War its architecture and ground plan offered 'a curious combination of the old and the new, the Orient and Occident.'[113] By far its most interesting districts were the old parts, notably the Čaršija. Sarajevo preserved its specificity until the 1990s, but during the siege not only were its inhabitants the victims of a merciless aggressor but the town itself was recreated by 'warchitecture' or, as some authors call it, urbicide.

Sarajevo remained under the control of the Bosnian government, albeit the target of heavy shelling. Though many of its mosques and other monuments of Muslim architecture were badly damaged they defied destruction. But the situation was quite different in towns under the control of the Republika Srpska. Among the mosques destroyed was the Aladža mosque, built in 1588, which was blown up after Foča was 'liberated.' The Aladža mosque was one of the most beautiful in Bosnia, and according to Evliya Çelebi was a more astoundingly graceful structure than had been 'built by any architect before on planet Earth.'[114] An even more appalling fate befell Banja Luka where, in 1993, all the mosques were razed to the ground, including the mosque of

Ferhad Pasha built in 1579, and, for many, the most beautiful and perfect
example of its kind in the country.[115] After the mosques had been demolished
their sites were mechanically levelled in groundwork for new buildings and
roads. A Serbian student in Banja Luka, commenting on the demolition of
the mosque of Ferhad Pasha, said that after it had been blown up, there was
a clear view of the town as the minaret no longer concealed it. When asked
why the Kastel had not also been demolished as it had been converted into
an arsenal and cannon store by Ferhad Pasha and then turned into a fortress
during the second half of the sixteenth century, she replied that, 'The fortress
was built on Roman foundations, and we respect their culture. For one thing,
we are Christians like them.'[116]

When the Turks overran Bosnia in the middle of the fourteenth century
Banja Luka, then a small village, began to thrive and eventually became a very
important town.[117] Although several attempts were made in the first half of
the twentieth century to turn it into a 'Christian' town it remained 'Turkish,'
as demonstrated by its forty-five mosques.[118]

The history of the Balkans thus explains why no architectural style worthy
of note can be traced between the ruins of the classical period and the
characterless buildings of the last century. Palaces and other solid buildings
arose, a few modern avenues and broad streets and an extended network of
tramlines were constructed, but during the process the Balkan towns lost their
pronounced architectural character. They all have wide, clean streets, solid
houses built of stone, a town hall or something more or less equivalent to
one, a marketplace and a church built as an outward and visible sign that this
land was Christian, not for any architectural merit. Even the smallest towns
in European Turkey in which Muslims lived had public baths. When they left,
the baths were no longer maintained or were even deliberately destroyed.[119]
Bath houses, aqueducts and even fountains built by the Ottomans have
vanished from Athens and Bucharest, Belgrade and Plovdiv, Pirot and Vranje,
and everywhere else. In Serbia, for instance, all traces of the Turks have been
wiped out so thoroughly that even the Turkish name of the Serbian capital,
which was under Turkish control from 1521 to 1867, has sunk into oblivion.
The contemporary Serbian author Miljana Laketić, writing in 1995 about the
history of the Serbian capital in the Belgrade magazine *Duga*, claimed that she
had been unable to discover its Turkish name.[120]

What 'modern' Balkan people liked was a perfectly straight street in which
all the houses were as similar as possible, on the European model of the
beginning of the twentieth century. As a British diplomat at the end of the
nineteenth century, William Miller, put it:

No one, of course, can defend the taste of the German architects, who laid out modern Athens on the model of Munich, and planted a brand-new European city by the side of the majestic ruins of antiquity. The wide streets, entirely destitute of shade, make the town in summer a veritable inferno, while the glare from the marble houses is most trying to the eye.[121]

There was no place for the mosque and minaret in the new architecture. They were perceived as symbols of a bygone age, indeed as symbols of backwardness,[122] as were all other Ottoman architectural features. In the southern republics of former Yugoslavia even 'the coffee houses of the lazy ones,' where once upon a time the 'Turks' congregated, were knocked down after the Second World War to make room for 'progress.'[123]

The Ousting of the Balkan spirit

In the middle of the nineteenth century, the Balkans at last became 'Balkan,' looking like a copy or even a caricature of western Europe. There was nothing original about the Balkan towns, nothing individual. Everything was borrowed. Instead of having their own identity the exteriors and interiors of dwellings, workshops and offices, and also the dress of the townspeople, followed fashions from Paris, Pest or Vienna. It was fashionable to look 'European' and this is what everyone tried to do. Townspeople affected a taste for modern art, modern music, the tango and the foxtrot, and ridiculed the songs and costumes of the peasants.[124] But Westerners saw them not as their equals but still as Eastern Other, though without their former charm:

> What a charming place Constantinople would be, were it a little less, or a great deal more, civilised! It is just too much European to be pleasant, and not enough so to make it perfection.[125]

However hard Easterners tried to look Western, travellers from the West often found them outlandish and ridiculous. When the sultan himself adopted a hussar jacket made in Paris and white kerseymere trousers trimmed with gold lace, some commented that 'an "infidel" could hardly have fancied a masquerade more calculated to make the Prophet's vicegerent appear ridiculous.'[126] The simple fact was that the Ottomans were called barbarians when they did not conform to Western ways; when they imitated the West, they were called rogues.[127] Ottoman ladies, sure enough, dressed their hair like 'a perfect caricature of some way in which it was worn in Paris or London a year ago, and consider themselves leaders of fashion.'[128] But even Balkan

Christians did not fare much better. When a new palace was built for the
Greek king in Athens, it was ridiculed as

> an enormous edifice of plaster, in a square containing six houses, three
> donkies, no roads, no fountains (except in the picture of the inn);
> backwards it seems to look straight to the mountain – on one side is
> a beggarly garden – the kings go out to drive (revolutions permitting)
> at five – some four and twenty blackguards saunter up to the huge
> sandhill of a terrace, as his majesty passes by in a gilt barouche and an
> absurd fancy dress.[129]

And some years later another traveller observed that the Greek army aped the
French, but were just 'a burlesque of the original.[130]

In spite of all the changes, the modern Balkan towns that grew exuberantly
on the ruins of the old ones were full of defects noticeable everywhere.
Modern houses, many of them only one storey high and mainly built of brick
encased in white plaster, gave an air of tawdry grandeur to the towns where
visitors experienced the lack of good hotel accommodation, drainage, lighting
and so on that make up 'the present-day ideas of comfort.'[131] British visitors
at the beginning of the twentieth century, for instance, informed their readers
that someone once argued with them that Niš would eventually develop into
a fine city. They agreed, 'for its situation is all that could be desired, but every
house of it would have to be pulled down first.'[132] At that time an anecdote
circulated in western Europe about a young Romanian who boasted to his
French friends that Bucharest was a little Paris, only to receive the immediate
retort: 'Perhaps – but thank God Paris is not a large Bucaresti!'[133]

The price of modernisation, that is 'Europeanisation,' was high: the history
embodied in mosques, minarets, bazaars, *hans*, graveyards, bridges, homes and
so on was destroyed as new ones, which substituted historic monuments with
'the ugliness of modernism,'[134] were rapidly built instead. Losing their former
appearance, the towns of the Balkans lost their spirit; losing their spirit,
they lost their history. The image was new but hollow. Western travellers
were the first to notice that the brand new Balkan towns and cities were
paved 'with good intentions, and nothing else.'[135] In the Balkan towns there
were practically no fine old buildings to be seen, for those built during the
Ottoman occupation were destroyed and the modern ones were more or less
'economical imitations of French and British buildings.'[136] Walking in their
streets, Westerners were able to admire some 'notable creations of the new
era' on the one hand and 'the other relics of an age that has already vanished
in western Europe' on the other.[137] The Balkans were trying hard to be
European and modern, and prove themselves so to the world. Since Europe

A Catholic couple from Bosnia, late 19th century

was seen as a foil to the Turks and as endowed with all conceivable positive attributes, the East was judged on its similarity to or difference from the West. To be less like Europe was to be Other, inferior, and to be more like Europe was to advance.[138] Or, as a Bosnian bey explained to Consul Gil'ferding: 'Well, long ago I realised that we, the Bosnians, are stupid people, that we know and understand nothing, but Germans and French and other nations, live well. From them I carried over whatever I could.'[139]

In former times a visitor to a Balkan town would be transported to 'the gorgeous East,' with mosques and minarets, veiled women and men in brilliant costumes with baggy knickerbockers, jackets and fezzes; only a few wore European dress. Christians were not immediately distinguishable from

Muslims by their dress. In Belgrade, for instance, in 1875 men still generally wore the fez, and with their general appearance and pompous display of old-fashioned firearms and knives they could easily be mistaken for Muslims.[140] In Bitola, Shköder and other Balkan capitals in the nineteenth century the women, whether Muslim or Christian, scrupulously concealed their faces; any woman who ventured out unveiled would became the target of insult, as appearing barefaced meant total loss of reputation.[141] But alongside changes in architecture, customs were changing too. An American missionary to the Mediterranean recorded that in the summer of 1827 the wives of the sultan and other ladies of rank appeared in public dressed entirely in the French style.[142] Others followed suit, the only exceptions being the Bosnian Muslims who retained Eastern dress even after the Young Turks had exchanged it 'for a monkey-like imitation of Europe.'[143] These changes failed to make a favourable impression on Western observers who thought that Muslims should never adopt European costume. The same men who appeared 'to be somebody' in the turban and voluminous garments of the East, reportedly, had an air 'of any thing but a gentleman' when wearing a European suit.[144]

The change was vast, and the Balkans was 'Europeanised' – outwardly. As we have seen, the most radical changes were in urban architecture and fashion. This outward change might have been expected to bring about a complete Europeanisation of the Balkan people: once they and their towns had become outwardly indistinguishable from 'others in Europe,' it was supposed that they would acquire all the other qualities that had brought prosperity to the Western world – without, of course, adopting its vices. However, where food and coffee houses were concerned, the Ottoman legacy seemed to be much more tenacious. More strenuous efforts were made to de-Ottomanise in the ideological sphere (popular beliefs, customs, attitudes, value system). But, as a British expert on the Balkans observed, a people cannot discard all its time-honoured habits at once:

> Though it has been the Turk's for five hundred years, he has set no visible mark upon it. Roughly speaking, he has spent those five centuries in camping out on it temporarily as an army of occupation! Nothing is more surprising about him than the speed with which all visible signs of his existence can be wiped out, but the stain he has left upon the souls of the people is, alas! harder to erase.[145]

For instance, one of the most important representatives of so-called Serbian Socialism, Dimitrije Tucović, writing on poverty in Serbia in 1902, described how once upon a time the 'lofty landlords' wearing jackets of crimson velvet embroidered with gold or silver rode 'spirited Arabs' striking sparks on the *kaldrmi* when they went to coffee houses or bazaars. As Benedetto Ramberti recorded in the sixteenth century, the Turks took great delight in their horses.[146] A good horse remained the most prized possession of the Turks until they left the Balkans.[147] On the other hand, according to an old rule Christians were not permitted to enter a town on horseback, nor were they permitted to bear arms or exhibit garments of too bright a hue. As late as the first half of the nineteenth century it was a strictly obeyed rule that the *rayah* halted as a lordly Muslim approached and dismounted as he passed by.[148]

Lattice windows were removed and the walls that surrounded houses in Balkan towns were demolished, but in domestic life new customs were adopted at a much slower pace. When Martin Gjurgjević visited an acquaintance, a Serbian merchant in Pristina, the host brought his young wife from the harem, unveiled, to kiss the visitor's hand, telling him that he had not done 'something like this before.' Apart from this woman, Gjurgjević saw no other unveiled in the town.[149]

Ottoman domination – or tyranny – was social as well as political, and not only manners and morals but also social life were deeply affected by it. Nevertheless, it is a singular fact that no determined attempt was made to assimilate the Balkan peoples to the Ottoman way of life or to Islam during all those centuries of occupation: 'Mahomet did not abuse his victory. The religious tolerating spirit of the Turks was seen in his first act. He left to the Christians their churches and the liberty of public worship; he maintained the Greek patriarch in his office.'[150]

A prominent natural scientist of the sixteenth century, Pierre Belon, was clearly impressed by the fact that 'the Turks force nobody to live according to the Turkish way, but all Christians are allowed to follow their own law.'[151] The Ottomans did not try to assimilate their subject peoples, and in this respect they differed greatly from the contemporary governments of western Europe. Where the Ottoman Empire followed a policy of non-interference, the European governments made every effort to extinguish the national spirit and the mother-tongue of their subject peoples.[152] In comparison, the attitude of the Porte towards the various creeds professed by its Christian subjects had 'ever been one of quite exceptional tolerance.'[153] Mother of the secretary at the British Embassy in Istanbul praised this tolerance: 'In no other country would unbelievers be appointed to the highest offices as in Turkey, where we find Christians not only among the Ministers, but among the Ambassadors, who of course must be trusted with the most important state secrets.'[154]

Notwithstanding its theocratic structure, the Ottoman Empire allowed the practice of any religion making the Balkans under its rule a vibrant example of multiculturalism: lands where 'all the nationalities of the world' carried on their normal lives as if 'immediately after the fall of the Tower of Babel.'[155]

Gypsy puppet theatre in the Balkans

It is well known that about 170,000 Jews were given asylum and granted freedom to practise their religion in Istanbul, Thessaloníki, Sarajevo and other Ottoman towns after they were expelled by the Spanish monarchs Ferdinand and Isabella in 1492.[156] According to a seventeenth-century French traveller, in the whole Ottoman Empire, 'no places but Athens and Trebizond have preserved the privilege of excluding the Jews, though the Turkish officers have attempted several times to introduce them.'[157] It is less well known that there was once a large Trappist monastery, Marija Zvijezda, near Banja Luka. The monks had been expelled from France during the Revolution; they first took refuge in Germany but were driven out in 1868. As no Christian state was willing to take them in, they asked and received the sultan's permission to purchase land in the neighbourhood of Banja Luka and build their monastery there.[158] Even less known is the story of the Spanish Admiral Don Ferrante Gonzaga. He captured Hercegnovi in 1538 and built the chapel of St Anna there but the following year the Ottomans retook the town. They not only spared the chapel but gave permission in 1550 for the body of their old enemy Don Ferrante to be buried there beside his wife and son.[159]

In 1788 an Italian traveller expressed great surprise at the religious tolerance he witnessed during his stay in Istanbul:

A stranger, who has beheld the intolerance of London and Paris, must be much surprised to see a church here between a mosque and a synagogue, and a dervise by the side of a capuchin friar. I know not how this government can have admitted into its bosom religions so opposite to its own. It must be from degeneracy of Mahommedanism, that this happy contrast can be produced. What is still more astonishing is to find that this spirit of toleration is generally prevalent among the people; for here you see Turks, Jews, Catholics, Armenians, Greeks, and Protestants conversing together, on subjects of business or pleasure, with as much harmony and good will as if they were of the same country and religion.[160]

In Sarajevo in the 1920s, Lester George Hornby witnessed a Bosnian peasant of the Orthodox faith dropping a coin into the begging-bowl of a blind Muslim squatting at the entrance to a mosque playing his *gusle*. Glancing at the peaceful little stalls where Muslims, Christians and Jews mingled at their work, each able to go his own way to cathedral, mosque or synagogue, he wondered 'if tolerance is not one of the greatest of virtues.'[161] The rash of new buildings and the many lasting symbols of the Balkan people's break with their 'unspeakable past' did not signify their happy reunion with Europe but marked the end of a specific Balkan history. As Mrs Scott-Stevenson put it, the Eastern lands restored to Western civilisation lost their picturesque quality but kept their dirt and squalor.[162] As soon as the Ottomans left, Europeanisation became the order of the day and the old Balkan spirit died. In the process, mythology replaced history; tolerance and multiculturalism were its first victims.[163]

We have seen how vigorously the people of 'the mountainous peninsula' struggled to progress and how splendid were the results of their efforts to Europeanise. But in the process the quality that present-day Europe proudly claims as its foremost virtue was eliminated: tolerance of diversity. Travellers on our Balkan tour may in addition notice a curious fact: while the Balkans is now making every effort to be part of Europe as it once was, Europe now defines itself on the basis of its difference from the East, the Balkans included, and claims to be what the Balkans used to be for centuries.

Notes

Chapter 1

1. Cf. *Eremiten, Reise nach dem Orient*, vol. I, p. 95; A. Boué, *La Turquie d'Europe*, vol. I, p. 4.
2. F. Calvert, *A Tour to the East, In the Years 1763 and 1764*, p. 139.
3. J. B. S. Morritt, The Letters of John B. S. Morrit of Rokeby, p. 65.
4. L. Hugonnet, *La Turquie inconnue*, pp. 25–6; J. Cvijić, *Nekolika promatranja o etnografiji makedonskih Slovena*, p. 3–4; see also A. Boué *La Turquie d'Europe*, vol. I, p. 90–7; H. Barth, *Reise durch das innere der Europäischen Türkei im Herbst 1862*, pp. 23, 117; and K. Braum-Wiesbaden, *Reise-Eindrücke aus dem Südosten*, vol. III, pp. 229–30.
5. See e.g. F. de Beaujour, *Voyages militaire dans l'Empire Othoman*, vol. I, p. 467; G. Keppel, *Narrative of a Journey across the Balcan*, vol. II, p. 10; G. T. Temple, *Travels in Greece and Turkey*, vol. II, p. 146; M. Marmont, *The Present State of the Turkish Empire*, p. 126; A. W. Kinglake, *Eōthen*, p. 32; C. White, *Three Years in Constantinople*, vol. I, p. vii; F. R. Chesney, *The Russo-Turkish Campaigns of 1828 and 1829*, pp. 26, 43, 53–4; A. F. Macintosh, *A Military Tour in European Turkey, the Crimea, and on the Eastern Shores of the Black Sea*, vol. I, pp. 92, 100, 103; A. Slade, *Records of Travels in Turkey and Greece, etc.*, pp. 160, 190, 192, 200; G. W. Valentini, *Description of the Seat of War in European Turkey*, p. 10; N. W. Senior, *A Journal kept in Turkey*, pp. 141–2; H. Leach, *A Bit of Bulgaria*, p. 34; F. S. Russell, *Russian Wars with Turkey*, pp. 64, 69–70, 104, 263; H. M. Hozier, *The Russo-Turkish War*, pp. 481–2; J. S. Stuart-Glennie, *Europe and Asia*, pp. 272, 277; J. Cuthbertson, *Sacred and Historic Lands*, p. 247; H. M. Field, *The Greek Islands and Turkey after the War*, p. 158; W. Huyshe, *The Liberation of Bulgaria*, pp. 84, 140; N. Buxton, *Europe and the Turks*, p. 30; E. Pears, *Forty Years in Constantinople*, pp. 26, 32.
6. J. O. Noyes, *Roumania*, p. 348.
7. B. Ruland, *Orient Express*, p. 27.
8. E. Scopetea, 'Greek and Serbian Enlightenment', p. 201.
9. T. Arnold, *History of Rome*, p. 492.
10. M. A. Walker, *Old Tracks and New Landmarks*, p. 252.
11. H. M. Brailsford, *Macedonia: Its Races and Their Future*, p. 263.
12. J. C. Hobhouse, *A Journey through Albania and other Provinces of Turkey in Europe and Asia, to Constantinople, during the years 1809 and 1810*, p. 585.

13. R. Walsh, *A Residence at Constantinople*, vol. I, p. 141.
14. N. Angell, *Peace Theories and the Balkan War*, p. 26.
15. H. Sandwith, *Notes on the South Slavonic countries in Austria and Turkey in Europe*, p. 25; S. G. St. Clair and C. A. Brophy, *A Residence in Bulgaria*, p. v.
16. A. J. Evans, *Illyrian Letters*, p. 26.
17. E. L. V. de Laveleye, *The Balkan Peninsula*, p. 127.
18. A. Upward, *The East End of Europe*, p. xvii.
19. H. C. Woods, *Washed by Four Seas*, pp. xiii-xiv.
20. H. Blount, *A Journey into the Levant*, p. 1.
21. E. Browne, *A Brief Account of some Travels in Hungaria, Servia, Bulgaria, Macedonia, Thessaly, Austria, Styria, Carinthia, Carniola, and Fruili*, p. 69.
22. J. Fuller, *Narrative of a tour through some parts of the Turkish Empire*, p. 25.
23. R. and K. Bruce, *Letters from Turkey*, p. 34.
24. N. Buxton, *Europe and the Turks*, p. 19.
25. A. W. Kinglake, *Eöthen*, pp. 3–4.
26. J. B. Fraser, *A Winter's Journey*, vol. I, p. 70.
27. J. Kristeva, *Strangers to Ourselves*, p. 201; M. Van De Port, *Gypsies, War, and other Instances of the Wild*, pp. 153–4.
28. R. D. Kaplan, *Balkan Ghosts*, p. xxiii.
29. H. F. Tozer, *Researches in the Highlands of Turkey*, vol. I, p. 233; C. N. E. Eliot, *Turkey in Europe*, p. 353; R. Wyon, *The Balkans from Within*, p. 423; R. Trevor, *My Balkan Tour*, pp. 31–2; A. Moore, *The Orient Express*, p. 210.
30. A. Grisebach, *Reise durch Rumelien und nach Brussa im Jahre 1839*, vol. II, p. 236; A. A. Paton, *Servia, the youngest member of the European family*, p. 216; N. W. Senior, *A Journal kept in Turkey*, p. 318; K. Braum-Wiesbaden, *Reise-Eindrücke aus dem Südosten*, p. 101; E. F. Knight, *Albania. A Narrative of Recent Travel*, p. 54; W. Miller, *Travels and Politics in the Near East*, p. xiii, 58; H. Renner, *Durch Bosnien und die Hercegovina kreuz und quer*, pp. 86, 485; H. O. Dwight, *Constantinople and its Problems*, p. 188; H. Vivian, *The Servian Tragedy with some Impressions of Macedonia*, p. 289; M. E. Durham, *The Burden of the Balkans*, p. 4; R. Trevor, *My Balkan Tour*, pp. 15, 31–2; R. Hichens, *The Near East*, p. 54; W. Morgan, *The New East*, p. 223; G. Melas, *The Turk as he is*, pp. 51–2; F. Thierfelder, *Schichsalstunden des Balkan*, p. 10; I. T. Sanders, *Balkan Village*, p. 69.
31. W. M. Leake, *Researches in Greece*, p. viii; H. A.V. Post, *A Visit to Greece and Constantinople*, p. 99; R. Pashley, *Travels in Crete*, vol. I, p. 65; H. Barth, *Reise durch das innere der Europäischen Türkei im Herbst 1862*, p. 105; D. Urquhart, *The Spirit of the East*, vol. I, pp. 422–3; L. Heuzey and H. Daumet, *Mission archéologique de Macédoine*, p. 321; A. Moore, *The Orient Express*, pp. ix, 178, 219, 236; R. Graves, *Storm Centres of the Near East*, p. 259.
32. G. J. Grelot, *A late voyage to Constantinople*, p. 78.
33. A. Hill, *A Full and Just Account of the Present State of The Ottoman Empire In all its Branches*, p. 149.
34. C. Thompson, *The Travels Of the Late Charles Thompson, Esq*, vol. II, p. 10.
35. W. Lithgow, *A Delectable, and true discourse, of an admired and painefull peregrination from Scotland, to the most famous Kingdomes in Europe, Asia, and Affricke*, H 3 – c.
36. A. Hill, *A Full and Just Account of the Present State of The Ottoman Empire In all its Branches*, p. 94.
37. H. O. Dwight, *Constantinople and its Problems*, p. 159.
38. J. C. Hobhouse, *A Journey through Albania and other Provinces of Europe and Asia, to Constantinople, during the years 1809 and 1810*, p. 830.
39. J. Galt, *Voyages and Travels, in the Years 1809, 1810, and 1811*, p. 282.

40. M. Todorova, *Imagining the Balkans*, p. 64.

41. R. Burton, *A Pilgrimage to Mecca and Medina*, vol. I, p. 84.

42. S. Kapper, *Südslavische Wanderungen im Sommer*, vol. I, p. 60; E. About, *Greece and the Greeks of the Present Day*, p. 29; K. Braum-Wiesbaden, *Reise-Eindrücke aus dem Südosten*, vol. III, p. 224; F. Kanitz, *Das Königreich Serbien und das Serbenvolk von der Römerzeit bis zur Gegenwart*, vol. I, p. 394; O. M. Aldridge, *The Retreat from Serbia Through Montenegro and Albania*, p. 16; A. Melik, *Do Ohrida in Bitolja*, p. 93; Earl of Cardigan, *Youth goes East*, pp. 135, 150; L. Kuba, *Cteni o Makedonii*, p. 15; M. Burr, *Slouch Hat*, p. 118; F. Bevk, *Deset dni v Bolgariji*, p. 79.

43. M. Golczewski, *Der Balkan in deutschen und österreichischen Reise- und Erlebnisberichten*, p. 194.

44. See e.g. A. Gil'ferding, *Poëzdka po Cercegovine, Bosnii i Staroj Serbii*, pp. 76–9, 120, 101–2.

45. G. F. Abbott, *The Tale of a Tour in Macedonia*, pp. 43–4, 276.

46. Ibid., p. 276.

47. T. Bevan, *The Insurgent Trail*, p. 35.

48. Jezernik, 'Zigeunerlager on the planet Auschwitz,' p. 352.

49. E. A. Brayley Hodgetts, *Round about Armenia*, p. 17.

50. See e.g. N. W. Senior, *A Journal kept in Turkey*, p. 286; F. Fox, *The Balkan Peninsula*, p. 167.

51. R. Pashley, *Travels in Crete*, vol. I, p. 232; F. W. Newman, *Personal Narrative, In Letters, Principally from Turkey, In the Years 1830 – 3*, pp. 113, 117; S. G. St. Clair and C. A. Brophy, *A Residence in Bulgaria*, p. 24; W. Forsyth, *The Slavonic Provinces South of the Danube*, p. 170; R. and K. Bruce, *Letters from Turkey*, p. 9; A. F. Townshend, *A Military Consul in Turkey*, pp. 60–1.

52. J. Creagh, *Over the Borders of Christendom and Eslamiah*, vol. II, p. 147.

53. See e.g. J. Burbury, *A Relation of a Journey of the Right Honourable My Lord Henry Howard*, p. 140; T. Smith, *Remarks Upon the Manners, Religion and Government of the Turks*, p. 12; J. B. Tavernier, 'Persian Travels', p. 45; P. Lucas, *Voyage du sieur Paul Lucas fait en M.DCCXIV*, vol. I, p. 31; A. Gislenius, *Travels into Turkey*, p. 22; R. G. Boscovich, *Giornale di un Viaggio da Constantinopoli in Polonia*, p. 7; C. F. Sutherland, *A Tour up the Straits, from Gibraltar to Constantinople*, p. 194; M. Jenour, *The Route to India*, p. 18; H. Holland, *Travels in the Ionian Isles*, p. 207; J. Hamilton, *Researches in Asia Minor, Pontus, and Armenia*, p. 120; W. Wratislaw, *Adventures of Baron Wenceslas Wratislaw of Mitrowitz*, pp. 27–9; P. de Fresne-Canaye, *Le Voyage du Levant (1573)*, pp. 23, 40; P. Mundy, *The Travels in Europe, 1608 – 1628*, p. 53.

54. T. Comyn-Platt, *The Turk in the Balkans*, p. 84.

55. L. Dunne, *A Trip to Constantinople*, p. 7.

56. A. Gil'ferding, *Poëzdka po Gercegovine, Bosnii i Staroj Serbii*, p. 91.

57. H. Sandwith, *Notes on the South Slavonic countries in Austria and Turkey in Europe*, p. 20.

58. J. G. Stephens, *Incidents of Travel in Greece, Turkey, Russia, and Poland*, vol. I, p. 160; J. G. C. Minchin, *The Growth of Freedom in the Balkan Peninsula*, p. 353; M. Burr, *Slouch Hat*, p. 267.

59. See e.g. L. Glück, *Albanien und Macedonien*, p. 44; W. Miller, *Travels and Politics in the Near East*, p. 180; W. E. Curtis, *The Turk and His Lost Provinces*, p. 199; M. M. Holbach, *Bosnia and Herzegovina*, pp. 107–8; B. Ruland, *Orient Express*, p. 13.

60. B. Ruland, *Orient Express*, p. 34; V. Goldsworthy, *Inventing Ruritania*, pp. 79, 103.

61. See e.g. A. de Vere, *Picturesque Sketches of Greece and Turkey*, vol. I, pp. 194–5.

62. A. Moore, *Orient Express*, p. 171.

63. G. F. Abbott, *The Tale of a Tour in Macedonia*, p. 4; W. E. Curtis, *The Turk and His Lost*

Provinces, p. 191; Earl of Cardigan, *Youth goes East*, p. 195; B. Newman, *Tito's Yugoslavia*, p. 18.

64. L. James, *With the Conquered Turk*, p. 30; T. Allen, *The Tracks They Trod*, p. 37.
65. B. Ruland, *Orient Express*, p. 13.
66. R. Chandler, *Travels in Asia Minor*, pp. 223, 230.
67. M. Šamić, *Francuski putnici u Bosni na pragu XIX stoljeća i njihovi utisci o njoj*, p. 182.
68. C. Pertusier, *La Bosnie considérée dans ses rapports avec l'empire Ottoman*, p. 94; cf. e.g. F. de Beaujour, *Voyages militaires dans l'Empire Othoman*, vol. I, pp. 416–7.
69. See e.g. J. de Thevenot, *The Travels of the Monsieur de Thevenot into the Levant*, p. 57; T. Smith, *Remarks Upon the Manners, Religion and Government of the Turks*, p. 5; N. Bisani, *A Picturesque Tour Through Part of Europe, Asia and Africa*, p. 44; E. Dodwell, *A Classical and Topographical Tour through Greece*, vol. I, p. 270; T. S. Hughes, *Travels in Siciliy, Greece and Albania*, p. 393; C. Pertusier, *La Bosnie Considérée dans ses rapports avec l'empire Ottoman*, pp. 95–6; C. C. Frankland, *Travels to and from Constantinople, in the years 1827 and 1828*, vol. I, p. 110; R. R. Madden, *Travels in Turkey, Egypt, Nubia, and Palestine, in 1824, 1825, 1826 and 1827*, vol. I, pp. 13–14; H. A. V. Post, *A Visit to Greece and Constantinople, in the year 1827–8*, p. 320; H. Bagge, *Reise nach dem Orient, der Europäischen, Türkei, Aegypten, Nubien und Palastina*, p. 55; A Lady, *Wayfaring Sketches among the Greeks and Turks*, p. 265; A. Smith, *A Month in Constantinople*, p. 124; S. Novaković, *Dva dana u Skoplju*, p. 39; V. Jelavić, 'Kratki francuski putopis kroz Hercegovinu i novopazarski sandžak iz godine 1611,' p. 337.
70. J. C. Hobhouse, *A Journey through Albania and other Provinces of Turkey in Europe and Asia, to Constantinople, during the years 1809 and 1810*, p. 823; J. J. Best, *Excursions in Albania*, p. 270; S. G. St. Clair and C. A. Brophy, *A Residence in Bulgaria*, p. 231; H. E. H. Jerningham, *To and from Constantinople*, p. 188; M. Müller, *Letters fom Constantinople*, p. 15; C. R. Cockerell, *Travels in Southern Europe and the Levant*, pp. 32–3, 112; A. Upward, *The East End of Europe*, p. 119; G. F. Abbott, *Under the Turk in Constantinople*, pp. 65–6.
71. J. Porter, *Observations on the Religion, Law, Government and Manners of the Turks*, p. 3.
72. H. A. Brown, *A Winter in Albania*, p. 90.
73. B. Ramberti, *Libri tre delle cose de Turchi*, p. 52; Quiclet, *Les voyages de M. Quiclet a Constantinople par terre*, pp. 65–6; E. Browne, *A Brief Account of some Travels in Hungaria, Servia, Bulgaria, Macedonia, Thessaly, Austria, Styria, Carinthia, Carniola, and Fruili*, p. 71; P. du Fresne-Canaye, *Le Voyage du Levant*, p. 30.
74. H. E. H. Jerningham, *To and from Constantinople*, p. 211.
75. J. B. S. Morritt, *The Letters of John B. S. Morritt of Rokeby*, p. 195.
76. See e.g. A. Chaumette, *Voyage en Bosnie dans les années 1807 et 1808*, p. 13; C. Pertusier, *La Bosnie considérée dans ses rapports avec l'empire Ottoman*, pp. 75, 86–7; E. Spencer, *Travels in European Turkey in 1850*, vol. II, p. 73; E. L. V. de Laveleye, *The Balkan Peninsula*, p. 85.
77. M. Šamić, *Francuski putnici u Bosni na pragu XIX stoljeća i njihovi utisci o njoj*, p. 221.
78. M. M. Holbach, *Bosnia and Herzegovina*, pp. 234–5.
79. See e.g. W. Turner, *Journal of a Tour in the Levant*, vol. I, pp. 88, 122; J. Fuller, *Narrative of a Tour through some parts of the Turkish Empire*, p. 23; J. Carne, *Letters fom the East*, vol. II, p. 312; M. J. Quin, *A Steam Voyage down the Danube*, vol. I, p. 91; G. Cochrane, *Wanderings in Greece*, vol. II, p. 238; W. W. Smith, *A Year with the Turks*, p. 198; H. E. H. Jerningham, *To and from Constantinople*, p. 85; J. S. Stuart-Glennie, *Europe and Asia*; L. Hugonnet, *La Turqie inconnue. Roumélie, Bulgarie, Macédoine, Albanie*, pp. 83, 1357; E. L. V. de Laveleye, *The Balkan Peninsula*, pp. 88–9; W. M. Ramsay, *Everyday Life in Turkey*, p. 168; F. K. Hutchinson, *Motoring in the Balkans*, p. 276.
80. W. W. Smith, *A Year with the Turks*, p. 198.
81. B. Ramberti, *Libre tre delle cose de Turchi*, p. 52.

82. E. L. V. de Laveleye, *The Balkan Peninsula*, pp. 168–9.
83. F. Kanitz, *Das Königreich Serbien und das Serbenvolk von der Römerzeit bis zur Gegenwart*, vol. III, p. 446.
84. E. Browne, *A Brief Account of some Travels in Divers Parts of Europe*, p. 34.
85. R. Burton, *Love, War and Fancy*, p. 238.
86. E. Çelebi, *Putopis*, pp. 208–9.
87. S. Purchas, *Relations of the world and religions observed in all ages*, p. 246.
88. J. de Thevenot, *The Travels of the Monsieur de Thevenot into the Levant*, p. 57.
89. C. N. E. Eliot, *Turkey in Europe*, p. 15; G. F. Abbott, *The Tale of a Tour in Macedonia*, p. 56.
90. E. Freeman, *The Ottoman Power in Europe*, p. 202.
91. M. E. Durham, *Twenty Years of Balkan Tangle*, p. 128; cf. W. W. Smith, *A Year with the Turks*, pp. vi-vii; W. H. C. Price, *The Balkan Cockpit*, p. 22.
92. M. E. Durham, *Twenty Years of Balkan Tangle*, p. 96.
93. R. Semple, *Observations on A Journey through Spain and Italy to Naples*, vol. II, pp. 221–2.
94. F. Calvert, *A Tour to the East, In the Years 1763 and 1764*, pp. 131–2.
95. C. C. Frankland, *Travels to and from Constantinople, in the years 1827 and 1828*, vol. I, p. 192.
96. F. Hervé, *A Residence in Greece and Turkey*, vol. II, p. 172.
97. M. Šamić, *Francuski putnici u Bosni na pragu XIX stoljeća i njihovi utisci o njoj*, pp. 265–6.
98. A. Chaumette, *Voyage en Bosnie dans les années 1807 et 1808*, p. 3.
99. A. J. Evans, *Through Bosnia and Herzegovina during the insurrection in 1875 on foot*, p. xcvi.
100. E. J. Lloyd, *British Journalists' tour in the Adriatic & Bosnia*, p. 35.
101. E. L. V. de Laveleye, *The Balkan Peninsula*, p. 96.
102. R. Munro, *Rambles and Studies in Bosnia-Herzegovina*, p. 395.
103. I. Sanderson, *Sundrie the personall Voyages performed by Iohn Sanderson of London, Merchant*, p. 1620; R. Withers, *The Grand Signiors Serraglio*, p. 1585; M. Baudier, *The History of the serrail, and of the Court of the Grand Seigneur, Emperour of the Turks*, p. 44; J. C. Hobhouse, *A Journey through Albania and other Provinces of Turkey in Europe and Asia, to Constantinople, during the years 1809 and 1810*, p. 999: P. du Fresne-Canaye, *Le Voyage du Levant*, p. 235; P. Mundy, *The Travels in Europe, 1608–1628*, p. 37; M. H. Omont, *Voyages a Athenes, Constantinople et Jerusalem de Francois Arnaud*, p. 7.
104. E. Barton, 'A description of a Voiage to Constantinople and Syria'; R. Walsh, *A Residence at Constantinople*, vol. II, pp. 296–7.
105. S. Crow, *Subtilty and Cruelty*, p. 13; P. Rycaut, *The History of the Turkish Empire From the Year 1623 to the Year 1677*, p. 75; H. N. Brailsford, *Macedonia: Its Races and Their Future*, p. 16.
106. A. Gislenius, *Travels into Turkey*, p. 137.
107. C. Haga, *A Trve Declaration of the ariuall of Cornelius Haga*, p. 6; R. Withers, *The Grand Signiors in Sarraglio*, p. 1585; M. Baudier, *The History of the serrail, and of the Court of the Grand Seigneur, Emperour of the Turks*, p. 44; J. Burbury, *A Relation of a Journey of the Right Honourable My Lord Henry Howard*, p. 156; T. Smith *RemarksUpon the Manners, Religion and Government Of the Turks*, p. 11; P. Rycaut, *The Present State of the Ottoman Empire*, p. 84; E. Veryard, *An Account on divers Choice Remarks, as well Geographical, as Historical, Political, Mathematical, Physical, and Moral*, p. 344; A. Hill, *A Full and Just Account of the Present State of the Ottoman Empire In all its Branches*, p. 154; J. P. Tournefort, *A Voyage into the Levant*, vol. I, p. 397; N. Rolamb, 'A relation of a Journey to Constantinople', p. 684; Tollot, *Nouveau voyage fait au Levant, ès années 1731 & 1732*, p. 285; J. Porter, *Observations on the Religion, Law, Government and Manner of the Turks*, p. 171; W. Eton, *A Survey of the Turkish Empire*, p. 112; G. Larpent, *Turky; Its History and Progress*, vol. I, p. 295.

108. E. Habesci, *The Present State of the Ottoman Empire*, p. 344; W. Eton, *A Survey of the Turkish Empire*, p. 111; J. C. Hobhouse, *A Journey through Albania and other Provinces of Turkey in Eurpe and Asia, to Constantinople, during the year 1809 and 1810*, pp. 996–7; W. Turner, *Journal of a Tour in the Levant*, vol. I, pp. 56–7; R. Walsh, *A Residence at Constantinople*, vol. I, p. 358; M. Marmont, *The Present State of the Turkish Empire*, p. 20; A. Slade, *Records of Travels in Turkey and Greece, etc.*, p. 165.

109. M. Baudier, *Histoire generall dv Serrail, et de la Covr Du Grand Seigneur Empereur de Turcs*, p. 39.

110. See e.g. I. Kukuljević, *Putovanje po Bosni*, p. 111.

111. J. Du Mont, *A New Voyage to the Levant*, p. 262.

112. W. Eton, *A Survey of the Turkish Empire*, pp. 195–6; C. C. Frankland, *Travels to and from Constantinople, in the years 1827 and 1828*, vol. I, pp. 191–2; E. Spencer, *Turkey, Russia, the Black Sea, and Circassia*, p. 158; W. Denton, *The Christians of Turkey*, p. 181; E. L. V. de Laveleye, *The Balkan Peninsula*, p. 138; F. Kanitz, *Das Königreich Serbien und das Serbenvolk von der Römerzeit bis zur Gegenwart*, vol.I, p. 420.

113. See e.g. H. H. Leech, *Letters of a Sentimental Idler*, p. 30; B. Schwarz, *Montenegro*, p. 92; E. L. V. de Laveleye, *The Balkan Peninsula*, p. 141; M. E. Durham, *Through the Lands of the Serb*, p. 240; M. M. Patrick, *Under Five Sultans*, p. 172.

114. See e.g. R. J. Curzon, *Visits to Monasteries in the Levant*, p. 244; J. O. Noyes, *Roumania*, p. 81; L. Dunne, *A Trip to Constantinople*, p. 7; B. Jaeckel, *The Lands of the Tamed Turk or the Balkan States Today*, p. 155; F. Kanitz, *Das Königreich Serbien und das Serbenvolk von der Römerzeit bis zur Gegenwart*, vol. I, pp. 322, 346; H. G. Dwight, *Constantinople, Old and New*, p. 31; W. Gordon, *A Woman in the Balkans*, p. 246.

115. See e.g. J. Lloyd, *British Journalists' tour in the Adriatic & Bosnia*, p. 41.

116. A. J. Evans, *Through Bosnia and Herzegovina during the insurrection in 1875 on foot*, pp. 311–2.

117. D. Walshe, *With the Serbs in Macedonia*, p. 201.

118. K. Bercovici, *The Incredible Balkans*, p. 46.

119. G. M. Mackenzie and A. P. Irby, *Travels in the Slavonic Provinces of Turkey-in-Europe*, p. 179.

120. F. Moore, *The Balkan Trail*, p. 58.

121. R. Burgess, *Greece and the Levant*, vol. II, p. 283.

122. N. Elias, *The History of Manners*, pp. 121–4.

123. F. Hervé, *A Residence in Greece and Turkey*, vol. II, pp. 216–7. See also E. About, *Greece and the Greeks of the Present Day*, p. 293.

124. G. F. Abbott, *The Tale of a Tour in Macedonia*, pp. 52–3; C. Matthews, *Experiences of a Woman Doctor in Serbia*, p. 80.

125. M. Baring, *Letters from the Near East 1909 and 1912*, p. 128.

126. J. P. de Tournefort, *A Voyage into the Levant*, vol. II, p. 79.

127. N. Elias, *The History of Manners*, p. 126.

128. J. G. Wilkinson, *Dalmatia and Montenegro: with a Journey to Mostar in Herzegovina*, vol. II, p. 130.

129. E. Browne, *A Brief Account of some Travels in Hungaria, Servia, Bulgaria, Macedonia, Thessaly, Austria, Styria, Carinthia, Carniola, and Friuli*, p. 80.

130. H. J. Boemus, *The Fardle of facions conteining the annciente maners, customes, and Lawes, of the peoples enhabiting the two partes of the earth, called Affrike and Asie*; T.Glover, 'The Journey of Edward Barton, Esq.', p. 1295; J. Burbury, *A Relation of a Journey of the Right Honourable My Lord Henry Howard*, p. 181; E. Browne, *A Brief Account of some Travels in Hungaria, Servia, Bugaria, Macedonia, Thessaly, Austria, Styria, Carinthia, Carniola, and Friuli*, p. 80; J. de Thevenot, *The Travels of the Monsieur de Thevenot into the Levant*, p. 47; A. Hill,

A Full and Just Account of the Present State of the Ottoman Empire In all its Branches, p. 122.
131. J. P. de Tournefort, *A Voyage into the Levant*, vol. II, p. 49.

Chapter 2

1. E. Veryard, *An Account on divers Choice Remarks, as well Geographical, as Historical, Political, Mathematical, Physical, and Moral*, p. 343.
2. J. Du Mont, *A New Voyage to the Levant*, p. 262.
3. A. Russell, *The Natural History of Aleppo*, p. 173; G. Keppel, *Narrative of a Journey across the Balcan*, vol. II, p. 421; Mrs Pardoe, *The City of the Sultan*, vol. I, p. 24; C. White, *Three Years in Constantinople*, vol. III, pp. 91–2; F. Elliot, *Diary of an Idle Woman in Constantinople*, pp. 307–8; F. Moore, *The Balkan Trail*, p. 175.
4. B. Ramberti, *Libri tre delle cose de Turchi*, p. 28.
5. T. Smith, *Remarks Upon the Manners, Religion and Government of the Turks*, pp. 147–8.
6. E. Veryard, *An Account of divers Choice Remarks, as well Geographical, as Hisorical, Political, Mathematical, Physical, and Moral*, p. 343.
7. J. Du Mont, *A New Voyage to the Levant*, p. 262.
8. J. P. Tournefort, *A Voyage into the Levant*, vol. I, p. 354.
9. T. Comyn-Platt, *The Turk in the Balkans*, p. 104.
10. E. Lear, *Journals of a Landscape Painter in Albania, etc.*, p. 144.
11. A. Chaumette, *Voyage en Bosnie dans les années 1807 et 1808*, pp. 51–2.
12. See e.g. W. Biddulph, *The Travels of certaine Englishmen*, p. 65; G. Sandys, *A relation of a iourney begvn Anno Dom. 1610*, p. 65; F. Moryson, *Itinerary*, vol. III, p. 119; M. Baudier, *Histoire générale du sérail et de la cour du grand seigneur empereur des Turcs*, p. 33; T. Glover, 'The Journey of Edward Barton, Esq.', p. 1296; R. Withers, *The Grand Signiors Serraglio*, p. 1584; L. Des Hayes, *Voiage de levant Fait par le Commandement dv Roy en lannée 1621*, pp. 63, 137; J. Burbury, *A Relation of a Journey of the Right Honourable My Lord Henry Howard*, pp. 121–3, 185–7; P. Rycaut, *The Present State of the Ottoman Empire*, p. 84; J. de Thevenot, *The Travels of the Monsieur de Thevenot into the Levant*, p. 33; J. Du Mont, *A Voyage to the Levant*, p. 262; E. Veryard, *An Account on divers Choice Remarks, as well Geographical, as Historical, Political, Mathematical, Physical, and Moral*, p. 343; C. Bruyn, *A Voyage to the Levant*, p. 93.
13. J. T. Bent, *Early Voyages and Travels in the Levant*, pp. 261–2.
14. T. Smith, *Remarks Upon the Manners, Religion and Government of the Turks*, p. 187.
15. See e.g. A. Hill, *A Full and Just Account of the Present State of the Ottoman Empire In all its Branches*, p. 118; N. Bisani, *A Picturesque Tour Through Part of Europe, Asia and Africa*, p. 38; J. Montague, *A Voyage Perfomed by the Late Earl of Sandwich Round the Mediterranean in the Years 1738 and 1739*, p. 165; J. Morier, *A Journey through Persia, Armenia, and Asia Minor, to Constantinople, in the Years 1808 and 1809*, p. 366; W. Macmichael, *Journey from Moscow to Constantinople, in the years 1817, 1818*, p. 143; W. Turner, *Journal of a Tour in the Levant*, vol. I, p. 45.
16. T. H. Hughes, *Travels in Greece and Albania*, vol. II, p. 51.
17. W. Hunter, *Travels in the Year 1792 through France, Turkey, and Hungary, to Vienna*, p. 283.
18. R. Walsh, *Narrative of a Journey from Constantinople to England*, pp. 157–8.
19. G. F. Abbott, *Under the Turk in Constantinople*, p. 142.
20. See e.g. C. Thompson, *The Travels Of the Late Charles Thompson, Esq.*, vol. II, p. 146; R. Walsh, *Narrative of a Journey from Constantinople to England*, p. 158; Mrs Pardoe, *The City of the Sultan*, vol. I, p. 24; J. Davy, *Notes and Observations on the Ionian Islands and Malta*, vol. II, p. 418; J. G. Wilkinson, *Dalmatia and Montenegro*, vol. II, p. 118; N. P. Willis, *Summer Cruise in the Mediterranean*, p. 240; W. Knighton, *European Turkey*, p. 28; M. A. Walker, *Through Macedonia to the Albanian Lakes*, p. 253; M. E. Durham, *High Albania*, p. 142.

21. R. R. Madden, *Travels in Turkey, Egypt, Nubia, and Palestine, in 1824, 1825, 1826 and 1827*, vol. I, pp. 47–8.
22. C. Hamlin, *Among the Turks*, pp. 175–6.
23. Mrs Pardoe, *The City of the Sultan*, vol. I, p. 71.
24. F. de Tott, *Memoirs of the Baron de Tott, on the Turks and the Tartars*, vol. I, p. 123.
25. See e.g. W. Turner, *Journal of a Tour in the Levant*, vol. I, p. 265; T. S. Hughes, *Travels in Greece and Albania*, vol. II, p. 48; T. Alcock, *Travels in Russia, Persia, Turkey, and Greece*, p. 170; R. Walsh, *A Residence at Constantinople*, vol. II, p. 311; R. T. Claridge, *A Guide along the Danube*, p. 133; M. Marmont, *The Present State of the Turkish Empire*, p. 39; A. Boué, *La Turquie d'Europe*, vol. II, p. 399; E. Spencer, *Travels in European Turkey in 1850*, vol. I, p. 363; W. Knighton, *European Turkey*, p. 37; Lady Hornby, *Constantinople during the Crimean War*, pp. 251–2, 330–1; R. J. More, *Under the Balkans*, pp. 201, 204; C. Hamlin, *Among the Turks*, p. 176.
26. A. Slade, *Records of Travels in Turkey and Greece*, p. 254.
27. T. Gautier, *Constantinople*, p. 116.
28. See e.g. C. White, *Three Years in Constantinople*, vol. III, p. 95; A. Gil'ferding, *Poëzdka po Gercegovine, Bosnii i Staroj Serbii*, p. 52; F. Elliot, *Diary of an Idle Woman in Constantinople*, p. 307.
29. A. Gil'ferding, *Poëzdka po Gercegovine, Bosnii i Staroj Serbii*, p. 52.
30. Ibid. pp. 80–1.
31. H. C. Barkley, *Between the Danube and the Black Sea*, p. 94.
32. N. W. Senior, *A Journal kept in Turkey*, p. 228.
33. R. Walsh, *A Residence at Constantinople*, vol. II, p. 311; Mrs Pardoe, *The City of the Sultan*, vol. I, p. 237; A. Gil'ferding, *Poëzdka po Gercegovine, Bosnii i Staroj Serbii*, p. 24; E. M. Pearson and L. E. McLaughlin, *Service in Serbia under the Red Cross*, p. 96; S. L. Poole, *The People of Turkey*, vol. II, pp. 34, 36; G. F. Abbott, *The Tale of a Tour in Macedonia*, pp. 254–5.
34. H. H. Leech, *Letters of a Sentimental Idler*, pp. 79–80.
35. A. Slade, *Records of Travels in Turkey and Greece*, p. 164.
36. J. S. Stuart-Glennie, *Europe and Asia*, p. 344.
37. R. Wyon, *The Balkans from Within*, p. 36.
38. P. Thornton, *Dead Puppets Dance*, p. 26.
39. N. Buxton, *Europe and the Turks*, p. 10.
40. N. Elias, *The History of Manners*, p. 99.
41. M. A. Walker, *Through Macedonia to the Albanian Lakes*, p. 250.
42. P. Edmonds, *The Land of the Eagle*, p. 169; cf. Earl of Cardigan, *Youth goes East*, p. 81.

Chapter 3
1. W. Raleigh, 'The English voyages of the sixteenth century', p. 100.
2. G. L. Buffon, 'How to Study Natural History', p. 161.
3. A. Cronia, *La conoscenza del mondo slavo en Italia*, pp. 305–6.
4. A. Fortis, *Viaggio in Dalmazia*, vol. II, p. 162.
5. Ibid., vol. II, p. 31.
6. See e.g. G. L. C. de Buffon, *Natural History*, pp. 325–6.
7. A. Fortis *Viaggio in Dalmazia*, vol. II, pp. 30–1.
8. A. Fortis, *Saggio d'osservazioni sopra l'isola di Cherso ed Osero*, p. 109; *Viaggio in Dalmazia*, vol. II, pp. 12, 14, 68.
9. A. Fortis, *Viaggio in Dalmazia*, vol. I, p. 131.
10. Ibid., vol. II, p. 10.
11. Ibid., vol. II, p. 79.

12. Ibid., vol. II, p. 30.
13. Ibid., vol. II, p. 47.
14. Ibid., vol. II, p. 2.
15. Ibid., vol. II, p. 31.
16. Ibid., vol. II, p. 30.
17. A. Fortis, *Saggio d'osservazioni sopra l'isola di Cherso ed Osero*, pp. 77–8.
18. Ibid., p. 102.
19. Ibid., p. 107.
20. S. Johnson, *The Philosophick Mirror*, vol. I, p. 93.
21. A. Fortis, *Viaggio in Dalmazia*, vol. I, p. 18, vol. II, pp. 119, 124; cf. *Saggio d'osservazioni sopra l'isola di Cherso ed Osero*, p. 117.
22. A. Fortis, *Viaggio in Dalmazia*, vol. II, p. 117.
23. Ibid., vol. I, p. 153, vol. II, pp. 59–60.
24. A. Fortis, *Saggio d'osservazioni sopra l'isola di Cherso ed Osero*, pp. 39–40.
25. J. G. Wilkinson, *Dalmatia and Montenegro*, vol. I, p. 41.
26. Ibid., vol. I, p. 49.
27. A. Fortis, *Saggio d'osservazioni sopra l'isola di Cherso ed Osero*, p. 113.
28. A. Fortis, *Travels into Dalmatia*, p. 543.
29. A. Fortis, *Viaggio in Dalmazia*, vol. II, p. 159.
30. A. Fortis, *Travels into Dalmatia*, p. 508.
31. A. Fortis, *Saggio d'osservazioni sopra l'isola di Cherso ed Osero*, p. 135.
32. A. Fortis, *Viaggio in Dalmazia*, vol. I, p. 131.
33. Ibid., vol. II, p. 179.
34. Ibid., vol. I, vol. VII, pp. 131–2; cf. A. Fortis, *Saggio d'osservazioni sopra l'isola di Cherso ed Osero*, p. 68.
35. A. Fortis, *Viaggio in Dalmazia*, vol. I, p. 31.
36. Ibid., vol. I, p. 160.
37. Ibid., vol. I, p. 161.
38. C. Gozzi, *Memorie inutile*, vol. I, pp. 67–70; cf. I. Reinsberg-Düringsfeld, *Aus Dalmatien*, vol. I, p. 1.
39. R. H. R., *Rambles in Istria, Dalmatia and Montenegro*, pp. 105–6.
40. A. Fortis, *Saggio d'osservazioni sopra l'isola di Cherso ed Osero*, pp. 43–4.
41. A. Fortis, *Viaggio in Dalmazia*, vol. I, p. 134.
42. A. Fortis, *Travels into Dalmatia*, p. 510.
43. A. Fortis, *Viaggio in Dalmazia*, vol. I, p. 15.
44. Ibid., vol. I, p. 162.
45. L. F. Cassas, *Travels in Istria and Dalmatia*, p. 74; see also F. de Beaujour, *Voyages militaire dans l'Empire Othoman*, vol. I, p. 382.
46. J. G. Wilkinson, *Dalmatia and Montenegro*, vol. II, pp. 6–7.
47. Ibid., vol. I, pp. 244–5.
48. Ibid., vol. I, p. 245; cf. G. Wheler, *A Journey into Greece*, p. 25; A. Fortis, *Viaggio in Dalmazia*, vol. II, p. 167.
49. M. Mirković, *Ekonomska historija Jugoslavije*, pp. 63–4.
50. A. Fortis, *Viaggio in Dalmazia*, vol. I, p. 52.
51. L. F. Cassas, *Travels in Istria and Dalmatia*, p. 8.
52. T. Allason, *Picturesque views of the antiquities of Pola and Istria*, p. 56.
53. J. G. Wilkinson, *Dalmatia and Montenegro*, vol. II, p. 173.
54. M. E. Durham, *High Albania*, p. 212.
55. A. Fortis, *Travels into Dalmatia*, p. 235.
56. A. Fortis, *Viaggio in Dalmazia*, vol. I, pp. 67–8; cf. L. F. Cassas, *Travels in Istria and*

Dalmatia, p. 9.

57. Ibid., vol. I, p. 59.

58. A. Cronia, *La conoscenza del mondo slavo in Italia*, pp. 307 f., 331 f.

59. A. Fortis, *Viaggia in Dalmazia*, vol. I, p. 81.

60. G. Lovrich, *Osservazioni di Giovanni Lovrich sopra diversi pezzi del Viaggio in Dalmazia del signor abate Alberto Fortis coll' aggiunta della vita di Socivizca*, pp. 69–70.

61. A. A. Paton, *Highlands and Islands of the Adriatic*, vol. II, p. 32.

62. Cf. S. Johnson, *The Prince of Abissinia*, p. 88; G. L. C. de Buffon, *Natural History*, vol. IV, p. 18; D. B. Jelliffe and E. F. P. Jelliffe, *Human Milk in the Modern World*, p. 170.

63. G. Lovrich, *Osservazzioni di Giovanni Lovrich sopra diversa pezzi del Viaggio in Dalmazia del signor abate Alberto Fortis coll' aggiunta della vita di Socivizca*, pp. 81–2.

64. A. Fortis, *L'abate Fortis al Signor Giovanni Lovrich*.

65. Ibid., p. v; cf. P. Sclamer, *Sermone parenetico di Pietro Sclamer Chersino al Signor Giovanni Lovrich*, p. 24.

66. A. Fortis, *Viaggio in Dalmazia*, vol. I, p. 56; vol. II, p. 144; cf. L. F. Cassas, *Travels in Istria and Dalmazia*, p. 10.

67. G. L. Buffon, *Natural History*, vol. IV, p. 193.

68. A. Fortis, *Viaggio in Dalmazia*, vol. I, p. 57.

69. Ibid., vol. II, p. 191.

70. A. A. Paton, *Highlands and Islands of the Adriatic*, vol. II, p. 33.

71. O. Dapper, 'Kaffraria or Land of the Kafris, otherwise named Hottentots', p. 45.

72. Cf. I. Schapera and B. Farrington, *The Early Cape Hottentots*, p. 268.

73. J. Ogilby, *Africa*, p. 590.

74. G. Fritsch, *Die Eingeborenen Süd-Afrika's*, p. 25.

75. G. E. Lessing, *Laookon*, p. 250.

76. See e.g. A. Montagu, *An introduction to Physical Anthropolgy*, p. 432; T. Lang Teslow, 'Reifying race', p. 75.

77. P. Hazard, *Evropska misel v XVIII. stoletju*, p. 343; S. L. Gilman, *Difference and Pathology*, p. 83.

78. G. Tachard, *A Relation of a Voyage to Siam*, p. 67.

79. S. Kern, *Anatomy and Destiny*, p. 97; R. Perry, 'Colonizing the breast', p. 131.

80. E. Tyson, *Orang-Outan, sive Homo Sylvestris*, p. 26.

81. M. Miles, 'The Virgin's one bare breast', p. 204; P. Weideger, *History's Mistress*, p. 60; cf. W. Eton, *A Survey of the Turkish Empire*, p. 346.

82. J. P. de Tournefort, *A Voyage into the Levant*, vol. II, p. 70.

83. E. Shorter, *A History of Women's Bodies*, p. 29.

84. P. Weideger, *History's Mistress*, pp. 59–60.

85. J. G. Wilkinson, *Dalmatia and Montenegro*, vol. I, p. 174.

86. J. Swift, *Travels into several Remote Nations of the World*, vol. IV, p. 9.

87. J. Rousseau, *A Discourse upon the Origin and Foundation of the Inequality among Mankind*, p. 3.

88. G. L. Buffon, *Natural History*, vol. III, p. 284.

89. J. Swift, *Travels into several Remote Nations of the World*, vol. IV, p. 120.

90. Ibid., vol. IV, p. 124.

91. G. L. Buffon, *Natural History*, p. 327.

92. S. Johnson, *The Philosophick Mirror*, vol. I, p. 73.

93. Ibid., pp. 73–4.

94. A. Fortis, *Viaggio in Dalmazia*, vol. I, p. 61; cf. G. Sandys, *A relation of a iourney begvn Anno. Dom. 1610*, p. 3; G. Wheler, *A Journey into Greece*, p. 9.

95. J. G. Wilkinson, *Dalmatia and Montenegro*, vol. II, pp. 363–4; S. Peričić, *Dalmacija uoči pada*

Mletačke Republike, p. 205.

96. D. Goldring, *Dream Cities*, p. 157.

97. E. F. Knight, *Albania*, p. 35; A. J. Evans, *Illyrian Letters*, p. 61; D. Goldring, *Dream Cities*, p. 166.

98. J. P. Barry, *At the Gates of the East*, p. 222.

99. W. I. Monson, *Extracts from a Journal*, p. 62.

100. R. Hichens, *The Near East*, p. 5.

101. H. Baerlein, *The Birth of Yugoslavia*, vol. II, p. 329.

102. R. Biasutti, *Le razze e i popoli della terra*, vol. II, p. 80.

103. Ibid., vol. II, pp. 324–6.

Chapter 4

1. P. Thornton, *Ikons and Oxen*, pp. 274–5.

2. Ibidem.

3. G. L. Buffon, *The Natural History of Animals, Vegetables, Minerals, &c.*, vol. I, p. 196.

4. C. Linnaeus, *Systema naturae*, 29.

5. Ptolemy, book 7, chap. iii, p. 157.

6. G. Neilson, *Caudatus Anglicus: A mediæval slander*, p. 2.

7. J. Bale, *The Actes of Englysh votaryes*, p. 76.

8. M. Polo, *The Travels of Marco Polo, a Venetian in the Thirteen Century, Being a Description, By That Early Traveller, of Remarkable Places and Things, in the Eastern Parts of the World*, p. 612.

9. J. Struys, *The Perillous and most Unhappy Voyages*, p. 57; G. F. Gemelli Careri, *Giro del Mondo*, vol. II, p. 67.

10. See e.g. U. Aldrovandi, *Monstrorum historia*, p. 12.

11. See e.g. W. Marsden *The History of Sumatra*, p. 35.

12. See e.g. F. de Castelnau, *Renseignements sur l'Afrique Centrale et sur une nation d'hommes a queue qui s'y trouverait, d'après le rapport des négres du Soudan, esclaves a Bahia*, p. 6; L. Ducouret, *Voyage au pais des Niams-Niams ou les homes a queue*, p. 35; d'Escayrac de Lauture, *Mémoire sur le Soudan*, p. 51; L Ch. Cuny, *Observations générales sur le Mémoire sur le Soudan de M. le comte d'Escayrac de Lauture*, p. 6; P. Garbiglietti, *I Pigmei della favola di Omero gli Akkà dell'Africa equatoriale*, p. 15.

13. L. Ducouret, *Voyage au pais des Niams-Niams ou les homes a queue*, p. 30.

14. G. Schweinfurth, *The Heart of Africa*, vol. II, p. 2.

15. L. Ducouret, *Voyage au pais des Niams-Niams ou les homes a queue*, p. 20.

16. J. Verne *Cinq semaines en ballon. Voyage de découvertes en Afrique*, p. 151.

17. P. Gleisberg, *Kritische Darlegung der Urgeschichte des Menschen nach Carl Vogt*, p. 33.

18. See e.g. G. Schweinfurth, *The Heart of Africa*, vol. II, p. 2; C. Chaillé Long, *Central Africa: naked truth of naked people*, p. 267.

19. C. Chaillé Long, *Central Africa: naked truth of naked people*, p. 267.

20. Cit. G. Neilson, *Caudatus Anglicus: A mediæval slander*, pp. 35–6.

21. A. Zimmerman, *Anthropology and Antihumanism in Imperial Germany*, p. 79.

22. G. Neilson, *Caudatus Anglicus: A mediæval slander*, p. 2.

23. H. H. Johnson, *Reminiscences of the Near East (1891–1913)*, p. 220.

24. Ibid., p. 221.

25. V. Georgevitch, *Die Albanesen und die Großmächte*, p. 4.

26. P. Siebertz, *Albanien und die Albanesen*, p. 186.

27. I. Jastrebov, *Stara Serbija i Albanija*, p. 226.

28. H. A. Brown, *A Winter in Albania*, pp. 235, 241.

29. Ibid., p. 175.

30. Ibid., p. 198.

31. B. Jezernik, *Non cogito ergo sum*, p. 93.

32. P. Gay, *The Cultivation of Hatred*, p. 82.

33. V. Đorđević, *Kuda si se uputila Austrijo?*, p. 6.

34. Ibid., p. 8.

35. P. H. B. Salusbury, *Two Months with the Tchernaieff in Servia*, p. 83.

36. See e.g. J. W. Gambier, *Servia*, p. 90; G. Marcotti, *Il Montenegro e le sue donne*, p. 21; V. Bérard, *La Macédoine*, p. 36; H. S. Edwards, *Sir William White*, pp. 83, 92; H. C. Woods, *War and Diplomacy in the Balkans*, p. 42; F. Valoušek, *Vzpominky na Bosnu*, pp. 122, 133, 138.

37. C. A. Dako, *Albania*, p. 165; A. N. Dragnich and S. Todorovich, *The Saga of Kosovo*, p. 109.

38. W. Peacock, *Albania, the foundling state of Europe*, p. 176; C. A. Dako, *Albania*, p. 57.

39. M. Baring, *Letters from the Near East 1909 and 1912*, p. 136.

40. R. W. Lane, *The Peaks of Shala*, pp. 14–5.

41. R. G. D. Laffan, *The Guardians of the Gate*, pp. 139–40.

42. C. A. Dako, *Albania*, p. 129.

43. S. Novaković, *Balkanska pitanja i manje istorijsko-političke beleške o Balkanskom poluostrvu 1886–1905*, p. 311; J. Tomić, *Rat na Kosovu i Staroj Srbiji 1912. godine*, p. 37; R. G. D. Laffan, *The Guardians of the Gate*, pp. 52, 138; W. Peacock, *Albania, the foundling state of Europe*, p. 202; J. Macdonald, *Turkey and the Eastern Question*, p. 88; H. C. Woods, *The Danger Zone of Europe*, p. 43; *War and Diplomacy in the Balkans*, p. 14; E. Bouchié de Belle, *La Macédoine et les Macédoinens*, p. 243; D. Alastos, *The Balkans and Europe*, p. 25; E. C. Helmreich, *The Diplomacy of the Balkan Wars 1912–1913*, p. 425.

44. R. G. D. Laffan, *The Guardians at the Gate*, p. 129.

45. See e.g. W. Peacock, *Albania, the foundling state of Europe*, p. 202; J. Macdonald, *Turkey and the Eastern Question*, p. 88; H. C. Woods, *The Danger Zone of Europe*, p. 43; *War and Diplomacy in the Balkans*, p. 14; R. G. D. Laffan, *The Guardians of the Gate*, p. 138; E. Bouchié de Belle, *La Macédoine et les Macédoinens*, p. 243; D. Alastos, *The Balkans and Europe*, p. 25; E. C. Helmreich, *The Diplomacy of the Balkan Wars 1912–1913*, p. 425.

Chapter 5

1. F. C. Pouqueville,*Travels in the Morea, Albania, and other parts of the Ottoman Empire*, p. 114.

2. A. Gil'ferding, *Poězdka po Gercegovine, Bosnii, i Staroj Serbii*, pp. 230, 313.

3. W. Denton, *Servia and the Servians*, pp. 90, 148, 197, 211.

4. I. Jastrebov, *Stara Serbija i Albanija*, p. 27.

5. N. P. Kondakov, *Makedonija*, pp. 131, 178.

6. F. Kanitz, *Das Königreich Serbien und das Serbenvolk von der Römerzeit bis zur Gegenwart*, vol. II, pp. 296, 358.

7. G. M. Mackenzie and A. P. Irby, *Travels in Slavonic Provinces of Turkey-in-Europe*, vol. I, pp. 195–6; M. E. Durham, *Through the Lands of the Serb*, p. 219; *The Burden of the Balkans*, p. 122; *The Struggle for Scutari*, p. 91; A. and C. Askew, *The Stricken Land*, p. 64.

8. G. M. Mackenzie and A. P. Irby, *Travels in Slavonic Provinces of Turkey-in-Europe*, vol. I, pp. 195–6.

9. R. Burton, *Love, War and Fancy*, p. 122.

10. M. Orbini, *Il regno de gli slavi*, pp. 271, 326, 357, 440.

11. V. Marković, *Pravoslavno monaštvo i monastiri u srednjevekovnoj Srbiji*, p. 36.

12. L. Glück, *Albanien und Macedonien*, p. 47.

13. Carnegie Endowment, *Report of the International Commisssion to inquire into the Causes and Conduct of the Balkan Wars* (1914), p. 105.
14. M. E. Durham, *High Albania*, p. 297.
15. M. Meslin, *Eye*, p. 236.
16. M. Orbini, *Il regno de gli slavi*, p. 450.
17. See e.g. Ibid., pp. 319–20.
18. G. M. Mackenzie and A. P. Irby, *Travels in Slavonic Provinces of Turkey-in-Europe*, vol. II, pp. 32–3; I. Jastrebov, *Stara serbija i Albanija*, p. 16; F. Kanitz, *Das Königreich Serbien und das Serbenvolk von der Römerzeit bis zur Gegenwart*, vol.I, p. 12.
19. F. Kanitz, *Das Königreich Serbien und das Serbenvolk von der Römerzeit bis zur Gegenwart*, vol. II, p. 358.
20. F. Kanitz, *Srbya*, vol. II, p. 361.
21. G. W. F. Hegel, *The Phenomenology of the Mind*, vol. II, pp. 762–3.
22. R. J. Curzon, *Visits to Monasteries in the Levant*, p. 364.
23. A. W. Kinglake, *Eōthen*, p. 1.
24. J. Du Mont, *A New Voyage to the Levant*, p. 161; Captain Sutherland, *A Tour up the Straits, from Gibraltar to Constantinople*, p. 190; W. Eton, *A Survey of the Turkish Empire*, pp. 213–14; N. Burton, *Narrative of a Voyage from Liverpool to Alexandria*, p. 281; A. W. Kinglake, *Eōthen*, p. 35; E. Spencer, *Travels in European Turkey in 1850*, vol. I, p. 5.
25. M. V. Chirol, *Twixt Greek and Turk*, p. 13.
26. H. A. Brown, *A Winter in Albania*, p. 101.
27. A. Gil'ferding, *Poězdka po Gercegovine, Bosnii i Staroj Serbii*, p. 91.
28. E. L. V. de Laveleye, *The Balkan Peninsula*, pp. 143–4.
29. E. Chishull, *Travels in Turkey and back to England*, p. 4; A. Gil'ferding, *Poězdka po Gercegovine, Bosnii i Staroj Serbii*, p. 460.
30. G. Wheler, *A Journey into Greece*, p. 195; R. G. Boscovich, *Giornale di un Viaggio da Constantinopoli in Polonia*, p. 31.
31. A. V. Amfiteatrov, *Strana Razdora*, p. 77.
32. E. Spencer, *Travels in European Turkey in 1851*, vol. I, pp. 232–3.
33. O. Oztürk, 'Folk Treatment of the Mental Illness in Turkey', p. 350.
34. F. Kanitz, *Das Königreich Serbien und das Serbenvolk von der Römerzeit bis zur Gegenwart*, vol. II, p. 358.
35. G. M. Mackenzie and A. P. Irby, *Travels in Slavonic Provinces of Turkey-in-Europe*, vol. II, p. 122.
36. B. Ramberti, *Libri tre delle cose de Turchi*, p. 6.
37. A. Gil'ferding, *Poězdka po Gercegovine, Bosnii i Staroj Serbii*, p. 314.
38. See e.g. R. Mandrou, *Possession et sorcellerie au XVIIe siecle*.
39. E. Çelebi, *Narrative of Travels in Europe, Asia, and Africa in the Seventeenth Century*, p. 117.
40. V. Ćurčić, 'Zanimljivi pabirci iz narodne medicine'.
41. R. Filipović-Fabijanić, ' "Domaći liekar" iz 1868. godine sa Širokog Brijega', p. 148.
42. A. Šimčik, 'Jesu li samo Turci kopali oči hrišćanskim ikonama'; V. Ćurčić, 'Zanimljivi pabirci iz narodne medicine'.
43. R. Filipović-Fabijanić, 'O narodnoj medicini stanovništva Lištice s okolinom', p. 324; S. Knežević, 'Kultna mesta i manastiri u tradicionalnoj zdravstvenoj kulturi Srba, Makedonaca i Arbanasa', p. 250.
44. Z. Kajmaković, *Zidno slikarstvo u Bosni i Hercegovini*, p. 153.
45. O. Kolberg, *Dzieła wszystkie*, p. 473.
46. A. Mrkun, 'Ljudska medicina v dobrépoljski dolini', pp. 9–10.
47. N. P. Kondakov, *Makedonija*, p. 131.

48. G. M. Mackenzie and A. P. Irby, *Travels in Slavonic Provinces of Turkey-in-Europe*, vol. II, p. 73.
49. De la Guilletiere, *Athenes ancienne et novelle*, pp. 192–3; cf. G. Wheler, *A Journey into Greece*, p. 364; Ch. Thompson, *The Travels Of the Late Charles Thompson, Esq*, vol. I, 323–4.
50. F. Kanitz, *Das Königreich Serbien und das Serbenvolk von der Römerzeit bis zur Gegenwart*, vol. III, p. 190.
51. A. Gil'ferding, *Poězdka po Gercegovine, Bosnii i Staroj Serbii*, p. 220.
52. M. E. Durham, *High Albania*, p. 160; K. Steinmetz, *Od Adrije do Crnoga Drima*, p. 59.
53. E. Pears, *Turkey and its People*, p. 79.
54. B. Randolph, *The Present State of the Morea*, p. 16.
55. H. N. Brailsford, *Macedonia: Its Races and Their Future*, p. 18.
56. L. Trotsky, *The Balkan Wars 1912–1913*, p. 127.
57. G. Ellison, *Yugoslavia. A New Country and Its People*, p. 84.
58. See e.g. M. E. Durham, *Through the Lands of the Serb*, pp. 119, 237–8; cf. C. Hamlin, *Among the Turks*, pp. 270–1.
59. H. Vivian, *Servia, the Poor Man's Paradise*, p. 74.
60. E. A. Bartlett, *The Battlefields of Thessaly*, pp. 211–2.
61. A. Šimčik, 'Jesu li samo Turci kopali oči hrišćanskim ikonama?' p. 193.

Chapter 6
1. A. A. Paton, *Highlands and Island of the Adriatic*, vol. I, p. 82.
2. G. Marcotti, *Il Montenegro e le sue donne*, p. 2; W. Gordon, *A Woman in the Balkans*, p. 256.
3. E. P. Kovalevski, *Četyre mesjaca v Černogorii*, p. 124.
4. W. Forsyth, *The Slavonic Provinces South of the Danube*, pp. 126–7.
5. R. Trevor, *My Balkan Tour*, p. 239.
6. V. B. Bronevsky, *Zapiski morskago oficera*, vol. I, p. 192.
7. V. de Sommières, *Travels in Montenegro*, p. 55.
8. R. H. R., *Rambles in Istria, Dalmatia and Montenegro*, p. 248.
9. G. Rasch, *Die Türken in Europa*, p. 227.
10. I. von Reinsberg-Düringsfeld, *Aus Dalmatien*, vol. I, p. 302; G. Rasch, *Die Türken in Europa*, p. 234.
11. R. H. R., *Rambles in Istria, Dalmatia and Montenegro*, p. 206.
12. D. Urquhart, *The Spirit of the East*, vol. I, p. 157.
13. G. M. Mackenzie and A. P. Irby, *Travels in Slavonic Provinces of Turkey-in-Europe*, vol. II, p. 263.
14. J. Creagh, *Over the Borders of Christendon and Eslamiah*, vol. II, p. 275; W. Y. Morgan, *The New East*, p. 207; M. E. Durham, *Twenty Years of Balkan Tangle*, p. 160; R. Landau, *Search for Tomorrow*, p. 298.
15. L. C. V. de Sommières, *Travels in Montenegro*, p. 12.
16. A. H. Layard, *Autobiography and Letters*, vol. I, p. 135.
17. W. Miller, *The Balkans*, pp. 354–5.
18. See e.g. G. Hertzberg, *Montenegro und sein Freiheitskampf*, p. 11; C. Prel, *Unter Tannen und Pinnien*, p. 300; W. Forsyth, *The Slavonic Provinces South of the Danube*, p. 103; J. Holeček, *Černa Hora*, p. 26; K. Braum-Wiesbaden, *Reise-Eindrücke aus dem Südosten*, vol. I, p. 167; C. Yriarte *Les bords de l'Adriatique et le Montenegro*, p. 389; G. Chiudina, *Storia del Montenero (Crnagora) da' tempi antichi fino a' nostri*, pp. 175–6; J. Frischauf, *Gebirgsführer durch die Österreichischen Alpen und die Thiele Bayern, Italien und Montenegro*, p. 265; B. Schwarz, *Montenegro*, p. 435; J. G. C. Minchin, *The Growth of Freedom in the Balkan Peninsula*, p. 7; R. J. Kennedy, *Montenegro and Its Borderland*, pp. 13–4; K. Baedeker, *Austria, including*

Hungary, Transsylvania, Dalmatia, and Bosnia, p. 307; L. Cappelletti, *Il Montenegro e i suoi principi*, p. 6; F. D. Erba, *Il Montenegro*, p. 7; V. Mantegazza, *Al Montenegro*, p. 1; A. Baldacci, *Crnagora*, p. 15; W. Miller, *The Balkans*, p. 354; A. Rossi, *Un'Escursione nel Montenegro*, p. 37; J. Lavtižar, *Pri Jugoslovanih*, p. 228; M. M. Holbach, *Dalmatia. The Land where East meets West*, p. 185; R. Trevor, *My Balkan Tour*, p. 248; B. G. Baker, *The Passing of the Turkish Empire in Europe*, pp. 281, 287; J. Macdonald, *Turkey and the Eastern Question*, p. 26; W. Gordon, *A Woman in the Balkans*, pp. 257–8, 266; R. G. D. Laffan, *The Guardians of the Gate*, p. 25; P. Edmonds, *The Land of the Eagle*, p. 43; A. Lyall, *The Balkan Road*, p. 144; E. Radovich, *Land of Destiny*, p. 10.

19. W. Miller, *Travels and Politics in the Near East*, p. 47.

20. M. E. Durham, *Twenty Years of Balkan Tangle*, p. 16.

21. W. J. Stillman, *Herzegovina and the late Uprising*, p. 9.

22. H. Sandwith, *Notes on the South Slavonic countries in Austria and Turkey in Europe*, p. 46.

23. See e.g. V. Karadžić, *Montenegro und die Montenegriner*, p. 5; J. G. Wilkinson, *Dalmatia and Montenegro*, vol. I, p. 412; J. G. Kohl, *Reisen nach Istria, Dalmatien und Montenegro*, vol. I, p. 374; H. Delarue, *La Monténégro*, p. 18; F. Lenormant, *Turks et Monténégrins*, p. iii; H. F. Tozer, *Researches in the Highlands of Turkey*, vol. I, p. 245; G. Frilley and J. Wlahovitj, *Le Monténégro contemporain*, p. 88; A. Meylan, *A travers l'Herzégovine*, p. 60; E. F. Knight, *Albania*, p. 65; D. Vaka, *The Eagle and the Sparrow*, pp. 83–4; W. Gordon, *A Woman in the Balkans*, p. 256.

24. A. Bashmakoff, *Through the Montenegro in the Land of the Geugeus, North Albania*, p. 3.

25. E. Radovich, *Land of Destiny*, p. 9.

26. J. Creagh, *Over the Borders of Christendom and Eslamiah*, vol. II, pp. 253–4.

27. K. Baedeker, *Austria, including Hungary, Transsylvania, Dalmatia, and Bosnia*, p. 307.

28. R. Trevor, *My Balkan Tour*, p. 240.

29. M. E. Durham, *Through the Lands of the Serb*, p. 6.

30. R. H. R., *Rambles in Istria, Dalmatia and Montenegro*, pp. 228–9.

31. J. T. Shotwell, *A Balkan Mission*, p. 46.

32. J. Holeček, *Černá Hora*, p. 25.

33. See e.g. V. de Sommières, *Travels in Montenegro*, p. 53; see also V. Karadžić, *Montenegro und die Montengriner*, p. 113; J. G. Wilkinson, *Dalmatia and Montenegro*, vol. I, p. 433; F. Lenormant, *Turcs et Monténégrins*, p. xvii; G. Rasch, *Die Türken in Europa*, p. 239; J. Holeček, *Černa Hora*. p. 63; R. Wyon, *The Balkans from Within*, p. 373.

34. M. E. Durham, *Through the Lands of the Serb*, p. 273.

35. V. Skarić, 'Trebinje u 18 vijeku', p. 64; H. Wendel, *Von Belgrade bis Buccari*, p. 112.

36. V. M. G. Medaković, *Život i običai Crnogoraca*, p. 24.

37. See V. Đorđević, *Evropa i Crna Gora*, p. 1; also e.g. V. Karadžić, *Montenegro und die Montenegriner*, p. 18; H. Stieglitz, *Ein Besuch auf Montenegro*, pp. 50–1; H. Delarue, *Le Monténégro*, p. 47; J. Creagh, *Over the Borders of Christendom and Eslamiah*, vol. II, p. 283; W. Forsyth, *The Slavonic Provinces South of the Danube*, p. 107; S. Gopčević, *Montenegro und die Montenegriner*, p. 9; *Geschichte von Montenegro und Albanien*, p. 168; D. Milaković, *Storia del Montenero*, p. 86; A. J. Evans, *Illyrian Letters*, p. 195; K. Braum-Wiesbaden, *Reise-Eindrücke aus dem Südosten*, vol. I, pp. 180–1; J. S. Stuart-Glennie, *Europe and Asia*, p. 133; G. Chiudina, *Storia del Montenero (Crnagora) da' tempi antichi fino a' nostri*, pp. 66, 101; J. Frischauf, *Gebirgsfuhrer durch die Osterreichischen Alpen und die Thiele Bayern, Italien und Montenegro*, p. 265; L. Cappelletti, *Il Montenegro e i suoi principi*, p. 8; V. Mantegazza, *Al Montenegro*, p. 89; G. Marcotti, *Il Montenegro e le sue donne*, p. 172; A. Baldacci, *Crnagora*, pp. 17–8; J. Lavtižar, *Pri Jugoslovanih*, pp. 195, 234; R. Trevor, *My Balkan Tour*, p. 344; M. E. Durham, *Twenty Years of Balkan Tangle*, p. 18.

38. M. E. Durham, *Twenty Years of Balkan Tangle*, p. 18.

39. M. E. Durham, *The Struggle for Scutari*, p. 253.
40. A. A. Paton, *Highlands and Islands of the Adriatic*, vol. I, p. 88.
41. G. M. Mackenzie and A. P. Irby, *Travels in Slavonic Provinces of Turkey-in-Europe*, vol. II, p. 277.
42. C. N. E. Eliot, *Turkey in Europe*, p. 14.
43. J. Holeček, *Černa Hora*, p. 31.
44. J. G. Wilkinson, *Dalmatia and Montenegro*, vol. I, pp. 420–1; H. F. Tozer, *Researches in the Highlands of Turkey*, vol. I, p. 270; G. Frilley and J. Wlahovitj, *Le Monténégro contemporain*, p. 434; A. Kutschbach, *In Montenegro und im Insurgentenlager der Herzegowizen*, p. 31; J. Frischauf, *Gebirgführer durch die Österreichischen Alpen und die Thiele Bayern, Italien und Montenegro*, p. 266; J. G. C. Minchin, *The Growth of Freedom in the Balkan Peninsula*, p. 16; D. Franić, *S giacima kroz Bosnu-Hercegovinu, Crnu Goru, Dalmaciju, Jadransko more, Istru (Trst, Mletke, Rijeku) i Hrvatsku*, p. 208; W. Le Queux, *An Observer in the Near East*, p. 23; P. Henderson, *A British Officer in the Balkans*, p. 48; R. Trevor, *My Balkan Tour*, pp. 281–2; A. B. Spens, *Half Hours in the Levant*, p. 11; A. Bashmakoff, *Through the Montenegro in the Land of the Geugeus, North Albania*, pp. 5–6; R. Peterlin-Petruška, *Ahasverjeva kronika*, p. 32.
45. V. Karadžić, *Montenegro und die Montenegriner*, p. 95; S. Gopčević, *Montenegro und die Montenegriner*, p. 75; R. Trevor, *My Balkan Tour*, p. 255.
46. V. Karadžić, *Montenegro und die Montenegriner*, p. 95; J. G. Wilkinson, *Dalmatia and Montenegro*, vol. I, p. 423; E. A. Strangford, *The Eastern Shores of the Adriatic in 1863 with a Visit to Montenegro*, p. 157; H. F. Tozer, *Researches in the Highlands of Turkey*, vol. I, p. 241; G. Rasch, *Die Türken in Europa*, p. 212; J. S. Stuart-Glennie, *Europe and Asia*, p.124; K. Steinmetz, *Eine Reise durch die Hochländergaue Oberalbaniens*, p. 26; P. Edmonds, *The Land of the Eagle*, pp. 52–3.
47. C. Yriarte, *Les bords de l'Adriatique et le Montenegro*, p. 106; F. D. Erba, *Il Montenegro*, p. 30.
48. See e.g. F. Valoušek, *Vzpomínky na Bosnu*, p. 85.
49. H. F. Tozer, *Researches in the Highlands of Turkey*, vol. I, p. 207.
50. A. Kutschbach, *In Montenegro und im Insurgentenlager der Herzegowizen*, p. 31.
51. J. S. Stuart-Glennie, *Europe and Asia*, pp. 162–3.
52. See e.g. V. Karadžić, *Montenegro und die Montenegriner*, p. 49; J. G. Wilkinson, *Dalmatia and Montenegro*, vol I, p. 424; G. Hertzberg, *Montenegro und sein Freiheitskampf*, p. 19; G. Frilley and J. Wlahovitj, *Le Monténégro contemporain*, pp. 147, 155; D. Franić, *S giacima kroz Bosnu-Hercegovinu, Crnu Goru, Dalmaciju, Jadransko more, Istru (Trst, Mletke, Rijeku) i Hrvatsku*, p. 209.
53. J. G. Wilkinson, *Dalmatia and Montenegro*, vol. I, p. 420.
54. S. Gopčević, *Montenegro und die Montenegriner*, p. 75.
55. J. G. C. Minchin, *The Growth of Freedom in the Balkan Peninsula*, p. 15.
56. R. Trevor, *My Balkan Tour*, p. 240.
57. E. P. Kovalevski, *Četyre mesjaca v Černogorii*, p. 60.
58. Cf. e.g. V. Mantegazza, *Macedonia*, p. 59.
59. A. V. Amfiteatrov, *Strana razdora*, p. 154.
60. Ibid., p. 106.
61. V. de Sommières, *Travels in Montenegro*, p. 26; R. Trevor, *My Balkan Tour*, p. 254.
62. S. Gopčević, *Montenegro und die Montenegriner*, p. 76.
63. V. de Sommières, *Travels in Montenegro*, p. 44; V. Karadžić, *Montenegro und die Montenegriner*, p. 95; D. Urquhart, *The Spirit of the East*, vol. I, p. 363; J. G. Wilkinson, *Dalmatia and Montenegro*, vol. I, p. 422; G. Frilley and J. Wlahovitj, *Le Monténégro contemporain*, p. 153; S. Gopčević, *Montenegro und die Montenegriner*, p. 76; G. M. Mackenzie and A. P. Irby, *Travels*

in Slavonic Provinces of Turkey-in-Europe, vol. II, p. 269; I. Jastrebov, *Stara Serbija i Albanija*, p. 190.

64. J. Holeček, *Černa Hora*, p. 32.

65. V. Karadžić, *Montenegro und die Montenegriner*, p. 90; E. P. Kovalevski, *Četyre mesjaca v Černogorii*, p. 34.

66. R. Burton, *Love, War and Fancy*, pp. 148–9.

67. V. Karadžić, *Montenegro und die Montenegriner*, p. 100; J. G. von Hahn, *Albanische Studien*, vol. I, p. 150; L. P. Nenadović, *O Crnogorcima*, p. 85; M. Gjurgjević, *Memoari sa Balkana 1858 – 1878*, pp. 134–5.

68. J. G. von Hahn, *Albanische Studien*, vol. I, p. 150.

69. I. Jastrebov, *Stara Serbija i Albanija*, p. 168.

70. See e g V. B. Bronevsky, *Zapiski morskago ofiera*, p. 109, J. G. Wilkinson, *Dalmatia and Montenegro*, vol. I, p. 421; V. M. G. Medaković, *Život i običai Crnogoraca*, pp. 21, 69; G. Frilley and J. Wlahovitj, *Le Monténégro contemporain*, p. 15; J. Holeček, *Černa Hora*, p. 32; S. Gopčević, *Montenegro und die Montenegriner*, p. 75; G. M. Mackenzie and A. P. Irby, *Travels in Slavonic Provinces of Turkey-in-Europe*, vol. II, p. 269; E. F. Knight, *Albania*, p. 83.

71. E. Dodwell, *A Classical and Topographical Tour through Greece*, vol. I, p. 169.

72. V. M. G. Medaković, *Život i običai Crnogoraca*, pp. 127–8; G. M. Mackenzie and A. P. Irby, *Travels in Slavonic Provinces of Turkey-in-Europe*, vol. II, p. 268.

73. V. M. G. Medaković, *Život i običai Crnogoraca*, p. 132.

74. E. F. Knight, *Albania*, p. 76.

75. M. Gjurgjević, *Memoari sa Balkana*, pp. 125–6.

76. M. Jelić, *Albanija*, p. 24.

77. F. C. Pouqueville, *Travels in the Morea, Albania, and other parts of the Ottoman Empire*, p. 452.

78. M. E. Durham, *Twenty Years of Balkan Tangle*, p. 17.

79. C. N. E. Eliot, *Turkey in Europe*, p. 383.

80. Ibid., p. 390.

81. J. G. Wilkinson, *Dalmatia and Montenegro*, vol. I, pp. 3–4.

82. W. Carr, *Montenegro*, p. 51.

83. V. de Sommières, *Travels in Montenegro*, p. 61.

84. L. P. Nenadović, *O Crnogorcima*, p. 26.

85. J. G. Wilkinson, *Dalmatia and Montenegro*, vol. I, p. 472; E. A. Strangford, *The Eastern Shores of the Adriatic in 1863 with a Visit to Montenegro*, p. 143; L. P. Nenadović, *O Crnogorcima*, p. 163.

86. G. T. Temple, *Travels in Greece and Turkey*, vol. II, p. 23.

87. V. Karadžić, *Montenegro und die Montenegriner*, p. 19.

88. W. Carr, *Montenegro*, p. 52.

89. A. V. Amfiteatrov, *V moih skitan'jah*, p. 103; W. Gordon, *A Woman in the Balkans*, p. 269; M. E. Durham, *Twenty Years of Balkan Tangle*, p. 32.

90. W. Gordon, *A Woman in the Balkans*, p. 272; L. P. Nenadović, *O Crnogorcima*, p. 163.

91. B. Newman, *Balkan Background*, p. 179.

92. M. Burr, *Slouch Hat*, p. 50; B. Newman, *Balkan Background*, p. 155.

93. W. E. Gladstone, 'Montenegro', p. 119.

94. W. Miller, *Travels and Politics in the Near East*, pp. 41–2.

95. A. Achleitner, *Reisen im slavischen Süden*, pp. 150–1; A. N. Dragnich and S. Todorovich, *The Saga of Kosovo*, p. 109.

96. W. Gordon, *A Woman in the Balkans*, p. 277.

97. M. Burr, *Slouch Hat*, p. 43.

98. G. M. Mackenzie and A. P. Irby, *Travels in Slavonic Provinces of Turkey-in-Europe*, vol. II,

p. 262.

99. A. Hill, *A Full and Just Account of the Present State of the Ottoman Empire in all its Branches*, p. 134.

100. K. Hassert, *Reise durch Montenegro nebst Bemerkungen über Land und Leute*, p. 7; V. Mantegazza, *Al Montenegro*, p. 217.

101. V. M. G. Medaković, *Život i običai Crnogoraca*, pp. 125–6; G. Rasch, *Die Türken in Europa*, p. 233; E. F. Knight, *Albania*, p. 80; B. Schwarz, *Montenegro*, p. 78; K. Hassert, *Reise durch Montenegro nebst Bemerkungen über Land und Leute*, pp. 6–7; A. G. Hulme-Beaman, *Twenty Years in the Near East*, p. 159; W. Miller, *The Balkans*, p. 436; R. Wyon and G. Prance, *The Land of the Black Mountain*, pp. 49–50; R. Wyon, *The Balkans from Within*, p. 309.

102. See e.g. F. Lenormant, *Turcs et Monténégrins*, p. lxvii; H. F. Tozer, *Researches in the Highlands of Turkey*, vol. I, p. 260; A. Meylan, *A travers l'Hercegovine*, p. 47; G. M. Mackenzie and A. P. Irby, *Travels in Slavonic Provinces of Turkey-in-Europe*, vol. II, p. 264; V. Mantegazza, *Al Montenegro*, p. 217; A. G. Hulme-Beaman, *Twenty Years in the Near East*, p. 159; L. Passarge, *Dalmatien und Montenegro*, p. 330.

103. See e.g. L. Passarge, *Dalmatien und Montenegro*, p. 335; R. Wyon, *The Balkans from Within*, p. 311.

104. J. G. Wilkinson, *Dalmatia and Montenegro*, vol. I, p. 468; G. M. Mackenzie and A. P. Irby, *Travels in Slavonic Provinces of Turkey-in-Europe*, vol. II, p. 264; V. Mantegazza, *Al Montenegro*, p. 220; L. Passarge, *Dalmatien und Montenegro*, p. 335; H. C. Woods, *Washed by Four Seas*, p. 110; M. Burr, *Slouch Hat*, p. 59.

105. G. M. Mackenzie and A. P. Irby, *Travels in Slavonic Provinces of Turkey-in-Europe*, vol. II, p. 117; R. J. More, *Under the Balkans*, pp. 198, 250, 256; A. J. Evans, *Illyrian Letters*, p. 237; S. L. Poole, *The People of Turkey*, vol. I, p. 46; J. G. C. Minchin, *The Growth of Freedom in the Balkan Peninsula*, p. 144; W. E. Curtis, *The Turk and His Lost Provinces*, p. 342; J. Andrejka, *Slovenski fantje v Bosni in Hercegovini 1878*, p. 298; M. E. Durham, *The Burden of the Balkans*, p. 146; R. and K. Bruce, *Letters from Turkey*, p. 56; M. Gjurgjević, *Memoari sa Balkana*, pp. 14, 69; A. F. Townshend, *A Military Consul in Turkey*, p. 106; A. Forder, *In Brigand's Hands and Turkish Prisons*, p. 38.

Chapter 7

1. G. Hertzberg, *Montenegro und sein Freiheitskampf*, p. 19.

2. M. E. Durham, *Twenty Years of Balkan Tangle*, p. 26.

3. A. H. Layard, *Autobiography and Letters*, vol. I, p. 128.

4. Ibid., vol. I, p. 132.

5. A. Mączak, *Travel in Early Modern Europe*, p. 223.

6. M. E. Durham, *The Burden of the Balkans*, p. 285 ; B. Bailey, *Hangmen of England*, p. 50.

7. C. Hibbert, *The Roots of Evil*, p. 43.

8. V. B. Bronevsky, *Zapiski morskago oficera*, vol. I, pp. 267–8.

9. V. de Sommières, *Travels in Montenegro*, p. 24.

10. Ibid., p. 35.

11. E. Dodwell, *A Classical and Topographical Tour through Greece*, vol. I, p. 19; B. Biasoletto, *Relazione del viaggio fatto nella primavera dell'anno 1838 dalla maestà del re Federico Augusto di Sassonia nell'Istria, Dalmazia e Montenegro*, pp. 95–6; A. Slade, *Records of travels in Turkey and Greece, etc.*, p. 134; W. Forsyth, *The Slavonic Provinces South of the Danube*, pp. 108–9; D. Milaković, *Storia del Montenero*, p. 161; G. Chiudina, *Storia del Montenero (Crnagora) da' tempi antichi fino a' nostri*, pp. 31, 75.

12. J. G. Wilkinson, *Dalmatia and Montenegro*, vol. I, pp. 511–2.

13. See e.g. V. Karadžić, *Montenegro und die Montenegriner*, pp. 29, 35, 53; G. Hertzberg,

Montenegro und sein Freiheitskampf, p. 19; V. Krasinski, *Montenegro, and the Slavonians of Turkey*, p. 50; C. Pelerin, *Excursion artistique en Dalmatie et au Montenegro*, p. 27; J. M. Neale, *Notes, Ecclesiological and Picturesque, on Dalmatia, Croatia, Italia, Styria, with a Visit to Montenegro*, p. 186; C. du Prel, *Unter Tannen und Pinnien*, p. 303; G. Frilley and J. Wlahovitj, *Le Montenegro contemporain*, pp. 437, 450; J. Andrejka, *Slovenski fantje v Bosni in Hercegovini 1878*, p. 344; M. E. Durham, *Some Tribal Origins, Laws and Customs of the Balkans*, p. 172; L. P. Nenadović, *O Crnogorcima*, p. 41.

14. M. E. Durham, *Some Tribal Origins, Laws and Customs of the Balkans*, pp. 172–3.

15. Ibid., pp. 175–6.

16. E. Dodwell, *A Classical and Topographical Tour through Greece*, vol. I, p. 20; V. de Sommières, *Travels in Montenegro*, p. 24; V. Karadžić, *Montenegro und die Montenegriner*, p. 53; J. G. Wilkinson, *Dalmatia and Montenegro*, vol. I, pp. 431, 562; J. G. Kohl, *Reisen nach Istrien, Dalmatien und Montenegro*, vol. I, pp. 271, 295, 336; G. Hertzberg, *Montenegro und sein Freiheitskampf*, p. 19; C. Pelerin, *Excursion artistique en Dalmatie et au Montenegro*, p. 27; F. Lenormant, *Turcs et Monténégrins*, p. xiv; H. F. Tozer, *Researchès in the Highlands of Turkey*, vol. I, p. 266; C. du Prel, *Unter Tannen und Pinien*, p. 302; W. Forsyth, *The Slavonic Provinces South of the Danube*, p. 126; E. Freeman, *The Ottoman Power in Europe*, p. 24; K. Braun-Wiesbaden, *Reise-Eindrücke aus dem Südosten*, vol. I, p. 192; G. Chiudina, *Storia del Montenero (Crnagora) da' tempi antichi fino a' nostri*, p. 25; J. Frischauf, *Gebirgsführer durch die Österreichischen Alpen und die Theile Bayern, Italien und Montenegro*, p. 268; G. Marcotti, *Il Montenegro e le sue donne*, p. 77; A. H. Layard, *Autobiography and Letters*, vol. I, p. 132; L. Passarge, *Dalmatien und Montenegro*, p. 333.

17. V. Karadžić, *Montenegro und die Montenegriner*, p. 113.

18. V. de Sommières, *Travels in Montenegro*, p. 24; G. Chiudina, *Storia del Montenero (Crnagora) da' tempi antichi fino a' nostri*, p. 79.

19. W. Miller, *The Balkans*, p. 414.

20. M. E. Durham, *Some Tribal Origins, Laws, and Customs of the Balkans*, p. 173.

21. G. Hertzberg, *Montenegro und sein Freiheitskapmf*, p. 19; V. Krasinski, *Montenegro, and the Slavonians of Turkey*, p. 51; F. Lenormant, *Turcs et Monténégrins*, p. xiv; K. Pieńkowski, *Czarnagora pod względen geographicznym, statystycznym i historycznym*, p. 7; C. du Prel, *Unter Tannen und Pinien*, p. 303; A. Kutschbach, *In Montenegro und im Insurgentenlager der Herzegowizen*, p. 82; G. M. Mackenzie and A. P. Irby, *Travels in Slavonic Provinces of Turkey-in-Europe*, vol. II, p. 202; R. Wyon, *The Balkans from Within*, p. 292; M. E. Durham, *Some Tribal Origins, Laws, and Customs of the Balkans*, pp. 173–4; G. Gesemann, *Heroische Lebensform*, p. 140.

22. V. B. Bronevsky, *Zapiski morskago oficera*, vol. I, p. 268.

23. L. P. Nenadović, *O Crnogorcima*, p. 41.

24. M. E. Durham, *Some Tribal Origins, Laws, and Customs of the Balkans*, p. 174; see also L. Glück, *Albanien und Macedonien*, p. 38.

25. M. E. Durham, *Through the Lands of the Serb*, p. 81.

26. G. Sandys, *A relation of a iourney begvn Anno. Dom. 1610*, p. 3; A. Hill, *A Full and Just Account of the Present State of the Ottoman Empire in all its Branches*, pp. 92–3; M. de Guys, *A Sentimental Journey Through Greece*, vol. I, pp. 133–4; R. Semple, *Observations on A Journey through Spain and Italy to Naples*, vol. II, p. 221; J. C. Hobhouse, *A Journey through Albania and other Provinces of Turkey in Europe and Asia*, p. 133; H. Holland, *Travels in the Ionian Isles, Albania, Thessaly, Macedonia, &c.*, p. 157; E. Dodwell, *A Classical and Topographical tour through Greece*, vol. I, pp. 133–4; C. C. Frankland, *Travels to and from Constantinople, in the years 1827 and 1828*, vol. I, p. 111; A. W. Kinglake, *Eōthen*, p. 77; G. F. Bowen, *Mount Athos, Thessaly, and Epirus*, p. 196; H. Hecquard, *Histoire et description de la Haute Albanie ou Guegarie*, p. 284; H. H. Leech, *Letters of a Sentimental Idler*, p. 17; P. du Fresne-Canaye,

Le Voyage du Levant, p. 36; H. N. Brailsford, *Macedonia: Its Races and Their Future*, p. 95; N. Buxton, *Europe and the Turks*, p. 9; Ruprecht, *Reise-Erinnirungen aus dem Süd-Osten Europas un dem Orient*, p. 32.

27. M. E. Durham, *Some Tribal Origins, Laws, and Customs of the Balkans*, p. 174.
28. Cf. D. Freeman, 'Severed Heads that Germinate', p. 245.
29. E. Dodwell, *A Classical and Topographical Tour of Greece*, vol. I, p. 138; W. Ebel, *Zwölf Tage auf Montenegro*, p. 44; J. Holeček, *Černa Hora*, pp. 43, 65; E. F. Knight, *Albania. A Narrative of Recent Travel*, p. 76; G. Marcotti, *Il Montenegro e le sue donne*, p. 14; M. Gjurgjević, *Memoari sa Balkana*, p. 101.
30. A. H. Layard, *Autobiography and Letters*, vol. I, pp. 132–3.
31. J. G. Wilkinson, *Dalmatia and Montenegro*, vol. I, pp. 475–6.
32. Ibid., vol. II, pp. 74–5.
33. V. Krasinski, *Montenegro, and the Slavonians of Turkey*, p. 56; W. F. Wingfield, *A tour in Dalmatia, Albania, and Montenegro with an historical sketch of the Republic of Ragusa*, p. 200; C. Pelerin, *Excursion artistique en Dalmatie et au Montenegro*, p. 24; E. A. Strangford, *The Eastern Shores of the Adriatic in 1863 with a Visit to Montenegro*, p. 164; H. F. Tozer, *Researches in the Highlands of Turkey*, vol. I, p. 308; G. Rasch, *Die Türken in Europa*, pp. 228, 246; G. Frilley and J. Wlahovitj, *Le Montenegro contemporain* , p. 437; S. Gopčević, *Montenegro und die Montenegriner*, p. 92; A. Rossi, *Un'Escursione nel Montenegro*, p. 25; A. G. Hulme-Beaman, *Twenty Years in the Near East*, p. 160; J. Lavtižar, *Pri Jugoslovanih*, pp. 200, 212.
34. S. Gopčević, *Geschichte von Montenegro und Albanien*, p. 330.
35. J. Creagh, *Over the Borders of Christendom and Eslamiah*, vol. II, p. 264; W. Denton, *Montenegro. Its People and Their History*, p. 138.
36. E. F. Knight, *Albania. A Narrative of Recent Travel*, pp. 65, 75.
37. M. Gjurgjević, *Memoari sa Balkana 1858–1878*, p. 119.
38. G. M. Mackenzie and A. P. Irby, *Travels in Slavonic Provinces of Turkey-in-Europe*, vol. II, p. 202.
39. E. A. Strangford, *The Eastern Shores of the Adriatic in 1863 with a Visit to Montenegro*, p. 335; J. S. Stuart-Glennie, *Europe and Asia*, pp. 362–3; E. F. Knight, *Albania. A Narrative of Recent Travel*, p. 90; P. Loti, *Turkey in Agony*, p. 88.
40. J. S. Stuart-Glennie, *Europe and Asia*, p. 374.
41. L. P. Nenadović, *O Crnogorcima*, p. 50.
42. L. P. Nenadović, *Memoari prote Matije Nenadovića*, p. 82; W. J. Stillman, *Herzegovina and the late uprising*, pp. 71–2; S. Gopčević, *Der turco-montenegrinische Kreig 1876–78*, vol. I, p. 103.
43. M. E. Durham, *Some Tribal Origins, Laws, and Customs of the Balkan People*, p. 179.
44. E. Freeman, *The Ottoman Power in Europe*, p. 24; S. Gopčević, *Der turco-montenegrinische Kreig 1876–78*, vol. I, p. 116.
45. J. Stillman, *Herzegovina and the late uprising*, pp. 107–8, 121–2; F. Garrido and C. B. Cayley, *A History of Political and Religious Persecutions*, p. 884.
46. A. Kutschbach, *In Montenegro und im Insurgentenlager der Herzegowizen*, p. 82.
47. L. P. Nenadović, *O Crnogorcima*, p. 50; cf. A. Baldacci *Crnagora*, p. 35.
48. M. E. Durham, Some Tribal Origins, Laws, and Customs of the Balkans, p. 177.
49. Cf. A. E. Jensen, *Myth and Cult Among Primitive Peoples*, p. 162.
50. M. E. Durham, *Some Tribal Origins, Laws, and Customs of the Balkans*, pp. 177–8.
51. J. Holeček, *Černa Hora*, p. 65.
52. J. Thevenot, *Travels of the Monsieur de Thevenot into the Levant*, vol. I, p. 279; F. M. A. Voltaire, *The Works*, vol. IV, p. 252; E. Dodwell, *A Classical and Topographical Tour of Greece*, vol. I, p. 59; S. Mazro, *Turkish Barbarity*, pp. 29–30; J. G. C. Minchin, *The Growth*

of Freedom in the Balkan Peninsula, p. 13.

53. P. Rycaut, *The History of the Turkish Empire From the Year 1623. to the Year 1677*, p. 70.

54. A. de Chaumette, *Voyage en Bosnie dans les années 1807 et 1808*, pp. 57–8; E. Dodwell, *A Classical and Topographical Tour through Greece*, vol. I, p. 20; V. M. G. Medaković, *Život i običai Crnogoraca*, pp. 127–8; V. Klaić, *Kosovo*, p. 15.

55. M. E. Durham, *Some Tribal Origins, Laws, and Customs of the Balkans*, p. 213.

56. M. E. Durham, *The Struggle for Scutari*, p. 185; Idem, *Some Tribal Origins, Laws, and Customs of the Balkans*, p. 177.

57. M. E. Durham *The Struggle for Scutari*, pp. 197, 218, 237–8.

58. M. E. Durham, *Some Tribal Origins, Laws, and Customs of the Balkans*, p. 177.

59. G. M. Mackenzie and A. P. Irby, *Travels in Slavonic Provinces of Turkey-in-Europe*, vol. II, p. 202.

60. W. Forsyth, *The Slavonic Provinces South of the Danube*, p. 126; J. G. C. Minchin, *The Growth of Freedom in the Balkan Peninsula*, pp. 13–4.

61. H. N. Brailsford, *Macedonia: Its Races and Their Future*, p. 96.

62. J. Gruden, *Zgodovina slovenskega naroda*, p. 581.

63. Cit. C. D. Rouillard, *The Turk in French History, Thought, and Literature*, p. 71.

64. Ibid., p. 79.

65. J. W. Valvasor, *Die Ehre deß Hertzogthums Crain*, vol. XII, pp. 63–5, 115–6.

66. Ibid., vol. XII, p. 93.

67. R. Palmer, *An Account Of the Present War Between the Venetians & Turk*, p. 40.

68. R. Knolles, *The Generall Historie of the Turke*, p. 1045.

69. T. Glover, 'The Journey of Edward Barton, Esq.', p. 1354; Quiclet, *Les Voyages de M. Quiclet a Constantinople par terre*, p. 126; J. Burbury, *A Relation of a Journey of the Right Honourable My Lord Henry Howard*, p. 212; B. Randolph, *The Present State of the Islands in the Archipelago, (Or Arches) Sea of Constantinople, and Gulf of Smyrna*, p. 89; E. Çelebi, *Putopis*, p. 63.

70. B. Randolph, *The Present State of the Islands in the Archipelago, (Or Arches), Sea of Constantinople, and Gulf of Smyrna*, p. 89.

71. H. Holland, *Travels in the Ionian Isles, Albania, Thessaly, Macedonia, &c. during the years 1812 and 1813*, p. 201; E. Dodwell, *A Classical and Topographical Tour through Greece*, p. 201; W. Turner, *Journal of a Tour in the Levant*, vol. I, p. 99, vol. III, p. 427; J. K. Weyand, *Reisen durch Europa, Asien, und Afrika von dem Jahre 1818 bis 1821 incl.*, vol. I, p. 13; J. Hartley, *Researches in Greece and The Levant*, p. 17; G. Keppel, *Narrative of a Journey across the Balcan*, vol. I, p. 18; J. G. Wilkinson, *Dalmatia and Montenegro*, vol. II, p. 69; E. Spencer, *Travels in European Turkey in 1850*, vol. I, p. 380; N. W. Senior, *A Journal kept in Turkey*, p. 106; A. Arnold, *From the Levant, the Black Sea, and the Danube*, vol. I, p. 161; L. Ross, *Erinnerungen und Mittheilungen aus Griechenland*, pp. 41, 272; M. M. S. Bašeskija, *Ljetopis (1746–1804)*, p. 118.

72. P. J. Green, *Sketches of War in Greece*, pp. 248, 250; T. Gordon, *History of the Greek Revolution*, vol. II, p. 265; D. Urquhart, *The Spirit of the East*, vol. I, p. 52; G. Levinge, *The Traveller in the East*, pp. 117–8; J. G. Stephens, *Incidents of Travel in the Russian and Turkish Empires*, vol. I, p. 11; J. O. Noyes, *Roumania: The Border Land of the Christian and the Turk*, p. 282.

73. V. Hugo, *Les Orientales*, p. 50.

74. E. Habesci, *The Present State of the Ottoman Empire*, pp. 144, 365; F. de Tott, *Memoirs of the Baron de Tott, on the Turks and Tartars*, vol. I, p. 63; W. Hunter, *Travels in the Year 1792 through France, Turkey, and Hungary, to Vienna*, p. 213; J. Dallaway, *Constantinople Ancient and Modern*, p. 21; T. Watkins, *Travels through Switzerland, Italy, Sicily, the Greek Islands to Constantinople*, vol. II, p. 231; J. C. Hobhouse, *A Journey through Albania and other Provinces*

of Turkey in Europe and Asia, to Constantinople, during the years 1809 and 1810, pp. 947, 992;
M. Tancoigne, *A Narration of a Journey into Persia, and Residences in Tehran,* p. 376; A. L.
Castellan, *Turkey,* vol. III, pp. 37–8; R. Wilson, *Travels in Egypt and the Holy Land,* p. 354;
P. J. Green, *Sketches of the War in Greece,* pp. 52–3; 246; M. Andreossy, *Constantinople et
Bosphore de Thrace,* p. 15; E. Blaquiere, *Letters from Greece,* p. 150; C. C. Frankland, *Travels
to and from Constantinople, in the years 1827 and 1828,* vol. I, p. 111; J. Fuller, *Narrative of a
tour through some parts of the Turkish Empire,* p. 90; C. Mac Farlane, *Constantinople in 1828,*
pp. 449–51.

75. G. Keppel, *Narrative of a Journey across the Balcan,* vol. I, pp. 85–7; T. Gordon, *History of
the Greek Revolution,* vol. I, pp. 377–8, 487; vol. II, pp. 140, 265; R. Burgess, *Greece and
the Levant,* vol. I, p. 74; vol. II, pp. 164, 185; G. T. Temple, *Travels in Greece and Turkey,*
vol. II, pp. 43–4, 251; R. Walsh, *A Residence at Constantinople,* vol. I, pp. 335–7, 349; R.
T. Claridge, *A Guide along the Danube,* pp. 127, 143; G. Levinge, *The Traveller in the East,*
p. 268; S. S. Wilson, *A Narrative of the Greek Mission,* pp. 508–9; A. Slade, *Records of
Travels in Turkey and Greece, etc.,* pp. 133, 231–2, 242; H. Bagge, *Reise nach dem Orient,
der Europäischen, Türkei, Aegypten, Nubien und Palastina,* p. 55; T. Gautier, *Constantinople,*
p. 289; Azaïs and C. Domergue, *Journal d'un voyage en Orient,* p. 302; N. W. Senior, *A
Journal kept in Turkey,* pp. 12, 39; C. W. Wutzer, *Reise in dem Orient Europa's und einen
Theil Westasien's,* vol. II, pp. 62–3; F. Bremer, *Greece and the Greeks,* vol. I, p. 195; E. de
Amicis, *Constantinople,* pp. 270, 312; F. Elliot, *Diary of an Idle Woman in Constantinople,* pp.
5, 258–9; P. Jousset, *Un tour de Méditerranée, de Venise à Tunis, par Athènes, Constantinople
et le Caire,* p. 101; C. E. Clement, *Constantinople. The City of the Sultans,* p. 179; E. A.
Grosvenor, *Constantinople,* vol. II, p. 716; W. J. J. Spry, *Life on the Bosphorus,* vol. I, p. 6; H.
S. Lunn, *How to visit the Mediterranean,* p. 129; C. R. Cockerell, *Travels in Southern Europe
and the Levant, 1810–1817,* p. 26; G. Young, *Constantinople,* p. 143; M. Reshid, *Tourist's
Practical Guide to Constantinople and Environs,* p. 62.

76. R. Walsh, *A Residence at Constantinople,* vol. I, p. 394.

77. R. Walsh, *Narrative of a Journey from Constantinople to England,* pp. 47–9.

78. See e.g. H. A. V. Post, *A visit to Greece and Constantinople, in the Year 1827–8,* pp. 323–4;
A. Smith, *A Month at Constantinople,* p. 57.

79. R. Walsh, *Narrative of a Journey from Constantinople to England,* pp. 49–50; G. F. Bowen,
Mount Athos, Thessaly, and Epirus, p. 202.

80. Le Croy, *An Account of the Turks Wars with Poland, Muscovy, and Hungary,* p. 191; A. Slade,
Travels in Germany and Russia, pp. 149–50; K. A. Schimmer, *The Sieges of Vienna by the
Turks,* p. 166; Anon., *The Siege of Vienna,* p. 188; W. J. J. Spry, *Life on the Bosphorus,* vol.
II, p. 117.

81. K. A. Schimmer, *The Sieges of Vienna by the Turks,* p. 166.

82. I. Smith, *The True Travels, Adventvres, and Observations of Captain Iohn Smith,* p. 19; P.
Rycaut, *The History of the Turkish Empire From the Year 1623. to the Year 1677,* p. 41;
S. Gerlach, *Deß Aeltern Tage-Buch,* pp. 132–3; G. Benaglia, *Relatione del Viaggio Fatto
a Constantinopoli, e Ritorno in Germania,* pp. 181, 225; J. W. Valvasor, *Die Ehre deß
Hertzogthums Crain,* vol. XII, pp. 30, 92; E. Çelebi, *Putopis,* pp. 183, 187, 193.

83. W. Eton, *A Survey of the Turkish Empire,* p. 80.

84. J. Burbury, *A Relation of a Journey of the Right Honourable My Lord Henry Howard,* p. 180.

85. J. W. Valvasor, *Die Ehre deß Hertzogthums,* vol. XI, p. 27; A. Dimitz, *Geschichte Krains von
der ältesten Zeit bis auf das Jahr 1813,* vol. III, p. 56; J. Gruden, *Zgodovina slovenskega naroda,*
pp. 774–6.

86. G. Stanojević, *Šćepan Mali,* p. 57.

87. J. K. Weyand, *Reisen Durch Europa, Asien, und Afrika von dem Jahre 1818 bis 1821 incl.,*
vol. I, p. 94; R. R. Madden, *Travels in Turkey, Egypt, Nubia, and Palestine, in 1824, 1825,*

1826, and 1827, vol. I, p. 76; A. Arnold, *From the Levant, the Black Sea, and the Danube*, vol. I, p. 129; F. Garrido and C. B. Cayley, *A History of Political and Religious Persecutions*, pp. liv-lvi, lxxix; R. J. More, *Under the Balkans*, pp. 87, 106, 109, 112, 224; A. Serristori, *La costa Dalmata e il Montenegro durante la guerra del 1877*, p. 15; S. Gopčević, *Der turco-montenegrinische Kreig 1876–78*, vol. I, pp. 134–5; vol. II, pp. 109, 156–7, 241, 244, 248, 266, 269–70; H. O. Dwight, *Turkish Life in War Time*, pp. 37, 55; A. J. Evans, *Illyrian Letters*, pp. 32, 77–8, 80–2, 96; W. Huyshe, *The liberation of Bulgaria*, pp. 85, 156–7, 241, 244, 248, 266, 269–73; H. S. Edwards, *Sir William White*, p. 104.

88. R. T. Claridge, *A Guide along the Danube*, pp. 127; 131–2; E. Freeman, *The Ottoman Power in Europe*, p. 24.

89. P. J. Green, *Sketches of the War in Greece*, pp. 25, 28, 44; E. Blaquiere, *Letters from Greece*, p. 149; T. Gordon, *History of the Greek Revolution*, vol. I, pp. 391, 396, 497; vol. II, pp. 132, 140, 216; R. Pashley, *Travels in Crete*, vol. I, p. 108; P. Čokorilo, *Türkisch Zustände*, p. 15; H. Hecquard, *Histoire et description de la Haute Albanie ou Guegarie*, p. 130; L. P. Nenadović, *Memoari prote Matije Nenadovića*, p. 82; A. J. Evans, *Through Bosnia and the Herzegovina On Foot During the Insurrection, August and September 1875*, pp. 352–3; Idem, *Illyrian Letters*, pp. 32, 77–82; F. Garrido and C. B. Cayley, *A History of Political and Religious Persecutions*, pp. 888–9; E. F. Knight, *Albania*, p. 90; G. M. Mackenzie and A. P. Irby, *Travels in Slavonic Provinces of Turkey-in-Europe*, vol. I, p. 52; R. Gossip, *Turkey and Russia*, vol. I, p. 84; J. Fife-Cookson, *With the Armies of the Balkans at Gallipoli in 1877–1878*, pp. 68–9; H. M. Field, *The Greek Islands and Turkey after the War*, pp. 177–8; Draganof, *Macedonia and the Reforms*, pp. 109, 204; Carnegie Endowment, *Report of the International Commission to Inquire into the Causes and Conduct of the Balkan Wars* (1914), p. 134; G. Melas, *The Turk as he is*, p. 45; C. Yriarte, *Bosna i Herzegovina*, pp. 82–3.

90. R. Wyon, *The Balkans from Within*, p. 68.

91. M. Gjurgjević, *Memoari sa Balkana*, p. 102.

92. V. Mantegazza, *Macedonia*, p. 227; F. Moore, *The Balkan Trail*, p. 259; A. Moore, *The Orient Express*, p. 179; R. Graves, *Storm Centres of the Near East*, p. 212a.

93. M. E. Durham, *The Struggle for Scutari*, p. 168.

94. A. Bashmakoff, *Through the Montenegro in the Land of the Geugeus, North Albania*, p. 62.

95. L. A. Matzhold, *Brandherd Balkan*, p. 42.

96. A. Svetek, 'Spomini na okupacijo Bosne', p. 669; J. Andrejka, *Slovenski fantje v Bosni in Herzegovini 1878*, pp. 43, 68, 121, 259, 261, 336; J. Alésovec, *Vojska na Turškem od leta 1875 do konca leta 1878*, pp. 97, 112.

97. E. Chaura, *Obrazky z okupace bosenske*, p. 38.

98. J. Reed, *The War in Eastern Europe*, p. 84.

99. W. Eton, *A Survey of the Turkish Empire*, p. 218; C. White, *Three Years in Constantinople*, vol. I, pp. 126–7; A. Slade, *Records of Travel in Turkey and Greece, etc.*, p. 329; J. O. Noyes, *Roumania: The Border Land of the Christian and the Turk*, p. 74; II, G. Geary, *Through Asiatic Turkey*, p. 335; W. Huyshe, *The Liberation of Bulgaria*, pp. 204–5; W. E. Curtis, *The Turk and His Lost Provinces*, p. 299; J. Alésovec, *Vojska na Turškem od leta 1875 do konca leta 1878*, p. 123; C. Yriarte, *Bosna i Herzegovina* 83; cf. B. Bailey, *Hangmen of England*, p. 23.

100. E. M. Pearson and L. E. McLaughlin, *Service in Serbia under the Red Cross*, p. 183; see also J. Fife-Cookson, *With the Armies of the Balkans at Gallipoli in 1877–1878*, p. 13; J. G. C. Minchin, *The Growth of Freedom in the Balkan Peninsula*, p. 19; M. E. Durham, *The Burden of the Balkans*, p. 149; N. Buxton, *Europe and the Turks*, p. 95; O. M. Aldridge, *The Retreat from Serbia Through Montenegro and Albania*, p. 54.

101. F. Fox, *The Balkan Peninsula*, p. 143.

102. J. G. C. Minchin, *The Growth of Freedom in the Balkan Peninsula*, p. 13.

103. W. Miller, *The Balkans*, pp. 414–15; G. Marcotti, *Il Montenegro e le sue donne*, p. 186.

104. L. P. Nenadović, *O Crnogorcima*, p. 42.

105. Ibid., p. 43.

106. S. Gopčević, *Montenegro und die Montenegriner*, p. 26.

107. L. Passarge, *Dalmatien und Montenegro*, p. 318.

108. S. Gopčević, *Montenegro und die Montenegriner*, p. 91.

109. W. J. Stillman, *Herzegovina and the late uprising*, p. 26.

110. C. Pelerin, *Excursion artistique en Dalmatie et au Montenegro*, p. 27.

111. J. Holeček, *Černa Hora*, p. 1.

112. E. P. Kovalevski, *Četyre mesjaca v Černogorii*, p. 108.

113. M. Borsa, *Dal Montenegro*, p. 54; G. Cerciello, *Uno sguardo al Montenegro (Cenno storico)*, pp. 20–1; F. Erba, *Il Montenegro*, p. 12; V. Mantegazza, *Al Montenegro*, p. 92; A. Rossi, *Un'Escursione nel Montenegro*, p. 25.

114. V. Mantegazza, *Al Montenegro*, p. 92.

115. G. Cerciello, *Uno sguardo al Montenegro (Cenno storico)*, pp. 20–1.

116. B. Jaeckel, *The Lands of the Tamed Turk or the Balkan States To-day*, p. 101.

117. H. De Windt, *Through Savage Europe*, p. 191.

118. A. Lamartine, *Visit to the Holy Land*, vol. II, pp. 235–6.

119. F. Hervé, *A Residence in Greece and Turkey*, vol. II, p. 300.

120. J. O. Noyes, *Roumania: The Border Land between the Christian and the Turk*, pp. 281–2.

121. A. W. Kinglake, *Eōthen*, p. 31.

122. A. Boué, *La Turquie d'Europe*, vol. II, p. 596; Idem, *Reccueil d'itineraires dans la Turquie d'Europe*, p. 241; E. Spencer, *Travels in European Turkey in 1850*, vol. I, p. 146; S. L. Popović, *Putovanje po novoj Srbiji*, p. 362; J. G. C. Minchin, *The Growth of Freedom in the Balkan Peninsula*, p. 133; A. Aškerc, *Izlet v Carigrad*, p. 63; H. De Windt, *Through Savage Europe*, p. 191; F. Kanitz, *Das Königreich Serbien und das Serbenvolk von der Römerzeit bis zur Gegenwart*, vol. II, pp. 144, 179–80; B. Jaeckel, *The Lands of the Tamed Turk or the Balkan States To-day*, p. 101; J. Reed, *The War in Eastern Europe*, pp. 47–8.

123. J. O. Noyes, *Roumania: The Border Land between the Christian and the Turk*, p. 282.

124. P. J. Green, *Sketches of the War in Greece*, p. 250; see also S. S. Wilson, *A Narrative of the Greek Mission*, p. 469.

125. K. Braun-Wiesbaden, *Reise-Endrücke aus dem Südosten*, vol. I, p. 192.

126. D. Urquhart, *The Spirit of the East*, vol. I, p. 52.

127. H. Levine, *The Broken Column*, p. 42.

128. P. Pomet, *A complete history of drugs*, p. 22.

129. M. B. Valentini, *Museum Museorum*, vol. I, p. 419.

130. P. Pomet, *Histoire generale des Drogues*, vol. II, p. 8; Idem, *A complete history of drugs*, p. 229.

131. M. B. Valentini, *Museum museorum*, vol. I, p. 419.

132. E. De Amicis, *Constantinople*, p. 314.

133. F. de Beaujour, *Voyages militaire dans l'Empire Othoman*, vol. I, pp. 367–8.

134. See e.g. A. Fabre, *Histoire du siège de Missolonghi, suivie de pièces justificatives*, pp. 316–7.

135. See e.g. T. Gordon, *History of the Greek Revolution*, vol. I, pp. 233, 236, 277, 338–9, 437; vol. II, p. 350.

136. W. Gell, *Narrative of a Journey in the Morea*, p. 365.

137. See A. J. Toynbee, *The Western Question in Greece and Turkey*, pp. 265–6.

Chapter 8

1. L. Rauwolf, *Aigentliche beschreibung der Raisz in die Morgenlander*, p. 108.

2. W. F. Wingfield, *A tour in Dalmatia, Albania, and Montenegro with an historical sketch of the Republic of Ragusa*, p. 121.

3. W. Biddulph, *The Travels of Certaine Englishmen*, p. 65; W. Lithgow, *A Delectable, and true discourse, of an admired and painefull peregrination from Scotland, to the most famous Kingdomes in Europe, Asia and Affricke*, pp. I-3; G. Sandys, *A relation of a iourney begvn Anno. Dom. 1610*, p. 66; T. Glover, 'The Journey of Edward Barton Esq.', pp. 1296–7; T. Herbert, *A Relation of some Yeares Travile, begvnne Anno 1626*, p. 150; H. Blount, *A Journey into the Levant*, p. 15; P. della Valle, *Viaggio*, p. 152; de la Guilletiere, *Athenes ancienne et novelle*, p. 98; T. Smith, *Remarks upon the Manners, Religion, and Government of the Turks*, p. 37; J. de Thevenot, *The Travels of the Monsieur de Thevenot into the Levant*, vol. I, p. 33; J. Du Mont, *A New Voyage to the Levant*, p. 171; F. B. Naironus, *A Discourse on Coffee*, p. 14.

4. T. Herbert, *A Relation of some Yeares Travile, begvnne Anno 1610*, p. 150.

5. E. C. P. Hull, *Coffee Planting in Southern India and Ceylon*, p. 10.

6. W. A. Alcott, *Tea and Coffee*, p. 63.

7. Poullet, *Nouvelle relations du Levant*, vol. I, pp. 52–3.

8. W. H. Ukers, *All About Coffee*, p. 23.

9. E. F. Robinson, *The Early History of Coffee Houses in England*, p. 87.

10. E. F. Robinson, *The Early History of Coffee Houses in England*, p. 48; W. H. Ukers, *All About Coffee*, p. 9; H. E. Jacob, *The Saga of Coffee*, p. 40.

11. V. Skarić, 'Uticaj turskog vladanja na društveni život', p. 137.

12. F. Spaho, 'Prve kafane su otvorene u našim krajevima', pp. 41–2; V. Skarić, 'Uticaj turskog vladanja na društveni život', p. 137.

13. E. Çelebi, *Putopis*, pp. 307, 567, 577.

14. A. Hangi, *Život i običaji Muslimana u Bosni i Hercegovini*, p. 78.

15. F. Valoušek, *Vzpomínky na Bosnu*, p. 42.

16. V. B. Bronevsky, *Zapiski morskago oficera*, p. 285.

17. F. Spaho, 'Prve kafane su otvorene u našim krajevima', p. 41.

18. M. Šamić, *Francuski putnici u Bosni na pragu XIX stoljeća i njihovi utisci o njoj*, p. 237.

19. J. Rośkiewicz, *Studien über Bosnien und die Herzegovina*, p. 190.

20. A. Hangi, *Život i običaji Muslimana u Bosni i Hercegovini*, p. 83.

21. H. C. Thomson, *The Outgoing Turk*, p. 121; W. E. Curtis, *The Turk and His Lost Provinces*, p. 285.

22. V. M. G. Medaković, *Život i običai Crnogoraca*, p. 165.

23. A. Hangi, *Život i običaji Muslimana u Bosni i Hercegovini*, pp. 78–85.

24. H. E. Jacob, *The Saga of Coffee*, p. 262.

25. M. Golczewski, *Der Balkan in deutschen und österreichischen Reise und Erlebnisberichten*, p. 133.

26. P. Henderson, *A British Officer in the Balkans*, pp. 99–100.

27. L. M. J. Garnett, *Turkish Life in Town and Country*, p. 40.

28. J. Galt, *Voyages and Travels, in the Years 1809, 1810, and 1811*, p. 249; H. Holland, *Travels in the Ionian Isles, Albania, Thessaly, Macedonia, &c. during the years 1812 and 1813*, p. 311; C. R. Cockerell, *Travels in Southern Europe and the Levant 1810–1817*, p. 109; J. B. S. Morritt, *The Letters of John B. S. Morritt of Rokeby*, p. 99.

29. A. Slade, *Turkey, Greece and Malta*, vol. I, p. 188; J. G. Stephens, *Incidents of travel in Greece, Turkey, Russia, and Poland*, vol. I, p. 76; A. Boué, *Le Turquie d'Europe*, vol. II, p. 296; A. A. Paton, *Servia, the youngest member of the European family*, p. 93; S. Kapper, *Südslavische Wanderungen im Sommer*, vol. I, p. 243; E. Spencer, *Travels in European Turkey in 1850*, vol. I, p. 15; H. H. Leech, *Letters of a Sentimental Idler*, p. 19; J. S. Stuart-Glennie, *Europe and Asia*, p. 154; E. L. V. de Laveleye, *The Balkan Peninsula*, pp. 75–6.

30. S. G. St Clair and C. A. Brophy, *A Residence in Bulgaria*, p. 165.

31. R. Walsh, *A Residence at Constantinople*, vol. II, p. 298.

32. H. G. Dwight, *Constantinople, Old and New*, p. 26.

33. A. Messner-Sporšić, *Od Bukurešta do Ankare*, pp. 47, 62, 108, 228, 239.

34. J. Du Mont, *A New Voyage to the Levant*, p. 172; J. Ellis, *An Historical Account of Coffee*, p. 9; C. Arendonk, 'Kahwa', p. 633.

35. J. Ellis, *An Historical Account of Coffee*, pp. 8–9; F. Spaho, 'Prve kafane su otvorene u našim krajevima', p. 42; G. Elezović, 'Kafa i kafana na balkanskom prostoru', pp. 619–20; B. Lewis, *Istanbul and the Civilization of the Ottoman Empire*, pp. 132–3.

36. W. H. Ukers, *All About Coffee*, p. 15; G. Elezović, 'Kafa i kafana na balkanskom prostoru', p. 631.

37. N. Nicolay de Dauphinoys, *Les quatre premiers livres des navigations et peregrinations Orientales*, p. 102.

38. E. Çelebi, *Putopis*, p. 632.

39. W. Biddulph, *The Travels of Certaine Englishmen*, p. 66.

40. F. Calvert, *A Tour to the East, in the Years 1763 and 1764*, p. 77; T. Gautier, *Constantinople*, p. 198.

41. R. Johnson, *Relations, Of the Most Famovs Kingdoms and Common-Weales Throvgh the World*, p. 267; J. de Thevenot, *The Travels of the Monsieur de Thevenot into the Levant*, pp. 34–5; C. Bruyn, *A Voyage to the Levant*, p. 95; C. Thompson, *The Travels of the Late Charles Thompson, Esq.*, vol. II, p. 149; J. Porter, *Observations on the Religion, Law, Government, and Manners of the Turks*, p. 297; N. Bisani, *A Picturesque Tour Through Part of Europe, Asia, and Africa*, p. 178; J. B. S. Morritt, *The Letters of John B. S. Morritt of Rokeby*, p. 231.

42. M. E. Durham, *The Struggle for Scutari*, p. 93.

43. J. E. P. Boulden, *An American among the Orientals*, p. 63; R. S. Hattox, *Coffee and Coffeehouses*, pp. 107–8.

44. J. Ellis, *An Historical Account of Coffee*, p. 8; I. de M. d'Ohsson, *Tableau general de l'Empire Othoman*, vol. II, p. 126; C. White, *Three Years in Constantinople*, vol. I, p. 280; E. F. Robinson, *The Early History of Coffee Houses in England*, p. 38; C. Arendonk, 'Kahwa', p. 633; W. H. Ukers, *All About Coffee*, p. 16; B. Lewis, *Istanbul and the Civilization of the Ottoman Empire*, p. 133.

45. C. Arendonk, 'Kahwa', p. 633.

46. J. Du Mont, *A New Voyage to the Levant*, p. 168.

47. P. Rycaut, *The Present State of the Ottoman Empire*, p. 165.

48. E. F. Robinson, *The Early History of Coffee Houses in England*, p. 39; W. H. Ukers, *All About Coffee*, p. 16; C. Roden, *Coffee*, p. 21.

49. A. Galland *De l'origine et du progrez du café*, p. 69.

50. J. de la Roque, *A Voyage to Arabia the Happy*, pp. 273–4.

51. A. Galland *De l'origine et du progrez du café*, p. 70.

52. J. de Thevenot, *The Travels of the Monsieur de Thevenot into the Levant*, vol. I, p. 33; J. de la Roque, *A Voyage to Arabia the Happy*, p. 275; J. Ellis, *An Historical Account of Coffee* 10–1.

53. B. Lewis, *Istanbul and the Civilization of the Ottoman Empire*, p. 135.

54. W. Y. Morgan, *The New East*, p. 234.

55. A. Chaumette, *Voyage en Bosnie dans les années 1807 et 1808*, p. 77.

56. V. Skarić, 'Uticaj turskog vladanja na društveni život', p. 137.

57. C. White, *Three Years in Constantinople*, vol. I, p. 282.

58. F. Kanitz, *Das Königreich Serbien und das Serbenvolk von der Römerzeit bis zur Gegenwart*, vol. I, p. 59.

59. J. de Asboth, *An Official Tour Through Bosnia and Herzegovina*, p. 177.

60. A. J. Evans, *Illyrian Letters*, pp. 53–4.

61. P. Henderson, *A British Officer in the Balkans*, p. 100.

62. H. Armstrong, *Turkey in Travail*, p. 71.

63. J. Griffiths, *Travels in Europe, Asia Minor, and Arabia*, p. 111; cf. R. Walsh, *A Residence at Constantinople*, vol. II, pp. 9–10.

64. Mrs Pardoe, *The Beauty of the Bosphorus*, p. 148.

65. G. Sandys, *A relation of a iourney begvn Anno. Dom. 1610*, p. 66.

66. R. S. Hattox, *Coffee and Coffeehouses*, p. 109.

67. J. Porter, *Observations on the Religion, Law, Government, and Manners of the Turks*, p. 298.

68. F. de Tott, *Memoirs of the Baron de Tott, on the Turks and Tartars*, vol. I, p. 46; F. Hervé, *A Residence in Greece and Turkey*, vol. II, p. 214; L. M. J. Garnett, *The Turkish People*, p. 79.

69. A. Russell, *The Natural History of Aleppo*, pp. 141–2.

70. C. Bruyn, *A Voyage to the Levant*, p. 96; C. Thompson, *The Travels of the Late Charles Thompson, Esq.*, vol. II, pp. 149–50; F. de Tott, *Memoirs of the Baron de Tott, on the Turks and Tartars*, vol. I, p. 157; C. Niebuhr, *Travels through Arabia, and the Other Countries of the East*, vol. I, pp. 139–40; J. T. Bent, *Early Voyages and Travels in the Levant*, p. 213.

71. J. de Thevenot, *The Travels of the Monsieur de Thevenot into the Levant*, vol. I, p. 35; J. Du Mont, *A New Voyage to the Levant*, pp. 276–7.

72. F. Kanitz, *Das Königreich Serbien und das Serbenvolk von der Römerzeit bis zur Gegenwart*, vol. II, p. 157; F. Doflein, *Mazedonien*, p. 253; T. O. Nishani, *Albanien, das Wunschland Mussolinis*, p. 137; F. A. Konitza, *The Rock Garden of Southeastern Europe*, p. 41.

73. R. West, *Black Lamb and Grey Falcon*, p. 308.

74. A. Messner-Sporšić, *Od Bukurešta do Ankare*, p. 142.

75. See e.g. J. K. Weyand, *Reisen durch Europa, Asien, und Afrika von dem Jahre 1818 bis 1821 incl.*, p. 52; J. G. Stephens, *Incidents of Travel in Greece, Turkey, Russia, and Poland*, vol. I, p. 157; C. White, *Three Years in Constantinople*, vol. I, pp. 281–2; A Lady, *Wayfaring Sketches among the Greeks and Turks*, pp. 100, 120; R. J. Curzon, *Visits to Monasteries in the Levant*, p. 244; A. Smith, *A Month at Constantinople*, p. 118; S. Kapper, *Südslavische Wanderungen im Sommer 1850*, vol. I, pp. 246–7; T. Gautier, *Constantinople*, p. 107; J. Sullivan, *Diary of a Tour in the Autumn of 1856*, p. 23; Azaïs and C. Domergue, *Journal d'un voyage en Orient*, p. 302; A. Gil'ferding, *Poězdka po Gercegovine, Bosnii i Staroj Serbii*, p. 80; J. Roškiewicz, *Studien über Bosnien und die Herzegovina*, p. 261; H. E. H. Jerningham, *To and from Constantinople*, p. 213; A. Janke, *Reise-Errinerungen aus Italien, Griechenland und dem Orient*, p. 147; A. J. Evans, *Through Bosnia and the Herzegovina On Foot During the Insurrection, August and September 1875*, p. 198; E. de Amicis, *Constantinople*, pp. 307–8; S. L. Poole, *The People of Turkey*, vol. II, p. 74; F. Kanitz, *Donau-Bulgarien und Balkan*, vol. I, p. 233; P. de Régla, *La Turquie Officielle*, pp. 114, 119; W. Huyshe, *The Liberation of Bulgaria*, p. 42; C. N. E. Eliot, *Turkey in Europe*, p. 100; H. O. Dwight, *Constantinople and its Problems*, pp. 160–1; G. F. Abbott, *The Tale of a Tour in Macedonia*, pp. 72–3; J. Lloyd Evans, *British journalists' Tour in the Adriatic and Bosnia*, p. 41; F. G. Aflalo, *An Idler in the Near East*, pp. 268–9; D. L. Neave, *Romance of the Bosphorus*, p. 56.

76. W. K. Loftus, *Travels and Researches in Chaldaea and Susianna*, p. 109.

77. E. L. V. de Laveleye, *The Balkan Peninsula*, p. 141.

78. R. R. Madden, *Travels in Turkey, Egypt, Nubia, and Palestine, in 1824, 1825, 1826, and 1827*, vol. I, pp. 16–7.

79. S. G. St Clair and C. A. Brophy, *A Residence in Bulgaria*, p. 238.

80. H. A. V. Post, *A Visit to Constantinople, in the Year 1827–8*, p. 269.

81. R. Burton, *Personal Narrative of a Pilgrimage to al-Madinah and Meccah*, vol. I, p. 9.

82. A. Smith, *A Month at Constantinople*, p. 118; S. G. W. Benjamin, *The Turk and the Greek*, p. 45; E. L. V. de Laveleye, *The Balkan Peninsula*, p. 141; D. Coufopoulos, *A Guide to Constantinople*, p. 23; M. Sykes, *Dar-ul-Islam*, p. 175; Ruprecht, *Reise-Erinnerungen aus dem Süd-Osten Europas un dem Orient*, p. 222.

83. R. Močnik, 'Temne zore'.
84. V. Karadžić, *Srpski rječnik, istolkovan njemačkim i latinskim riječima*, p. 839.
85. M. E. Durham, *Through the Lands of the Serb*, p. 204.
86. E. L. V. de Laveleye, *The Balkan Peninsula*, pp. 75–6.
87. J. Lloyd Evans, *British journalists' tour in the Adriatic and Bosnia*, p. 41.
88. C. White, *Three Years in Constantinople*, vol. I, p. 281.
89. P. Edmonds, *The Land of the Eagle*, p. 78.
90. F. X. Zedtwitz, *Zaubervoller Balkan*, p. 88.

Chapter 9
1. T. Comyn-Platt, *The Turk in the Balkans*, p. 11.
2. S. Pribichevich, *Macedonia*, pp. 4, 38.
3. M. B. Cosmopoulos, *Macedonia*, p. 13.
4. L. Hugonnet, *La Turquie inconnue*, p. 90; C. von Goltz, *Ein Ausflag nach Macedonien*, pp. 14–15; V. Bérard, *La Macédoine*, pp. 43–4, 171; V. Mantegazza, *Macedonia*, p. 12; H. N. Brailsford, *Macedonia: Its Races and Their Future*, p. 80.
5. A. Miecznik, 'Macedonia i Macedonczycy', p. 77.
6. C. N. E. Eliot, *Turkey in Europe*, p. 17; H. N. Brailsford, *Macedonia: Its Races and Their Future*, p. 77; Z. Duckett Ferriman, *Turkey and the Turks*, p. 80; L. Villari, *The Balkan Question*, p. 121; B. G. Baker, *The Passing of the Turkish Empire in Europe*, p. 259.
7. L. M. Danforth, *The Macedonian Conflict*, p. 57; c.f. Novaković 1906: 393; A. Goff and H. A. Fawcett, *Macedonia. A Plea for the Primitive*, pp. 6–7; D. M. Perry, *The Politics of Terror*, p. 24.
8. See e.g. Baudier 1624: 31; E. Browne, *A Brief Account of some Travels in Hungaria, Servia, Bulgaria, Macedonia, Thessaly, Austria, Styria, Carinthia, Carniola, and Fruili*, p. 45; Mahmut, *Letters Written by a Turkish Spy*, p. 137; A. Hill, *A Full and Just Account of the Present State of the Ottoman Empire in all its Branches*, p. 69; R. R. Madden, *Travels in Turkey, Egypt, Nubia, and Palestine, in 1824, 1825, 1826, and 1827*, vol. I, p. 74; V. Grigorovič, *Očerk putešestvija po evropejskoj Turcii*, p. 164.
9. V. Mantegazza, *Macedonia*, p. 7; H. N. Brailsford, *Macedonia: Its Races and Their Future*, p. 103; N. Buxton, *Europe and the Turks*, p. 45; A. Moore, *The Orient Express*, p. 265; J. Reed, *The War in Eastern Europe*, p. 14.
10. G. F. Abbott, *The Tale of a Tour in Macedonia*, p. 278; M. E. Durham, *The Burden of the Balkans*, p. 6; H. N. Brailsford, *Macedonia: Its Races and Their Future*, p. 103; A. Upward, *The East End of Europe*, pp. 28, 162.
11. H. F. Tozer, *Researches in the Highlands of Turkey*, vol. I, p. 214; B. Nušić, *Kosovo*, p. 87; J. Slišković, *Albanija i Macedonija*, p. 86; E. E. F. Descamps, *L'avenir de l'Albanie*, p. 21; C. A. Dako, *Albania*, pp. 17, 29; R. W. Lane, *The Peaks of Shala*, p. 16; R. Matthews, *Sons of the Eagle*, pp. 5, 42.
12. S. L. Popović, *Putovanje po novoj Srbiji*, p. 281.
13. L. Kuba, *Čtení o Makedonii*, p. 213.
14. See e.g. K. Jireček, *Cesty po Bulharsku*, p. 307; A. Upward, *The East End of Europe*, pp. 162–3.
15. See e.g. R. Walsh, *Narrative of a Journey from Constantinople to England*, p. 168; E. M. Cousinéry, *Voyage dans La Macédoine*, vol. I, p. 15; E. R. Friedrichsthal, *Reise in den südlichen Theilen von Neu-Griechenland*, p. 36; A. Boué, *La Turqui d'Europe*, vol. II, p. 5; V. Grigorovič, *Očerk putešestvija po evropejskoj Turcii*, pp. 105, 121, 127; N. Heuzey, *Mission archeologique de Macedoine*, p. 309; L. Glück, *Albanien und Macedonien*, p. 65; A. Moore, *The Orient Express*, p. 181; Carnegie Endowment, *Report of the International Commission to Inquire into the Causes and Conduct of the Balkan Wars* (1914), pp. 26, 30; 1925: 12; A

Diplomatist, *Nationalism and War in the Near East*, p. 89.

16. V. Mantegazza, *Macedonia*, p. 2; H. F. B. Lynch, *Europe in Macedonia*, p. 12–3; cf. J. Reuter, 'Policy and Economy in Macedonia', p. 29.

17. A. Miecznik, *Macedonja i Macedonczycy*, p. 5; A. Upward, *The East End of Europe*, p. 26; G. B. Zotiades, *The Macedonian Controversy*, p. 12.

18. F. Moore, *The Balkan Trail*, p. 156.

19. S. Gopčević, *Makedonien und Alt-Serbien*, pp. 501–3.

20. C. Nicolaides, *Macedonien*, pp. 25–8.

21. V. Kŭnčov, *Makedonija*, p. 289.

22. See e.g. M. V. Chirol, *Twixt Greek and Turk*, p. 74; V. Mantegazza, *Macedonia*, p. 232; L. Villari, *The Balkan Question*, p. 138; F. Moore, *The Balkan Trail*, p. 156; A. V. Amfiteatrov, *Slavjanskoe gore*, p. 247, D. G. Baker, *The Passing of the Turkish Empire in Europe*, pp. 235–6; J. Reed, *The War in Eastern Europe*, p. 319; L. W. W. Buxton, *The Black Sheep of the Balkans*, pp. 146–7; M. E. Durham, *Twenty Years of Balkan Tangle*, pp. 93–4; V. Sís, *Novy Balkan*, p. 151; S. Christowe, *Heroes and Assassins*, pp. 45–6; R. Matthews, *Sons of the Eagle*, p. 215; M. B. Cosmopoulos, *Macedonia*, pp. 86–7.

23. H. F. Tozer, *Researches in the Highlands of Turkey*, vol. I, p. 182.

24. C. A. Vavouskos, *Macedonia's Struggle for Freedom*, p. 9; N. K. Martis, *The Falsification of Macedonia's History*, p. 109; M. B. Cosmopoulos, *Macedonia*, p. 57.

25. C. A. Vavouskos, *Macedonia's Struggle for Freedom*, pp. 22–3.

26. E. L. V. de Laveleye, *The Balkan Peninsula*, p. 290.

27. C. Nicolaides, *Macedonien*, p. 25.

28. E. L. V. de Laveleye, *The Balkan Peninsula*, pp. 290–2.

29. D. Misheff, *The Truth about Macedonia*, p. 31.

30. E. L. V. de Laveleye, *The Balkan Peninsula*, p. 293.

31. Ibidem.

32. See e.g. E. Habesci, *The Present State of the Ottoman Empire*, p. 289; N. Bisani, *A Picturesque Tour Through Part of Europe, Asia, and Africa*, p. 129; T. S. Hughes, *Travels in Sicily Greece and Albania*, p. 442; D. Ross, *Opinions of the European Press on the Eastern Question*, p. 273; J. S. Stuart-Glennie, *Europe and Asia*, p. 189; R. Gossip, *Turkey and Russia*, vol. II, p. 300; A. de Lusignan, *A Word about Turkey and Her Allies*, p. 10; G. Young, *Constantinople*, pp. 164–5; H. Edib, *Turkey Faces West*, p. 53; R. L. Wolff, *The Balkans in Our Time*, p. 71; cf. T. Mastnak, *Evropa: med evolucijo in evtanazijo*, p. 122.

33. A. J. Toynbee, *The Western Question in Greece and Turkey*, p. 17.

34. C. Hamlin, *Among the Turks*, p. 268.

35. H. N. Brailsford, *Macedonia: Its Races and Their Future*, p. 107.

36. Carnegie Endowment, *Report of the International Commission to Inquire into the Causes and Conduct of the Balkan Wars* (1914), p. 22.

37. Ibidem.

38. H. N. Brailsford, *Macedonia: Its Races and Their Future*, p. 107; L. S. Stavrianos, *The Balkans since 1453*, p. 518.

39. K. Bercovici, *The Incredible Balkans*, pp. 93–4; G. B. Zotiades, *The Macedonian Controversy*, p. 57.

40. M. V. Chirol, *Twixt Greek and Turk*, pp. 64, 168; G. F. Abbott, *The Tale of a Tour in Macedonia*, p. 79; V. Mantegazza, *Macedonia*, p. 265; A. Miecznik, *Macedonja i Macedonczycy*, p. 4; N. Buxton, *Europe and the Turks*, p. 49; W. Le Queux, *An Observer in the Near East*, p. 147; H. F. B. Lynch, *Europe in Macedonia*, pp. 34–5; A. Upward, *The East End of Europe*, p. 179; A. Moore, *The Orient Express*, pp. 171–2; J. Reed, *The War in Eastern Europe*, p. 305; E. Bouchié de Belle, *La Macédoine et les Macédoinens*, pp. 25, 129–30; K. Bercovici, *The Incredible Balkans*, pp. 90, 93; R. Graves, *Storm Centres of the Near East*, p. 196.

41. E. L V. de Laveleye, *The Balkan Peninsula*, p. 290; J. Samuelson, *Bulgaria Past and Present*, p. 218; E. A. Barlett, *The Battlefields of Thessaly*, p. 45; J. P. Barry, *At the Gaes of the East*, p. 251; T. Comyn-Platt, *The Turk in the Balkans*, p. 51; N. Buxton, *Europe and the Turks*, p. 55; A. F. Townshend, *A Military Consul in Turkey*, p. 321; E. Bouchié de Belle, *La Macédoine et les Macédoinens*, p. 96; M. B. Cosmopoulos, *Macedonia*, p. 74.
42. A. G. Hulme-Beaman, *Twenty Years in the Near East*, p. 137.
43. W. Le Queux, *An Observer in the Near East* 285; E. About, *Greece and the Greeks of the Present Day*, pp. 42, 305.
44. T. Gordon, *History of the Greek Revolution*, vol. I, p. 321; N. W. Senior, *Diary of a Journal kept in Turkey*, pp. 358–9, 364; F. Bremer, *Greece and the Greeks*, vol. II, pp. 85, 285; A. Arnold, *From the Levant, the Black Sea, and the Danube*, vol. I, pp. 11–3; J. S. Stuart-Glennie, *Europe and Asia*, pp. 244; L. Hugonnet, *La Turquie inconnue*, p. 284; Kesnin bey, *The Evil of the East*, p. 209; J. Samuelson, *Bulgaria, Past and Present*, p. 216; G. Horton, *Constantine*, p. 9; H. S. Edwards, *Sir William White*, p. 248; L. Villari, *The Balkan Question*, p. 137; H. N. Brailsford, *Macedonia: Its Races and Their Future*, p. 122; S. Novaković, *Balkanska pitanja i manje istorijsko-političke beleške o Balkanskom poluostrvu 1886–1905*, p. 368; A. Upward, *The East End of Europe*, p. 26; J. A. Douglas, *The Redemption of Saint Sophia*, p. 67; L. Ostrorog, *The Turkish Problem*, p. 178; M. D. Volonakis, *Saint Sophia and Constantinople*, p. 50; E. Bouchié de Belle, *La Macédoine et les Macédoinens*, p. 248; C. Price, *The Rebirth of Turkey*, p. 52; H. Armstrong, *Turkey in Travail*, p. 233.
45. G. T. Temple, *Travels in Greece and Turkey*, vol. I, p. 22; A. Arnold, *From the Levant, the Black Sea, and the Danube*, vol. I, pp. 119, 124; K. Braum-Wiesbaden, *Eine Türkische Reise*, vol. II, p. 156; H. O. Dwight, *Turkish Life in War Time*, p. 243.
46. D. Vaka, *The Eagle and the Sparrow*, pp. 2–3.
47. See e.g. M. V. Chirol, *Twixt Greek and Turk*, pp. 79, 86; N. Buxton, *Europe and the Turks*, pp. 49–50; W. Le Queux, *An Observer in the Near East*, p. 294; Draganof, *Macedonia and the Reforms*, pp. 231–92; H. F. B. Lynch, *Europe in Macedonia*, p. 35; A. V. Amfiteatrov, *Slavjanskoe gore*, p. 254; Carnegie Endowment, *Report of the International Commission to Inquire into the Causes and Conduct of the Balkan Wars* (1914), p. 56; Carnegie Endowment, *Report of the International Commission to Inquire into the Causes and Conduct of the Balkan Wars* (1925), p. 43; J. Reed, *The War in Eastern Europe*, p. 319; L. W. W. Buxton, *The Black Sheep of the Balkans*, pp. 146–7.
48. H. Edib, *Turkey Faces West*, p. 68.
49. A. H. Layard, *Autobiography and Letters*, vol. II, p. 125; I. Ivanić, *Maćedonija i Maćedonci*, pp. 98, 126; H. N. Brailsford, *Macedonia: Its Races and Their Future*, pp. 62, 80; A. V. Amfiteatrov, *Slavjanskoe gore*, pp. 244–5; B. G. Baker, *The Passing of the Turkish Empire in Europe*, pp. 54–5; E. Maliszewski, *Albania*, pp. 41–2; W. Gordon, *A Woman in the Balkans*, p. 258; J. A. Douglas, *The Redemption of Saint Sophia*, p. 59; H. R. Wilkinson, *Maps and Politics*, p. 17.
50. J. B. S. Morritt, *The Letters of John B. S. Morritt of Rokeby*, p. 60.
51. F. Hervé, *A Residence in Greece and Turkey*, vol. II, p. 286.
52. H. Vivian, *Servia, the Poor Man's Paradise*, p. 100; *The Servian Tragedy with some Impressions of Macedonia*, p. 227; C. N. E. Eliot, *Turkey in Europe*, p. 347; H. S. Edwards, *Sir William White*, pp. 123, 248; B. G. Baker, *The Passing of the Turkish Empire in Europe*, p. 239.
53. S. M. Protić, *O Makedoniji i Macedoncima*, pp. 87–90, 94–5; K. P. Misirkov, *Za makedonckite raboti*, p. 123; L. M. J. Garnett, *Turkish Life in Town and Country*, pp. 160–1; I. Ivanić, *Maćedonija i Maćedonci*, pp. 16, 72–3, 105; M. Plut, *Po macedonskem bojišču*, p. 126; S. Tomitch, 'Who are the Macedonian Slavs?', p. 110; S. Pribichevich, *Macedonia*, p. 108; see also J. K. Cowan, *Macedonia*, p. xv.
54. A. V. Amfiteatrov, *Strana razdora*, p. 26.

55. A. Upward, *The East End of Europe*, p. 76.
56. H. N. Brailsford, *Macedonia: Its Races and Their Future*, pp. 62–3, 102; N. Buxton, *Europe and the Turks*, p. 52; H. A. Franck, *The Fringe of the Moslem World*, p. 316.
57. J. F. Fraser, *Pictures from the Balkans*, p. 11.
58. A. J. Toynbee, *The Western Question in Greece and Turkey*, pp. 15–6.
59. V. Vodovozov, *Na Balkanah*, pp. 76–7.
60. S. Gopčević, *Makedonien und Alt-Serbien*, p. 325; A. V. Amfiteatrov, *Strana razdora*, p. 17; K. P. Misirkov, *Za makedonckite raboti*, p. 122; H. N. Brailsford, *Macedonia: Its Races and Their Future*, p. 99.
61. A. V. Amfiteatrov, *Strana Razdora*, p. 13.
62. G. F. Abbott, *The Tale of a Tour in Macedonia*, p. 77; F. Moore, *The Balkan Trail*, p. 187.
63. A. V. Amfiteatrov, *Strana Razdora*, p. 17.
64. P. A. Rittih, *Po Balkanam*, p. 199.
65. Ibid., p. 214.
66. A. G. Hulme-Beaman, *Twenty Years in the Near East*, p. 143; G. F. Abbott, *The Tale of a Tour in Macedonia*, p. 110; A. V. Amfiteatrov, *Strana razdora*, p. 14; L. W. W. Buxton, *The Black Sheep of the Balkans*, pp. 146–7.
67. S. Tomitch, 'Who are the Macedonian Slavs?', p. 118.
68. C. N. E. Eliot, *Turkey in Europe*, p. 298; L. Villari, *The Balkan Question*, p. 122; H. N. Brailsford, *Macedonia: Its Races and Their Future*, p. 167.
69. See e.g. H. N. Brailsford, *Macedonia: Its Races and Their Future*, p. 101.
70. G. F. Abbott, *The Tale of a Tour in Macedonia*, pp. 9–10.
71. H. N. Brailsford, *Macedonia: Its Races and Their Future*, p. 103.
72. A. V. Amfiteatrov, *Strana Razdora*, p. 20.
73. E. Dicey, *The Peasant State*, pp. 104, 123; K. Kirkness, *Ferdinand of Bulgaria*, pp. 104, 123.
74. A. G. Hulme-Beaman, *Twenty Years in the Near East*, p. 143; G. F. Abbott, *The Tale of a Tour in Macedonia*, p. 110; H. N. Brailsford, *Macedonia: Its Races and Their Future*, p. 132; F. Moore, *The Balkan Trail*, p. 157; R. and K. Bruce, *Letters from Turkey*, p. 64; A. Upward, *The East End of Europe*, pp. 21–2; L. M. Garnett, *Turkey of the Ottomans*, p. 124; M. J. Andonović, *Makedonski su Sloveni Srbi*, p. 10; R. Graves, *Storm Centres of the Near East*, p. 193.
75. W. Le Queux, *An Observer in the Near East*, p. 207.
76. M. B. Cosmopoulos, *Macedonia*, p. 72.
77. E. A. Barlett, *The Battlefields of Thessaly*, pp. 16–23, 125–7; C. Bigham, *With the Turkish Army in Thessaly*, pp. 3–4; V. Mantegazza, *Macedonia*, p. 226; H. F. B. Lynch, *Europe in Macedonia*, p. 35; M. B. Cosmopoulos, *Macedonia*, pp. 74–5.
78. See e.g. V. Bérard, *La Macédoine*, p. 36; H. N. Brailsford, *Macedonia: Its Races and Their Future*, p. 104; N. Buxton, *Europe and the Turks*, p. 48; Carnegie Endowment, *Report of the International Commission to Inquire into the Causes and Conduct of the Balkan Wars* (1914), pp. 25–6; Carnegie Endowment, *Report of the International Commission to Inquire into the Causes and Conduct of the Balkan Wars* (1925), pp. iv, 6; J. Reed, *The War in Eastern Europe*, p. 317; D. Misheff, *The Truth About Macedonia*, p. 29; F. Valoušek, *Vzpomínky na Bosnu*, p. 49.
79. L. Villari, *The Balkan Question*, p. 83; A. Upward, *The East End of Europe*, p. 271.
80. J. Cvijić, *Nekolika promatranja o etnografiji makedonskih Slovena*, p. 5; cf. R. A. Reiss, *The Kingdom of Serbia*, p. 39.
81. S. M. Protić, *O Macedoniji i Macedoncima*, pp. 41, 83–7; M. V. Veselinović, *Srbi u Makedoniji i u južnoj Staroj Srbiji*, p. 3; S. Gopčević, *Makedonien und Alt-Serbien*, p. 37; M. J. Andonović, *Makedonski su Sloveni Srbi*, p. 6; J. Cvijić, *Nekolika promatranja o*

etnografiji makedonskih Slovena, p. 12; idem, *La péninsule balkanique*, p. 480; Balkanicus, *The Aspirations of Bulgaria*, pp. 230–1.

82. J. Reed, *The War in Eastern Europe*, p. 55.
83. M. E. Durham, *The Burden of the Balkans*, pp. 91–2.
84. F. M. Wilson, *Portraits and Sketches of Serbia*, p. 64; see also Carnegie Endowment, *Report of the International Commission to Inquire into the Causes and Conduct of the Balkan Wars* (1914), p. 180.
85. Carnegie Endowment, *Report of the International Commission to Inquire into the Causes and Conduct of the Balkan Wars* (1914), p. 164.
86. Carnegie Endowment, *Report of the International Commission to Inquire into the Causes and Conduct of the Balkan Wars* (1914), pp. 174–7; J. Reed, *The War in Eastern Europe*, p. 319; V. Vodovozov, *Na Balkanah*, p. 82; L. Kuba, *Čtení o Makedonii*, pp. 38, 211; S. Christowe, *Heroes and Assassins*, p. 145; S. K. Pavlowitch, *A History of the Balkans 1804–1945*, p. 177.
87. L. Kuba, *Čtení o Makedonii*, pp. 40, 226.
88. S. Christowe, *Heroes and Assassins*, p. 45.
89. V. Vodovozov, *Na Balkanah*, pp. 76, 90.
90. F. Moore, *The Balkan Trail*, pp. 185–6.
91. A. G. Hulme-Beaman, *Twenty Years in the Near East*, p. 146.
92. D. J. Popović, *O Cincarima*, pp. 276–7.
93. F. Tućan, *Po Makedoniji*, p. 96.
94. Cf. N. K. Martis, *The Falsification of Macedonia History*, p. 109; M. B. Cosmopoulos, *Macedonia*, p. 57.
95. J. F. Fraser, *Pictures from the Balkans*, p. 6.
96. Đ. M. Puljevski, *Rečnik od tri jezika s. makedonski, arbanski i turski*, p. 49.
97. K. P. Misirkov, *Za makedonckite raboti*, p. 101.
98. A. Miecznik, *Macedonja i Macedonczycy*, p. 66; A. Upward, *The East End of Europe*, pp. 59, 204; R. G. D. Laffan, *The Guardians of the Gate*, p. 66; E. Bouchié de Belle, *La Macédoine et les Macédoinens*, p. 44.
99. P. A. Rittih, *Po Balkanam*, p. 178.
100. S. K. Salgŭndžijev, *Lični dela i spomeni po vŭzroždaneto na solunskiot i serski Bulgari ili 12–godišna žestoka neravna borca s gŭrckata propaganda*, pp. 34–5.
101. V. Vodovozov, *Na Balkanah*, p. 30.
102. See e.g. Horn, *Das Volksthum der Slaven Makedoniens. Ein Beitrag zur Klärung der Orientfrage*, pp. 19–20.
103. J. F. Fraser, *Pictures from the Balkans*, p. 6.
104. T. Comyn-Platt, *The Turk in the Balkans*, pp. 33–4.
105. G. F. Abbott, *The Tale of a Tour in Macedonia*, p. 80.

Chapter 10
1. R. Trevor, *My Balkan Tour*, p. 166.
2. R. West, *Black Lamb and Grey Falcon*, p. 288.
3. A. Nametak, 'Mostarski stari most', p. 137; Idem, *Islamski kulturni spomenici turskoga perioda u Bosni i Hercegovini*, p. 28; F. Babinger, 'Die Brücke von Mostar', p. 11.
4. See F. K. Hutchinson, *Motoring in the Balkans*, p. 244.
5. F. de Beaujour, *Voyages militaire dans l'Empire Othoman*, vol. I, p. 389; G. Capus, *A travers la Bosnie et l'Herzegovine*, p. 303; D. Franić, *S giacima kroz Bosnu-Hercegovinu, Crnu Goru, Dalmaciju, Jadransko more, Istru (Trst, Mletke, Rijeku) i Hrvatsku*, p. 108; J. Koetschet, *Osman Pascha*, p. 58; A. Nametak, 'Mostarski stari most', p. 140; H. Kreševljaković and H. Kapidžić, 'Stari hercegovački gradovi', p. 11.

6. M. A. Mujić, 'Krivi most na Radobolji u Mostaru', p. 215.
7. M. Ajkić, *Stari most – simbol Mostara*, p. 5.
8. H. Renner, *Durch Bosnien und die Hercegovina kreuz und quer*, pp. 307–8; R. Michel, *Auf der Südbastion unseress Reiches*, p. 29; M. Ajkić, *Mostarski stari most*, p. 12; Idem, *Stari most – simbol Mostara*, p. 16.
9. E. Çelebi, *Putopis*, p. 470.
10. M. Ajkić, *Mostarski stari most*, p. 13; D. Čelić and M. Mujezinović, *Stari mostovi u Bosni i Herzegovini*, p. 188.
11. H. Hasandedić, *Spomenici kulture turskog doba u Mostaru*, p. 111.
12. C. J. Jireček, *DieHeerstrassse von Belgrad nach Constantinopel und die Balkanpässe*, p. 79; J. de Asboth, *An Official Tour through Bosnia and Herzegovina*, p. 258; C. Peez, *Mostar und sein Culturkreis*, p. 15; H. Renner, *Durch Bosnien und die Hercegovina kreuz und quer*, p. 307; R. Michel, *Mostar*, p. 14; Idem, *Auf der Südbastion unsereß Reiches*, p. 30; M. Ajkić, *Mostarski stari most*, p. 8; Idem, *Stari most – simbol Mostara*, p. 7; F. Bajraktarević, *Mostar*, vol. III, pp. 608–9; D. Čelić and M. Mujezinović, *Stari mostovi u Bosni i Herzegovini*, p. 184; H. Hasandedić, *Spomenici kulture turskog doba u Mostaru*, p. 112.
13. D. Čelić and M. Mujezinović, *Stari mostovi u Bosni i Herzegovini*, p. 187.
14. E. Çelebi, *Putopis*, p. 470.
15. G. Capus, *A travers la Bosnie et l'Herzegovine*, p. 304; H. Renner, *Durch Bosnien und die Hercegovina kreuz und quer*, p. 307; R. Michel, *Auf der Südbastion unsereß Reiches*, p. 30; M. Ajkić, *Mostarski stari most*, p. 13; D. Čelić and M. Mujezinović, *Stari mostovi u Bosni i Herzegovini*, p. 187; H. Hasandedić, *Spomenici kulture turskog doba u Mostara*, p. 114.
16. J. de Asboth, *An Official Tour through Bosnia and Herzegovina*, p. 258; H. Renner, *Durch Bosnien und die Herzegovina kreuz und quer*, p. 307; M. H. Muhibić, 'Stara ćuprija u Mostaru', p. 13; R. Trevor, *My Balkan Tour*, pp. 166–7; R. Michel, *Auf der Südbastion unsereß Reiches*, p. 30; J. Neidhardt and D. Čelić, 'Stari most u Mostaru', p. 135; H. Hasandedić, *Spomenici kulture turskog doba u Mostaru*, p. 116.
17. M. H. Muhibić, 'Stara ćuprija u Mostaru', p. 13.
18. M. Ajkić, *Mostarski stari most*, p. 6; Idem, *Stari most – simbol Mostara*, p. 15.
19. J. de Asboth, *An Official Tour through Bosnia and Herzegovina*, p. 258; G. Capus, *A travers la Bosnie et l'Herzegovine*, p. 304; H. Renner, *Durch Bosnien und die Hercegovina kreuz und quer*, p. 307; M. H. Muhibić, 'Stara ćuprija u Mostaru', p. 13; R. Michel, *Mostar*, p. 14; Idem, *Auf der Südbastion unsereß Reiches*, p. 31; R. Trevor, *My Balkan Tour*, p. 167; J. and C. Gordon, *Two Vagabonds in the Balkans*, p. 193; M. Ajkić, *Mostarski stari most*, p. 5; Idem, *Stari most – simbol Mostara*, p. 14; J. Neidhardt and D. Čelić, 'Stari most u Mostaru', p. 135; D. Čelić and M. Mujezinović, *Stari mostovi u Bosni i Hercegovini*, p. 196; H. Hasandedić, *Spomenici kulture turskog doba u Mostaru*, p. 116.
20. See e.g. K. Jireček, *Cesty po Bulharsku*, pp. 444–5; M. A. Walker, Untrodden Path in Roumania, pp. 50–2; H. Vivian, *The Servian Tragedy with some Impressions of Macedonia*, pp. 250–1; B. Newman, *Albanian Journey*, p. 75.
21. J. Creagh, *Over the Borders of Christendom and Eslamiah*, vol. II, pp. 331–3; L. Hugonnet, *La Turquie inconnue*, p. 253; L. Glück, *Albanien und Macedonien*, p. 14; P. Edmonds, *The Land of the Eagle*, p. 240.
22. H. Renner, *Durch Bosnien und die Hercegovina kreuz und quer*, p. 195; R. Trevor, *My Balkan Tour*, p. 133.
23. J. de Asboth, *An Official Tour through the Balkans*, p. 258; H. Renner, *Durch Bosnien und die Hercegovina kreuz und quer*, pp. 197, 358.
24. C. Edsman, 'Bridges', p. 313.
25. A. Chaumette, *Voyage en Bosnie dans las années 1807 et 1808*, pp. 25, 43.
26. A. Gil'ferding, *Poězdka po Gercegovine, Bosnii, i Staroj Serbii*, p. 43; J. Creagh, *Over the*

Borders of Christendom and Eslamiah, vol. II, p. 171; J. de Asboth, *An Official Tour through Bosnia and Herzegovina*, p. 257; G. Capus, *A travers la Bosnie et l'Herzegovine*, p. 304; H. Renner, *Durch Bosnien und die Hercegovina kreuz und quer*, p. 306; M. H. Muhibić, 'Stara ćuprija u Mostaru', p. 12; J. Lavtižar, *Pri Jugoslavanih*, p. 131; J. Wester, *Iz domovine in tujine*, p. 214.

27. G. Thoemmel, *Geschichtliche, politische und topographisch-statische Beschreibung des Vilajet Bosnien*, p. 130; W. Forsyth, *The Slavonic Provinces South of the Danube*, p. 85; H. Renner, *Durch Bosnien und die Hercegovina kreuz und quer*, p. 306; J. Andrejka, *Slovenski fantje v Bosni in Hercegovini 1878*, p. 187.

28. C. Pertusier, *La Bosnie considérée dans ses rapports avec l'empire Ottoman*, pp. 265, 356.

29. A. Boué, *La Turquie d'Europe*, p. II, 384; B. Biasoletto, *Relazione del viaggio fatto nella primavera dell'anno 1838 dalla maestâ del re Federico Augusto di Sassonia nell'Istria, Dalmazia e Montenegro*, p. 129; J. G. Wilkinson, *Dalmatia and Montenegro*, vol. II, pp. 59–60; I. Reinsberg-Düringsfeld, *Aus Dalmatien*, vol. III, p. 327; C. De Lazen, *L'Herzegovine et le pont de Mostar*, p. 2; G. Arbuthnot, *Herzegovina*, p. 89; J. Rośkiewicz, *Studien über Bosnien und die Herzegovina*, p. 140; A. J. Evans, *Through Bosnia and the Herzegovina On Foot During the Insurrection, August and September 1875*, pp. 348–9; J. S. Stuart-Glennie, *Europe and Asia*, p. 383; G. Capus, *A travers la Bosnie et l'Herzegovine*, p. 304; R. Trevor, *My Balkan Tour*, p. 166; A. Blunt, *Where the Turk Trod*, p. 47.

30. A. Boué, *Recueil d'itineraires dans la Turquie d'Europe*, vol. II, p. 211.

31. G. Capus, *A travers la Bosnie et l'Herzegovine*, p. 304.

32. B. Jaeckel, *The Lands of the Tamed Turk or the Balkan States To-day*, p. 171.

33. C. Yriarte, *Les bords de l'Adriatique et le Montenegro*, p. 6; J. S. Stuart-Glennie, *Europe and Asia*, p. 383.

34. Quiclet, *Les Voyages de M. Quiclet a Constantinople par terre*, p. 60.

35. J. G. Wilkinson, *Dalmatia and Montenegro*, vol. II, pp. 59–60.

36. J. G. Wilkinson, *Dalmatia and Montenegro*, vol. II, p. 60; C. de Lazen, *L'Herzegovine et le pont de Mostar*, p. 2; G. Arbuthnot, *Herzegovina*, p. 89; A. J. Evans, *Through Bosnia and the Herzegovina On Foot During the Insurrection, August and September 1875*, p. 348; H. M. Muhibić, 'Stara ćuprija u Mostaru', p. 11; G. Capus, *A travers la Bosnie et l'Herzegovine*, p. 304; H. De Windt, *Through Savage Europe*, p. 83.

37. O. Blau, *Reisen in Bosnien und der Hertzegovina*, p. 36; J. de Asboth, *An Official Tour through Bosnia and Herzegovina*, p. 257.

38. J. G. Wilkinson, *Dalmatia and Montenegro*, vol. II, pp. 61: G. Arbuthnot, *Herzegovina*, p. 89; J. Rośkiewicz, *Studien über Bosnien und die Herzegovina*, p. 140.

39. A. Boué, *Recueil d'itineraires dans la Turquie d'Europe*, vol. II, p. 212; G. Arbuthnot, *Herzegovina*, p. 89.

40. J. Hartley, *Researches in Greece and the Levant*, p. 37; cf. e.g. G. Benaglia, *Relatione del Viaggio Fatto a Constantinopoli, e Ritorno in Germania*, p. iii.

41. E. Browne, *A Brief Account of some Travels in Hungaria, Servia, Bulgaria, Macedonia, Thessaly, Austria, Styria, Carinthia, Carniola, and Fruili*, p. 82.

42. N. Buxton, *Europe and the Turks*, p. 24.

43. See e.g. R. Johnson, *Relations, Of the Most Famovs Kingdoms and Common-Weales Throvgh the World*, p. 268; J. Howell, *Instructions and Dierections For Forren Travell*, p. 134; J. Burbury, *A Relation of a Journey of the Right Honourable My Lord Henry Howard*, pp. 142, 173; F. Gemelli Careri, *Giro del Mondo*, vol. I, pp. 241, 295–6.

44. Poullet, *Nouvelles relations du Levant*, vol. I, p. 75.

45. R. Semple, *Observations on A Journey through Spain and Italy to Naples*, vol. II, p. 180.

46. W. Knighton, *European Turkey*, p. 153.

47. R. Walsh, *Narrative of a Journey from Constantinople to England*, p. 191.

48. J. Hartley, *Researches in Greece and the Levant*, p. 37.
49. A. Boué, *La Turquie d'Europe*, vol. II, p. 415.
50. G. Rasch, *Die Türken in Europa*, p. v; P. Loti, *Turkey in Agony*, p. 40.
51. C. R. Cockerell, *Travels in Southern Europe and the Levant, 1810–1817*, pp. 26–7.
52. A. Boué, *La Turquie d'Europe*, vol. III, p. 73; M. Borsa, *Dal Montenegro*, p. 63.
53. N. Angell, *Peace Theories and the Balkan War*, p. 33.
54. C. de Lazen, *L'Herzegovine et le pont de Mostar*, p. 2.
55. F. Gemelli Careri, *Giro del Mondo*, vol. VI, pp. 200–1.
56. I. F. Jukić, 'Putovanje po Bosni godine 1843', p. 26; I. Kukuljević, *Putovanje po Bosni*, p. 74; H. De Windt, *Through Savage Europe*, p. 107; P. Šolta, *Bosniski kraj a raj*, p. 26.
57. I. Reinsberg-Düringsfeld, *Aus Dalmatien*, vol. III, p. 194.
58. Ibid., vol. III, p. 327.
59. O. Blau, *Reisen in Bosnien und der Hertzegovina*, p. 36.
60. A. J. Evans, *Through Bosnia and the Herzegovina On Foot During the Insurrection, August and September 1875*, pp. 348–9.
61. R. Munro, *Rambles and Studies in Bosnia-Herzegovina*, p. 181.
62. J. de Asboth, *An Official Tour through Bosnia and Herzegovina*, p. 257; H. De Windt, *Through Savage Europe*, p. 83.
63. E. Styx, *Das Bauwesen in Bosnien und der Hercegovina vom Beginn der Occupation durch die österreichisch-ungarische Monarchie bis in das Jahr 1887*, p. 14.
64. M. H. Muhibić, 'Stara ćuprija u Mostaru', p. 13.
65. M. Ajkić, *Stari most – simbol Mostara*, pp. 3, 17.
66. See e.g. A. F. Schweiger-Lerchenfeld, *Bosnien, das Land und seine Bewohnen*, p. 89; C. Peez, *Mostar und sein Culturkreis*, p. 15; H. C. Thomson, *The Outgoing Turk*, p. 94; H. De Windt, *Through Savage Europe*, p. 83; R. Michel, *Mostar*, p. 14; Mrs E. R. Whitwell, *Through Bosnia and Herzegovina*, p. 51; B. Jaeckel, *The Lands of the Tamed Turk or the Balkan States To-day*, p. 172; R. Trevor, *My Balkan Tour*, p. 166; J. and C. Gordon, *Two Vagabonds in the Balkans*, p. 194; A. Köhler, *Sonne über dem Balkan*, p. 91; G. Ellison, *Yugoslavia*, p. 258; M. Burr, *Slouch Hat*, p. 31; J. I. B. McCulloch, *Drums in the Balkan Night*, p. 103.
67. S. Stanojević, *Narodna enciklopedija srpsko-hrvatska-slovenačka*, vol. II, p. 1049.
68. L. A. Matzhold, *Brandherd Balkan*, p. 39.
69. B. Curipeschitz, *Itinerarivm Wegrayß kün. May. potschaft gen Constantinopel zudem Türkischen keiser Soleyman*.
70. M. Plut, *Po macedonskem bojišču*, p. 53; A. Melik, *Do Ohrida in Bitolja*, p. 20.
71. F. Tućan, *Po Makedoniji*, p. 36; see also Novaković, *Balkanska pitanja i manje istorijsko-političke beleške o Balkanskom poluostrvu 1886–1905*, p. 30.
72. C. J. Jireček, *Die Heerstrasse von Belgrad nach Constantinopel und die Balkanpässe*, p. 79; D. Čelić and M. Mujezinović, *Stari mostovi u Bosni i Hercegovini*, p. 184; H. Hasandedić, *Spomenici kulture turskog doba u Mostaru*, p. 5.
73. C. J. Jireček, *Die Heerstrasse von Belgrad nach Constantinopel und die Balkanpässe*, p. 79; E. Styx, *Das Bauwesen in Bosnien und der Hercegovina vom Beginn der Occupation durch die österreichisch-ungarische Monarchie bis in das Jahr 1887*, p. 10; H. Renner, *Durch Bosnien und die Hercegovina kreuz und quer*, p. 306; H. Šabanović, *Bosanski pašaluk*, p. 142; D. Mandić, 'Mostar u Hercegovini, njegov postanak i značenje imena', pp. 96–7; H. Hasandedić, *Spomenici kulture turskog doba u Mostaru, pp. 6, 9.
74. A. Nametak, 'Mostarski stari most', p. 135.
75. E. Çelebi, *Putopis*, p. 469.
76. A. Chaumette, *Voyage en Bosnie dans les années 1807 et 1808*, p. 25; J. G. Wilkinson, *Dalmatia and Montenegro*, vol. II, pp. 59–60; A. Boué, *Recueil d'itineraires dans la Turquie d'Europe*, vol. II, p. 212; A. Gil'ferding, *Poězdka po Gercegovine, Bosnii, i Staroj Serbii*, p. 43;

G. Arbuthnot, *Herzegovina*, p. 89; J. Rośkiewicz, *Studien über Bosnien und die Herzegovina*, p. 140; O. Blau, *Reisen in Bosnien und der Hertzegovina*, p. 34; J. S. Stuart-Glennie, *Europe and Asia*, p. 383; J. de Asboth, *An Official Tour through Bosnia and Herzegovina*, p. 260; M. H. Muhibić, 'Stara ćuprija u Mostaru', p. 13; G. Capus, *A travers la Bosnie et l'Herzegovine*, p. 303; J. Lavtižar, *Pri Jugoslavanih*, p. 129; J. Wester, *Iz domovine in tujine*, p. 214; A. Blunt, *Where the Turk Trod*, p. 42.

77. G. Arbuthnot, *Herzegovina*, p. 89.

78. A. F. Schweiger-Lerchenfeld, *Bosnien, das Land und seine Bewohnen*, p. 89; C. Peez, *Mostar und sein Culturkreis*, p. 18.

79. A. Gil'ferding, *Poëzdka po Gercegovine, Bosnii, i Staroj Serbii*, p. 43.

80. C. Peez, *Mostar und sein Culturkreis*, p. 18.

81. V. Ćorović, *Mostar i njegovi književnici*, p. 4; M. Žunkovič, *Die Slaven, ein Urvolk Europas*, p. 165; A. Ajkić, *Mostarski stari most*, p. 11; idem, *Stari most – simbol Mostara*, p. 21; H. Kreševljaković, 'Esnafi i obrti u Bosni i Hercegovini'. P. 61; H. Hasandedić, *Spomenici kulture turskog doba u Mostaru*, p. 6.

82. D. Mandić, 'Mostar u Hercegovini, njegov postanak i značenje imena', p. 107.

83. M. Ajkić, *Stari most – simbol Mostara*, p. 21; D. Mandić, 'Mostar u Hercegovini, njegov postanak i značenje imena', p. 103.

84. M. Ajkić, *Stari most – simbol Mostara*, p. 13.

85. M. Burr, *Slouch Hat*, p. 31; J. Neidhardt and D. Čelić, 'Stari most u Mostaru', p. 134; I. Zdravković, 'Opravka kula kod Starog mosta u Mostaru', p. 141; M. Dizdar and D. Pilja, *The District of Mostar*, p. 13.

86. J. Neidhardt and D. Čelić, 'Stari most u Mostaru', p. 134.

Chapter 11

1. H. De Windt, *Through Savage Europe*.

2. W. M. Sloane, *The Balkans*.

3. Cit. L. Villari, *The Balkan Question*, pp. 33–4.

4. E. Spencer, *Travels in European Turkey in 1850*, vol. II, pp. 74.

5. A. Vambéry, *Western Culture in Eastern Lands*, p. 281; E. Pears, *Turkey and its People*, p. 318.

6. S. Gopčević, *Makedonien und Alt-Serbien*, p. 182.

7. H. Austell, 'The voyage of M. Henry Austell by Venice to Ragusa, and thence ouer-land to Constantinople: and from thence through Moldauia, Polonia, Silesia, and Germany into England, Anno 1586', p. 320.

8. G. Sandys, *A relation of a iourney begvn Anno. Dom. 1610*, p. 36.

9. See e.g. A. Russell, *The Natural History of Aleppo*, p. 14; E. D. Clarke, *Travels in various countries of Europe, Asia and Africa*, vol. I, p. 691; W. R. Greg, *Sketches in Greece and Turkey*, p. 28; E. Spencer, *Travels in European Turkey in 1850*, vol. II, pp. 371–2; W. Knighton, *European Turkey*, p. 110; A. Gil'ferding, *Poëzdka po Gercegovine, Bosnii i Staroj Serbii*, p. 311; L. Jeran, *Potovanje v Sveto Deželo, v Egipt, Fenicijo, Sirijo, na Libanon, v Carigrad in druge kraje*, p. 356; W. T. Adams, *Cross and Crescent*, p. 145; H. De Windt, *Through Savage Europe*, pp. 63, 216; F. Fox, *The Balkan Peninsula*, p. 90.

10. Mrs Pardoe, *The City of the Sultan*, vol. I, p. 1; A Lady, *Wayfaring Sketches among the Greeks and Turks*, p. 173; H. H. Leech, *Letters of a Sentinmental Idler*, p. 37; E. A. Bartlett, *The Battlefields of Thessaly*, p. 325; J. A. Douglas, *The Redemption of Saint Sophia*, p. 18; D. L. Neave, *Romance of the Bosphorus*, p. 11.

11. T. Gautier, *Constantinople*, p. 76.

12. L. James, *With the Conquered Turk*, p. 184.

13. See e.g. G. Sandys, *A relation of a iourney begvn Anno. Dom. 1610*, p. 36; E. Veryard, *An

Account on divers Choice Remarks, p. 341; C. Thompson, *The Travels Of the Late Charles Thompson, Esq.*, vol. II, p. 43; F. Calvert, *A Tour to the East, In the Years 1763 and 1764*, p. 56; F. de Tott, *Memoirs of the Baron de Tott, on the Turks and the Tartars*, vol. I, p. 41; Captain Sutherland, *A Tour up the Straits, from Gibraltar to Constantinople*, p. 348; M. Jenour, *The Route to India*, p. 19; T. Watkins, *Travels through Switzerland, Italy, Sicily, the Greek Islands to Constantinople*, vol. II, p. 244; W. Wittman, *Travels in Turkey, Asia-Minor, Syria, and Across the Desert into Egypt During the Years 1799, 1800, and 1801*, p. 13; E. D. Clarke, *Travels in various countries of Europe, Asia and Africa*, vol. I, p. 687; J. Galt, *Voyages and Travels, in the Years 1809, 1810, and 1811*, p. 255; E. Spencer, *Travels in Circassia, Krim Tartary, &c.*, vol. I, p. 129; I. Pfeiffer, *Reise eine Wienerin in das heilige Land*, p. 16; M. A. Titmarsh, *Notes of a Journey from Cornhill to Grand Cairo*, p. 100; J. G. Wilkinson, *Dalmatia and Montenegro*, vol. II, p. 88; A. de Vere, *Picturesque Sketches of Greece and Turkey*, vol. II, p. 114; L. Dunne, *A Trip to Constantinople*, p. 4; A. P. Black, *A Hundred Days in the East*, p. 499; Mrs W. Grey, *Journal of a Visit to Egypt, Constantinople, the Crimea, Greece, &c.*, p. 154; H. C. Barkley, *Between the Danube and the Black Sea*, p. 7; G. M. Mackenzie and A. P. Irby, *Travels in Slavonic Provinces of Turkey-in-Europe*, vol. I, pp. 54–5; F. Elliot, *Diary of an Idle Woman in Constantinople*, p. 230; W. E. Curtis, *The Turk and His Lost Provinces*, p. 95; F. G. Aflalo, *An Idler in the Near East*, p. 9.

14. J. Du Mont, *A New Voyage to the Levant*, p. 148.
15. P. H. Bruce, *Memoirs*, pp. 48–9.
16. A. Upward, *The East End of Europe*, p. 185.
17. R. Johnson, *Relations, Of the Most Famovs Kingdoms and Common-Weales Throvgh the World*, p. 268; A. Hill, *A Full and Just Account of the Present State of the Ottoman Empire in all its Branches*, p. 129; A. Gislenius, *Travels into Turkey*, pp. 14–5; J. Davy, *Notes and Observations on the Ionian Isles and Malta*, vol. II, p. 416.
18. M. W. Montague, *Letters*, vol. II, pp. 69–70.
19. J. Montague, *A Voyage Performed by the Late Earl of Sandwich*, p. 168; J. C. Hobhouse, *A Journey through Albania and other Provinces of Turkey in Europe and Asia*, p. 513; A. de Vere, *Picturesque Sketches of Greece and Turkey*, vol. II, pp. 119–20; J. T. Bent, *Early Voyages and Travels in the Levant*, p. 178.
20. G. F. Abbott, *Under the Turk in Constantinople*, p. 33.
21. M. A. Titmarsh, *Notes of a Journey from Cornhill to Grand Cairo*, p. 74; H. C. Thomson, *The Outgoing Turk*, p. 11; W. Miller, *Travels and Politics in the Near East*, pp. 365–6; C. N. E. Eliot, *Turkey in Europe*, p. 92; G. F. Abbott, *The Tale of a Tour in Macedonia*, p. 74; W. E. Curtis, *The Turk and His Lost Provinces*, p. 297.
22. See e.g. W. Macmichael, *Journey from Moscow to Constantinople*, p. 117; J. Bramsen, *Travels in Egypt, Syria, Cyprus, the Morea, Greece, Italy &c.*, vol. II, p. 90; W. Turner, *Journal of a Tour in the Levant*, vol. I, p. 86; J. E. Alexander, *Travels from India to England*, p. 253; E. Blaquiere, *Letters from Greece*, p. 110; G. Cochrane, *Wanderings in Greece*, vol. I, p. 202; Eremiten, *Reise nach dem Orient*, vol. I, p. 107; W. Mure, *Journal of a Tour in Greece and the Ionian Islands*, vol. II, p. 51; O. T. Parnauvel, *A Trip to Turkey*, p. 46; H. E. H. Jerningham, *To and from Constantinople*, p. 203; H. M. Field, *The Greek Islands and Turkey after the War*, p. 81; J. Samuelson, *Bulgaria, Past and Present*, p. 118; E. A. Brayley Hodgetts, *Round about Armenia*, p. 7; H. O. Dwight, *Constantinople and its Problems*, p. 180–2; C. R. Cockerell, *Travels in Southern Europe and the Levant, 1810–1817*, p. 46; W. E. Curtis, *The Turk and His Lost Provinces*, pp. 95, 196; I. Jastrebov, *Stara Serbija i Albanija*, p. 38; J. P. Barry, *At the Gates of the East*, p. 52; N. Buxton, *Europe and the Turks*, p. 15; F. Kanitz, *Das Königreich Serbien und das Serbenvolk von der Römerzeit bis zur Gegenwart*, vol. III, p. 125; L. M. Garnett, *Turkey of the Ottomans*, p. 154; J. B. S. Morritt, *The Letters of John B. S. Morritt of Rokeby*, p. 232; H. G. Blackwood, *My Russian and Turkish Journals*, p. 196; R. Graves,

Storm Centres of the Near East, p. 36.

23. A. Chaumette, *Voyage en Bosnie dans les années 1807 et 1808*, p. 77; A. Boué, *La Turquie d'Europe*, vol. II, p. 296; E. L. V. de Laveleye, *The Balkan Peninsula*, p. 74; J. Rośkiewicz, *Studien über Bosnien und die Herzegovina*, pp. 190–1; J. de Asboth, *An Official Tour through Bosnia and Herzegovina*, p. 177; D. Coufopoulos, *A Guide to Constantinople*, p. 36; B. Nušić, *Kosovo*, p. 14; M. E. Durham, *Through the Lands of the Serb*, p. 193; M. M. Holbach, *Bosnia and Herzegovina*, pp. 166–7; F. Fox, *The Balkan Peninsula*, pp. 159–60; R. West, *Black Lamb and Grey Falcon*, p. 308; M. Golczewski, *Der Balkan in deutschen und österreichischen Reise und Erlebnisberichten*, p. 133.

24. The Man, *My Secret Service*, p. 43.

25. J. E. Alexander, *Travels from India to England*, p. 253; R. Walsh, *Narrative of a Journey from Constantinople to England*, p. 208–9; A. Slade, *Travels in Germany and Russia*, pp. 170–1; W. W. Smith, *A Year with the Turks*, p. 11.

26. P. Ustinov, 'A country with too much past tries to come to terms with the present'.

27. W. Wratislaw, *Adventures of Baron Wenceslas Wratislaw of Mitrowitz*, p. 15.

28. J. Burbury, *A Relation of a Journey of the Right Honourable My Lord Henry Howard*, p. 88; E. Browne, *A Brief Account of some Travels in Hungaria, Servia, Bulgaria, Macedonia, Thessaly, Austria, Styria, Carinthia, Carniola, and Fruili*, pp. 32–5; G. Benaglia, *Relatione del Viaggio Fatto a Constantinopoli, e Ritorno in Germania*, p. 21.

29. S. Lusignan, *A Series of Letters*, vol. I, p. 254; W. Hunter, *Travels in the Year 1792*, p. 418; R. Townson, *Travels in Hungary*, p. 83; J. B. S. Morritt, *The Letters of John. B. S. Morritt of Rokeby*, p. 46; A Lady, *Wayfaring Sketches among the Greeks and Turks*, p. 320.

30. E. Spencer, *Travels in Circassia, Krim Tartary, &c.*, vol. I, p. 18.

31. J. Bramsen, *Travels in Egypt, Syria, Cyprus, the Morea, Greece, Italy, &c.*, vol. I, pp. 117–8; R. Burgess, *Greece and the Levant*, vol. II, p. 306.

32. J. Creagh, *Over the Borders of Christendom and Eslamiah*, vol. I, p. 33.

33. E. Çelebi, *Putopis*, p. 376.

34. R. Trevor, *My Balkan Tour*, p. 379.

35. *An Itinerary from London to Constantinople*, p. 45; W. Hunter, *Travels in the Year 1792*, p. 412; J. J. Best, *Excursions in Albania*, p. 327.

36. A. A. Paton, *Researches on the Danube and the Adriatic*, vol. II, pp. 37–8.

37. Ibid., vol. II, p. 254.

38. *An Itinerary from London to Constantinople*, p. 58; J. E. Alexander, *Travels from India to England*, p. 250; A British Resident, *The Frontier Lands of the Christian and the Turk*, p. 213; E. E. Johnson, *On the Track of the Crescent*, p. 115.

39. R. Walsh, *Narrative of a Journey from Constantinople to England*, p. 206.

40. C. C. Frankland, *Travels to and from Constantinople*, vol. I, p. 37.

41. N. Burton, *Narrative of a voyage from Liverpool to Alexandria*, p. 276; A British Resident, *The Frontier Lands of the Christian and the Turk*, p. 213.

42. See e.g. A Lady, *Wayfaring Sketches among the Greeks and Turks*, p. 231; W. Knighton, *European Turkey*, p. 103; J. O. Noyes, *Roumania*, p. 179; A. De Burton, *Ten Months' Tour in the East*, p. 41; H. M. Field, *The Greek Islands and Turkey after the War*, pp. 211–3; A. G. Hulme-Beaman, *Twenty Years in the Near East*, p. 117; A. Moore, *The Orient Express*, p. 174; J. Reed, *The War in Eastern Europe*, p. 295; The Man Who Dined with Kaiser, *My Secret Service*, p. 43.

43. W. M. Sloane, *The Balkans*, p. 125.

44. J. R. Colville, *Fools' Pleasure*, p. 63.

45. A. Messner-Sporšić, *Od Bukurešta do Ankare*, p. 18.

46. P. Mundy, *The Travels in Europe, 1608–1628*, p. 152.

47. F. Bevk, *Deset dni v Bolgariji*, p. 15.

48. J. G. C. Minchin, *The Growth of Freedom in the Balkan Peninsula*, p. 361.
49. K. Jireček, *Cesty po Bulharsku*, p. 26; A. Aškerc, *Izlet v Carigrad*, p. 59; W. Huyshe, *The Liberation of Bulgaria*, pp. 90, 94; W. Miller, *Travels and Politics in the Near East*, pp. 456–8; G. Modrich, *Nella Bulgaria Unita*, p. 20; W. E. Curtis, *The Turk and His Lost Provinces*, p. 199; J. F. Fraser, *Pictures from the Balkans*, pp. 66–8; W. Von Herbert, *By-paths in the Balkans*, p. 20; F. Moore, *The Balkan Trail*, pp. 56–8; H. De Windt, *Through Savage Europe*, p. 200; H. C. Woods, *Washed by Four Seas*, pp. 219–20; W. Gordon, *A Woman in the Balkans*, p. 68; R. Graves, *Storm Centres of the Near East*, p. 36; H. Hauser, *Süd- Ost-Europa ist erwacht*, p. 174.
50. J. L. C. Booth, *Trouble in the Balkans*, p. 16; F. Moore, *The Balkan Trail*, p. 69; H. De Windt, *Through Savage Europe*, p. 200; H. C. Woods, *Washed by Four Seas*, p. 227; P. A. Rittih, *Po Balkanam*, p. 19; R. G. Thomsett, *A Trip through the Balkan*, pp. 66–7; E. Pears, *Turkey and Its People*, p. 223; A. Messner-Sporšić, *Od Bukurešta do Ankare*, p. 75.
51. See e.g. R. J. More, *Under the Balkans*, pp. 9–10; A. Messner-Sporšić, *Od Bukurešta do Ankare*, p. 146.
52. F. Fox, *The Balkan Peninsula*, p. 91.
53. Hadži-Kalfa, *O balkanskom poluostrvu*, p. 36.
54. N. Bisani, *A Picturesque Tour Through Part of Europe, Asia, and Africa*, p. 36.
55. H. Holland, *Travels in the Ionian Isles, Albania, Thessaly, Macedonia, &c.*, pp. 315–6; E. M. Cousinéry, *Voyage dans La Macedoine*, vol. I, p. 41; W. M. Leake, *Travels in Northern Greece*, vol. III, pp. 239–41; A. Grisebach, *Reise durch Rumelien und nach Brussa im Jahre 1893*, vol. II, p, 61; M. A. Walker, *Through Macedonia to the Albanian Lakes*, p. 42; H. F. Tozer, *Researches in the Highlands of Turkey*, vol. I, p. 143; C. von Goltz, *Ein Ausflug nach Macedonien*, p. 10; V. Bérard, *La Macédoine*, p. 166; J. F. Fraser, *Pictures from the Balkans*, p. 184; N. P. Kondakov, *Makedonija*, pp. 74, 113–20; F. G. Aflalo, *An Idler in the Near East*, p. 265; A. Barker, *Memoire of Macedonia*, p. 17; Anon., *Fusilier Bluff*, p. 30.
56. W. Miller, *Travels and Politics in the Near East*, pp. 365–6.
57. J. F. Fraser, *Pictures from the Balkans*, p. 184.
58. J. Reed, *The War in Eastern Europe*, pp. 22–3; A. E. Conway, *A Ride Through the Balkans*, p. 53; E. Bouchié de Belle, *La Macédoine et les Macédoinens*, p. 173; A. Köhler, *Sonne über dem Balkan*, p. 167.
59. C. T. Newton, *Travels and Discoveries in the Levant*, vol. I, p. 121; J. G. C. Minchin, *The Growth of Freedom in the Balkan Peninsula*, p. 148; C. von Goltz, *Ein Ausflug nach Macedonien*, p. 12; V. Bérard, *La Macédoine*, pp. 22, 186; C. Bigham, *With the Turkish Army in Thessaly*, p. 8; G. F. Abbott, *The Tale of a Tour in Macedonia*, p. 19; H. Vivian, *The Servian Tragedy with some Impressions of Macedonia*, p. 268; H. N. Brailsford, *Macedonia: Its Races and Their Future*, p. 83; S. K. Salgŭndžijev, *Lični dela i spomeni po vŭzroždaneto na solunskiot i serski Bulgari ili 12-godišna žestoka neravna borca s gŭrckata propaganda*, p. 24; A. Köhler, *Sonne über dem Balkan*, p. 166.
60. C. von Goltz, *Ein Ausflug nach Macedonien*, p. 12.
61. N. Bisani, *A Picturesque Tour Through Part of Europe, Asia, and Africa*, p. 42; G. F. Abbott, *The Tale of a Tour in Macedonia*, p. 75.
62. M. Gilbert, *The Holocaust*, p. 551; R. Hilberg, *The Destruction of European Jews*, pp. 239, 295; L. S. Stavrianos, *The Balkans since 1453*, p. 11.
63. De la Guilletiere, *Athenes ancienne et novvelle*, p. 148; G. Wheler, *A Journey into Greece*, pp. 350–2; B. Randolph, *The Present State of the Morea*, p. 23; Thompson 1774: I, 332.
    R. Chandler, *Travels in Greece*, p. 34; F. de Chateaubriand, *Travels in Greece, Palestine, Egypt, and Barbary, during the years 1806 and 1807*, vol. I, pp. 186–7; J. Galt, *Voyages and Travels*, p. 184; H. Holland, *Travels in the Ionian Isles, Albania, Thessaly, Macedonia &c.*, p. 412; G. de Vaudoncourt, *Memoirs of the Ionian Islands*, p. 178; L. N. P. A. Forbin, *Travels in*

Greece, Turkey, and the Holy Land, in 1817–18, p. 3; T. S. Hughes, *Travels in Sicily Greece and Albania*, p. 246; W. M. Leake, *The Topography of Athens*, p. xcvi; G. Keppel, *Narrative of a Journey across the Balcan*, vol. I, p. 19; M. J. Quin, *A Steam Voyage Down the Danube*, vol. II, p. 196; J. Röser, *Tagebuch meiner Reise nach Griechenland*, p. 88; R. Walsh, *A Residence at Constantinople*, vol. I, p. 124; G. Cochrane, *Wanderings in Greece*, vol. I, p. 147; L. von Klenze, *Aphoristische Bemerkungen gesammelt auf seiner Reise nach Griechenland*, p. 404; W. F. Cumming, *Notes of a Wanderer*, vol. II, p. 108; G. Levinge, *The Traveller in the East*, p. 131; J. L. Stephens, *Incidents of travel in the Russian and Turkish Empires*, p. 41; E. Zachariá, *Reise in den Orient in den Jahren 1837 und 1838*, p. 112; N. P. Willis, *Summer Cruise in the Mediterranean*, p. 209.

64. R. Chandler, *Travels in Greece*, p. 34; F. de Chateaubriand, *Travels in Greece, Palestine, Egypt, and Barbary, during the years 1806 and 1807*, vol. I, pp. 186–7; J. Galt, *Voyages and Travels*, p. 184; H. Holland, *Travels in the Ionian Isles, Albania, Thessaly, Macedonia &c.*, p. 412; G. de Vaudoncourt, *Memoirs of the Ionian Islands*, p. 178; L. N. P. A. Forbin, *Travels in Greece, Turkey, and the Holy Land, in 1817–18*, p. 3; T. S. Hughes, *Travels in Sicily Greece and Albania*, p. 246; W. M. Leake, *The Topography of Athens*, p. xcvi; G. Keppel, *Narrative of a Journey across the Balcan*, vol. I, p. 19; M. J. Quin, *A Steam Voyage Down the Danube*, vol. II, p. 196; J. Röser, *Tagebuch meiner Reise nach Griechenland*, p. 88; R. Walsh, *A Residence at Constantinople*, vol. I, p. 124; G. Cochrane, *Wanderings in Greece*, vol. I, p. 147; L. von Klenze, *Aphoristische Bemerkungen gesammelt auf seiner Reise nach Griechenland*, p. 404; W. F. Cumming, *Notes of a Wanderer*, vol. II, p. 108; G. Levinge, *The Traveller in the East*, p. 131; J. L. Stephens, *Incidents of travel in the Russian and Turkish Empires*, p. 41; E. Zachariá, *Reise in den Orient in den Jahren 1837 und 1838*, p. 112; N. P. Willis, *Summer Cruise in the Mediterranean*, p. 209.

65. S. S. Wilson, *A Narrative of the Greek Mission*, p. 426.

66. M. A. Titmarsh, *Notes of a Journey from Cornhill to Grand Cairo*, pp. 74, 81; Mrs R. Barrington, *Through Greece and Dalmatia*, p. 84.

67. C. B. Stark, *Nach dem Griechischen Orient*, p. 301; A. De Burton, *Ten Months' Tour in the East*, p. 334.

68. C. Wordsworth, *Greece: Pictoral, Descriptive, and Historical*, p. 138.

69. F. Vernon, 'Francis Vernon's Letter, written to Mr Oldenburg', p. 357.

70. G. Wheler, *A Journey into Greece*, pp. 360–1.

71. L. Des Hayes, *Voiage de levant Fait par le Commandement dv Roy en lannée 1621*, p. 474; Du Loir, *Les voyage dv sievr dv Loir*, p. 312; Guilletiere, *Athenes ancienne et novvelle*, p. 178; G. Wheler, *A Journey into Greece*, pp. 363–4; B. Randolph, *The Present state of the Morea*, p. 23; C. Perry, *A View of the Levant*, p. 506; C. Thompson, *The Travels of the Late Charles Thompson, Esq.*, vol. I, pp. 323–4; R. Chandler, *Travels in Greece*, p. 47; N. Bisani, *A Picturesque Tour Through Part of Europe, Asia, and Africa*, p. 84; S. Pomardi, *Viaggio nella Grecia Fatto Negli Anni 1804, 1805, e 1806*, vol I, p. 124; W. Turner, *Journal of a Tour in the Levant*, vol. I, p. 326; J. Auldjo, *Journal of a Visit to Constantinople*, p. 24; E. Zachariá, *Reise in den Orient in den Jahren 1837 und 1838*, p. 139; Mrs G. L. D. Damer, *Diary of a Tour in Greece, Turkey, Egypt, and the Holy Land*, vol. I, p. 19; W. Mure, *Journal of a Tour in Greece and the Ionian islands*, vol. II, pp. 73, 76–7; W. D. Stent, *Egypt and the Holy Land in 1842*, p. 61; Miss Plumley, *Days and Nights in the East*; N. P. Willis, *Summer Cruise in the Mediterranean*, p. 208; A. Arnold, *From the Levant, the Black Sea, and the Danube*, vol. I, pp. 55–6.

72. B. Randolph, *The Present State of the Islands in the Archipeligo*, p. 23; C. Perry, *A View of the Levant*, p. 507; R. Pococke, *A Description of the East, and Some other Countries*, p. 162; F. M. A. Voltaire, *The Works*, vol. VI, p. 111; R. Chandler, *Travels in Greece*, pp. 42, 47; E. Craven, *A Journey Through the Crimea to Constantinople*, pp. 256–7; Captain Sutherland,

A Tour up the Straits, from Gibraltar to Constantinople, p. 226; T. Watkins, *Travels through Switzerland, Italy, Sicily, the Greek Islands to Constantinople*, vol. II, p. 294; J. Montague, *A Voyage Performed by the Late Earl of Sandwich*, p. 62; F. de Chateaubriand, *Travels in Greece, Palestine, Egypt, and Barbary*, vol. I, pp. 211–2; J. C. Hobhouse, *A Journey through Albania and other Provinces of Turkey in Europe and Asia*, p. 340; T. S. Hughes, *Travels in Sicily Greece and Albania*, p. 256; W. Colton, *Visit to Constantinople and Athens*, p. 259; J. Röser, *Tagebuch meiner Reise nach Griechenland*, p. 91; A. Slade, *Turkey, Greece and Malta*, vol. II, p. 303; G. Levinge, *The Traveller in the East*, p. 136; E. Zachariá, *Reise in den Orient in den Jahren 1837 und 1838*, p. 139; W. D. Stent, *Egypt and the Holy Land in 1842*, p. 60; A. de Vere, *Picturesque Sketches of Greece and Turkey*, vol. I, pp. 82–3; A. Arnold, *From the Levant, the Black Sea, and the Danube*, vol. I, p. 55; P. Jousset, *Un tour de Méditerranée, de Venise à Tunis, par Athènes, Constantinople et le Caire*, p. 59; W. E. Curtis, *The Turk and His Lost Provinces*, p. 371.

73. E. Dodwell, *A Classical and Topographical Tour through Greece*, vol. I, pp. 323–4; E. E. Crowe, *The Greek and the Turk*, p. 110.

74. A. Michaelis, *Ancient Marbles in Great Britain*, pp. 142, 150–1; see also E. Dodwell, *A Classical and Topographical Tour through Greece*, pp. 322–3; T. S. Hughes, *Travels in Sicily Greece and Albania*, p. 261; W. Turner, *Journal of a Tour in the Levant*, vol. I, p. 325; J. Fuller, *Narrative of a tour through some parts of the Turkish Empire*, pp. 540–1; R. Burgess, *Greece and the Levant*, vol. I, p. 279; W. Colton, *Visit to Constantinople and Athens*, pp. 259–61; J. Röser, *Tagebuch meiner Reise nach Griechenland*, p. 91; R. Walsh, *A Residence at Constantinople*, vol. I, p. 125; J. G. Stephens, *Incidents of Travel in Greece, Turkey, Russia, and Poland*, vol. I, p. 74; Mrs Russell Barrington, *Through Greece and Dalmatia*, pp. 52–4.

75. E. Spencer, *Travels in European Turkey in 1850*, vol. II, pp. 266–7.

76. E. E. Johnson, *On the Track of the Crescent*, p. 70.

77. J. Galt, *Voyages and Travels*, p. 164.

78. R. Graves, *Storm Centres of the Near East*, p. 265; R. Matthews, *Sons of the Eagle*, p. 22; V. Robinson, *Albania's Road to Freedom*, p. 18; W. Kollegger, *Albaniens wiedergeburt*, p. 72; E. von Luckwald, *Albanien*, p. 16.

79. J. Müller, *Albanien, Rumelien und die österreichisch-montenegrische Gränze*, p. 71; J. G. von Hahn, *Albanische Studien*, p. 85; H. Hecquard, *Histoire et description de la Haute Albanie ou Guegarie*, p. 255; M. E. Durham, *The Burden of the Balkans*, p. 301; P. Edmonds, *The Land of the Eagle*, p. 119; V. Robinson, *Albania's Road to Freedom*, p. 19.

80. See e.g. J. Müller, *Albanien, Rumelien und die österreichisch-montenegrische Gränze*, pp. 48–9; E. Lear, *Journals of a Landscape Painter in Albania, etc.*, pp. 23–5; E. Spencer, *Travels in European Turkey in 1850*, vol. II, p. 141; J. G. von Hahn, *Albanische Studien*, vol. I, p. 95; H. Hecquard, *Histoire et description de la Haute Albanie ou Guegarie*, p. 21; W. F. Wingfield, *A Tour in Dalmatia, Albania, and Montenegro*, p. 155; E. A. Strangford, *The Eastern Shores of the Adriatic in 1863 with a Visit to Montenegro*, p. 178; L. Hugonnet, *La Turquie inconnue*, p. 238; L. Glück, *Albanien und Macedonien*, p. 11; M. E. Durham, *Through the Lands of the Serb*, p. 107; R. Trevor, *My Balkan Tour*, p. 350; W. Peacock, *Albania, the foundling state of Europe*, p. 52; A. E. Conway, *A Ride through the Balkans*, p. 180; R. W. Lane, *The Peaks of Shala*, p. 12.

81. R. Trevor, *My Balkan Tour*, p. 351.

82. B. Newman, *Albanian Journey*, p. 26.

83. W. Peacock, *Albania, the foundling state of Europe*, p. 52.

84. F. Hervé, *A Residence in Greece and Turkey*, vol. II, pp. 315–6; E. Spencer, *Travels in Circassia, Krim Tartary, &c.*, vol. I, p. 53; A. A. Paton, *Servia, the youngest member of the European family*, p. 53; A Lady, *Wayfaring Sketches among the Greeks and Turks*, pp. 302–3; A. de Lamartine, *Visit to the Holy Land*, vol. II, p. 239; S. Kapper, *Südslavische*

Wanderungen im Sommer 1850, vol. I, p. 51; J. O. Noyes, *Roumania*, p. 42.

85. S. Kapper, *Südslavische Wanderungen im Sommer 1850*, vol. I, p. 107.

86. E. Browne, *A Brief Account of some Travels in Hungaria, Servia, Bulgaria, Macedonia, Thessaly, Austria, Styria, Carinthia, Carniola, and Fruili*, p. 39; idem, *A Brief Account of some Travels in Divers Parts of Europe*, p. 21; Hadži-Kalfa, *O balkanskom poluostrvu*, p. 65; P. Mundy, *The Travels in Europe, 1608–1628*, p. 74.

87. Rašid-bey, *Istorija čudnovatih događaja u Beogradu i Srbiji*, pp. 2, 10, 55.

88. P. Milosavljević, 'Ruski putešestvenici u Srbiji', p. 142.

89. A. Aškerc, *Izlet v Carigrad*, p. 68.

90. A. A. Paton, *Servia, the youngest member of the European family*, pp. 59, 256.

91. A. G. Hulme-Beaman, *Twenty Years in the Near East*, pp. 119–20.

92. A. A. Paton, *Servia, the youngest member of the European family*, pp. 53–4; E. Spencer, *Travels in European Turkey in 1850*, vol. I, pp. 15–6; W. Denton, *Servia and the Servians*, pp. 53–4; J. G. C. Minchin, *The Growth of Freedom in the Balkan Peninsula*, p. 188; E. L. V. de Laveleye, *The Balkan Peninsula*, pp. 172–3; H. Vivian, *Servia, the Poor Man's Paradise*, pp. 199–200; Idem, *The Servian Tragedy with some Impressions of Macedonia*, p. 170; V. Mantegazza, *Macedonia*, pp. 30–1; M. E. Durham, *Through the Lands of the Serb*, p. 143; J. F. Fraser, *Pictures from the Balkans*, p. 19; H. De Windt, *Through Savage Europe*, pp. 112–6; W. Y. Morgan, *The New East*, p. 63; F. Fox, *The Balkan Peninsula*, pp. 124–5; W. Gordon, *A Woman in the Balkans*, p. 9.

93. W. Y. Morgan, *The New East*, pp. 68–9.

94. W. W. Smith, *A Year with the Turks*, p. 272; A. Arnold, *From the Levant, the Black Sea, and the Danube*, vol. II, p. 277; J. Creagh, *Over the Borders of Christendom and Eslamiah*, vol. I, pp. 82, 96; E. L. V. de Laveleye, *The Balkan Peninsula*, p. 174; J. Samuelson, *Bulgaria, Past and Present*, pp. 55, 118; H. Vivian, *Servia, the Poor Man's Paradise*, pp. 199–200; V. Mantegazza, *Macedonia*, pp. 31, 170; A. G. Hulme-Beaman, *Twenty Years in the Near East*, pp. 119–20; M. E. Durham, *Through the Lands of the Serb*, p. 146; E. Karić, *Essays (on behalf) of Bosnia*, p. 59.

95. F. Kanitz, *Das Königreich Serbien und das Serbenvolk von der Römerzeit bis zur Gegenwart*, vol. I, p. 40.

96. See e.g. E. L. V. de Laveleye, *The Balkan Peninsula*, p. 174; F. Kanitz *Das Königreich Serbien und das Serbenvolk von der Römerzeit bis zur Gegenwart*, vol. I, pp. 40, 131.

97. A. A. Paton, *Servia, the youngest member of the European family*, p. 50; W. Denton, *Servia and the Servians*, p. 59; F. Kanitz, *Das Königreich Serbien und das Serbenvolk von der Römerzeit bis zur Gegenwart*, vol. II, p. 45.

98. H. S. Edwards, *Sir William White*, p. 93.

99. J. Creagh, *Over the Borders of Christendom and Eslamiah*, vol. I, p. 96.

100. G. Ellison, *Yugoslavia*, p. 82.

101. S. Gopčević, *Makedonien und Alt-Serbien*, p. 89; F. Kanitz, *Das Königreich Serbien und das Serbenvolk von der Römerzeit bis zur Gegenwart*, vol. II, p. 158.

102. M. E. Durham, *Through the Lands of the Serb*, pp. 175–7; H. Vivian, *The Servian Tragedy with some Impressions of Macedonia*, p. 199; S. Novaković, *Balkanska pitanja i manje istorijsko-političke beleške o Balkanskom poluostrvu 1886–1905*, p. 49.

103. A. J. Evans, *Illyrian Letters*, p. 161; E. F. Knight, *Albania*, p. 177; B. Schwarz, *Montenegro*, p. 238; K. Hassert, *Reise durch Montenegro nebst Bemerkungen über Land und Leute*, p. 14; M. Borsa, *Dal Montenegro*, p. 67; W. Miller, *Travels and Politics in the Near East*, p. 78; M. E. Durham, *Through the Lands of the Serb*, p. 21; Idem, *The Struggle for Scutari*, p. 303; H. De Windt, *Through Savage Europe*, p. 63; R. Trevor, *My Balkan Tour*, pp. 296–8; W. Gordon, *A Woman in the Balkans*, p. 276; P. Edmonds, *The Land of the Eagle*, p. 98; M. Burr, *Slouch Hat*, p. 67; R. Peterlin-Petruška, *Ahasverjeva kronika*, p. 76.

104. A. Lyall, *The Balkan Road*, p. 168.
105. M. E. Durham, *Through the Lands of the Serb*, p. 51.
106. E. Browne, *A Brief Account of some Travels in Hungaria, Servia, Bulgaria, Macedonia, Thessaly, Austria, Styria, Carinthia, Carniola, and Friuli*, p. 48.
107. W. Knighton, *European Turkey*, p. 118; C. von Goltz, *Ein Ausflug nach Macedonien*, p. 123; V. Bérard, *La Macédoine*, p. 53; S. Novaković, *Dva dana u Skoplju. 14–15–16 jul 1905*, p.12; Idem, *Balkanska pitanja i manje istorijsko-političke beleške o Balkanskom poluostrvu 1886–1905*, p. 49; N. P. Kondakov, *Makedonija*, p. 169; M. Baring, *Letters from the Near East 1909 and 1912*, p. 129; F. Doflein, *Mazedonien*, p. 257.
108. F. Tućan, *Po Makedoniji*, p. 45; L. Kuba, *Čteni o Makedonii*, p. 128.
109. G. Ellison, *Yugoslavia*, pp. 91–2.
110. R. West, *Black Lamb & Grey Falcon*, p. 634.
111. A. A. Paton, *Servia, the youngest member of the European family*, p. 101; J. G. C. Minchin, *The Growth of Freedom in the Balkan Peninsula*, p. 45; J. S. Stuart-Glennie, *Europe and Asia*, p. 277; W. E. Curtis, *The Turk and His Lost Provinces*, p. 281.
112. .111 J. de Asboth, *An Official Tour through Bosnia and Herzegovina*, p. 14.
113. J. G. C. Minchin, *The Growth of Freedom in the Balkan Peninsula*, p. 45; W. E. Curtis, *The Turk and His Lost Provinces*, p. 279; P. Henderson, *A British Officer in the Balkans*, p. 93; A. Zavadil, *Obrazky z Bosny*, p. 22.
114. E. Çelebi, *Putopis*, p. 405.
115. V. Klaić, *Bosna*, p. 177–8; J. de Asboth, *An Official Tour through Bosnia and Herzegovina*, p. 383; H. Renner, *Durch Bosnien und die Hercegovina kreuz und quer*, p. 496; R. Trevor, *My Balkan Tour*, p. 30; I. F. Jukić, *Putopisi i istorisko-etnografski radovi*, pp. 83, 377; I. Horozović and M. Vukmanović, *Banja Luka i okolina*, p. 56.
116. U. Komlenović, 'Rolling Stones na Vrbasu', pp. 30–1.
117. H. Renner, *Durch Bosnien und die Hercegovina kreuz und quer*, p. 493; M. Džaja, *Banja Luka u putopisima i zapisima*, p. 8.
118. G. Ellison, *Yugoslavia*, pp. 264–5.
119. J. E. Alexander, *Travels from India to England*, p. 251; E. E. Johnson, *On the Track of the Crescent*, p. 21; E. L. V. de Laveleye, *The Balkan Peninsula*, p. 97.
120. M. Laketić, 'Kalemegdanci i Beograđani', p. 90.
121. W. Miller, *Travels and Politics in the Near East*, p. 258.
122. See e.g. J. Pahor, *Hodil po zemlji sem naši*, p. 126.
123. Ibid., pp. 106, 180.
124. D. Urquhart, *The Spirit of the East*, vol. I, p. 368; W. Richter, *Serbiens Zustände unter dem Fürsten Milosch*, p. 44; C. Mac Farlane, *Turkey and Its Destiny*, vol. I, pp. 50–1; I. Kukuljević, *Putovanje po Bosni*, p. 31; Lady Hornby, *Constantinople during the Crimean War*, pp. 171–2; A. P. Black, *A Hundred Days in the East*, p. 499; H. Sandwith, *Notes on the South Slavonic countries in Austria and Turkey in Europe*, p. 38; S. L. Poole, *The People of Turkey*, vol. II, p. 53; B. Nušić, *Kraj obala Ohridskoga Jezera*, p. 160; M. E. Durham, *Through the Lands of the Serb*, p. 280; L. Mihačević, *Po Albaniji*, p. 49; J. Reed, *The War in Eastern Europe*, pp. 52–3; A. Köhler, *Sonne über dem Balkan*, p. 87.
125. H. E. H. Jerningham, *To and from Constantinople*, p. 202.
126. A. Slade, *Travels in Germany and Russia*, p. 188.
127. Ibid., p. 220.
128. Lady Hornby, *Constantinople during the Crimean War*, p. 174.
129. M. A. Titmarsh, *Notes of a Journey from Cornhill to Grand Cairo*, p. 72.
130. E. E. Johnson, *On the Track of the Crescent*, p. 5.
131. H. C. Woods, *Washed by Four Seas*, pp. 220, 226; A. and C. Askew, *The Stricken Land*, pp. 72–3.

132. A. and C. Askew, *The Stricken Land*, p. 154.
133. P. Thornton, *Dead Puppets Dance*, p. 272.
134. P. Loti, *Turkey in Agony*, p. 63.
135. E. A. Brayley Hodgetts, *Round about Armenia*, p. 5.
136. F. Fox, *The Balkan Peninsula*, p. 158.
137. J. R. Colville, *Fools' Pleasure*, p. 65.
138. R. Kabbani, *Europe's Myths of Orient*, p. 6.
139. A. Gil'ferding, *Poëzdka po Gercegovine, Bosni i Staroj Serbii*, pp. 311–2.
140. J. Creagh, *Over the Borders of Christendom and Eslamiah*, vol. I, p. 92.
141. A. Chaumette, *Voyage in Bosnie dans les années 1807 et 1808*, p. 63; C. Pertusier, *La Bosnie consideree dans ses rapports avec l'empire Ottoman*, p. 99; R. Pashley, *Travels in Crete*, vol. I, p. 181; I. Kukuljević, *Putovanje po Bosni*, p. 40; A. Gil'ferding, *Poëzdka po Gercegovine, Bosnii i Staroj Serbii*, p. 158; M. A. Walker, *Through Macedonia to the Albanian Lakes*, p. 257; H. F. Tozer, *Researches in the Highlands of Turkey*, vol. I, p. 175; J. Creagh, *Over the Borders of Christendom and Eslamiah*, vol. II, p. 327; R. Munro, *Rambles and Studies in Bosnia-Herzegovina*, pp. 176–7; N. Buxton, *Europe and the Turks*, p. 16; M. M. Holbach, *Bosnia and Herzegovina*, p. 33.
142. J. Brewer, *A Residence at Constantinople, in the Year 1827*, p. 128.
143. H. Sandwith, *Notes on the South Slavonic countries in Austria and Turkey in Europe*, p. 38.
144. W. F. Cumming, *Notes of a Wanderer*, vol. II, p. 165.
145. M. E. Durham, *Through the Lands of the Serb*, p. 318.
146. B. Ramberti, *Libri tre delle cose de Turchi*, p. 29.
147. T. Glover, *The Journey of Edward Barton Esq.*, p. 1296; F. Kanitz, *Das Königreich Serbien und das Serbenvolk von der Römerzeit bis zur Gegenwart*, vol. I, p. 173; M. M. Holbach, *Bosnia and Herzegovina*, p. 226.
148. .See e.g. A. Russell, *The Natural History of Aleppo*, pp. 222–3; J. C. Hobhouse, *A Journey through Albania and other Provinces of Turkey in Europe, and Asia to Constantinople, during the years 1809 and 1810*, p. 513; E. D. Clarke *Travels in various countries of Europe, Asia and Africa*, vol. III, p. 478; E. Dodwell, *A Classical and Topographical Tour through Greece*, vol II, p. 275; F. C. Pouqueville, *Travels in Epirus, Albania, Macedonia, and Thessaly*, p. 24; J. Vujić, *Putešestvie po Serbii*, pp. 194–5; E. Spencer, *Travels in European Turkey in 1850*, vol. I, p. 244; J. Roškiewicz, *Studien über Bosnien und die Herzegovina*, p. 251; W. Forsyth, *The Slavonic Provinces South of the Danube*, pp. 33, 159; G. M. Mackenzie and A. P. Irby, *Travels in Slavonic Provinces of Turkey-in-Europe*, vol. I, p. 11; C. Hamlin, *Among the Turks*, p. 334; B. Nušić, *Kraj obala Ohridskoga Jezera*, pp. 136–7; F. Kanitz, *Das Königreich Serbien und das Serbenvolk von der Römerzeit bis zur Gegenwart*, vol. III, p. 125; O. Knezović, Ali-paša Rizvanbegović-Stoičević, hercegovački vezir 1832–1851, p. 16.
149. M. Gjurgjević, *Memoari sa Balkana*, pp. 55–6.
150. A. Lamartine, *Visit to the Holy Land*, vol. II, p. 163.
151. P. Belon, *Les observations de plvsievrs singvlatitez & chosez memorables, trouuées en Greece, Asie, Iudée, Egypte, Arabie, & autres pays estranges, redigées en trois liures*, p. 180.
152. D. Urquhart, *The Spirit of the East*, vol. II, pp. 236–7.
153. L. M. Garnett, *Turkey of the Ottomans*, p. 141.
154. Mrs M. Müller, *Letters from Constantinople*, p. 18.
155. See e.g. J. Boemus, *The Fardle of factions*; G. Sandys, *A relation of a iourney begvn Anno. Dom. 1610*, p. 81; P. Rycaut, *The Present State of the Ottoman Empire*, p. 103; J. Burbury, *A Relation of a Journey of the Right Honourable My Lord Henry Howard*, p. 114; J. de Thevenot, *Travels of the Monsieur de Thevenot into the Levant*, p. 94; B. Randolph, *The Present State of the Morea*, p. 15; J. Du Mont, *A New Voyage to the Levant*, pp. 185–6; M. W. Montague, *Letters*, vol. II, p. 44; Captain Sutherland, *A Tour up the Straits, from Gibraltar*

to Constantinople, pp. 186–7; T. Watkins, *Travels through Switzerland , Italy, Sicily, the Greek Islands to Constantinople*, vol. II, p. 227; T. MacGill, *Travels in Turkey, Italy, and Russia, During the Years 1803, 1804, 1805, & 1806*, p. 84; D. Ross, *Opinions of the European Press on the Eastern Question*, pp. 8, 118; Mrs. Pardoe, *The City of the Sultan*, vol. I, p. 50; D. Urquhart, *The Spirit of the East*, vol. I, p. 340; H. A. Munro-Butler-Johnstone, *The Turks*, p. 27; M. V. Chirol, *Twixt Greek and Turk*, p. 185; L. Hugonnet, *La Turquie inconnue*, p. 216; A. de Lusignan, *The Twelve Years' Reign of His Imperial Majesty Abdul Hamid*, p. 130; Mrs. M. Müller, *Letters from Constantinople*, p. 11; C. N. E. Eliot, *Turkey in Europe*, p. 17; G. F. Abbott, *The Tale of a Tour in Macedonia*, p. 20; A. Upward, *The East End of Europe*, p. 233; J. Koetschet, *Osman Pascha*, p. 25; B. Jaeckel, *The Lands of the Tamed Turk or the Balkan State To-day*, p. 118; P. Loti, *Turkey in Agony*, p. 87; M. Plut, *Po macedonskem bojišču*, p. 126; W. M. Sloane, *The Balkans. A laboratory of history*, p. 27; R. G. D. Laffan, *The Guardians of the Gate*, p. 22; Ruprecht, *Reise-Erinnirungen aus dem Süd-Osten Europas un dem Orient*, pp. 127, 196.

156. See e.g. N. Nicolay, *Les quatre premieres livres des navigations et peregrinations Orientales*, p. 149; J. Dallaway, *Constantinople Ancient and Modern*, p. 389; J. O. Noyes, *Roumania*, p. 504; H. F. Tozer, *Researches in the Highlands of Turkey*, vol. I, p. 146; J. Brown, *Eastern Christianity and the War*, p. 51; J. S. Stuart-Glennie, *Europe and Asia*, p. 266; M. V. Chirol, *Twixt Greek and Turk*, p. 9; G. F. Abbott, *The Tale of a Tour in Macedonia*, p. 20; H. N. Brailsford, *Macedonia: Its Races and Their Future*, p. 82; A. Wherry, *From Old to New*, p. 17; L. M. Garnett, *Turkey of the Ottomans*, p. 38; B. G. Baker, *The Passing of the Turkish Empire in Europe*, p. 194; P. Loti, *Turkey in Agony*, p. 60.

157. De la Guilletiere, *Athenes ancienne et novvelle*, p. 152.

158. F. Ruthner, *Un Viaggio a Maria Stella convento dei trappisti*, p. 20; J. de Asboth, *An Official Tour through Bosnia and Herzegovina*, p. 389; H. Renner, *Durch Bosnien und die Hercegovina kreuz und quer*, p. 499; H. C. Thomson, *The Outgoing Turk*, p. 167; M. M. Holbach, *Dalmatia*, p. 75; R. Trevor, *My Balkan Tour*, p. 29; A. Zavadil, *Obrazky z Bosny*, pp. 3, 36; P. Šolta, *Bosniski kraj a raj*, p. 26.

159. A. Lyall, *The Balkan Road*, p. 179.

160. N. Bisani, *A Picturesque Tour through part of Europe, Asia, and Africa*, p. 152.

161. L. G. Hornby, *Balkan Sketches*, p. 153.

162. E. Scott-Stevenson, *On Summer Seas*, p. 217.

163. See e.g. D. Rihtman-Auguštin, *Ulice moga grada*, p. 193.

Bibliography

Abbott, George Frederick *The Tale of a Tour in Macedonia*, London, Edward Arnold 1903.

Abbott, George Frederick *Under the Turk in Constantinople. A Record of Sir John Finch's Embassy 1674–1681*, London, Macmillan & Co. 1920.

About, Edmond *Greece and the Greeks of the Present Day*, Edinburgh, Thomas Constable and Co.; London, Hamilton, Adams and Co. 1855.

Achleitner, Arthur *Reisen im slavischen Süden (Dalmatien und Montenegro)*, Berlin, Verlag von Gebrüder Paetel 1913.

Adams, William T. *Cross and Crescent*, Boston, Lee and Shepard 1873.

Aflalo, F. G. *An Idler in the Near East*, London, John Milne 1910.

Ajkić, Muhamed *Mostarski stari most*, Mostar, Hrvatska tiskara F. P. 1936.

Ajkić, Muhamed *Stari most – simbol Mostara*, Mostar 1955.

Alastos, Doros *The Balkans and Europe. A Study of Peace and the Forces of War*, London, John Lane and Bodley Head 1937.

Alcock, Thomas *Travels in Russia, Persia, Turkey, and Greece. In the years 1828–29*, London, E. Clarke and Son 1831.

Alcott, William Andrus *Tea and Coffee, Their Physical, Intellectual, and Moral Effects on the Human System*, New York, Fowlers and Wells 1850.

Aldridge, Olive M. *The Retreat from Serbia Through Montenegro and Albania*, London, The Minerva Publishing 1916.

Aldrovandi, Ulyssis *Monstrorum Historia*, Bononiæ, Nicolai Tebaldini 1642.

Alésovec, Jakob *Vojska na Turškem od leta 1875 do konca leta 1878*, Ljubljana, Janez Giontini 1908.

Alexander, James Edward *Travels from India to England; Comprehending a Visit to the Burman Empire, and a Journey through Persia, Asia Minor, European Turkey, &c. In the Years 1825–26*, London, Parbury, Allen, and Co. 1827.

Allason, Thomas *Picturesque views of the antiquities of Pola and Istria*, London, John Murray 1819.

Allcock, John, and Antonia Young eds *Black Lambs and Grey Falcons*, Bradford, University of Bradford Press 1991.

Allen, Trevor *The Tracks They Trod. Salonica and the Balkans, Gallipoli, Egypt and Palestine Revisited*, London, Herbert Joseph 1932.

Amfiteatrov, Aleksandr *Strana razdora*, S.- Peterburg, I. V. Rajskoj 1903.

Amfiteatrov, Aleksandr *V moih skitan'jah*, S.- Peterburg, I. V. Raiskoj 1903.

Amfiteatrov, Aleksandr *Slavjanskoe gore*, Moskva, Moskovskoe knigoizdatel'stvo 1912.

Amicis, Edmondo de *Constantinople*, London, Sampson Low, Marston, Searle & Co. 1878.

Anastosoff, Christ *The Tragic Peninsula. A History of the Macedonian Movement for Independence since 1878*, St Louis, Blackwell Wielandly Co. 1938.

Andonović, M. J. *Makedonski su Sloveni Srbi. U odbranu opravdanih srpskih prava i interesa na Balkanu*, Beograd, Naumović i Stefanović 1913.

Andreas (Mui Shuko) *With Gypsies In Bulgaria*, Liverpool, Henry Young and Sons 1916.

Andrejka, Jernej pl. *Slovenski fantje v Bosni in Hercegovini 1878*, Celovec, Družba sv. Mohorja 1904.

Andreossy, M. Le Comte *Constantinople et Bosphore de Thrace, pendant les annés 1812, 1813 et 1814, et pendant l'anné 1826*, Paris, Théophile Barrois et Benj. Duprat; J. S. Merlin 1828.

Angell, Norman *Peace Theories and the Balkan War*, London, Horace Marshall & Son 1912.

Anon. *The Siege of Vienna. A Story of the Turkish War in 1683*, Edinburgh, William Oliphant 1880.

Anon. *The Near East from within*, London, Cassell and Company 1915.

Anon. *Fusilier Bluff. The Experiences of an Unprofessional Soldier in the Near East 1918 to 1919*, London, Geoffrey Bles 1934.

An Arabian Phisician *The Nature of the drink kauhi, or coffee, and the Berry of which it is made, Described by an Arabian Phisician*, Oxford 1659.

Arbuthnot, George *Herzegovina; or Omer Pasha and the Christian Rebels*, London, Longman, Green, Longman, Roberts & Green 1862.

Arendonk, C. van 'Kahwa', in Th. Houtsma et al. eds *The Encyclopaedia of Islam* II, pp. 630–5. Leiden, Late E. J.Brill; London, Luzac & Co. 1927.

Armstrong, Harold *Turkey in Travail. The Birth of a New Nation*, London, John Bodley; The Bodley Head 1925.

Arnold, Arthur *From the Levant, the Black Sea, and the Danube*, London, Chapman & Hall 1868.

Arnold, Thomas *History of Rome*, London, B. Fellows; J. G. Rivington; J. Duncan; E. Hodgson; G. Lawford; J. M. Richardson; J. Boin; J. Bain; S. Hodgson; F. C. Westley; and L. A. Lewis 1838–43.

Asboth, Johann de *An Official Tour through Bosnia and Herzegovina*, London, Swan Sonnenschein, 1890.

Aškerc, Anton *Izlet v Carigrad*, Ljubljana, Narodna tiskarna 1893.

Askew, Alice and Claude *The Stricken Land. Serbia as we saw it*, London, Eveleigh Nash Company 1916.

Auldjo, John *Journal of a Visit to Constantinople, and Some of the Greek Islands, in the Spring and Summer of 1833*, London, Longman, Rees, Omre, Brown, Green, & Longman 1835.

Austell, Henry 'The voyage of M. Henry Austell by Venice to Ragusa, and thence ouer-land to Constantinople: and from thence through Moldauia, Polonia, Silesia, and Germany into England, Anno 1586', in Hakluyt's *Collection of the Early Voyages, Travels, and Discoveries, of the English Nation* II, pp. 318–39. London, R. H. Evans, J. Mackinlay, and R. Priestley 1810.

Avril, Father *Travels Into divers Parts of Europe and Asia, Undertaken by the French King's Order to discover a new Way by Land into China*, London, Tim Goodwin 1693.

Azaïs, l'Abbé and C. Domergue, *Journal d'un voyage en Orient*, Avignon, F. Seguin Ainé 1858.

Babinger, Franz 'Die Brücke von Mostar', in *Morgenblatt* 53/115: 11. Zagreb 1938.

Baedeker, Karl *Austria, including Hungary, Transsylvania, Dalmatia, and Bosnia. Handbook for travellers*, Leipsic, Karl Baedeker; London, Dulan & Co. 1896.

Baerlein, Henry *The Birth of Yugoslavia*, London, Leonard Parsons 1922.

Bagge, Harald *Reise nach dem Orient, der Europäischen, Türkei, Aegypten, Nubien und Palästina*, Frankfurt am Main, Verlag der Johann Christian Hermann'schen Buchhandlung 1847.

Bailey, Brian *Hangmen of England. A History of Execution from Jack Ketch to Albert Pierrepoint*, London, W H Allen 1989.

Bajraktarević, Fehim *Mostar*, in M. Th. Houtsma et al. eds, Vol. III 1936.

Baker, B. Granville *The Passing of the Turkish Empire in Europe*, London, Seeley, Service & Co. 1913.

Baldacci, Antonio *Crnagora. Memorie di un botanico*, Bologna, Ditta Nicola Zanichelli 1897.

Bale, Johan *The Actes of Englysh notaryes, comprehendynge their unchaste practises and examples by all ages, from the worldes begynnge to thys present yeare, collected out of their owne legends and chronicles*, London 1546.

Balkanicus *Albanski problem i Srbija i Austro-Ugarska*, Beograd, Dositije Obradović 1913.

Balkanicus *The Aspirations of Bulgaria*, London, Simpkin, Marshall, Hamilton, Kent & Co. 1915.

Baring, Maurice *Letters from the Near East 1909 and 1912*, London, Smith, Elder & Co. 1913.

Barker, Albert *Memoire of Macedonia*, London, Arthur H. Stockwell 1917.

Barker, Elizabeth *Macedonia. Its Place in Balkan Power Politics*, London and New York, Royal Institute of International Affairs 1950.

Barkley, Henry C. *Between the Danube and Black Sea*, London, John Murray 1876.

Barlett, Ellis Ashmead *The Battlefields of Thessaly. With Personal Experiences in Turkey and Greece*, London, John Murray 1897.

Barnes, Harry Elmer, and Negley K. Teeters *New Horizons in Criminology*, Englewood Cliffs, Prentice-Hall 1959.

Barrington, Mrs. Russell *Through Greece and Dalmatia. A diary of impressions recorded by pen & picture*, London, Adam and Charles Black 1912.

Barry, J. P. *At the Gates of the East: A Book of Travel among Historic Wonderlands*, London, Longmans, Green, and Co. 1906.

Barth, Heinrich *Reise durch das Innere der Europäischen Türkei von Rutschuk über Philippopel, Rilo (Monastir), Bitolia und den Thessalischen Olymp nach Saloniki im Herbst 1862*, Berlin, Verlag von Dietrich Reimer 1864.

Barton, Edward 'A description of a Voiage to Constantinople and Syria, begun the 21. of March 1593. and ended the 9. of August, 1595; wherein is shewed the order of deliuering the second Present by Master Edward Barton her maiesties Ambassador, which was sent from her Maiestie to Sultan Murad Can, Emperor of Turkie', in *Hakluyt's Collection of the Early Voyages, Travels, and Discoveries, of the English Nation* II, pp. 443–53. London, R. H. Evans, J. Mackinlay, and R. Priestley 1810.

Bašeskija, Mula Mustafa Ševki *Ljetopis (1746–1804)*, Sarajevo, Veselin Masleša 1987.

Bashmakoff, Aleksandr *Through the Montenegro in the Land of the Geugeus, North Albania*, 1915.

Bašmakov, Aleksandr *Bulharsko a Makedonie*, Praha, E. Beaufort 1903.

Baudier, Michel *Histoire generall dv Serrail, et de la Covr Du Grand Seigneur Empereur de Turcs*, Paris 1635.

Beaujour, Félix de *Voyage militaire dans l'Empire Othoman, ou description de ses frontières et de ses principales défenses, soit naturelles soit artificielles, avec cinq cartes géographiques*, Paris, Firmin Didot, Bossange, Delaunay 1829.

Belon du Mans, Pierre *Les observations de plvsievrs singvlatitez & chosez memorables, trouées en Greece, Asie, Iudée, Egypte, Arabie, & autres pays estranges, redigées en trois liures*, Paris, Gilles Corrozer 1554.

Benaglia, Giovanni *Relatione del Viaggio Fatto a Constantinopoli, e Ritorno in Germania, dell'Illustruissimo Sig. Conte Alberto Caprara, Gentilhuomo della Camera dell'Imperatore. E da Esso Mandato come Internuntio Straordinario, e Plenipotentiorio per Trattore le Continuatione della Tregna*, Bologna, Per gli Heredi di gio. Recaldini 1684.

Benjamin, S. G. W. *The Turk and the Greek; or, Creeds, Races, Society, and Scenery in Turkey, Greece, and the Isles of Greece*, New York, Hurd and Houghton 1867.

Bent, J. Theodore *Early Voyages and Travels in the Levant* London, Hakluyt Society 1893.

Bérard, Victor *La Macédoine*, Paris, Calmann Lévy 1897.

Bercovici, Konrad *The Incredible Balkans*, New York, G. P. Putnam's Sons 1932.

Best, J. J. *Excursions in Albania; comprising a description of the wild boar, deer, and woodcock shooting in that country; and a journey from thence to Thessalonica & Constantinople, and up the Danube to Pest*, London, Wm. H. Allen and Co. 1842.

Bevan, Tom *The Insurgent Trail. A Story of the Balkans*, London, Thomas Nelson and Sons 1910.

Bevk, France *Deset dni v Bolgariji*, Gorizia, Unione editoriale Goriziano 1938.

Bezenšek, Anton *Bolgarija in Srbija*, Celovec, Družba sv. Mohorja 1897.

Biasoletto, Bartolomeo *Relazione del viaggio fatto nella primavera dell'anno 1838 dalla maestà del re Federico Augusto di Sassonia nell'Istria, Dalmazia e Montenegro*, Trieste, Tipografia Weis 1841.

Biasutti, Renato *Le razze e i popoli della terra*, Torino, Unione tipografico – Editrice torinese 1967.

Biddulph, William *The Travels of certaine Englishmen into Africa, Asia, Troy, Bythinia, Thracia, and to the Black Sea, and into Syria, Cilicia, Pisidia, Mesopotamia, Damascus, Canaan, Galile, Samaria, Iudea, Palestina, Ierusalem, Iericho, and to the Red Sea: and to sundry other places. Begunne in the yeere of Iubile 1600. and by some of them finished this yeere 1608. The others not yet returned*, London, W. Aspley 1609.

Bigham, Clive *With the Turkish Army in Thessaly*, London, Macmillan and Co.; New York, The Macmillan Company 1897.

Bisani, N. *A Picturesque Tour Through Part of Europe, Asia, and Africa: Containing Many New Remarks on the Present State of Society, Remains of Ancient Edifices, &c.*, London, R. Faulder 1793.

Black, Archibald Pollok *A Hundred Days in the East: A Diary of a Journey to Egypt, Palestine, Turkey in Europe, Greece, the Isles of Archipelago, and Italy*, London, John F. Shaw 1865.

Blackwood, Hariot Georgina *My Russian and Turkish Journals*, London, John Murray 1916.

Blaquiere, Edward *Letters from Greece: With Remarks on the Treaty of Intervention*, London, James Ilbery 1828.

Blau, Otto *Reisen in Bosnien und der Hertzegovina*, Berlin, Dietrich Reimer 1877.

Blount, Henry *A Journey into the Levant*, London, Andrew Crooke 1636.

Blowitz, M. de *Une course a Constantinople*, Paris, E. Plon, Nourrit et Cie 1884.

Blunt, Anthony *Where the Turk Trod. A Journey to Sarajevo with a Slavonic Mussulman*, London, Weidenfeld and Nicolson 1956.

Boemus, Joanne *The Fardle of facions conteining the annciente maners, customes, and Lawes, of the peoples enhabiting the two partes of the earth, called Affrike and Asie*, London, John Kingstone, and Henry Sutton 1555.

Booth, John L. C. *Trouble in the Balkans*, London, Hurst and Blackett 1905.

Borsa, Mario *Dal Montenegro*, Bergamo, Istituto italiano d'arti grafiche 1896.

Boscovich, Ruggiero Giuseppe *Giornale di un Viaggio da Constantinopoli in Polonia dell'Abate Ruggiero Giuseppe Boscovich. Con una sua Relazione delle Rovine di Troja, e in fine il Prospetto delle Opere nuove Matematiche del Medesimo Autore, contenute in cinque tomi, che attualmente lui presente si stampano*, Bassano, A spese Remondini di Venezia 1784.

Bouchié de Belle, Edmond *La Macédoine et les Macédoinens*, Paris, Librairie Armand Colin 1922.

Boué, Ami *Le Turquie d'Europe ou observations sur la géographie, la géologie, l'histoire naturelle, la statistique, les moeurs, les coutumes, l'archéologie, l'agriculture, l'industrie, le commerce, les governments divers, le clergé, l'histoire et l'état politique de cet empire*, Paris, Arthus Bertrand 1840.

Boué, Ami *Recueil d'itinéraires dans la Turquie d'Europe. Détails géographiques, topographiques et statistiques sur cet empire*, Vienne, W. Braunmüller 1854.

Boulden, James E. P. *An American among the Orientals: Including an Audience with the Sultan, and a*

Visit to the Interior of a Turkish Harem, Philadelphia, Lindsay & Blakiston 1855.

Bowen, George Ferguson *Mount Athos, Thessaly, and Epirus: A Diary of a Journey from Constantinople to Corfu*, London, Francis & John Rivington 1852.

Brailsford, Henry Noel *Macedonia: Its Races and Their Future*, London, Methuen & Co. 1906.

Bramsen, John *Travels in Egypt, Syria, Cyprus, the Morea, Greece, Italy &c. &c. In a Series of Letters. Interspersed with Anecdotes of Distinguished Persons, and Illustrations of Political Occurrences*, London, Henry Colburn &. Co. 1820.

Brassey, Annie *Sunshine and Storm in the East, or Cruises to Cyprus and Constantinople*, London, Longmans, Green, and Co. 1880.

Braum-Wiesbaden, Karl *Eine Türkische Reise*, Stuggart, Verlag von August Auerbach 1876.

Braun-Wiesbaden, Karl *Reise-Eindrücke aus dem Südosten. Ungarn, Istrien, Montenegro, Griechenland, Türkei*, Stuttgart, Aug. Berth. Auerbach 1878.

Brayley Hodgetts, E. A. *Round about Armenia. The Record of a Journey across The Balkans, through Turkey, The Caucasus, and Persia in 1895*, London, Sampson, Low, Marston and Company 1896.

Bremer, Fredrika *Greece and the Greeks. The Narrative of a Winter Residence and Summer Travel in Greece and Its Islands*, London, Hurst and Blackett 1863.

Brewer, Josiah *A Residence at Constantinople, in the Year 1827. With the Notes to the Present Time*, New-Haven, Durrie and Peck 1830.

A British Resident of Twenty Years in the East *The Frontier Lands of the Christian and the Turk; Comprising Travels of the Regions of the Lower Danube, In 1850 and 1851*, London, Richard Bentley 1853.

Bronevsky, Vladimir *Zapiski morskago oficera, v prodolženii kampanii na Sredizemnom more pod načal'stvom Vice-Admirala Dmitrija Nikolaeviča Senjavina ot 1805 do1810 god*, Sanktpeterburg, Tipografija Imperatorskoj Rossijskoj Akademii 1818.

Bronevsky, Vladimir *Pis'ma morskago oficera*, Moskva, Vysochajshie povelenie 1826.

Brown, H. A. *A Winter in Albania*, London, Griffith, Farran, Okeden & Welsch 1888.

Brown, Joseph *Eastern Christianity and the War. The Idolatry, Superstition, and Corruption of the Christians of Turkey, Greece, and Asia, Exposed and Considered with the Present War, and the Prospects of a Reformation*, London, Edward Stanford 1877.

Browne, Edward *A Brief Account of some Travels in Hungaria, Servia, Bulgaria, Macedonia, Thessaly, Austria, Styria, Carinthia, Carniola, and Friuli*, London, Benj. Tooke 1673.

Browne, Edward *A Brief Account of some Travels in Divers Parts of Europe*, London, Benj. Tooke 1685.

Bruce, Peter Henry *Memoirs. Containing An Account of his Travels in Germany, Russia, Tartary, Turkey, the West Indies, &c. as also Several very interesting private Anecdotes of the Czar, Peter I. of Russia*, London, Printed for the Author's Widow 1782.

Bruce, Rosslyn, and His Sister Kathleen *Letters from Turkey: Being Glimpses of Macedonian Misery*, Nottingham, Henry B. Saxton 1907.

Bruyn, Corneille le *A Voyage to the Levant, or, Travels in the Principal Parts of Asia Minor, the Islands of Scio, Rhodes, Cyprus, &c. With An Account of the most Considerable Cities of Egypt, Syria and the Holy Land*, London, Jacob Tonson and Thomas Bennet 1702.

Buffon, Georges Louis Le Clerc de 'How to Study Natural History', in Simon Eliot and Beverley Stern eds *The Age of Enlightenment*, London, Open University Press 1979.

Buffon, Georges Louis Le Clerc de *The Natural History of Animals, Vegetables, Minerals, &c.*, London, T. Bell 1775.

Buffon, Georges Louis Le Clerc de *Natural History*, London, J. S. Barr 1792.

Burbury, John *A Relation of a Journey of the Right Honourable My Lord Henry Howard, From London to Vienna, and thence to Constantinople*, London, T. Collins and I. Ford, and S. Hickman 1671.

Burgess, Richard *Greece and the Levant; or, Diary of a Summer's Excursion in 1834; with Epistolary Supplements*, London, Longman, Rees, Orme, Brown, Green, & Longman 1835.

Burr, Malcolm *Slouch Hat*, London, George Allen & Unwin 1935.

Burt, George *Notes of a Three Months' Trip to Egypt, Greece, Constantinople, and the Eastern Shores of the Mediterranean Sea, etc., etc.*, London, Marchant Singer & Co. 1878.

Burton, Nathanael *Narrative of a Voyage from Liverpool to Alexandria, Touching at the Island of Malta, From thence to Beirout in Syria; With a Journey to Jerusalem, Voyage from Jaffa to Cyprus and Constantinople, and a Pedestrian Journey from Constantinople, through Turkey, Wallachia, Hungary, and Prussia, to the Town of Hamburg, in the Years 1836–37*, Dublin, John Yates 1838.

Burton, Richard *Personal Narrative of a Pilgrimage to al-Madinah and Meccah*, London, Longmans and Co. 1855–6

Burton, Richard *A Pilgrimage to Mecca and Medina* Leipzig, Bernhard Tauchnitz 1874.

Burton, Richard *Love, War and Fancy. The Customs and Manners of the East from Writings on the Arabian Nights*, London, William Kimber 1964.

Buxton, Leland William Wilberforce *The Black Sheep of the Balkans*, London, Nisbet & Co. 1920.

Buxton, Noel *Europe and the Turks*, London, John Murray 1907.

Calvert, Frederick, Lord of Baltimore *A Tour to the East, In the Years 1763 and 1764. With remarks on the City of Constantinople and the Turks*, London, W. Richardson and S. Clark 1767.

Cantemir, Demetrius *The History of the Growth and Decay of the Othman Empire*, London, A. Millar 1756.

Cappelletti, Licurgo *Il Montenegro e i suoi principi*, Livorno, Tipografia di Raff. Giusti 1896.

Capus, Guillaume *A travers la Bosnie et l'Herzégovine*, Paris, Hachette et Cie 1896.

Cardigan, The Earl of *Youth Goes East*, London, Eveleigh Nash & Grayson 1928.

Carne, John *Letters from the East: Written during a Recent Tour through Turkey, Egypt, Arabia, the Holy Land, Syria, and Greece*, London, Henry Colburn and Richard Bentley 1830.

Carnegie Endowment for International Peace *Report of the International Commission to Inquire into the Causes and Conduct of the Balkan Wars*, Washington, The Carnegie Endowment 1914.

Carnegie Endowment for International Peace *Report of the International Commission to Inquire into the Causes and Conduct of the Balkan Wars. Chapter 1: Macedonia*, Sofia, Al. Paskaleff & Co. 1925.

Carr, William *Montenegro*, Oxford, James Thornton 1884.

Cassas, Louis François *Travels in Istria and Dalmatia*; A Collection of Modern and Contemporary Voyages and Travels, Vol. I, London, Richard Phillips 1805.

Castellan, Antoine Laurent *Turkey, Being a Description of the Manners, Customs, Dresses, and other Peculiarities Characteristic of the Inhabitants of the Turkish Empire*, London, R. Ackerman 1821.

Castellan, Francis des *Renseignements sur l'Afrique Centrale et sur une nation d'hommes à queue qui s'y trouverait d'après le rapport des nègres du Soudan, esclaves à Bahia*, Paris, chez P. Bertnard 1851.

Čelebi, Evliyá *Narrative of Travels in Europe, Asia, and Africa in the Seventeenth Century*, London, Oriental Translation Fund of Great Britain and Ireland 1834.

Čelebī, Evlija *Putopis*, Sarajevo, Veselin Masleša 1979.

Čelić, Džemal, and Mehmed Mujezinović *Stari mostovi u Bosni i Hercegovini*, Sarajevo, Veselin Masleša 1969.

Cerciello, Giuseppe *Uno sguardo al Montenegro (Cenno storico)*, Naples, Stabilimento Tipografico G. Cerciello 1896.

Chaillé Long, Charles *Central Africa: naked truth of naked people. An account of expeditions to the Lake Victoria Nyaza and the Makraka Niam-Niam, west of the Bahr-el-Abiad (White Nile)*, London Sampson Low, Marston, Searle & Rivington 1876.

Chandler, Richard *Travels in Asia Minor: or, An Account of a Tour Made at the Expence of the Society of Dilettanti*, Dublin, R. Marchbank 1775.

Chandler, Richard *Travels in Greece: or, An Account of a Tour Made at the Expence of the Society of Dilettanti*, London, J. Dodsley, J. Robson, T. Cadell, P. Elmsly, and G. Robinson. Oxford, D. Prince 1776.

Chateaubriand, François de *Travels in Greece, Palestine, Egypt, and Barbary, during the years 1806 and 1807*, London, Henry Colburn 1812.

Chaumette des Fossés, Amédée *Voyage en Bosnie dans les années 1807 et 1808*, Paris, F. – Didot 1816.

Chaura, Edmund *Obrázky z okupace bosenské*, Prague 1893.

Chesney, F. R. *The Russo-Turkish Campaigns of 1828 and 1829: With a View of the Present State of Affairs in the East*, London, Smith, Elder & Co. 1854.

Chirol, M. Valentine *'Twixt Greek and Turk*, Edinburgh and London, William Blackwood and Sons 1881.

Chiudina, Giacomo *Storia del Montenero (Crnagora) da' tempi antichi fino a' nostri*, Spalato, Antonio Zannoni – Tipografo Editore 1882.

Chishull, Edmund *Travels in Turkey and back to England*, London, W. Bowyer 1747.

Chrismar, F. S. *Skizzen einer Reise durch Ungarn in die Türkei*, Pesth, Georg Kilian, jun. 1834.

Christowe, Stoyan *Heroes and Assassins*, London, Victor Gollancz 1935.

Claridge, R. T. *A Guide along the Danube, from Vienna to Constantinople, Smyrna, Athens, the Morea, the Ionian Islands, and Venice. From the Notes of a Journey Made in the Year 1836*, London, F. C. Westley 1837.

Clarke, Edward Daniel *Travels in various countries of Europe, Asia and Africa*, Cambridge, T. Cadell and W. Davies 1810–23.

Clement, Clara Erskine *Constantinople. The City of the Sultans*, Boston, Estes and Lauriat 1895.

Cochrane, George *Wanderings in Greece*, London, Henry Colburn 1837.

Cockerell, Charles Robert *Travels in Southern Europe and the Levant, 1810–1817*, New York and Bombay, Longmans, Green, and Co. 1903.

Čokorilo, P. *Türkische Zustände. Schilderungen von Fremden Denkschriften von Eingeboren*, Bautzen, J. C. Schmaler 1858.

Colbeck, Alfred *A Summer's Cruise in the Waters of Greece, Turkey, and Russia*, London, T. Fisher Unwin 1887.

Colton, Walter *Visit to Constantinople and Athens*, New York, Leavitt, Lord & Co.; Boston, Crocker & Brewster 1836.

Colville, J. R. *Fools' Pleasure. A leisurely journey down the Danube, to the Black Sea, the Greek Islands and Dalmatia*, London, Methuen and Company 1935.

Comyn-Platt, T. *The Turk in the Balkans*, London, Alston Rivers 1906.

Conway, Agnes Ethel *A Ride Through the Balkans. On Classic Ground with a Camera*, London, Robert Scott 1917.

Ćorović, Vladimir *Mostar i njegovi književnici*, Mostar 1907.

Ćorović, Vladimir *Bosna i Hercegovina*, Beograd, Srpska književna zadruga 1925.

Cosmopoulos, Michael B. *Macedonia*, Winnipeg, Manitoba Studies in Classical Civilization 1992.

Coufopoulos, Demetrius *A Guide to Constantinople*, London, Adam and Charles Black 1895.

Cousinéry, Esprit Marie *Voyage dans La Macédoine, contenant des recherches sur l'histoire, la géographie et les antiquités de ce pays*, Paris, Imprimierie royale 1831.

Cowan, Jane K. ed *Macedonia. The Politics of Identity and Difference*, London and Sterling, Pluto Press 2000.

Craven, Elizabeth *A Journey Through the Crimea to Constantinople. In Series of Letters from the Right Honourable Elizabeth Lady Craven, to His Serene Highness the Margrave of Brandenbourg, Anspach, and Bareith*, London, G. G. J. and J. Robinson 1789.

Creagh, James *Over the Borders of Christendom and Eslamiah*, London, Samuel Tinsley 1876.

Cronia, Arturo *La conoscenza del mondo slavo in Italia*, Padova, Instituto di studi adriatici Venezia 1958.

Crow, Sackvile *Subtilty and Cruelty: or a Trve Relation of the Horrible and unparalleld abuses and intolerable Oppressions*, London, R. Cotes 1646.

Crowe, Eyre Evans *The Greek and the Turk, or, Power and prospects in the Levant*, London, Richard Bentley 1853.

Cumming, W. F. *Notes of a Wanderer, in Search of Health, through Italy, Egypt, Greece, Turkey, up the Danube, and down the Rhine*, London, Saunders and Otley; Edinburgh, Blackwood and Sons 1839.

Cuni, Ch. *Observations générales sur le Mémoire sur le Soudan de M. le comte d'Escayrac de Lauture*, Paris, Arthus Bertrand 1858.

Ćurčić, Vejsil 'Zanimljivi pabirci iz narodne medicine', in *Gajret* 7–8, pp. 127–9. Sarajevo 1933.

Curipeschitz, Benedict *Itinerarivm Wegrayß kün. May. potschaft gen Constantinopel zudem Türkischen keiser Soleyman*, Vienna 1531.

Curtis, William Eleroy *The Turk and His Lost Provinces*, Chicago, Fleming H. Revell Company 1903.

Curzon, Robert Jun. *Visits to Monasteries in the Levant*, London, John Murray 1849.

Cuthbertson, James *Sacred and Historic Lands, Being a Record of Travels in Egypt, Palestine, Syria, Greece, Constantinople, &c*, London, Wesleyan Conference Office 1885.

Cvijić, Jovan *Nekolika promatranja o etnografiji makedonskih Slovena*, Beograd 1906.

Cvijić, Jovan *La Péninsule Balkanique. Géographie humaine*, Paris, Librairie Armand Colin 1918.

Dako, Christo A. *Albania. The Master Key to the Near East*, Boston, E. L. Grimes Company 1919.

Dallaway, James *Constantinople Ancient and Modern, with Excursions to the Shores and Islands of the Archipelago and to the Troad*, London, T. Cadell Jun. & W. Davies 1797.

Damer, Mrs. G. L. Dawson *Diary of a Tour in Greece, Turkey, Egypt, and the Holy Land*, London, Henry Colburn 1841.

Danforth, Loring M. *The Macedonian Conflict. Ethnic Nationalism in a Transnational World*, Princeton, Princeton University Press 1995.

Daniel, Glyn *A Hundred and Fifty Years of Archaeology*, Cambridge, Duckworth 1975.

Dapper, Olbert. (1668) 'Kaffraria or Land of the Kafris, otherwise named Hottentots', in Isaac Schapera and B. Farrington *The Early Cape Hottentots*, Cape Town, The Van Riebeeck Society 1933.

Davy, John *Notes and Observations on the Ionian Islands and Malta: With Some Remarks on Constantinople and Turkey, and on the System of Quarantine as at Present Conducted*, London, Smith, Elder & Co. 1842.

De Burton, Albert *Ten Months' Tour in the East. Being A Guide to all that is Most Worth Seeing in Turkey in Europe, Greece, Asia Minor, Palestine, Egypt, and the Nile*, London, F. Bowyer Kitto 1870.

De Bunsen, Victoria, and Noel Buxton *Macedonian Massacres. Photos from Macedonia*, London, The Balkan Committee 1907.

De Windt, Harry *Through Savage Europe*, London, T. Fisher Unwin 1907.

Delarue, Henri *Le Monténégro: Histoire, description, moeurs, usages, législation*, Paris, Benjamin Duprat 1862.

Denton, William *Servia and the Servians*, London, Bell and Daldy 1862.

Denton, William *The Christians of Turkey. Their condition under Musliman rule*, London, Daldy, Isbister & Co. 1876.

Denton, William *Montenegro. Its People and their History*, London, Daldy, Isbister & Co. 1877.

Des Hayes, Louis, Baron de Courmemin *Voiage de levant Fait par le Commandement dv Roy en lannée*

1621, Paris, Adrian Tavpinar 1632.

D'Escayrac de Lauture *Mémoire sur le Soudan*, Paris, Imprimerie I. Martinet 1855.

Descamps, Édouard Eugène François *L'avenir de l'Albanie*, Louvain, Charles Peeters 1913.

Dicey, Edward *The Peasant State. An Account of Bulgaria in 1894*, London, John Murray 1894.

Dimitz, August *Geschichte Krains von der ältesten Zeit bis auf das Jahr 1813*, Laibach, Ig. V. Kleinmayr & Fed. Bamberg 1876.

A Diplomatist *Nationalism and War in the Near East*, Oxford, Claredon Press 1915.

Dizdar, Mak, and Dušan Pilja *The District of Mostar*, Sarajevo, Narodna prosvjeta 1959.

D'Ohsson, Ignace de Mouradja *Tableau général de l'Empire Othoman, divisé en deux parties, Don't l'une comprend la Législation Mahométane; l'autre l'Histoire de l'Empire Othoman*, Paris, L'imprimerie de Monsieur 1790.

Dodwell, Edward *A Classical and Topographical Tour through Greece, During the Years 1801, 1805, and 1806*, London, Rodwell and Martin 1819.

Doflein, Franz *Mazedonien. Erlebnisse und Beobachtungen eines Naturforschers im Gefolge des deutschen Heeres*, Jena, Verlag von Gustav Fisher 1921.

Đorđević, Vladan *Evropa i Crna Gora*, Beograd, Sv. Sava 1912.

Đorđević, Vladan *Kuda si se uputila Austrijo?*, Beograd, Štampa 1913.

Dorr, Benjamin *Notes of Travel in Egypt, the Holy Land, Turkey, and Greece*, Philadelphia, J. B. Lippincott & Co. 1856.

Douglas, J. A. *The Redemption of Saint Sophia. An Historical & Political Account of the Subject*, London, The Faith Press 1919.

Draganof *Macedonia and the Reforms*, London 1908.

Dragnich, Alex N., and Slavko Todorovich *The Saga of Kosovo*, Boulder, East European Monographs 1984.

Du Mont, Jean *A New Voyage to the Levant*, London, M. Gillyflower, T. Goodwin, M. Wotton, J. Walthoe, and R. Parker 1696.

Duckett Ferriman, Z. *Turkey and the Turks*, London, Mills & Boon 1911.

Ducoret, Louis *Voyage au pays des Niams-Niams ou les hommes à queue avec le portrait d'un Niam-Niam, et une notice biographique sur l'auteur par Alexandre Dumas, par Hadji-Abd-El-Hamid-Bey*, Paris, Martinon 1854.

Dunne, L. *A Trip to Constantinople*, London, J. Sheppard 1862.

Durham, Mary Edith *Through the Lands of the Serb*, London, Edward Arnold 1904.

Durham, Mary Edith *The Burden of the Balkans*, London, Edward Arnold 1905.

Durham, Mary Edith *High Albania*, London, Edward Arnold 1909.

Durham, Mary Edith *The Struggle for Scutari*, London, Edward Arnold 1914.

Durham, Mary Edith *Twenty Years of Balkan Tangle*, London, George Allen & Unwin 1920.

Durham, Mary Edith *Some Tribal Origins, Laws, and Customs of the Balkans*, London, Allen & Unwin 1928.

Dwight, H. G. *Constantinople, Old and New*, London, Longmans, Green & Co. 1915.

Dwight, Henry Otis *Turkish Life in War Time*, London, Wm. H. Allen & Co. 1881.

Dwight, Henry Otis *Constantinople and its Problems. Its Peoples, Customs, Religions and Progress*, London and Edinburgh, Oliphant, Anderson & Ferrier 1901.

Džaja, Mato *Banja Luka u putopisima i zapisima*, Banja Luka, Glas 1973.

Ebel, Wilhelm *Zwölf Tage auf Montenegro*, Königsberg, Verlag von J. H. Bon 1842.

Edib, Halidé *Turkey Faces West. A Turkish View on Recent Changes and Their Origin*, New Haven, Yale University Press 1930.

Edmonds, Paul *The Land of the Eagle*, London, George Rouledge & Sons; New York, E. P. Dutton & Co. 1927.

Edsman, Carl-Martin 'Bridges', in Mircea Eliade ed, *The Encyclopedia of Religion* 2, pp. 310–14. New York and London, Macmillan 1987.

Edwards, H. Sutherland *Sir William White. For Six Years Ambassador at Constantinople. His Life and Correspondence*, London, John Murray 1902.

Eisenstein, Richard, Freiherr von und zu *Reise nach Malta, Tripolitanien und Tunesien*, Vienna, Commissionsverlag von Carl Gerold's Sohn 1902.

Elezović, Gliša 'Kafa i kafana na balkanskom prostoru', in *Prilozi za istoriju, književnost i folklor* XVIII, pp. 617–37. Beograd 1938.

Elias, Norbert *The History of Manners*, Oxford, UK, and Cambridge, USA, Blackwell 1983.

Eliot, Charles Norton Edgeumbe *Turkey in Europe*, London, Edward Arnold 1900.

Eliot, William *A Letter to the Right Honourable The Earl of D***, on the Political Relations of Russia, in Regard to Turkey, Greece, and France*, London, T. Cadell and W. Davies 1807.

Elliot, Frances *Diary of an Idle Woman in Constantinople*, London, John Murray 1893.

Ellis, John *An Historical Account of Coffee*, London, Edward and Charles Dilly 1774.

Ellison, Grace *Yugoslavia. A New Country and Its People*, London, John Lane The Bodley Head 1933.

Emerson, James, and W. H. Humpreys *A Picture of Greece in 1825*, London, Henry Colburn 1826.

Erba F. Dell' *Il Montenegro*, Napoli, Casa editrice E. Pietrocola 1896.

Eremiten von Gauting *Reise nach dem Orient*, Stuggart, Hallberger'sche Verhandlung 1839.

Eton, William *A Survey of the Turkish Empire*, London, T. Cadell, jun. and W. Davies 1798.

Evans, Arthur John *Through Bosnia and the Herzegovina On Foot During the Insurrection, August and September 1875*, London, Longmans, Green, and Co. 1877.

Evans, Arthur John *Illyrian Letters*, London, Longmans, Green, and Co. 1878.

Fabre, Auguste *Histoire du siège de Missolonghi, suivie de pièces justificatives*, Paris, Moutardier 1827.

Farrer, Richard Ridley *A Tour in Greece 1880*, Edinburgh and London, William Blackwood and Sons 1882.

Fiedler, Karl Gustav *Reise durch alle Theile des Königsreiches Griechenland in Auftrag der Königl. Griechischen Regierung in den Jahren 1834 bis 1837*, Leipzig, Friedrich Fleischer 1840–1.

Field, Henry M. *The Greek Islands and Turkey after the War*, New York, Charles Scribner's Sons 1885.

Fife-Cookson, John *With the Armies of the Balkans and at Gallipoli in 1877–1878*, London, Cassell, Petter, Galpin & Co. 1879,

Filipović, Milenko *Prilozi etnološkom poznavanju Severoistočne Bosne*, Sarajevo, Akademija nauka i umjetnosti Bosne i Hercegovine 1969.

Filipović-Fabijanić, Radmila 'O narodnoj medicini stanovništva Lištice s okolinom', in *Glasnik Zemaljskog muzeja Bosne i Hercegovine* XXIV/XXV, pp. 319–35. Sarajevo 1970.

Filipović-Fabijanić, Radmila '"Domaći liekar" iz 1868. godine sa Širokog Brijega', in *Glasnik Zemaljskog muzeja Bosne i Hercegovine* XXVI, pp. 117–83. Sarajevo 1971.

Forbin, Louis N. P. A. *Travels in Greece, Turkey, and the Holy Land, In 1817–18*, London, Sir Richard Phillips 1820.

Forder, A. *In Brigand's Hands and Turkish Prisons 1914–1919*, London, Marshall Brothers 1920.

Forsyth, William *The Slavonic Provinces South of the Danube. A Sketch of Their History and Present State in Relation to the Ottoman Porte*, London, John Murray 1876.

Fortis, Alberto *Saggio d'osservazioni sopra l'isola di Cherso ed Osero*, Venice, Gaspare Storti 1771.

Fortis, Alberto *Viaggio in Dalmazia*, Venice, Alvise Milocco 1774.

Fortis, Alberto *L'abate Fortis al Signor Giovanni Lovrich*, Brescia 1777.

Fortis, Alberto *Travels into Dalmatia*, London, J. Robson 1778.

Fox, Frank *The Balkan Peninsula*, London, A. & C. Black 1915.

Franck, Harry A. *The Fringe of the Moslem World*, New York and London, The Century Co. 1928.

Franić, Dragutin *S gjacima kroz Bosnu-Hercegovinu, Crnu Goru, Dalmaciju, Jadransko more, Istru (Trst,*

Mletke, Rijeku) i Hrvatsku, Donja Tuzla 1901.

Frankland, Charles Colville *Travels to and from Constantinople, in the_years 1827 and 1828: or Personal narrative of a journey from Vienna, through Hungary, Transylvania, Wallachia, Bulgaria, and Roumelia, to Constantinople*, London, Henry Colburn 1829.

Fraser, James Baillie *A Winter's Journey (TATAR) from Constantinople to Tehran*, London, Richard Bentley 1838.

Fraser, John Foster *Pictures from the Balkans*, London, Cassell and Company 1906.

Freeman, Derek 'Severed Heads that Germinate', in R. H. Hook ed *Fantasy and Symbol. Studies in Anthropological Interpretation*, London and New York, Academic Press 1979.

Freeman, Edward *The Ottoman Power in Europe*, London, Macmillan & Co. 1877.

Fresne-Canaye, Philippe de *Le Voyage du Levant (1573)*, (Publié et annoté par M. H. Hauser.) Paris, Ernest Leroux 1897.

Friedrichsthal, E. R. *Reise in den südlichen Theilen von Neu-Griechenland. Beiträge zur Charakteristik dieses Landes*, Leipzig, Verlag von Wilhelm Engelmann 1838.

Frilley, G., and Jovan Wlahovitj *Le Monténégro contemporain*, Paris, E. Plon et Cie 1876.

Frischauf, J. *Gebirgsführer durch die Österreichischen Alpen und die Theile Bayern, Italien und Montenegro*, Vienna, Verlag des Österreichischen Touristen-Club 1883.

Fritsch, Gustav *Die Eingeborenen Süd-Afrika's*, Breslau, Ferdinand Hirt 1872.

Fuller, John *Narrative of a tour through some parts of the Turkish Empire*, London, Richard Taylor 1829.

Gaber, Slavko, and Tonči Kuzmanić eds *Kosovo – Srbija – Jugoslavija*, Ljubljana, Univerzitetna konferenca ZSMS 1989.

Galland, Antoine *De l'origine et du progrez du café*, Caen, Jean Cavelier; Paris, Florentin & Pierre Delauline 1699.

Galt, John *Voyages and Travels, in the Years 1809, 1810, and 1811; Containing Statistical, Commercial, and Miscellaneous Observations on Gibraltar, Sardinia, Sicily, Malta, Serigo, and Turkey*, London, T. Cadell and W. Davies 1812.

Galton, Francis, ed *Vacation Tourists and Notes of Travel in 1862–3*, London and Cambridge, Macmillan and Co. 1864.

Gambier, J. W. *Servia*, London, C. Kegan Paul & Co. 1878.

Garbiglietti, Paolo *I Pigmei della Favola di Omero gli Akkà dell'Africa Equatoriale*, Torino, Vincenzo Bona 1877.

Garnett, Lucy M. J. *Turkish Life in Town & Country*, London, George Newnes 1904.

Garnett, Lucy M. J. *The Turkish people. Their social Life, Religious Beliefs and Institutions and Domestic Life*, London, Methuen & Co. 1909.

Garnett, Lucy M. J. *Turkey of the Ottomans*, London, Sir Isaac Pitman 1911.

Garrido, Fernando, and C. B. Cayley *A History of Political and Religious Persecutions: From the Earliest Days of the Christian Church*, London, The London Printing and Publishing Company 1876–9.

Gautier, Théophile *Constantinople*, Paris, Michel Lévy Frère, Libraires-Editeurs 1853.

Gay, Peter *The Cultivation of Hatred*, New York, W. W. Norton 1993.

Geary, Grattan *Through Asiatic Turkey. Narrative of a Journey from Bombay to the Bosphorus*, London, Sampson Low, Marston, Searle, & Rivington 1878.

Gell, William *Narrative of a Journey in the Morea*, London, Longman, Hurst, Rees, Orme, and Brown 1823.

Gemelli Careri, Gio. Francesco *Giro del mondo*, Naples, Giuseppe Roselli 1699–1700.

Georgevitch, Vladan *Die Albanesen und die Großmächte*, Leipzig, S. Hirzel 1913.

Georgieuiz, Bartholomeus *Offspring of the House of Ottomano*, London 1570.

Gesemann, Gerhard *Heroische Lebensform. Zur Literatur und Wesenkunde der Balkanischen Patriarchalität*, Berlin, Wiking Verlag 1943.

Gibson, W. J. *In the Near East. Holiday Letters for Lewis Readers*, Stornoway 1926.

Giffard, Edward *A Short Visit to the Ionian Islands, Athens, and the Morea*, London, John Murray 1837.

Gilbert, Martin *The Holocaust: a history of the Jews of Europe during the Second World War*, New York, Henry Holt and Company 1985.

Gil'ferding, Aleksandr *Poězdka po Gercegovine, Bosnii i Staroj Serbii*, St Peterburg, Zapiski imperatorskago russkago geografičeskago obščestva XIII 1859.

Gilman, Sander L. *Difference and Pathology*, Ithaca, Cornell University Press 1985.

Gislenius, Augerius *Travels into Turkey: Containing the most accurate Account of the Turks, and Neighbouring Nations, Their Manners, Customs, Religion, Superstition, Policy, Riches, Coins, &c*, London, J. Robinson 1744.

Gjurgjević, Martin *Memoari sa Balkana 1858–1878*, Sarajevo 1910.

Gladstone, William Ewert 'Montenegro', in Edward L. Burlingame ed *Current Discussion* I, pp. 119–53, New York 1878.

Glazebrook, Philip *Journey to Kars*, Harmondsworth, Penguin 1985.

Gleisberg, Johann Paul *Kritische Darlegung und Urgeschichte des Menschen nach Carl Vogt*, Dresden, Conrad Weiske 1868.

Glover, Thomas 'The Journey of Edward Barton Esq., her Majesties Ambassador with the Grand Signor, otherwise called the Great Turke, in Constantinople, Sultan Mahumet Chan', in Samuel Purchas, *Purchas his Pilgrimage* VIII, pp. 1293–333. London 1625.

Glück, L. *Albanien und Macedonien. Eine Reiseskizze*, Würzburg and Vienna, Verlag von Leo Woerl 1892.

Goff, A., and Hugh A. Fawcett *Macedonia. A Plea for the Primitive*, London, John Lane The Bodley Head; New York, John Lane Company 1921.

Golczewski, Mechthild *Der Balkan in deutschen und österreichischen Reise- und Erlebnisberichten 1912–1918*, Wiesbaden, Steiner 1981.

Goldring, Douglas *Dream Cities*, London, T. Fisher Unwin 1913.

Goldsworthy, Vesna *Inventing Ruritania. The Imperialism of Imagination*, New Haven and London, Yale University Press 1998.

Goltz, Colmar von *Ein Ausflug nach Macedonien. Besuch der deutschen Eisenbahn von Salonik nach Monastir*, Berlin, R. v. Decker's Verlag 1894.

Gopčević, Spiridon *Montenegro und die Montenegriner*, Leipzig, Hermann Fries 1877.

Gopčević, Spiridon *Der turco-montenegrinische Krieg 1876–78*, Wien, L. W. Seidel & Sohn 1879.

Gopčević, Spiridon *Makedonien und Alt-Serbien*, Wien, L. W. Seidel & Sohn 1889.

Gopčević, Spiridon *Geschichte von Montenegro und Albanien*, Gotha, Friedrich Andreas Perthes 1914.

Gordon, Jan and Cora *Two Vagabonds in the Balkans*, New York, Robert M. Mc Bride and Company 1925.

Gordon, Thomas *History of the Greek Revolution*, Edinburgh, William Blackwood; London, T. Cadell 1832.

Gordon, Will *A Woman in the Balkans*, New York, Dodd, Mead & Company 1916.

Gossip, Robert *Turkey and Russia. Their Races, History, and Wars. Embracing a Graphic Account of the Great Crimean War and of the Russo-Turkish War*, Edinburgh, Thomas C. Jack 1878.

Gozzi, Carlo *Memorie inutile della vita di Carlo Gozzi scritte da lui medesimo e pubblicate per umiltà*, Bari, Gius. Laterza & Figli 1910.

Graves, Robert *Storm Centres of the Near East. Personal Memories 1879–1929*, London, Hutchinson & Co. 1933.

Gray, Arthur *Over the Black Coffee*, New York, The Baker and Taylor Company 1902.

Green, Philip James *Sketches of the War in Greece, In a Series of Extracts, from the Private Correspondence*, London, Thomas Hurst and Co. 1827.

Greg, William Rathbone *Sketches in Greece and Turkey: with the Present Condition and Future Prospects of the Turkish Empire*, London, James Ridgway 1833.

Grelot, Guillaume Joseph *A late voyage to Constantinople*, London, Henry Bonwicke 1683.

Grey, Hon. Mrs. William *Journal of a Visit to Egypt, Constantinople, the Crimea, Greece, &c. In the Suite of the Prince and Princess of Wales*, London, Smith, Elder & Co. 1869.

Griffiths, Julius *Travels in Europe, Asia Minor, and Arabia*, London, T. Cadell and W. Davies; Edinburgh, Peter Hill; John Crown 1805.

Grigorovič, Viktor *Očerk putešestvija po evropejskoj Turcii*, Kazan 1848.

Grisebach, August *Reise durch Rumelien und nach Brussa im Jahre 1839*, Göttingen, Vandenhoeck und Ruprecht 1841.

Grosvenor, Edwin A. *Constantinople*, London, Sampson Low; Marston and Company 1895.

Gruden, Josip *Zgodovina slovenskega naroda*, Celje, Družba sv. Mohorja 1941.

Guilletiere, De la *Athenes ancienne et novvelle. Et l'estat present de l'empire des Turcs, contenant la vie du Sultan Mahomet IV*, Paris, Estienne Michallet 1675.

Guys, M. de *A Sentimental Journey Through Greece. In a series of letters, written from Constantinople*, London, T. Cadell 1772.

Habesci, Elias *The Present State of the Ottoman Empire. Containing a More Accurate and Interesting Account of the Religion, Manners, Government, Customs, Military Establishments and Amusements, of the Turks Than Any Yet Extant. Including a Particular Description of the Court and Seraglio of the Grand Signior*, London, R. Baldwin 1784.

Hadži-Kalfa ili Ćatib-Čelebija *O balkanskom poluostrvu*, Beograd, Spomenik Srpske kraljevske akademije XVIII 1892.

Haga, Cornelius *A Trve Declaration of the arriuall of Cornelius Haga, (with others that accompanied him) Ambassador for the generall States of the Vnited Netherlands, at the great Citie of Constantinople*, London, Thomas Archer 1613.

Hahn, Johann Georg von *Albanische Studien*, Jena, Verlag von Friedrich Mauke 1854.

Halpern, Joel M. *The Changing Village Community*, Englewood Cliffs, Prentice Hall 1967.

Hamilton, William J. *Researches in Asia Minor, Pontus, and Armenia; with some Accounts of their Antiquities and Geology*, London, John Murray 1842.

Hamlin, Cyrus *Among the Turks*, London, Sampson Low, Marston, Searle, & Rivington 1878.

Hangi, Antun *Život i običaji Muslimana u Bosni i Hercegovini*, Sarajevo, Naklada Daniel A. Kajona 1906.

Hartley, John *Researches in Greece and the Levant*, London, Hatchard and Son; and Seeley and Sons 1831.

Hasandedić, Hivzija *Spomenici kulture turskog doba u Mostaru*, Sarajevo, Veselin Masleša 1980.

Hassert, Kurt *Reise durch Montenegro nebst Bemerkungen über Land und Leute*, Wien, A. Hartleben's Verlag 1893.

Hattox, Ralph S. *Coffee and coffeehouses*, Seattle and London, University of Washington Press 1985.

Hauser, Heinrich *Süd- Ost-Europa ist erwacht*, Berlin, Rowohlt 1938.

Haynes, James *Travels in several Parts of Turkey, Egypt, and the Holy Land*, London, Printed for the Author 1774.

Hazard, Paul *Kriza evropske zavesti*, Ljubljana, Državna založba Slovenije 1959.

Hazard, Paul *Evropska misel v XVIII. stoletju* Ljubljana, Državna založba Slovenije 1960.

Hecquard, Hyacinthe *Histoire et description de la Haute Albanie ou Guégarie*, Paris, Chez Arthus Bertrand 1858.

Hegel, Georg Wilhelm Friedrich *The Phenomenology of Mind*, London, Swan Sonneschen Co. 1910.

Helmreich, Ernst Christian *The Diplomacy of the Balkan Wars 1912–1913*, Cambridge, Harvard University Press 1938.

Henderson, Percy *A British Officer in the Balkans*, London, Seeley & Co. 1909.

Herbert, Thomas *A Relation of some Yeares Travile, begvnnee Anno 1626*, London, William Stansby, and Jacob Bloome 1634.

Herbert, William Von *By-paths in the Balkans*, London, Chapman & Hall 1906.

Hertzberg, Gustav *Montenegro und sein Freiheitskampf*, Halle, Schrödel & Simon 1853.

Hervé, Francis *A Residence in Greece and Turkey; with notes of the Journey through Bulgaria, Servia, Hungary, and the Balkan*, London, Whittaker & Co. 1837.

Heuzney, Léon, and H. Daumet *Mission archéologique de Macédoine,* Paris, Librairie de Firmin-Didot et Cie 1876.

Heyerdahl, Thor *Aku-aku. The secret of Easter Island*, London, George Allen & Unwin 1958.

Hibbert, Christopher *The Roots of Evil. A Social History of Crime and Punishment*, Harmondsworth, Penguin Books 1966.

Hichens, Robert *The Near East. Dalmatia, Greece and Constantinople*, New York, The Century Co. 1913.

Hilberg, Raul *The Destruction of the European Jews*, New York and London, Holmes & Meier 1985.

Hill, Aaron *A Full and Just Account of the Present State of The Ottoman Empire In all its Branches: with The Government, and Policy, Religion, Customs, and Way of Living of the Turks, in General. Faithfully Related From a Serious Observation, taken in many Years Travels thro' those Countries*, London, Printed for the Author 1709.

Hitti, Philip K. *History of the Arabs*, London, Macmillan 1970.

Hobhouse, John Cam. *A Journey through Albania and other Provinces of Turkey in Europe and Asia, to Constantinople, during the years 1809 and 1810*, London, J. Cawthorn 1813.

Hobhouse, John Cam. *Travels in Albania and other Provinces of Turkey in 1809 & 1810*, London, John Murray 1855.

Hobsbawn, Eric, and Terence Ranger eds, *The Invention of Tradition*, Cambridge, Cambridge University Press 1983.

Hogarth, David George *A Wandering Scholar in the Levant*, London, John Murray 1896.

Hogarth, David George *Accidents of an Antiquarian's Life*, London, Macmillan & Co. 1900.

Holbach, Maude M. *Dalmatia. The Land where East Meets West*, London, John Lane The Bodley Head; New York, John Lane Company 1908.

Holbach, Maude M. *Bosnia and Herzegovina*, London, John Lane The Bodley Head; New York, John Lane Company 1910.

Holeček, Josef *Černá Hora*, Praha, Spolek pro vydávání laciných knih českých 1876.

Holland, Henry *Travels in the Ionian Isles, Albania, Thessaly, Macedonia, &c. during the years 1812 and 1813*, London, Longman, Hurst, Rees, Orme, and Brown 1815.

Hornby, Lady *Constantinople during the Crimean War*, London, Richard Bentley 1863.

Hornby, Lester George *Balkan Sketches*, London, Brentano's 1927.

Horozović, Irfan, and Milan Vukmanović *Banja Luka i okolina*, Zagreb, Turistkomerc 1984.

Horton, George *Constantine. A Tale of Greece under King Otho*, London, T. Fisher Unwin 1896.

Howell, James *Instructions and Dierections For Forren Travell*, London, Humphrey Maseley 1650.

Hozier, H. M. *The Russo-Turkish War: Including an Account of the Rise and Decline of the Ottoman Power, and the History of the Eastern Question*, London, William Mackenzie 1877–9.

Hron, Karl *Das Volksthum der Slaven Makedoniens. Ein Beitrag zur Klärung der Orientfrage*, Wien, Selbstverlag 1890.

Hughes, Thomas Smart *Travels in Sicily Greece and Albania*, London, J. Mawman 1820.

Hugo, Victor *Les Orientales*, Paris, Charles Gosselin 1829.

Hugonnet, Léon *La Turqie inconnue. Roumélie, Bulgarie, Macédoine, Albanie*, Paris, L. Frinzine et Cie 1886.

Hull, Edmund C. P. *Coffee Planting in Southern India and Ceylon*, Madras, Higginbotham and Co. 1877.

Hulme-Beaman, Aredern G. *Twenty Years in the Near East*, London, Methuen & Co. 1898.

Hunter, William *Travels in the Year 1792 through France, Turkey, and Hungary, to Vienna: Concluding with an Account of that City*, London, B. and J. White 1794.

Hutchinson, Frances Kinsley *Motoring in the Balkans*, Chicago, A. C. McClurgh & Co. 1909.

Hutton, James *Theory of the Earth; or an Investigation of the Laws observable in the Composition, Dissolution, and Restoration of Land upon the Globe*, Edinburgh, Royal Society of Edinburgh 1785.

Huyshe, Wentworth *The Liberation of Bulgaria. War Notes in 1877*, London, Bliss, Sands and Foster 1894.

An Itinerary from London to Constantinople, in sixty days; taken in the suite of his excellency, the British Ambassador to the Ottoman Porte, in the year 1794, London, Richard Phillips 1805.

Ivanić, Ivan *Iz crkvene istorji Srba u Turskoj*, Beograd and Novi Sad, Rad 1902.

Ivanić, Ivan *Maćedonija i Maćedonci*, Beograd 1906.

Jackson, Thomas Graham *Dalmatia, the Quarnero and Istria with* Cettigne in Montenegro and the Island of Grado, Oxford, Claredon Press 1887.

Jacob, Heinrich Eduard *The Saga of Coffee*, London, George Allen & Unwin 1935.

Jaeckel, Blair *The Lands of the Tamed Turk or the Balkan States To-day*, Boston, L. C. Page and Company 1910.

Jahoda, Gustav *Images of Savages. Ancient Roots of Modern Prejudice in Western Culture*, London and New York, Routledge 1999.

James, Lionel *With the Conquered Turk. The Story of a Later-day Adventurer*, London, Thomas Nelson and Sons 1913.

James, Norman George Brett *My Term Off*, London, George Allen & Unwin 1921.

Janke, Arthur *Reise-Erinnerungen aus Italien, Griechenland und dem Orient*, Berlin, J. Schneider & Comp. 1874.

Jastrebov, Ivan *Stara Serbija i Albanija*, Beograd, Spomenik Srpske Kraljevske Akademije 41 1904.

Jelavić, Vjekoslav Kratki francuski putopis kroz Hercegovinu i novopazarski sandžak iz godine 1611, in *Glasnik zemaljskog muzeja Bosne i Hercegovine* XIX, pp. 471–82. Sarajevo 1907.

Jelić, Ilija *Šta znači kamen o vratu?* Beograd, Rajković i Čuković 1931.

Jelić, Milosav *Albanija*, Beograd, Geca Kon 1933.

Jelliffe, Derrick B., and E. F. Patrice Jelliffe *Human Milk in the Modern World*, Oxford 1978.

Jenour, Matthew *The Route to India through France, Germany, Hungary, Turkey, Natolia, Syria, and the Desart of Arabia, Delineated in a Clear Concise Manner, With the Distances, Time, Mode, and Expence of Travelling*, London, Printed for the Author 1791.

Jensen, Adolf E. *Myth and Cult among Primitive Peoples*, Chicago and London, The University of Chicago Press 1963.

Jeran, L. *Potovanje v Sveto Deželo, v Egipt, Fenicijo, Sirijo, na Libanon, v Carigrad in druge kraje*, Ljubljana, Založil pisatelj 1872.

Jerningham, Hubert E. H. *To and from Constantinople*, London, Hurst and Blackett 1873.

Jezernik, Božidar *Non cogito ergo sum: arheologija neke šale*, Ljubljana, Društvo za preučevanje zgodovine, literature in antropologije 1994.

Jezernik, Božidar 'Zigeunerlager on the planet Auschwitz', in *Acta Ethnographica Hungarica* 46, pp. 343–68, Budapest 2001.

Jireček, Constantin Jos. *Die Heerstrasse von Belgrad nach Constantinopel und die Balkanpässe*, Prag, F. Tempsky 1877.

Jireček, Konstantin *Cesty po Bulharsku*, Praha, Matica česká 1888.

Johnson, Clarence Richard, ed *Constantinople To-day or The Pathfinder Survey of Constantinople*, New York, The Macmillan Company 1922.

Johnson, E. E. *On the Track of the Crescent*, London, Hurst and Blackett 1885.

Johnson H. H. (Yahya Effendi) *Reminiscences of the Near East (1891–1913)*, London, Henry J. Drane 1920.

Johnson, Robert *Relations, Of the Most Famous Kingdoms and Common-weales Throvgh the World. Discoursing of their Scituations, Manners, Customes, Strengthes and Pollicies*, London, Iohn Iaggard 1608.

Johnson, Samuel *The Prince of Abissinia*, London, R. and J. Dodsley, and W. Johnston 1759.

Johnson, Samuel *The Philosophick Mirror*, Dublin, M. Williamson 1759.

Jousset, Paul *Un tour de Méditerranée, de Venise à Tunis, par Athènes, Constantinople et le Caire*, Paris 1893.

Jukić, Ivan Frano 'Putovanje po Bosni godine 1843', in *Kolo* 3, pp. 3–32. Zagreb 1847.

Jukić, Ivan Frano *Putopisi i istorisko-etnografski radovi*, Sarajevo, Svjetlost 1953.

Kabbani, Rana *Europe's Myths of Orient*, London, Macmillan 1986.

Kajmaković, Zdravko *Zidno slikarstvo u Bosni i Hercegovini*, Sarajevo, Veselin Masleša 1971.

Kanitz, Felix *Das Königreich Serbien und das Serbenvolk von der Römerzeit bis zur Gegenwart*, Leipzig, Bernh. Meyer 1904–9.

Kanitz, Felix *Srbija. Zemlja i stanovništvo*, Beograd, Srpska književna zadruga & Rad 1985.

Kaplan, Robert D. *Balkan Ghosts*, New York, Vintage Books 1994.

Kapper, Siegfried *Südslavische Wanderungen im Sommer 1850*, Leipzig, Friedr. Ludw. Herbig 1851.

Karadžić, Vuk *Srpski rječnik, istolkovan njemačkim i latinskim riječima*, Beč, P. P. Armeniern 1818.

Karadžić, Vuk *Montenegro und die Montenegriner*, Stuttgart and Tübingen, Verlag der J. G. Gott'schen Buchhandlung 1837.

Karić, Enes *Essays (on behalf) of Bosnia*, Sarajevo, El-Kalem 1999.

Kennedy, Robert J. *Montenegro and Its Borderland*, London, Hatchards 1894.

Keppel, George *Narrative of a Journey across the Balcan, by the two Passes of Selimo and Pravadi; also of a Visit to Azani, and other Newly Discovered Ruins in Asia Minor, in the Years 1829–1830*, London, Henry Colburn and Richard Bentley 1831.

Kern, Stephen *Anatomy and destiny*, Indianapolis, Bobbs-Merrill 1975.

Kesnin bey *The Evil of the East; or, Truth about Turkey*, London, Vizetelly & Co. 1888.

Kinglake, Alexander William *Eōthen, or Traces of Travel Brought Home from the East*, London, John Ollivier 1844.

Kirkness, Kenneth *Ferdinand of Bulgaria. The Dream of Byzantium*, London, Hurst & Blackett 1933.

Klaić, Vjekoslav *Bosna*, Zagreb, Matica Hrvatske 1878.

Klaić, Vjekoslav *Kosovo. Geografijsko-historijske crtice*, Zagreb, Dionička tiskara 1889.

Klenze, Leo von *Aphoristische Bemerkungen gesammelt auf seiner Reise nach Griechenland*, Berlin, G. Reimer 1838.

Kmet, Marija 'Iz Bosne', in *Ljubljanski zvon* XXXIV, pp. 214–219. Ljubljana 1914.

Knezović, Oton 'Ali-paša Rizvanbegović-Stoičević, hercegovački vezir 1832–1851', in *Glasnik zemaljskog muzeja Bosne i Hercegovine* XL, pp. 11–52. Sarajevo 1928.

Knežević, Srebrica 'Kultna mesta i manastiri u tradicionalnoj zdravstvenoj kulturi Srba, Makedonaca i Arbanasa', in *Bigorsko naučno-kulturni_sobiri, Gostivar, 21–22. X 1971*, pp. 243–55. Skopje 1973.

Knight, E. F. *Albania. A Narrative of Recent Travel*, London, Sampson Low, Marston, Searle & Rivington 1880.

Knighton, William *European Turkey; Its People, Its Provinces, and Its History*, London, John Cassell 1854.

Knolles, Richard *The Generall Historie of the Turkes, from the First beginning of that Nation to the rising of the Othoman Familie: with all the notable expeditions of the Christian Princes against them. Together with The Lives and Conquests of the Othman Kings and Emperous*, London, Adam Islip 1631.

Koetschet, Josef *Aus Bosniens letzter Türkenzeit*, Wien and Leipzig, A. Hartleben's Verlag 1905.

Koetschet, Josef *Osman Pascha, der letzte Grosse Wesier Bosniens, und seine Nachfolger*, Sarajevo, Daniel A. Kajon 1909.

Kohl, Johann Georg *Reisen nach Istrien, Dalmatien und Montenegro*, Dresden, Arnoldische Buchhandlung 1851.

Köhler, Albert *Sonne über dem Balkan*, Dresden, Carl Reissner 1930.

Kohn, Hans *Western Civilization in the Near East*, London, George Routledge and Sons 1936.

Kolberg, Oskar *Dzieła wszyskie*, Vol. 46, Wrocław and Poznań, Ludow Spolz. Wydawn. 1967.

Kollegger, Willibald *Albaniens wiedergeburt*, Wien, Wiener Verlagsgesellschaft 1942.

Komlenović, Uroš Rolling Stones na Vrbasu, in *Vreme* 199, pp. 28–31. Beograd 1994.

Kondakov, Nikodim Pavlovič *Makedonija. Arheologičeskoe putešestvie*, Sanktpeterburg, Imperatorskaja Akademija Nauk 1909.

Konitza, Faik *Albania: The Rock Garden of Southeastern Europe and Other Essays* 1957.

Kovalevskij, Egor Petrovič *Četyre mesjaca v Černogorii*, S.-Peterburg, A. A. Pljušar 1841.

Krasinski, Valerian *Montenegro, and the Slavonians of Turkey*, London, Chapman and Hall 1853.

Kreševljaković, Hamdija 'Esnafi i obrti u Bosni i Hercegovini (1463–1878)', in *Zbornik za narodni život i običaje Južnih Slavena* 35, pp. 61–138. Zagreb 1951.

Kreševljaković, Hamdija, and Hamdija Kapidžić 'Stari hercegovački gradovi', in *Naše starine* II, pp. 9–21. Sarajevo 1954.

Kristeva, Julia *Strangers to Ourselves*, New York, Harvester Wheatsheaf 1991.

Krumbacher, Karl *Griechische Reise. Blätter aus dem Tagebuche einer Reise in Griechenland und in der Türkei*, Berlin, August Hettler 1886.

Kuba, Ludvík *Čtení o Makedonii. Cesty a studie z roku 1925–1927*, Praha, Družstevní práce 1932.

Kukuljević Sakcinski, Ivan *Putovanje po Bosni*, Zagreb, Lavoslav Župan 1858.

Kůnčov, Vasil *Makedonija. Etnografija i statistika*, Sofia, Državna pečatnica 1900.

Kutschbach, Albin *In Montenegro und im Insurgentenlager der Herzegowizen. Reiseskizze eines Kriegsberichterstatters*, Dortmund, Verlag C. L. Krüger 1877.

La Roque, Jean de *A Voyage to Arabia the Happy, and the Eastern Ocean, and the Streigths of the Red-Sea Perform'd by the French for the first time, A.D. 1708, 1709, 1710*, London, G. Strahan and R. Williamson 1726.

A Lady *Wayfaring Sketches among the Greeks and Turks, and on the Shores of the Danube*, London, Chapman and Hall 1847.

Laffan, R. G. D. *The Guardians of the Gate. Historical Lectures on the Serbs*, Oxford, Claredon Press 1918.

Laketić, Miljana 'Kalemegdanci i Beograđani', in *Duga* 1555, pp. 90–93. Beograd 1995.

Lamartine, Alphonse de *Visit to the Holy Land: or, Recollections of the East*, London, George Virtue 1847.

Landau, Rom *Search for Tomorrow. The things which are and the things which shall be hereafter*, London, Nicholson and Watson 1938.

Lane, Rose Wilder *The Peaks of Shala*, London, Chapman & Dodd 1922.

Lang Teslow, Tracy 'Reifying race. Science and art in *Races of Mankind* at the Field Museum of Natural History', in Sharon Macdonald ed *The Politics of Display. Museums, science, culture*, London and New York, Routledge 1998.

Larpent, George *Turkey; Its History and Progress: From the Journals and Correspondence of Sir James Porter, Fifteen Years Ambassador at Constantinople; Continued to the Present Time, With a Memoir of Sir James Porter*, London, Hurst and Blackett 1854.

Laskaris, Mihailo *Vizantijske princeze u srednjevekovnoj Srbiji*, Beograd, Knjižara Franje Baha 1926.

Laveleye, Emile Louis Victor de *The Balkan Peninsula*, London, T. Fisher Unwin 1887.

Lavtižar, Josip *Pri Jugoslovanih*, Ljubljana, Slovenska Matica 1903.

Layard, Austen Henry *Autobiography and Letters*, London, John Murray 1903.

Lazen, Charlotte de *L'Herzegovine et le pont de Mostar*, Vienne, Gérold 1861.

Le Croy *An Account of the Turks Wars with Poland, Muscovy, and Hungary*, London, J. King and Bible 1711.

Le Queux, William *An Observer in the Near East*, London, Eveleigh Nash 1907.

Leach, Harry *A Bit of Bulgaria*, London, Simpkin, Marshall, & Co. 1877.

Leake, William Martin *Researches in Greece*, London, John Booth 1814.

Leake, William Martin *The Topography of Athens. With some remarks on its antiquities*, London, John Murray 1821.

Leake, William Martin *Travels in Northern Greece*, London, J. Rodwell 1835.

Lear, Edward *Journals of a Landscape Painter in Albania, etc.*, London, Richard Bentley 1851.

Leech, Harry Harewood *Letters of a Sentimental Idler, From Greece, Turkey, Egypt, Nubia, and the Holy Land*, New York, D. Appleton and Company 1869.

Lenormant, F. *Turcs et Monténégrins*, Paris, Didier et Cie 1866.

Lessing, Gottlob Ephraïm *Laookon: oder über der Grenzen der Malerei und Poesie*, Berlin, Christian Friedrich Gotz 1766.

Levin, Harry *The Broken Column*, Cambridge, MA, Harvard University Press 1931.

Levinge, Godfrey *The Traveller in the East; Being a Genuine Guide through the Levant, Syria and Palestine, Egypt and Nubia, With practical Information; Containing Descriptions of the principal Cities, Antiquities, and Interesting Localities: Excursions through the Southern Provinces of the Kingdom of Naples, Albania, the Ionian Islands, and the Principal Islands of the Archipelago; and A Variety of Tours, with Distances*, London, Printed by the Author 1839.

Lewis, Bernard *Istanbul and the Civilization of the Ottoman Empire*, Norman, University of Oklahoma Press 1963.

Lewis, Raphaela *Everyday Life in Ottoman Turkey*, London, Batsford 1971.

Linnaei, Caroli *Systema naturae*, Lugduni Batavorum (Leyden), Theodorus Haak 1735.

Linnaeus, Carolus *Systema naturae*, Nieuwkoop, B. de Graaf. (Facsimile of the first edition.) 1964.

Linton, William *The scenery of Greece and its islands, illustrated by fifty views, sketched from nature, executed on steel, and described en route, with a map of the country*, London, published by the artist 1856.

Lithgow Scotus, William *A Delectable, and true discourse, of an admired and painefull peregrination from Scotland, to the most famous Kingdomes in Europe, Asia, and Affricke*, London, Thomas Archer 1614.

Lloyd Evans, J. *British Journalists' tour in the Adriatic & Bosnia*, Warwick 1907.

Loftus, William Kennett *Travels and Researches in Chaldaea and Susianna*, London, James Nisbet and Co. 1857.

Loir, du *Les voyage dv sievr dv Loir, Ensemble de ce qui se passa à la mort du feu Sultan Mourat dans le Serrail, les ceremonies de ses funerailles; & celles de l'auenement à l'Empire de Sultan Hibraim son frete, qui luy succeda. Avec la relation du Siege de Babylone fait en 1639. par Sultan Mourat*, Paris, Francois Clovzier 1654.

Loti, Pierre *Turkey in Agony*, London, The Ottoman Committee 1913.

Lovrich, Giovanni *Osservazioni di Giovanni Lovrich sopra diversi pezzi del Viaggio in Dalmazia del signor abate Alberto Fortis coll' aggiunta della vita* di Soçivizca, Venizia, Francesco Sansoni 1776.

Lucas, Paul *Voyage du sieur Paul Lucas fait en M.DCCXIV, &c. par ordre de Louis XIV dans la Turquie, l'Aise, Sourie, Palestine, Haute & Basse Egypte, &c*, Rouen, Robert Machuel 1719.

Luckwald, Erich von *Albanien. Land zwischen Gestern und Morgen*, München, F. Bruckmann Verlag 1942.

Lunn, Henry S. *How to Visit the Mediterranean. A Guide-Book to Jerusalem, Cairo, Constantinople, Athens, and other Places of Interest on the Littoral of the Mediterranean*, London, Horace Marshall and Son 1896.

Lusignan, Annie de *A Word about Turkey and Her Allies*, London, Chapman and Hill 1885.

Lusignan, Annie de *The Twelve Years' Reign of His Imperial Majesty Abdul Hamid II. Sultan of Turkey*, London, Sampson Low, Marston, Searle, & Rivington 1889.

Lusignan, S. *A Series of Letters*, London, Printed for the Author 1788.

Lyall, Archibald *The Balkan Road*, London, Methuen & Co. 1930.

Lynch, H. F. B. *Europe in Macedonia. Being Five Articles Reprinted from the "Morning Post"*, London, Edward Stanford 1908.

Lynch, Henry Blosse, ed. *Constantinople in 1887. Leaves from the Diary of Thomas Kerr Lynch*, Printed for Private Circulation Only 1887.

Macdonald, John *Turkey and the Eastern Question*, London, T. C. & E. C. Jack 1913.

MacGill, Thomas *Travels in Turkey, Italy, and Russia, During the Years 1803, 1804, 1805, & 1806. With an Account of Some of the Greek Islands*, London, John Murray; Edinburgh, Archibald Constable & Co. 1808.

Mac Farlane, Charles *Constantinople in 1828. A Residence of Sixteen Months in the Turkish Capital and Provinces: With an Account of the present State of the Naval and Military Power, and of the resources of the Ottoman Empire*, London, Saunders and Otley 1829.

Mac Farlane, Charles *Turkey and Its Destiny*, London, John Murray 1850.

Macintosh, A. F. *A Military Tour in European Turkey, the Crimea, and on the Eastern Shores of the Black Sea: Including Routes across the Balkan into Bulgaria, and Excursions in the Turkish, Russian, and Persian Provinces of the Caucasian Range; With Strategical Observations on the Probable Scene of the Operations of the Allied Expeditionary Force*, London, Longman, Brown, Green, and Longmans 1854.

Mackenzie, Georgina Muir, and Adeline Paulina Irby *Travels in Slavonic Provinces of Turkey-in-Europe*, London, Daldy, Isbister & Co. 1878

Macmichael, William *Journey from Moscow to Constantinople, in the Years 1817, 1818*, London, John Murray 1819.

Mączak, Antoni *Travel in Early Modern Europe*, Cambridge, Polity Press 1995.

Madden, Richard Robert *Travels in Turkey, Egypt, Nubia, and Palestine, in 1824, 1825, 1826 and 1827*, London, Henry Colburn 1829.

Mahmut *Letters Written by a Turkish Spy, Who lived Five and Forty Years, Undiscovered, at Paris: Giving an Impartial Account to the Divan at Constantinople, of the most Remarkable Transactions of Europe; And discovering several Intrigues and Secrets of the Christian Courts, (especially of that of France) from the Year 1637, to the Year 1682*, London, Henry Rhodes 1691.

Maliszewski, Edward *Albania*, Warszawa, Wincent Jakowicki; Poznań, M. Niemierkiewicz 1913.

Mandić, Dominik 'Mostar u Hercegovini, njegov postanak i značenje imena', in *Hrvatski kalendar* 1968, pp. 96–105. Chicago 1968.

Mandrou, Robert *Possession et sorcellerie au XVIIe siécle*, Paris, Fayard 1979.

Mantegazza, Vico *Al Montenegro. Note ed impressioni (agosto-settembre 1896)*, Florence, Successori le Monnier 1896.

Mantegazza, Vico *Macedonia*, Milano, Fratelli Treves 1903.

Marcotti, G. *Il Montenegro e le sue donne*, Milano, Fratelli Treves 1896.

Marković, Vasilije *Pravoslavno monaštvo i monastiri u srednjevekovnoj Srbiji*, Sremski Karlovci, Srpska manastirska štamparija 1920.

Markovich, Slobodan G. *British Perceptions of Serbia and the Balkans, 1903–1906*, Paris, Dialogue 2000.

Marmont, Marshal, Duc de Raguse *The Present State of the Turkish Empire*, London, John Olivier 1839.

Marsden, William *The History of Sumatra, Containing an Account of the Government, Laws, Customs and Manners of the Native Inhabitants, with a Description of the Natural Productions, a Relation of the Ancient Political State of that Island*, London, Printed for the Author 1783.

Martis, Nicolaos K. *The Falsification of Macedonian History*, Athens 1984.

Mastnak, Tomaž *Kristjanstvo in muslimani*, Ljubljana, Znanstveno in publicistično središče 1996.

Mastnak, Tomaž *Evropa: med evolucijo in evtanazijo*, Ljubljana, Studia humanitatis 1998.

Matthews, Caroline *Experiences of a Woman Doctor in Serbia*, London, Mills & Boon 1916.

Matthews, Ronald *Sons of the Eagle. Wanderings in Albania*, London, Methuen & Co. 1937.

Matzhold, Louis A. *Brandherd Balkan*, Wien, L. W. Seidel & Sohn 1936.

Mazro, Sophia *Turkish Barbarity. An Affecting Narrative of the Unparalleled Sufferings of Mrs. Sophia Mazro, a Greek Lady of Missolonghi*, Providence, G. C. Jennings 1828.

McCulloch, John I. B. *Drums in the Balkan Night*, New York, G. P. Putnam's Sons 1936.

Medaković, V. M. G. *Život i običai Crnogoraca*, Novi Sad, Episkopska kn'igopečatna 1860.

Melas, G. *The Turk as he is. Answer to a libel*, Hove, Emery & Son 1922.

Melik, Anton *Do Ohrida in Bitolja*, Ljubljana, Jutro 1926.

Mérimée, Prosper *La Guzla*, Paris, Charpentier 1842.

Meslin, Michael 'Eye', in Mircea Eliade ed 5, pp. 236–9.

Meslin, Michael 'Head', in Mircea Eliade ed 6, pp. 221–5.

Messner-Sporšić, Ante *Od Bukurešta do Ankare*, Zagreb 1937.

Meylan, A. *A travers l'Herzégovine*, Paris, Sandoz et Fischbacher 1876.

Michaelis, Adolf *Ancient Marbles in Great Britain*, Cambridge, Cambridge University Press 1822.

Michel, Robert *Mostar*, Prag, Carl Bellmann 1909.

Michel, Robert *Auf der Südbastion unsereß Reiches*, Leipzig, Insel-Verlag 1915.

Miecznik, Antoni *Macedonja i Macedonczycy*, Warszawa, M. Arct 1904.

Mihačević, Lovro *Po Albaniji*, Zagreb, Matica Hrvatske 1911.

Milaković, Demetrio *Storia del Montenegro*, Ragusa, Carlo Pretner Tip. Editore 1877.

Miles, Margaret M. 'The Virgin's one bare breast', in Susan Robin Suleiman ed *The Female Body in Western Culture*, Cambridge and London, Harvard University Press 1986.

Miller, William *The Balkans*, London, T. Fisher Unwin; New York, G. P. Putnam's Sons 1896.

Miller, William *Travels and Politics in the Near East*, London, T. Fisher Unwin 1898.

Milojević, M. S. *Odlomci istorije Srba i srpskih-jugoslavenskih-zemalja u Turskoj i Austriji*, Beograd, Državna štamparija 1872.

Milosavljević, Petar 'Ruski putešestvenici u Srbiji', in *Balcanica* XII, pp. 131–47. Beograd 1981.

Minchin, James George Cotton *The Growth of Freedom in the Balkan Peninsula*, London, John Murray 1886.

Mirković, Mijo *Ekonomska historija Jugoslavije*, Zagreb, Informator 1968.

Misheff, D. *The Truth about Macedonia*, Berne, Pochon-Jent & Bühler 1917.

Misirkov, Krste P. *Za makedonckite raboti*, Sofia, Liberalni klub 1903.

Močnik, Rastko 'Temne zore', in *Razledi* 3, p. 11. Ljubljana 1995.

Modrich, Giuseppe *Nella Bulgaria Unita. Note di Viaggio*, Trieste, Tipografia di A. Levi 1902.

Monson, W. I. *Extracts from a Journal*, London, Rodwell and Martin 1820.

Montagu, Ashely *An Introduction to Physical Anthropology*, Illinois 1960.

Montague, John, Earl of Sandwich *A Voyage Performed by the Late Earl of Sandwich Round the Mediterranean in the Years 1738 and 1739*, London, T. Cadell Jun. and W. Davies 1799.

Montague, Mary Wortley *Letters, written during her travels in Europe, Asia and Africa*, London, T. Becket and P. A. De Hondt 1763.

Moore, Arthur *The Orient Express*, London, Constanble & Company 1914.

Moore, Frederick *The Balkan Trail*, London, Smith, Elder, & Co. 1906.

More, Robert Jasper *Under the Balkans. Notes of a Visit to the District of Philippolis in 1876*,

London, Henry S. King & Co. 1877.

Morgan, William Y. *The New East*, Topeka, Crane & Company 1913.

Morier, James *A Journey through Persia, Armenia, and Asia Minor, to Constantinople, in the Years 1808 and 1809*, London, Longman, Hurst, Rees, Orme, and Brown 1812.

Morritt, John B. S. *The Letters of John B. S. Morritt of Rokeby Descriptive of Journeys in Europe and Asia Minor in the Years 1794–1796*, London, John Murray 1914.

Moryson, Fynes *Itinerary. Containing His ten yeers travell through the twelve dominio of Germany, Bohmerland, Sweitzerland, Netherland, Denmarke, Poland, Italy, Turky, France, England, Scotland, and Ireland*, London, John Beale 1617.

Mrkun, Anton 'Ljudska medicina v dobrépoljski dolini', in *Etnolog* X-XI, pp. 1–10. Ljubljana 1939.

Muhibić, Mustafa Hilmi 'Stara ćuprija u Mostaru', in *Glasnik zemaljskog muzeja Bosne i Hercegovine* III, pp. 10–13. Sarajevo 1889.

Mujić, Muhamed A. 'Krivi most na Radobolji u Mostaru', in *Naše starine* II, pp. 213–15. Sarajevo 1954.

Müller, Joseph *Albanien, Rumelien und die österreichisch-montenegrinische Gränze, oder statistisch-topographische Darstellung der Paschaliks Skutari, Priserend, Ipek, Toli-Monastir, Jakova, Tirana, Kavaja, Elbassan und Ohrida, so wie des Gränzdistricts von Budua in Österreichisch-Albanien, nach eigenen Beobachtungen dargestellt*, Prag, Verlag von J. E. Calve'shcn Buchhandlung 1844.

Müller, Max, Mrs *Letters from Constantinople*, London, Longmans, Green, and Co. 1897.

Mundy, Peter *The Travels in Europe and Asia, 1608–1628*, Cambridge, Hakluyt Society 1907.

Munro, Robert *Rambles and Studies in Bosnia-Herzegovina*, Edinburgh and London, W. Blackwood & Sons 1895.

Munro-Butler-Johnstone, H. A. *The Turks: Their Character, Manners, and Institutions*, Oxford and London, James Parker and Co. 1876.

Mure, William *Journal of a Tour in Greece and the Ionian Islands, with Remarks on the Recent History – Present State – and Classical Antiquities of Those Countries*, Edinburgh and London, William Blackwood and Sons 1842.

Murray, David *Museums. Their History and their Use*, Glasgow, James MacLehose and Sons 1904.

Naironus, Faustus Banesius *A Discourse on Coffee: Its Description and Vertues*, London, Abel Roper 1710.

Nametak, Alija 'Mostarski stari most', in *Napredak* 11–12, pp. 135–42. Sarajevo 1932.

Nametak, Alija *Islamski kulturni spomenici turskoga perioda u Bosni i Hercegovini*, Sarajevo, Državna štamparija 1939.

Neale, J. M. *Notes, Ecclesiological and Picturesque, on Dalmatia, Croatia, Italia, Styria, with a Visit to Montenegro*, London, J. T. Hayes 1861.

Neave, Dorina Lady *Romance of the Bosphorus*, London, Hutchinson & Co. 1949.

Neilson, George *Caudatus Anglicus: A Mediæval Slander*, Edinburgh, George J. Johnston 1896.

Neidhardt, Juraj, and Džemal Čelić 'Stari most u Mostaru', in *Naše starine* I, pp. 133–140. Sarajevo 1953.

Nenadović, Ljubomir P. ed *Memoari prote Matije Nenadovića*, Beograd, Državna kn'igopečatnija 1867.

Nenadović, Ljubomir P. *O Crnogorcima. Pisma iz Cetinja 1878. Godine*, Cetinje, Obod 1975.

Newman, Bernard *Albanian Journey*, London, Sir Isaac Pitman & Sons 1938.

Newman, Bernard *Balkan Background*, London, Robert Hale 1944.

Newman, Bernard *Tito's Yugoslavia*, London, Robert Hale 1952.

Newman, F. W. *Personal Narrative, In Letters, Principally from Turkey, In the Years 1830–3*, London, Holyoake and Co. 1856

Newton, Charles Thomas *Travels and Discoveries in the Levant*, London, Day & Son 1865.

Nicolaides, Cleanthes *Macedonien. Die geschichtliche Entwicklung der macedonischen Frage im Altertum, im Mittelalter und in der neueren Zeit*, Berlin, Verlag von Johannes Räde 1899.

Nicolay de Dauphinoys, N. *Les quatre premiers livres des navigations et peregrinations Orientales*, Lyon, Gvillavme Roville 1568.

Niebuhr, Carsten *Travels through Arabia, and the other Countries of the East*, Edinburgh, R. Morison and Son, G. Mudie, and T. Vernor 1792.

Nikitin, Sergej *Slavjanskie komitety v Rosii*, Moskva, Moskovskij universitet 1960.

Nishani, Trandafile Omer *Albanien, das Wunschland Mussolinis*, Halle, Akademischer Verlag 1936.

Novaković, Stojan *Vaskrs države srpske. Političko-istorijska studija o prvom srpskom ustanku 1804–1813*, Novi Sad, Srpska knjižara Braće M. Popovića 1904.

Novaković, Stojan *Dva dana u Skoplju. 14–15–16 jul 1905. Beleške i razmišljanja s puta*, Beograd, Državna štamparija Kraljevine Srbije 1905.

Novaković, Stojan *Balkanska pitanja i manje istorijsko-političke beleške o Balkanskom poluostrvu 1886–1905*, Beograd, Zadužbina I. M. Kolarca 114 1906.

Noyes, James O. *Roumania: The Border Land of the Christian and the Turk, Comprising Adventures of Travel in Eastern Europe and Western Asia*, New York, Rudd & Carleton 1858.

Nušić, Branislav *Kraj obala Ohridskoga Jezera*, Beograd, Državna štamparija Kraljevine Srbije 1894.

Nušić, Branislav *Kosovo. Opis zemlje i naroda*, Novi Sad, Matica srpska 1902–3.

Ogilby, John *Africa*, London, Printed for the author 1670.

Omont, M. H. *Voyages à Athènes, Constantinople et Jérusalem de François Arnaud (1602–1605)*, Paris 1909.

Orbini, Mauro *Il regno de gli slavi*, Pesaro, Girolamo Concordia 1601.

Ostrorog, Léon *The Turkish Problem. Things Seen and a Few Deductions*, London, Chatto & Windus 1919.

Oztürk, Orhan 'Folk Treatment of the Mental Illness in Turkey', in Ari Kiev, *Magic, Faith & Healing*, pp. 343–63. New York, Free Press; London, Collier – Macmillan 1974.

Pahor, Jože *Hodil po zemlji sem naši...*, Ljubljana, Mladinska knjiga 1951.

Palerne, Iean *Peregrinations*, Lyon, Iean Pillehotte 1606.

Palmer, Roger *An Account Of the Present War Between the Venetians & Turk; With the State of Candie: (In a Letter to the King, from Venice.)*, London, H. Herringman 1666.

Pardoe, Mrs *The City of the Sultan; and Domestic Manners of the Turks, in 1836*, London, Henry Colburn 1837.

Pardoe, Mrs *The Beauties of the Bosphorus*, London, George Virtue 1838.

Parnauvel, Omney Tcherson *A Trip to Turkey, and Traveller's Guide to the Turkish Capital, By Way of Gibraltar, Malta, Syra, and Alexandria*, London, Houlston & Stoneman 1855.

Pashley, Robert *Travels in Crete*, Cambridge and London, John Murray 1837.

Pašić, Amir *The Old Bridge (Stari Most) in Mostar*, Istanbul, Research Centre for Islamic History, Art and Culture 1995.

Passarge, Louis *Dalmatien und Montenegro. Reise- und Kulturbilder*, Leipzig, Verlag von B. Elischer Nachfolger 1904.

Paton, Andrew Archibald *Servia, the youngest member of the European family: or, a residence in Belgrade, and travels in highlands and woodlands of the interior, during the years 1843 and 1844*, London, Longman, Brown, Green, and Longmans 1845.

Paton, Andrew Archibald *Highlands and Islands of the Adriatic*, London, Chapman and Hall 1849.

Paton, Andrew Archibald *Researches on the Danube and the Adriatic; or, the contributions to the modern history of Hungary and Transylvania, Dalmatia and Croatia, Servia and Bulgaria*, Leipzig, F. A. Brockhaus 1861.

Patrick, Mary Mills *Under Five Sultans*, New York and London, The Century Co. 1929.

Pavićević, Mićun *Crnogorke u pričama i anegdotama*, Zagreb 1930.

Pavlowitch, Stevan K. *A History of the Balkans 1804–1945*, London and New York, Longman 1999.

Peacock, Wadham *Albania, the foundling state of Europe*, London, Chapman & Hall 1914.

Pears, Edwin *Turkey and its People*, London, Methuen & Co. 1911.

Pears, Edwin *Forty Years in Constantinople*, London, Herbert Jenkins 1915.

Pearson, Emma Maria, and Louisa Elisabeth McLaughlin *Service in Serbia under the Red Cross*, London, Tinsley Brothers 1877.

Peez, Carl *Mostar und sein Culturkreis*, Leipzig, J. U. Brockhaus 1891.

Pelerin, Charles *Excursion artistique en Dalmatie et au Montenegro*, Paris, Imprimerie de Dubuisson & Co. 1860.

Pénel, Jean-Dominique *Homo Candatus. Les hommes à queue d'Afrique Centrale: un avatar de l'imaginaire occidental*, Paris, Société d'Etudes Linguistiques et Anthropologiques de France 1982.

Peričić, Šime *Dalmacija uoči pada Mletačke Republike*, Zagreb, Sveučilište u Zagrebu 1980.

Perry, Charles *A View of the Levant: Particularly of Constantinople, Syria, Egypt, and Greece. In which Their Antiquities, Government, Politics, Maxims, Manners, and Customs, (with many other Circumstances and Contigencies) are attempted to be Described and Treated on*, London, T. Woodward, and C. Davis, and J. Shuckburgh 1743.

Perry, Duncan M. *The Politics of Terror. The Macedonian Liberation Movements 1893–1903*, Durham and London, Duke University Press 1988.

Perry, Ruth 'Colonizing the breast. Sexuality and maternity in eighteenth-century England', in John C. Fout ed *Forbidden History*, pp. 107–37. Chicago and London, University of Chicago Press 1992.

Pertusier, Charles *La Bosnie considérée dans ses rapports avec l'empire Ottoman*, Paris, Librairie de Charles Gosselin 1822.

Peterlin-Petruška, Radivoj *Ahasverjeva kronika*, Ljubljana, Odmevi 1936.

Pfeiffer, Ida *Reise eine Wienerin in das heilige Land, Unternommen in März bis Dezember 1842*, Wien, Verlag von Jakob Dirnböck 1846.

Pieńkowski, Karol *Czarnagóra pod względem geograficznym, statystycznym i historycznym*, Lwów, Nakładem autora 1869.

Plamenac, Jovan 'Koze muslimanske, koze pravoslavne', in *Duga* 8, pp. 29–32. Beograd 1988.

Plumley, Matilda *Days and Nights in the East; from the Original Notes of a Recent Traveller through Egypt, Arabia-Petra, Syria, Turkey and Greece*, London, T. C. Newby 1845.

Plut, Milan *Po macedonskem bojišču*, Ljubljana, Samozaložba 1913.

Pococke, Richard *A Description of the East, and Some other Countries. Vol. II Part II. Observations on the Islands of the Archipelago, Asia Minor, Thrace, Greece, and some other Parts of Europe*, London, Printed for the Author 1745.

Pomardi, Simone *Viaggio nella Grecia Fatto Negli Anni 1804, 1805, e 1806*, Roma, Vincenzo Poggioli 1820.

Pomet, Pierre *Histoire generale des Drogues, traitant des Plantes, des Animaux, & des Mineraux; Ouvrage enrichy de plus de quatre cent Figures en Taille-douce tirées d'aprés Nature; avec un discours qui explique leurs differens Noms, les Pays d'où elles viennent, la maniere de connoître les Veritables d'avec les Falsifiées, & leurs proprietez, où l'on découvre l'erreur des Anciens & des Modernes; Le tout tres utile au Public*, Paris, Jean-Baptiste Loyson, & Augustin Pillon; Estienne Ducastin 1694.

Pomet, Pierre *A Compleat History of Drugs*, London, R. and J. Bonwicke, and R. Wilkin; John Walthoe and Tho. Ward 1725.

Poole, Stanley Lane ed *The People of Turkey: Twenty Years Residence among Bulgarians, Greeks, Albanians, Turks, and Armenians. By a Consul Daughter and Wife*, London, John Murray 1878.

Popović, Dušan J. *O Cincarima*, Beograd, Drag. Gregorić 1937.

Popović, Pavle *Serbian Macedonia. An Historical Survey*, London The Near East 1916.

Popović, Sreten L. *Putovanje po novoj Srbiji*, Beograd, Srpska knjižara Braće M. Popovića 1879–84.

Port, Mattijs van de *Gypsies, War and Other Instances of the Wild*, Amsterdam, Amsterdam University Press 1998.

Porter, James *Observations on the Religion, Law, Government, and Manners of the Turks*, London, J. Nourse 1771.

Post, Henry A. V. *A Visit to Greece and Constantinople, in the Year 1827–8*, New York, Sleight & Robinson 1830.

Poullet *Nouvelles relations du Levant, qui continent pluieurs remarques fort curieuses non encore obseruées, touchant la Religion, les mœurs & le politique de diuers Peuples. Aues un Discours sur le Commerce des Anglois & des Hollandois*, Paris, L. Billaine 1667–8.

Pouqueville, François Charles *Travels in the Morea, Albania, and other parts of the Ottoman Empire*, London, Henry Colburn 1813.

Pouqueville, François Charles *Travels in Epirus, Albania, Macedonia, and Thessaly*, London, Sir Richard Phillips 1820.

Poynter Mary A. *When Turkey Was Turkey. In and around Constantinople*, London, George Routledge and Sons; New York, E. P. Dutton and Co. 1921.

Pribichevich, Stoyan *Macedonia. Its People and History*, University Park and London, The Pennsylvania State University Press 1982.

Prel, Carl du *Unter Tannen und Pinien. Wanderungen in den Alpen, Italien, Dalmatien und Montenegro*, Berlin, Denicke's Verlag 1875.

Price, Clair *The Rebirth of Turkey*, New York, Thomas Seltzer 1923.

Price, W. H. Crawford *The Balkan Cockpit. The Political and Military Story of the Balkan Wars in Macedonia*, London, T. Werner Laurie 1914.

Prime, E. D. G. *Forty Years in the Turkish Empire; or, Memoirs of Rev. William Goodell, D. D.*, New York, Robert Carter and Brothers 1876.

Protić, Stojan M. *O Makedoniji i Makedoncima*, Beograd, K. S. Taumanović 1888.

Puljevski, oorpe M. *Rečnik od tri jezika s. makedonski, arbanski i turski*, Beograd, Državna štamparija 1875.

Purchas, Samuel *Relations of the world and religions observed in all ages*, London, H. Fetherstone 1613.

Quiclet *Les voyages de M. Quiclet a Constantinople par terre*, Paris, Pierre Promé 1664.

Quin, Michael J. *A Steam Voyage Down the Danube. With Sketches of Hungary, Wallachia, Servia, and Turkey, &c*, London, Richard Bentley 1835.

R. H. R. *Rambles in Istria, Dalmatia and Montenegro*, London, Hurst and Blackett 1875.

Radovich, Eugene *Land of Destiny*, New York, Philosophical Library 1951.

Rajić, Milan *Srpski pakao u komunističkoj Jugoslaviji*, Čikago 1975.

Raleigh, Walter 'The English voyages of the sixteenth century', in Rychard Hakluyt, *The Principal Navigations Voyages Traffiques & Discoveries of the English Nation*, Vol. 12. London, James MacLehose & Sons 1905.

Ramberti, Benedetto *Libri tre delle cose de Turchi*, Vinegia, Casa de' figliuoli di Aldo 1539.

Ramsay, W. M. Mrs *Everyday Life in Turkey*, London, Hodder and Stoughton 1897.

Randolph, Bernard *The Present State of the Islands in the Archipelago, (Or Arches) Sea of Constantinople, and Gulph of Smyrna; With the Islands of Candia, and Rhodes*, Oxford, The Theater 1687.

Randolph, Bernard *The Present State of the Morea, Called Anciently Peloponnesus: Together with a Description of the City of Athens, Islands of Zant, Strafades, and Serigo*, London, Will. Notts, Tho. Basset, and Thomas Bennet 1689.

Rasch, Gustav *Die Türken in Europa*, Prag, Skrejšovský 1873.

Rašid-bej *Istorija čudnovatih događaja u Beogradu i Srbiji*, Beograd, Spomenik Srpske kraljevske akademije XXIII 1894.

Rauwolf, Leonhart *Aigentliche beschreibung der Raisz in die Morgenländer*, Laugingen 1582.

Reed, John *The War in Eastern Europe*, London, Eveleigh Nash 1916.

Régla, Paul de *La Turquie officielle. Constantinople, son governement ses habitants, son présent et son avenir*, Geneva, C.-E. Alioth et Cie 1890.

Reinsberg-Düringsfeld, Ida von *Aus Dalmatien*, Prag, Carl Bellman's Verlag 1857.

Reiss, R. A. *The Kingdom of Serbia. Infringements of the Rules and Laws of War Committed by the Austro-Bulgaro-Germans: Letters of a Criminologist on the Serbian Macedonian Front*, London, George Allen & Unwin 1919.

Renner, Heinrich *Durch Bosnien und die Hercegovina kreuz und quer*, Berlin, Dietrich Riemer 1897.

Reshid, Mehmed *Tourist's Practical Guide to Constantinople and Environs*, Constantinople 1925.

Reuter, Jens 'Policy and Economy in Macedonia', in James Pettifer ed. *The New Macedonian Question*, pp, 28–46. Basingstoke and London, Macmillan Press 1999.

Richer, Christophle *Des Covstvmes et manieres de viure des Turcs*, Paris, Robert Estienne 1540.

Richter, Wilhelm *Serbiens Zustände unter dem Fürsten Milosch*, Leipzig, Adolf Frohberger 1840.

Rihtman Auguštin, Dunja *Ulice moga grada*, Beograd, Biblioteka XX. vek 2000.

Rihtman Auguštin, Dunja *Etnologija i etnomit*, Zagreb, Publica 2001.

Rittih, Petr Aleksandrovič *Po Balkanam*, S.-Peterburg, V. F. Kiršbaum 1909.

Robert, Cyprien *Les Slaves de Turquie*, Paris, L. Passard et Jules Labitte 1852.

Robinson, Edward Forbes *The Early History of Coffee Houses in England*, London, Kegan Paul, Trench, Trübner & Co. 1893.

Robinson, Vandeleur *Albania's Road to Freedom*, London, George Allen & Unwin 1941.

Roden, Claudia *Coffee*, London, Faber & Faber 1977.

Rolamb, Nicholas 'A Relation of a Journey to Constantinople', in Churchill, *A Collection of Voyages and Travels, some Now first Printed from Original Manuscripts, others Now First Published in English*, V, pp. 669–716. London, John Walthoe, Tho. Wotton, Samuel Birt, Daniel Browne, Thomas Osborne, John Shuckburgh, and Henry Lintot 1732.

Röser, Jacob *Tagebuch meiner Reise nach Griechenland, in die Türkei, nach Aegypten und Syrien, im Jahre 1834 bis 1835*, Mergentheim, Neue Buch- und Kunsthandlung 1836.

Rośkiewicz, Johann *Studien über Bosnien und die Herzegovina*, Leipzig and Wien, F. A. Brockhaus 1868.

Ross, David, of Bladensburg *Opinions of the European Press on the Eastern Question. Translated and extracted from Turkish, German, French, and English papers and reviews*, London, James Ridgway and Sons 1836.

Ross, Ludwig *Erinnerungen und Mittheilungen aus Griechenland*, Berlin, Verlag von Rudolph Gaertner 1863.

Rossi, Adolfo *Un'Escursione nel Montenegro*, Milano, Carlo Aliprandi 1897.

Rouillard, Clarence Dana *The Turk in French History, Thought, and Literature (1520–1660)*, Paris, Boivin & Cie 1941.

Rousseau, Jean-Jacques *A Discourse upon the Origin and Foundation of the Inequality among Mankind*, London, R. & J. Dodsley 1761.

Ruland, Bernd *Orient Expreß*, Bayreuth, Hestia 1967.

Ruprecht, Kronprinz von Bayern *Reise-Erinnerungen aus dem Süd-Osten Europas un dem Orient*, München, Josef Kösel & Friedrich Pustet 1923.

Russell, Alex *The Natural History of Aleppo*, London, G. G. and J. Robinson 1794.

Russell, Frank S. *Russian Wars with Turkey*, London, Henry S. King & Co. 1877.

Russell Barrington, Mrs *Through Greece and Dalmatia. A Diary of Impressions Recorded by Pen & Picture*, London, Adam and Charles Black 1912.

Ruthner, Francesco *Un Viaggio a Maria Stella convento dei trappisti nella valle dell'Urbas presso Banjaluka in Bosnia colla descrizione della vita e delle opere dei poveri monaci di San Bernardo*, Venezia, L. Merlo 1877.

Rycaut, Paul *The Present State of the Ottoman Empire. Containing the Maxims of the Turkish Politie, The most material Points of the Mahometan Religion, Their Sects and Heresies, their Convents and Religious Votaries, Their Military Discipline, With an exact Computation of their Forces both by Land and Sea*, London, John Starkey and Henry Brome, and The Star 1668.

Rycaut, Paul *The History of the Turkish Empire From the Year 1623. to the Year 1677. Containing the Reigns Of the three last Emperours, viz. Sultan Morat or Amurath IV. Sultan Ibrahim, and Sultan Mahomet IV. his Son, The XIII. Emperour now Reigning*, London, John Starkey 1680.

Šabanović, Hazim *Bosanski pašaluk*, Sarajevo, Naučno društwo NR Bosne i Hercegovine 1959.

Saint Clair, S. G., and Charles A. Brophy *A Residence In Bulgaria; or, Notes on the resources and Administration of Turkey: The Condition and Character, Manners, Customs, Language of the Christian and Mussulman Populations, with Reference to the Eastern Question*, London, John Murray 1869.

Salgündžijev, Stefan K. *Lični dela i spomeni po vuzroždaneto na solunskiot i serski Bulgari ili 12–godišna žestoka neravna borca s gürckata propaganda*, Plovdiv, Trud 1906.

Salusbury, Philip H. B. *Two Months with Tchernaieff in Servia*, London, Chapman and Hall 1877.

Šamić, Midhat *Francuski putnici u Bosni na pragu XIX stoljeća i njihovi utisci o njoj*, Sarajevo, Veselin Masleša 1966.

Šamić, Midhat *Francuski putnici u Bosni i u Hercegovini u XIX stoljeću 1836–1878*, Sarajevo, Veselin Masleša 1981.

Samuelson, James *Bulgaria, Past and Present. Historical, Political, and Descriptive*, London, Trübner & Co. 1888.

Sanders, Irwin T. *Balkan Village*, Lexington, The Kentucky University Press 1949.

Sanderson, Iohn *Sundrie the personall Voyages performed by Iohn Sanderson of London, Merchant, Begun in October 1584. Ended in October 1602. With an historical Description of Constantinople*, in 'Purchas His Pilgrimes V', pp. 1614–40. London, Henrie Fetherstone 1625.

Sandwith, Humpry *Notes on the South Slavonic countries in Austria and Turkey in Europe*, Edinburgh and London, William Blackwood and Sons 1865.

Sandys, George *A relation of a iourney begvn Anno Dom. 1610*, London, W. Barrett 1615.

Schapera, Isaac, and B. Farrington *The Early Cape Hottentots*, Cape Town, The Van Riebeeck Society 1933.

Schimmer, Karl August *The Sieges of Vienna by the Turks*, London, John Murray 1847.

Schwarz, Bernhard *Montenegro. Schilderung einer Reise durch das Innere nebst Entwurf einer Geographie des Landes*, Leipzig, Verlag von Paul Frohberg 1883.

Schweinfurth, Georg *The Heart of Africa. Three Years' Travels and Adventures in the Unexplored Regions of Central Africa. From 1868 to 1871*, London, Sampson Low, Marston, Low, and Searle 1873.

Sclamer, Pietro *Sermone parenetico di Pietro Sclamer Chersino al Signor Giovanni Lovrich, Nativo di Sign in Morlacchia, Autore delle Osservazioni sopra il Viaggio in Dalmazia del sig. Abate Alberto Fortis*, Modena 1776.

Schweiger-Lerchenfeld, Amand Freiherr von *Bosnien, das Land und seine Bewohnen*, Wien, L. C. Zamarski 1878.

Scopetea, Ellie 'Greek and Serbian enlightenment: a comparative approach', in *Proceedings of the Fifth Greek-Serbian symposyum*, pp. 201–9. Thessaloniki, Institute for Balkan Studies 1991.

Scott-Stevenson, Esmé *On Summer Seas*, London, Chapman and Hall 1883.

Semple, Robert *Observations on A Journey through Spain and Italy to Naples; and thence to Smyrna and Constantinople*, London, C. and R. Baldwin 1807.

Senior, Nassau W. *A Journal Kept in Turkey and Greece in the Automn of 1857 and the Beginning of 1558*, London, Longman, Brown, Green, Longmans, and Roberts 1859.

Serristori, Alfredo *La costa Dalmata e il Montenegro durante la guerra del 1877*, Firenze, Tipografia di G. Barbera 1877.

Shorter, Edward *A History of Women's Bodies*, London, Allen Lane 1983.

Shotwell, James Thompson *A Balkan Mission*, New York, Columbia University Press 1949.

Siebertz, Paul *Albanien und die Albanesen*, Wien, Verlag der Manz'schen k.u.k. Hofverlags- und Universitätsbuchhandlung 1910.

Šimčik, Antun 'Jesu li samo Turci kopali oči hrišćanskim ikonama?', in *Novi behar* 13–18, p. 193. Sarajevo 1932.

Sís, Vladimír *Nový Balkán*, Praha 1924.

Skarić, Vladislav 'Trebinje u 18 vijeku', in *Glasnik zemaljskog muzeja Bosne i Hercegovine* VL, pp. 39–70. Sarajevo 1933.

Skarić, Vladislav 'Uticaj turskog vladanja na društveni život', in *Knjiga o Balkanu* II, pp. 134–42. Beograd, Balkanski institut 1937.

Skene, James Henry *The Frontier Lands of the Christian and the Turk*, London, Richard Bentley 1853.

Skene, James Henry *With Lord Stratford in the Crimean War*, London, Bentley & Son 1883.

Slade, Adolphus *Turkey, Greece and Malta*, London, Saunders and Otley 1837.

Slade, Adolphus *Travels in Germany and Russia: Including a Steam Voyage by the Danube and the Euxine from Vienna to Constantinople, In 1838–39*, London, Longman, Orme, Brown, Green, and Longmans 1840.

Slade, Adolphus *Records of Travels in Turkey and Greece, etc. And of a Cruise with the Capitan Pacha*, London, Saunders and Otley 1854.

Slišković, Jakov *Albanija i Macedonija*, Sarajevo, Vlastita naklada 1904.

Sloane, William M. *The Balkans. A laboratory of history*, New York, The Abingdon Press 1914.

Smith, Albert *A Month at Constantinople*, London, David Bogue 1850.

Smith, Iohn *The True Travels, Adventvres, and Observations of Captain Iohn Smith, In Europe, Asia, Affrica, and America, from Anno Domini 1593. to 1629*, London, Thomas Slater 1630.

Smith, Thomas *Remarks Upon the Manners, Religion and Government Of the Turks. Together with A Survey of the Seven Churches of Asia, As they now lye in their Ruines: and A Brief Description of Constantinople*, London, Moses Pitt 1678.

Smith, Warington W. *A Year with the Turks or Sketches of Travel in the European and Asiatic Dominions of the Sultan*, London, John W. Parker and Son 1854.

Snow, Robert *Journal of Steam Voyage down the Danube to Constantinople, and thence by way of Malta and Marseilles to England*, London, Moyes and Barclay 1842.

Šolta, Pawol *Bosniski kraj a raj*, Budyšin 1918.

Sommières, L. C. Vialla de *Travels in Montenegro*, London, Richard Phillips 1820.

Spaho, Fehim 'Prve kafane su otvorene u našim krajevima', in *Novi behar* 3, pp. 41–2. Sarajevo 1931.

Spencer, Edmund *Travels in Circassia, Krim Tartary, &c. Including a steam voyage down the Danube, from Vienna to Constantinople and round the Black Sea*, London, Henry Colburn 1837.

Spencer, Edmund *Travels in European Turkey in 1850*, London, Colburn and Co. 1851.

Spencer, Edmund *Turkey, Russia, the Black Sea, and Circassia*, London, George Routledge & Co. 1854.

Spencer, Edmund *Travels in France and Germany in 1865 and 1866*, Vol. II, London, Hurst and Blackett 1866.

Spens, Archibald B. *Half Hours in the Levant. Personal Impressions of Cities & Peoples of the Near East*, London, Stanley Paul & Co. 1912.

Spry, William J. J. *Life on the Bosphorus. Doings in the City of Sultan. Turkey Past and Present. Including Chronicles of the Caliphs from Mahomet to Abdul Hamid II*, London, H. S. Nichols. 1895.

Stanojević, Gligor *Šćepan Mali*, Beograd, Srpska akademija nauka i umetnosti 1957.

Stanojević, Stanoje ed *Narodna enciklopedija srpsko-hrvatska-slovenačka* II, Zagreb, Bibliografski zavod 1925.

Stark, Carl Bernhard *Nach dem Griechischen Orient, Reise-Studien*, Heildelberg, Carl Winter's Universitätsbuchhandlung 1874.

Stavrianos, L. S. *The Balkans since 1453*, New York, Rinehart & Company 1958.

Steinmetz, Karl *Eine Reise durch die Hochländergaue Oberalbaniens*, Wien and Leipzig, A. Hartleben's Verlag 1904.

Steinmetz, Karl *Od Adrije do Crnoga Drima*, Skoplje 1910.

Stent, W. Drew *Egypt and the Holy Land in 1842, With Sketches of Greece, Constantinople, and the Levant*, London, Richard Bentley 1843.

Stephens, John G. *Incidents of Travel in Greece, Turkey, Russia, and Poland*, Dublin, William Curry, Jun. and Company 1839.

Stephens, J. L. *Incidents of Travel in the Russian and Turkish Empires*, London, Richard Bentley 1839.

Stieglitz, Heinrich *Ein Besuch auf Montenegro*, Stuttgart and Tübingen, J. G. Cotta'scher 1841.

Stillman, William James *Herzegovina and the late uprising: the causes of the later and the remedies*, London, Longmans, Green, and Co. 1877.

Stomma, Ludwik *Antropologia kultury wsi polskiej XIX w*, Warszawa, Instytut Wydawniczy Pax 1986.

Strangford, Emily Anne *The Eastern Shores of the Adriatic in 1863. With a Visit to Montenegro*, London, Richard Bentley 1864.

Struys, John *The Perillous and most Unhappy Voyages*, London, Samuel Smith 1683.

Stuart-Glennie, J. S. *Europe and Asia. Discussions of the Eastern Question in Travels through Independent, Turkish, and Austrian Illyria*, London, Chapman Hall 1879.

Stucley, Peter *Two Months' Grace*, London, Selwyn & Blount 1935.

Styx, Edmund *Das Bauwesen in Bosnien und der Hercegovina vom Beginn der Occupation durch die österreichisch-ungarische Monarchie bis in das Jahr 1887*, Wien, Hölder 1887.

Sullivan, James *Diary of a Tour in the Autumn of 1856 to Gibraltar, Malta, Smyrna, Dardanelles, Marmora, Constantinople, Scutari, Sweet Waters, Greece, Italy, and France*, Printed for Presentation to His Friends 1857.

Sutherland, Captain *A Tour up the Straits, from Gibraltar to Constantinople. With the Leading Events in the Present War between the Austrians, Russians, and the Turks, to the Commencement of the Year 1789*, London, Printed for the Author 1790.

Svetek, Anton 'Spomini na okupacijo Bosne', in *Ljubljanski zvon* VIII, Ljubljana 1888.

Swift, Johnatan *Travels into several Remote Nations of the World*, London, Benj. Motte 1726.

Sykes, Mark *Dar-ul-Islam. A Record of a Journey through Ten of the Asiatic Provinces of Turkey* London, Bickers & Son 1904.

Tachard, Gui *A Relation of Voyage to Siam*, London, J. Robinson and A. Churchill 1688.

Tancoigne, M. *A Narration of a Journey into Persia, and Residence in Teheran: Containing A Descriptive Itinerary from Constantinople to the Persian Capital*, London, William Wright 1820.

Tannahill, Raey *History of Food*, London, Eyre Methuen 1973.

Tavernier, Jean Baptiste de 'Persian Travels', in *Collection of Travels through Turkey into Persia, and the East-Indies*, Vol. I, London 1684.

Temple, Grenville T. *Travels in Greece and Turkey*, London, Saunders and Otley 1836.

The Man Who Dined with Kaiser *My Secret Service*, London, Herbert Jenkins 1916.

Thevenot, Jean de *The Travels of the Monsieur de Thevenot into the Levant*, London, John Taylor 1687.

Thierfelder, Franz *Schichsalstunden des Balkan*, Wien and Leipzig, Adolf Inser Verlag 1941.

Thoemmel, Gustav *Geschichtliche, politische und topographisch-statistische Beschreibung des Vilajet Bosnien*, Wien, Albert A. Wenedikt 1867.

Thompson, Charles *The Travels Of the Late Charles Thompson, Esq; Containing his Observations on France, Italy, Turkey in Europe, The Holy Land, Egypt, And many other Parts of the World: Giving A particular and faithful Account of what is most remarkable in the Manners, Religion, Polity, Antiquities, And Natural History of those Countries: With a Curious Description of Jerusalem*, London, J.

Newberry and C. Micklewright 1744.

Thomsett, Richard Gillham *A Trip through the Balkan*, London, Digby, Long & Co. 1909.

Thomson, Harry Craufuird *The Outgoing Turk. Impression of a Journey through the Western Balkans*, London, William Heinemann 1897.

Thornton, Philip *Dead Puppets Dance*, London, Collins 1937.

Thornton, Philip *Ikons and Oxen*, London, Collins 1939.

Tischendorf, Constantin *Reise in den Orient*, Leipzig, Verlag von Bernh. Tauschwitz, jun. 1846.

Titmarsh, M. A. *Notes of a Journey from Cornhill to Grand Cairo, by Way of Lisbon, Athens, Constantinople, and Jerusalem: Performed in the Steamers of the Peninsular and Oriental Company*, London, Chapman and Hall 1846.

Tobin, Catherine *Shadows of the East; or Slight Sketches of Scenery, Persons, and Customs, from Observations during a Tour in 1853 and 1854, in Egypt, Palestine, Syria, Turkey, and Greece*, London, Longman, Brown, Green, and Longmans 1855.

Todorova, Maria *Imagining the Balkans*, New York and Oxford, Oxford University Press 1997.

Tollot *Nouveau voyage fait au Levant, ès années 1731 & 1732*, Paris, Andre Cailleau 1742.

Tomić, Jaša *Rat na Kosovu i Staroj Srbiji 1912. godine*, Novi Sad 1913.

Tomić, Jaša *Rat u Albaniji i oko Skadra 1912. i 1913. godine*, Novi Sad 1913.

Tomitch, Svet 'Who are the Macedonian Slavs', in J. T. Markovitch ed *Macedonia and Macedonians*, pp. 43–124. Rome, Printing-office C. Colombo 1918.

Tooke, William *Russia: or, A Complete Historical Account of All the Nations Which Compose that Empire*, London, J. Nichols, T. Cadell, H. Payne, and N. Conant 1780.

Tott, François de *Memoirs of the Baron de Tott, on the Turks and the Tartars*, Dublin, L. White, J. Cash, and R. Marchbank 1785.

Tournefort, Joseph Pitton de *A Voyage into the Levant: Perform'd by Command of the Late French King*, London, D. Browne, A. Bell, J. Darby, A. Bettesworth, J. Pemberton, C. Rivington, J. Hooke, D. Cruttenden and T. Cox 1718.

Townshend, A. F. *A Military Consul in Turkey. The Experiences & Impressions of a British Representative in Asia Minor*, London, Seeley & Co. 1910.

Townson, Robert *Travels in Hungary, with a short account of Vienna in the year 1793*, London, G. G. and J. Robinson 1797.

Toynbee, Arnold J. *The Western Question in Greece and Turkey. A Study in the Contact of Civilisations*, London, Constable and Company 1922.

Tozer, Henry Fanshawe *Researches in the Highlands of Turkey; Including Visit to Mounts Ida, Athos, Olympus, and Pelion, the Mirdite Albanians, and Other Remote Tribes. With Notes on the Ballads, Tales, and Classical Superstitions of the Modern Greeks*, London, John Murray 1869.

Trevor, Roy *My Balkan Tour*, London, John Lane The Bodley Head; New York, John Lane Company 1911.

Trotsky, Leon *The Balkan Wars 1912–1913*, New York and Sidney, Monad Press 1980.

Tucović, Dimitrije 'Srpska sirotinja', in *Sabrana dela* I, pp. 64–71. Beograd, Rad 1975.

Tućan, Fran *Po Makedoniji*, Zagreb, Hrvatska tiskarna 1920.

Turner, William *Journal of a Tour in the Levant*, London, John Murray 1820.

Tyson, Edward *Orang-Outan, sive Homo Sylvestris; or the Anatomy of a Pygmie Compared with that of a Monkey, an Ape, and a Man*, London, T. Bennett and D. Brown 1699.

Ukers, William H. *All About Coffee*, New York, The Tea & Coffee Trade Journal Company 1935.

Upward, Allen *The East End of Europe*, London, John Murray 1908.

Urošević, Atanasije *Etnički procesi na Kosovu tokom turske vladavine*, Beograd, Srpska akademija nauka i umetnosti 1987.

Urquhart, David *The Spirit of the East, Illustrated in a Journal of Travels through Roumeli During an Eventful Period*, London, Henry Colburn 1838.

Ustinov, Peter 'A country with too much past tries to come to terms with the present', in *The European* 256, pp. 7–11. London 1995.

Vaka, Demetra *The Eagle and the Sparrow*, Boston 1913.

Vaka, Demetra *The Unveiled Ladies of Stamboul*, Boston, Houghton Mifflin Company 1923.

Valentini, George Wilhelm de *Description of the Seat of War in European Turkey*, London, James Ridgway 1854.

Valentini, Michael Bernhard *Museum museorum, oder Vollständige Schau-Bühne Aller Materialien und Specereyen Nebst deren Natürlichen Beschreibung /Election, Nutzen und Gebrauch/ Aus andern Material – Kunst- und Naturalien-Kammern Oost-und West-Indischen Reisz-Beschreibungen*, Franckfurt am Mäyn, Johann David Zunners 1704.

Valle, Pietro della *Viaggi*, Roma, Vitale Mascardi 1650.

Valoušek, František *Vzpomínky na Bosnu*, Brno, Společnost přátel jižních Slovanu v česke republice 1999.

Valvasor, Johann Weichard *Die Ehre deß Hertzogthums Crain*, Laybach and Nürnberg 1689.

Vambéry, Arminius *Western Culture in Eastern Lands. A Comparison of the Methods Adopted by England and Russia in the Middle East*, London, John Murray 1906.

Vaudoncourt, Guillaume de *Memoirs of the Ionian Islands, Considered in a Commercial, Political, and Military, Point of View; In which Their Advantages of Position Are Described, As Well As Their Relations with the Greek Continent; Including the Life and Character of Ali Pasha, the Present Ruler of Greece; Together with a Comparative Display of the Ancient and Modern Geography of the Epirus, Thessaly, Morea, Part of Macedonia, &c. &c.*, London, Baldwin, Cradock, and Joy 1816.

Vane, C. W., Marquess of Londonderry *A Steam Voyage to Constantinople, by the Rhine and the Danube, In 1840–41, and to Portugal, Spain, &c., In 1839*, London, Henry Colburn 1842.

Vasić, Milan 'O gradnji starog mosta u Mostaru', in *Balcanica* VIII, pp. 189–95. Beograd 1977.

Vavouskos, C. A. *Macedonia's Struggle for Freedom*, Thessaloníki, Institute for Balkan Studies 1973.

Vere, Aubrey de *Picturesque Sketches of Greece and Turkey*, London, Richard Bentley 1850.

Verne, Jules *Cinq semaines en ballon. Voyage de découvertes en Afrique. Par trios Anglais. Rédigé sur les notes de docteur Fergusson*, Paris, J. Hetzel 1863.

Vernon, Francis 'Francis Vernon's Letter, written to Mr. Oldenburg, Ja. 10. 1675/6, giving a short account of some of his Observations in his travels from Venice through Istria, Dalmatia, Greece, and the Archipelago, to Smyrna', in Rev. John Ray, *A Collection of Curious Travels and Voyages. Containing Dr. Leonhart Rauwolf's Journey Into the Eastern Countries* II, pp. 355–63. London, 1738, J. Walthoe, D. Midwinter, A. Bettesworth, and C. Hitch, W. Innys, R. Robinson, J. Wilford, A. Ward, J. and P. Knapton, T. Longman, O. Payne, W. Shropshire, J. and R. Tonson, T. Woodman, R. Chandler, and J. Wellington 1675–6.

Veryard, E. *An Account on divers Choice Remarks, as well Geographical, as Historical, Political, Mathematical, Physical, and Moral; Taken in a Journey through the Law-Countries, France, Italy, and Part of Spain; With the Isles of Sicily and Malta. As also, A Voyage to the Levant*, London, S. Smith and B. Walford 1701.

Veselinović, Milojko V. *Srbi u Maćedoniji i u južnoj Staroj Srbiji*, Beograd, Štamparija Kraljevine Srpske 1888.

Villari, Luigi ed *The Balkan Question. The present condition of the Balkans and of European responsibilities*, London, John Murray 1905.

Vivanti, Anna *A Journey to Crete, Constantinople, Naples, and Florence. Three Months Abroad*, London, Printed for Private Circulation 1865.

Vivian, Herbert *Servia, the Poor Man's Paradise*, London, Longmans, Green, and Co. 1897.

Vivian, Herbert *The Servian Tragedy with some Impressions of Macedonia*, London, Grant Richards 1904.

Vodovozov, Vasil *Na Balkanah*, Petrograd, Ogni 1917.

Volonakis, Michael D. *Saint Sophia and Constantinople. History and Art*, London, Hesperia Press 1920.

Voltaire, Francois Marie Arouet de *The Works. With Notes, Historical and Critical*, London, J. Newbery, R. Baldwin, W. Johnston, S. Crowder, T. Davies, J. Coote, G. Kearsley, and B. Collins 1761.

Vujić, Joakim *Putešestvie po Serbii*, Budim grad 1828.

Walker, Mary Adeleide *Through Macedonia to the Albanian Lakes*, London, Chapman and Hall 1864.

Walker, Mary Adeleide *Untrodden Path in Roumania*, London, Chapman and Hall 1888.

Walker, Mary Adeleide *Old Tracks and New Landmarks*, London, Richard Bentley and Son 1897.

Wallisch, Friedrich *Die Pforte zum Orient*, Innsbruck, Tyrolia 1917.

Wallisch, Friedrich *Der Atem des Balkans*, Leipzig, Dieterich'sche 1928. Verlagsbuchhandlung.

Walsh, Robert *Narrative of a Journey from Constantinople to England*, London, Frederick Westley 1828.

Walsh, Robert *A Residence at Constantinople, During a Period Including the Commencement, Progress, and Termination of the Greek and Turkish Revolutions*, London, Frederick Westley and A. H. Davis 1836.

Walshe, Douglas *With the Serbs in Macedonia*, London, John Lane The Bodley Head; New York, John Lane Company 1920.

Watkins, Thomas *Travels through Switzerland, Italy, Sicily, the Greek Islands to Constantinople; through Part of Greece, Ragusa, and the Dalmatian Isles*, London, J. Owen 1794.

Watson, Robert William Seton *The Rise of Nationality in the Balkans*, London, Constable & Co. 1917.

Weideger, Paula *History's Mistress*, Harmondsworth, Penguin 1986.

Weigand, Gustav *Ethnographie von Makedonien. Geschichtlich-nationaler, sprachlich-statistischer Teil*, Leipzig, Friedrich Brandstetter 1924.

Wendel, Hermann *Von Belgrad bis Buccari. Ein unphilosophische Reise durch Westserbien, Bosnien, Hercegovina, Montenegro und Dalmatien*, Frankfurt am Main, Frankfurt Societäts-Druckerei 1922.

West, Rebecca *Black Lamb & Grey Falcon*, London, Macmillan 1977.

Wester, Josip *Iz domovine in tujine*, Ljubljana, Slovensko planinsko društvo 1944.

Weyand, Johann Karl *Reisen durch Europa, Asien, und Afrika von dem Jahre 1818 bis 1821 incl.*, Amberg, Auf Kosten des Verfasers 1822–5.

Wheler, George *A Journey into Greece. In Company of Dr Spon of Lyons*, London, William Cademan, Robert Kettlewel, and Awnsham Churchill, the Hand and Scepter, and the Black Swan 1682.

Wherry, Albinia *From Old To New; being some personal experiences at Constantinople in April, 1909*, Cambridge, Bowes and Bowes 1909.

White, Charles *Three Years in Constantinople; or, Domestic Manners of the Turks in 1844*, London, Henry Colburn 1845.

Whitwell, Mrs. E. R. *Through Bosnia and Herzegovina*, London, Dresser 1909.

Wilkinson, Henry Robert *Maps and Politics. A Review of the Ethnographic Cartography of Macedonia*, Liverpool, The University Press 1951.

Wilkinson, John Gardner *Dalmatia and Montenegro: with a Journey to Mostar in Herzegovina*, London, John Murray 1848.

Willis, N. Parker *Summer Cruise in the Mediterranean, on board an American Frigate*, New York, Charles Scribner 1853.

Wilson, Francesca M. *Portraits and Sketches of Serbia*, London, The Swarthmore Press 1920.

Wilson Rae *Travels in Egypt and the Holy Land. With A Journey through Turkey, Greece, the Ionian

Islands, Sicily, Spain, &c, London, Longman, Hurst, Rees, Orme, Brown, and Green 1824.

Wilson, S. S. *A Narrative of the Greek Mission; or, Sixteen Years in Malta and Greece; Including Tours in the Peloponnesus in the Ægean and Ionian Isles,* London, John Snow 1839.

Wingfield, William Frederick *A tour in Dalmatia, Albania, and Montenegro with an historical sketch of the Republic of Ragusa,* London, Richard Bentley 1859.

Withers, Robert *The Grand Signiors Serraglio* in 'Purchas His Pilgrimes', vol. V, pp. 1580–1613. London, Henrie Fetherstone 1625.

Wittman, William *Travels in Turkey, Asia-Minor, Syria, and Across the Desert into Egypt During the Years 1799, 1800, and 1801, in Company with the Turkish Army and the British Military Mission,* London, Richard Phillips 1803.

Wolff, Robert Lee *The Balkans in Our Time,* Cambridge, Harvard University Press 1956.

Woods, Henry Charles *Washed by Four Seas,* London, T. Fisher Unwin 1908.

Woods, Henry Charles *The Danger Zone of Europe,* London, T. Fisher Unwin 1911.

Woods, Henry Charles *War and Diplomacy in the Balkans,* London, The Field & Queen (Horace Cox) 1915.

Wordsworth, Christopher *Greece: Pictorial, Descriptive, and Historical,* London, William S. Orr and Co. 1839.

Wratislaw, Wenceslas *Adventures of Baron Wenceslas Wratislaw of Mitrowitz. What he saw in the Turkish metropolis, Constantinople; experienced in his captivity; and after his happy return to his country, committed to writing in the year of Our Lord 1599,* London, Bell and Daldy 1862.

Wutzer, Carl Wilhelm *Reise in dem Orient Europa's und einen Theil Westasien's zur Untersuchung des Bodens und seiner Producte, des Klima's, der Salubrität – Verhältnisse und Vorhenschenden Krankheiten. Mit Beiträgen zur Geschichte, Charakteristik und Politik der Bewohner,* Elberfeld, Bädeker'schen Buch- und Kunsthandlung 1860–1.

Wyon, Reginald *The Balkans from Within,* London, James Finch & Co. 1904.

Wyon, Reginald, and Gerald Prance *The Land of Black Mountain,* London, Methuen & Co. 1903.

Young, George *Constantinople,* London, Methuen & Co. 1926.

Yriarte, Carlo *La Dalmazia,* Milan, Fratelli Treves 1878.

Yriarte, Charles *Les bords de l'Adriatique et le Montenegro,* Paris, Hachette 1878.

Yriarte, Charles *Bosna i Hercegovina – putopis iz vremena ustanka 1875–1876,* Sarajevo, Veselin Masleša 1981.

Zachariá, E. *Reise in den Orient in den Jahren 1837 und 1838. Ueber Wien, Venedig, Florenz, Rom, Neapel, Malta, Sicilien and Griechenland nach Saloniki, dem Berge Athos, Konstantinopel und Trapezunt,* Heidelberg, J. C. B. Mohr 1840.

Zavadil, Antonín *Obrázky z Bosny,* Praha, Josef Pelcl 1911.

Zdravković, Ivan 'Opravka kula kod Starog mosta u Mostaru', in *Naše starine* I, pp. 141–3. Sarajevo 1953.

Zedtwitz, Franz X. *Zaubervoller Balkan,* Berlin, Ullstein 1937.

Zimermann, Andrew *Anthropology and Antihumanism in Imperial Germany,* Chicago and London, The University of Chicago Press 2001.

Zotiades, George B. *The Macedonian Controversy,* Thessaloniki, Society of Macedonian Studies 1954.

Žunkovič, Martin *Die Slaven, ein Urvolk Europas,* Kremser, A Piša 1910.

Index

and Bosnia 106
bowling with heads 126
Christianity in 115
Christmas massacre 108–9
and coffee 152
corporal punishment in 114–15
and death 21
decapitation in 121–30, 140–5
gender behaviour in 109–15
heroism in 21, 108, 112, 123, 130–31, 142
and Herzegovina 106
and Kosovo 106
landscape of 106–8
and liberty 105–6, 128
marriage in 112–13, 130
and Muslims 108–9
nose cutting in 20, 129–32
and Orthodox Christianity 108
prisons in 118–20
and romanticism 103–5
rulers of 115–17
and Serbs 106
and Slavs 105
and spitting 45
women in 109–15
Moore, Frederick 44, 186
Moors 16
Morača 142
Morlaks 45, 56, 62–7, *69*, 105
    childrearing 67–71
    and Venetians 73–5
Morosini, Francesco 219
Morritt, John 23, 180
mosques, removal of 212–26
Mostar 32, 128, 130, *194*
    derivation of name 203–5
    Old Bridge 13, 14, 15, 20, 191–205, *192*
mourning 113
Mrkun, Anton 96
Murat III, Sultan 192, 212
Murat IV, Sultan 158, 159
Muromeć, Ilja 104
music *102*, 162–5
Muslims 14–18, 35, 39, 43, 97–8, 127, *194*, 205, 207, 230
    Christmas massacre of 108–9
    and coffee 151–2, 157–8, 165
    ethnicity of 179
    and games 157
    iconoclasm 92, 100
    and illness 95–6
    in Macedonia 171, 175, 179, 185
    and marriage 113
    and religious tolerance 233

see also Albania; Macedonia; Ottoman
    Empire; Turks

nationality and religion 105–6, 179–90
NATO occupation 14
natural history 35–9, 55–9
Natural History
    Buffon 79–80
    Pliny 59
Nazism 29
Nenadović, Ljubomir 141
Neretva river 58, 191, 196
    see also Mostar, Old Bridge
Nevrokop 184
Niam-Niam 82, 83, 84
Nicolaides, Dr Cleanthes 174, 175
Nicophorus, Emperor 132
Nikola, King 105, 106, 107, 117, 125, 129
Nikolić, Fra 96
Nikšić 223
Niš 143–4, 186, 223, 228
Non cogito ergo sum 85
nose removal 20, 114, 129–32, 134, 138
Novaković, Stojan 185
Novi Pazar *161*

Obilić, Miloš 108
Ohrid 151, 174–5, 176, 179, 184, 188
Olympias 173
Omar Pasha 128
Orbini, Mauro 91, 92
Orient Express 34
Orthodox Christianity *see* Christians and
    Christianity
Osijek 213
Ossero 60
Ossory, Bishop of 81
Othman, Seliman 133
Ottoman Empire
    attitudes to 42–3
    bridge building in 198–9, 200
    capital 24
    Christians in 39–40, 98, 99, 104, 115
    economy of 40–41
    expansion of 151
    fashion 42
    heads as trophies 136–9
    occupation, end of 42, 198, 212–24
    prisons in 120
    rule of 13–14, 16, 24, 40–2, 171, 179–81,
        197, 203, 206–9, 231
    Serbia, defeat of 105
Our Slavic Fellow Citizens 17–18
Oxford 149